Understanding English Grammar

Understanding English Grammar

SIXTH EDITION

Martha Kolln

The Pennsylvania State University

Robert Funk

Eastern Illinois University

New York San Francisco Boston
London Toronto Sydney Tokyo Singapore Madrid
Mexico City Munich Paris Cape Town Hong Kong Montreal

Vice President and Editor-in-Chief: Joseph Opiela
Vice President and Publisher: Eben W. Ludlow
Marketing Manager: Carlise Paulson
Production Manager: Ellen MacElree
Project Coordination, Text Design, and Electronic Page Makeup:
 Electronic Publishing Services Inc., NYC
Cover Designer/Manager: Nancy Danahy
Senior Manufacturing Buyer: Dennis J. Para
Printer and Binder: Courier-Westford
Cover Printer: Coral Graphic Services, Inc.

Library of Congress Cataloging-in-Publication Data

Kolln, Martha.
  Understanding English grammar / Martha Kolln, Robert Funk.
  --6th ed.
    p. cm.
  Includes index.
  ISBN 0-205-33622-1
  1. English language--Grammar. I. Funk, Robert. II. Title.

PE1112 .K64 2001
428.2--dc21
                                                        2001029562

Please visit our website at http://www.ablongman.com

ISBN 0-205-33622-1

1 2 3 4 5 6 7 8 9 10—CRW—04 03 02 01

Contents

Chapter 3
Expanding the Main Verb   60

Chapter 4
Transforming the Basic Patterns   90

PART III
Expanding the Sentence   107

Chapter 9
Coordination   213

PART IV
Words and Word Classes   229

Chapter 10
Morphemes   232

Chapter 13
Pronouns   293

PART VI
Glossary of Grammatical Terms   351

Appendix
An Introduction to Transformational Grammar   367

Answers to the Exercises   383

Index   441

Preface

Knowing a language and knowing about that language are two very different kinds of knowledge. The ability to speak perfectly grammatical English sentences in no way guarantees that the speaker knows enough *about* English to discuss what makes those sentences grammatical. Our purpose in this book is to help students achieve that knowledge.

Understanding English Grammar begins at the beginning. That is, we assume no prior knowledge on the readers' part beyond, perhaps, vague recollections of long-ago grammar lessons. But we do assume that, as speakers of the language, readers will learn to draw on their unconscious knowledge of English as they learn about English in a conscious way. This sixth edition, then, retains the underlying purpose of the book, which has remained constant since its first edition in 1982: to help students understand the systematic nature of language and to appreciate their own language expertise.

This edition also retains the eclectic methods of previous editions, drawing upon all of the grammatical theories, old and new. The basic framework of the book is that of the structural linguists, with their descriptive sentence patterns and classifications of words based on English (rather than on the Latin-based eight parts of speech). We also make use of early transformational theory, especially in the chapters covering expanded verbs and transformed sentences. Throughout the book, traditional diagrams will help the student visualize sentence structure.

Because we know that many students bring little or no background in the study of grammar from their middle school or high school classes, we have tried to look at every topic, every paragraph, every explanation and description through the eyes of those novice readers. This scrutiny has resulted in refinements in every chapter, new and updated exercises as well as several major changes:

- A somewhat scaled-down Chapter 1, with its description of grammar history and pedagogy and its discussion of language issues that teachers encounter in the classroom;

- A new section in Chapter 2 covering the basic word classes and phrases to prepare the reader for the sentence patterns (this section may satisfy those instructors who in the past have felt the need to review the parts of speech in Part IV before taking up syntax in Chapter 2);

- New step-by-step explanations in Chapter 3, which help to clarify the description of the verb system;

- A return of the chapter on nominals to its former position following adverbials and adjectivals, where it appeared in earlier editions, along with the return of the appositive discussion to that chapter;

- A new look for Chapter 14, with the discussion of rhetorical grammar now following the same organization as the chapters on syntax, moving from sentence patterns to the rhetorical effects of various sentence expansions.

Teachers who are familiar with the previous editions of *Understanding English Grammar* will find the same organization in this new one: We begin with an overview of grammar in Part I, followed by the study of sentence patterns in Part II; Part III describes the expansion of sentences with modifiers, nominals, and coordinate structures; Part IV covers morphemes and word classes. Instructors who prefer the more traditional approach of studying words before sentence patterns will find it easy to begin the course with Part IV. The occasional references to the sentence patterns in those chapters should not be a problem for the students. Part V covers rhetorical grammar, the application of grammar knowledge to writing.

There are exercises throughout the chapters to reinforce the principles of grammar as they are introduced. Answers to the exercises, which are provided in a section at the end, give the book a strong self-instructional quality. The exercises entitled "Investigating Language" will stimulate class discussion, calling on students to tap their innate language ability.

Each chapter ends with a list of key terms, a section of practice sentences (for which answers are provided only in the *Instructor's Manual*), a series of discussion questions that go beyond the concepts covered in the text, and several classroom applications that can be used in your college classes as well as in the future classrooms of your students. In addition to the main text, there is an appendix with a brief introduction to transformational grammar. The students will also find the glossary of terms extremely helpful.

Supplementing the sixth edition of the text, the *Instructor's Manual* includes analyses of the practice sentences, suggested answers for the discussion questions, and suggestions for using the book. The *Instructor's Manual* is available from your Longman representative.

A student supplement to the text is the third edition of *Exercises for Understanding English Grammar,* with exercises that go beyond those found in the text, many of which call for the students to compose sentences. To keep the self-instructional quality that teachers appreciate, answers for half of the items are included, where answers are appropriate. In addition, there are chapter-ending "test exercises" without answers, which can be used for testing and review. An Answer Key to *Exercises for Understanding English Grammar* is also available from your Longman representative.

The study of grammar is not just for English majors or for future teachers: It is for people in business and industry, in science and engineering, in law and politics. Every user of the language, in fact, will benefit from the consciousness-raising that results from the study of grammar. The more that speakers and writers and readers know consciously about their language, the more power they have over it and the better they can make it serve their needs. It is very gratifying to know that many thousands of students in schools throughout the country have experienced their consciousness-raising with *Understanding English Grammar.*

ACKNOWLEDGMENTS

Understanding English Grammar has once again been revised, corrected, and shaped by the questions and comments of students and colleagues who use the book. We are particularly grateful to the following reviewers for their thoughtful assessments of the previous edition and their recommendations for revision:

Vicki M. Adams, Kent State University

Rosemary Buck, Eastern Illinois University

Jena A. Burges, Longwood College

Lee Campbell, Valdosta State University

Fredric Dolezal, University of Georgia

Susan Fitzmaurice, Northern Arizona University

John Hagge, Iowa State University

Linda Hagge, Iowa State University

Victoria W. Massey, Howard University

Nicole Pepinster Greene, University of Louisiana—Lafayette

Margie Rauls, Florida A&M University

Joseph Sawicki, California State University—Fullerton

Gerald J. Schiffhorst, University of Central Florida

John W. Schwetman, Sam Houston State University

Jerome Shea, University of New Mexico

Riley B. Smith, Bloomsburg University

Connie Wasem, University of Texas at El Paso

Special thanks go to the four reviewers who read the final manuscript and offered many useful suggestions:

Rosemary Buck, Eastern Illinois University

John Hagge, Iowa State University

Linda Hagge, Iowa State University

Jerome Shea, University of New Mexico

Finally, our undiminished gratitude to Eben Ludlow, our good friend and incomparable editor.

Martha Kolln

Robert Funk

PART

I

Introduction

The subject of grammar differs markedly from every other subject in the curriculum—far different from history or math or biology or mechanical drawing. What makes it different? You do. If you're a native speaker of English, you're already an expert. You bring to the study of grammar a lifetime of "knowing" it—except for your first couple of years, a lifetime of producing grammatical sentences.

Modern scholars call this expertise your "language competence." Unlike the competence you have in your other subjects, your grammar competence is innate. Although you were not born with a vocabulary (it took a year or so before you began to perform), you were born with a language potential just waiting to be triggered. By the age of two you were putting words together into sentences, following your own system of rules: "Cookie all gone"; "Go bye-bye." Before long, your sentences began to resemble those of adults. By the time you started school, you were an expert in your native language—whatever that language happens to be.

Well, almost an expert. There were still a few gaps in your system. For example, you didn't start using verb phrases as direct objects (I like *reading books*) until perhaps second grade; and not until third or fourth grade did you use *although* or *even if* to introduce clauses (I'm going home *even if you're not*). But for the most part, your grammar system was in place on your first day of kindergarten.

At this point you may be wondering why you're here—in this class, reading this textbook—if you're already such an expert. You're here to learn in a conscious way the grammar that you use, expertly but subconsciously, every day. You'll learn to think about language and to talk about it, to understand and sharpen your own language skills and, if your future plans include teaching, to help others understand and sharpen theirs.

In Chapter 1 we will look briefly at the ways in which grammar has been studied in the past; we'll look also at the issues of correctness and standards and language change. In all of these discussions—in all of the chapters—a key word is *awareness*. The goal of *Understanding English Grammar* is to help you become consciously aware of your innate language competence.

The Study of Grammar: An Overview

The study of grammar has a long recorded history, stretching back well over twenty centuries to the great philosopher/teachers of Ancient Greece and Rome. For them grammar occupied a central role in the language arts. And for them the highest form of the language arts—the purpose for studying grammar—was the art of oratory, or public speaking.

For us, that purpose has changed somewhat, although of course public speech of many kinds remains an important part of our lives—from the spontaneous remarks we make in group discussions to prepared reports for classes or club meetings or the workplace. Rather than serving the art of oratory, however, today the purpose for studying grammar is more closely connected to improving the art of written composition. In fact, much of what you may remember about grammar from middle school or high school probably deals directly with writing and its correctness—usage rules, punctuation rules, a list of do's and don'ts.

Despite the difference in purpose, despite the passage of centuries, there still exists a clear connection between your grammar lessons and those learned by Greek and Roman schoolboys long ago (yes, only boys!). The standard Latin textbook, written by the grammarian Donatus around A.D. 350, described eight parts of speech, almost identical to the traditional eight parts of speech in grammar books today. And history tells us that Donatus borrowed his description for Latin from the word categories of Greek, written down even earlier.

So it turns out that what we call traditional English grammar is essentially a translation of traditional Latin grammar. Although in our own century language scholars have rejected that Latin framework in describing English, many textbooks and handbooks still follow the course that Donatus charted so long ago.

MODERN LINGUISTICS

The twentieth century witnessed important new developments in linguistics, the scientific study of language. Perhaps the first important trend, carried over from the work of nineteenth-century scholarly grammarians, was the emphasis on objectivity in describing language, together with a rejection of **prescriptivism.**[1] The term *prescriptivism* refers to the focus and purpose of many early grammar books: passing judgment on language rather than objectively describing it; promoting a particular variety, or **dialect,** of a language as the "correct" one. Often the purpose of such books was self-improvement, to instruct readers in "proper" English, to help them move up in the world. In his popular textbook *An English Grammar,* first published in 1795, Lindley Murray defined grammar as "the art of speaking and writing the English language with propriety."

By contrast, linguists today understand their job as that of description, the purpose being to *de*scribe how people actually use language, not to *pre*scribe how they *should* use it. Modern linguists emphasize the primacy of speech, recognizing that every dialect is equally grammatical.

In the early part of the twentieth century, a great deal of linguistic research was carried out by anthropologists studying Native American languages, many of which were in danger of being lost. It was not unusual for a few elders to be the only remaining speakers of a tribe's language. When they died, the language would die with them.

To understand the structure underlying languages unknown to them, researchers could not rely on their knowledge of Western languages: They could not assume that the language they were hearing was related either to Latin or to the Germanic roots of English. Nor could they assume that word classes like adjective and pronoun and preposition were part of the sentences they were hearing. To be objective in their description, they had to start from scratch in their thinking about word categories and sentence structure.

Structural Grammar. The same kind of objectivity needed to study the grammar of an unknown language was applied to English grammar by a group of linguists who came to be known as structuralists. Their description of grammar is called **structuralism.** Like the anthropologists studying the speech of Native Americans, the structuralists too recognized the importance of describing language on its own terms. Instead of assuming

---

[1] Words in boldface type are defined in the Glossary of Grammatical Terms, beginning on page 351.

that English words could be fit into the traditional eight word groups of Latin, the structuralists examined sentences objectively, paying particular attention to how words change in sound and spelling (their form) and how they are used in sentences (their function).

You will see the result of that examination in the next chapter, where a clear distinction is drawn between the large open **form classes** (nouns, verbs, adjectives, and adverbs) and the small closed **structure classes**, such as prepositions and conjunctions.

Another important feature of structuralism, which came to be called "new grammar," is its emphasis on the systematic nature of English. The description of the form classes is a good case in point. Their formal nature is systematic; for example, words that have a plural and possessive form are nouns; words that have an *-ed* form (past tense) and an *-ing* form are verbs. For the structuralists, this systematic description of the language includes an analysis of the sound system (**phonology**), then the systematic combination of sounds into meaningful units and words (**morphology**), and, finally, the systematic combination of words into meaningful sentence patterns (**syntax**).

Transformational Grammar.   In the late 1950s, at a time when structuralism was beginning to have an influence on textbooks, a new approach came into prominence. Called transformational generative grammar, this new linguistic theory, along with changes in the language arts curriculum, finally led to the diminishing influence of structuralism. Linguistic research today carries forward what can only be called a linguistic revolution.

The new linguistics, which began in 1957 with the publication of Noam Chomsky's *Syntactic Structures,* deserves the label "revolutionary." After 1957, the study of grammar would no longer be limited to what is said and how it is interpreted. In fact, the word *grammar* itself took on a new meaning. The new linguists defined *grammar* as our innate, subconscious ability to generate language, an internal system of rules that constitutes our human language capacity. The goal of the new linguistics was to describe this internal grammar.

Unlike the structuralists, whose goal was to examine the sentences we actually speak and to describe their systematic nature, the transformationalists wanted to unlock the secrets of language: to build a model of our internal rules, a model that would produce all of the grammatical—and no ungrammatical—sentences. It might be useful to think of our built-in language system as a computer program. The transformationalists are trying to describe that program.

Our internal grammar rules bear little or no resemblance to the kinds of rules we traditionally associate with grammar, such as subject–verb agreement. In fact, the transformationalists have identified rules that native speakers never think about. For example, consider that we say,

Don gave Karen a present

and

Don gave a present to Karen

and

Don gave it to Karen,

but we do not say,

*Don gave Karen it.[2]

(If you do hear someone say *Don gave Karen it*, you can be quite sure you're hearing a non-native speaker, one who has not yet mastered, or internalized, this particular rule.)

Transformational linguists want to know how our internal linguistic computer recognizes and rules out that variation. They also wonder how it can interpret a sentence such as

I enjoy visiting relatives

as ambiguous—that is, as having more than one possible meaning. (To figure out the two meanings, think about who is doing the visiting.)

In the Appendix ("An Introduction to Transformational Grammar") you can read about the distinction between "deep" and "surface" structure, a concept that may hold the key to ambiguity. This feature is also the basis for the label *transformational,* the idea that meaning, generated in the deep structure, can be *transformed* into a variety of surface structures, the sentences we actually speak. The model in the Appendix provides only a brief, as well as highly simplified, early version of transformational grammar. The theory has undergone evolutionary changes during the past three decades, and it continues to evolve.

Although these theoretical models reach far beyond the scope of classroom grammar, there are nevertheless several important concepts of the transformationalists that we have integrated into the description of grammar you will be studying in these chapters. The idea of transformation itself is certainly one of them, as you will see in Chapter 4—the recognition that a basic sentence can be transformed into a variety of forms, depending on intent or emphasis, while retaining its essential meaning. Another major adoption from transformational grammar is the description of our system for expanding the verb in Chapter 3.

[2.]An asterisk (*) marks a sentence as ungrammatical or questionable.

THE ISSUE OF CORRECTNESS

The structural linguists, who had as their goal the objective description of language, recognized that no one variety of English can lay claim to the label "best" or "correct," that the **dialects** of all native speakers are equally **grammatical**. (We define *dialect* as the variety of a language spoken in a particular region or community.)

We all know, of course, that there are many variations of English. Different parts of the country, different levels of education, different ethnic backgrounds—all of these factors produce differences in language communities. One of the positive contributions that television has made to our education is the demonstration of such differences. At times the English we hear sounds so different from our own that it seems almost like another language. Some of the dialogue in British programs, for example, can be downright indecipherable. In reality, however, even though dialects may seem far apart, most of their structural rules, their grammar, are exactly the same.

But can the linguists be right when they say that all dialects are equally grammatical? Surely some of those variations are **ungrammatical,** aren't they? What else are we to think when we hear people say "He just upped and left" or "I might could go" or "Y'all come back soon" or "He be working"? We don't hear such sentences in television news reports or in presidential addresses to Congress, nor do we see them in formal writing. Can such sentences really be grammatical? To discover the answer, imagine yourself in the role of the linguistic anthropologist.

Imagine that your job is to record the speech of Pennsylvanians. In Pittsburgh and its surrounding areas, you hear such sentences as "My car needs fixed" and "My hair needs washed" and "Let the door open." In Philadelphia, three hundred miles to the east, you hear instead "My car needs to be fixed" and "My hair needs washing" and "Leave the door open." As a linguist, are you going to judge one group's speech as grammatical and the other's as ungrammatical? Of course not. You have no basis for doing so. The anthropologists who recorded Menomini and Navajo did not ask, "Is this correct Menomini?" or "Is this version of Navajo grammatical?" Their job was to describe the language that native speakers actually used.

Many of the sentences that get labeled "ungrammatical" are simply usages that vary from one dialect to another, what we sometimes call regionalisms. The Southern *y'all* or *you all* and the Philadelphia *yous* and the Appalachian *you-uns* (or *y'uns*) are all ways of pluralizing the pronoun *you*. It's probably accurate to say that the majority of speech communities in this country have no plural form of *you*—but some do, and these plurals are part of their grammar.

THE QUESTION OF STANDARDS

You won't be surprised to learn that the structuralists, after describing the language of all native speakers as grammatical, were themselves called "permissive," charged with advocating a policy of "anything goes." After all, for three hundred years an important goal of school grammar lessons and textbooks had been to teach "proper" grammar. Proper grammar implies standards, and the structuralists appeared to be rejecting standards and ignoring rules. But what the structural linguists were actually doing was making a distinction between two kinds of rules: grammar rules and the social rules of usage, sometimes called "linguistic etiquette."

In his textbook, *English Sentences* (Harcourt, 1962), Paul Roberts labeled the following sentences "Grammar 1" and "Grammar 2," representing two dialects of English, equally grammatical:

1. Henry brought his mother some flowers.

2. Henry brung his mother some flowers.

Roberts explains that if we prefer sentence 1

> we do so simply because in some sense we prefer the people who say sentence 1 to those who say sentence 2. We associate sentence 1 with educated people and sentence 2 with uneducated people….But mark this well: educated people do not say sentence 1…because it is better than 2. Educated people say it, *and that makes it better.* That's all there is to it. (7)

The well-known issue of *ain't* provides another illustration of the difference between our internal rules of grammar and our external, social rules of usage. You may have assumed that pronouncements about *ain't* have something to do with incorrect or ungrammatical English—but they don't. The word itself, the contraction of *am not*, is produced by an internal rule, the same rule that gives us *aren't* and *isn't.* Any negative bias you may have against *ain't* is strictly a matter of linguistic etiquette. And, as you can hear for yourself, many speakers of English harbor no such bias.

Written texts from the seventeenth and eighteenth centuries show that *ain't* was once a part of conversational English of educated people in England and America. It was sometime during the nineteenth century that the word became stigmatized for public speech and marked a speaker as uneducated or ignorant. It's still possible to hear *ain't* in public speech, but only as an attention-getter:

If it ain't broke, don't fix it.

You ain't seen nothin' yet.

And of course it occurs in written dialogue and in written and spoken humor. But despite the fact that the grammar rules of millions of people produce *ain't* as part of their native language, for many others it carries a stigma.

Investigating Language **1.1**

The stigma attached to *ain't* has left a void in our language: We now have no first-person equivalent of the negative questions *Isn't it?* and *Aren't they?* You will discover how we have filled the void when you add the appropriate tag questions to three sentences. The tag question is a common way we have of turning a statement into a question. Two examples will illustrate the structure:

> Your mother is a nice person, isn't she?
>
> Your brother is still in high school, isn't he?

Now write the tag for these three sentences:

1. The weather is nice today, ___*isn't it*___?
2. You are my friend, ___*aren't you*___?
3. I am your friend, ___*aren't I*___?

You'll notice that you can turn those tag questions into statements by reversing them. Here are the examples:

> *She isn't.*
>
> *He isn't.*

Now reverse the three that you wrote:

1. ___*it isn't*___.
2. ___*You aren't*___.
3. ___*I aren't*___.

In trying to reverse the third tag, you have probably discovered the problem that the banishment of *ain't* has produced. It has left us with something that sounds like an ungrammatical structure. Given the linguists' definition of *ungrammatical,* something that a native speaker wouldn't say, would you call *"Aren't I?"* ungrammatical? Explain.

In summary, then, our attitude toward *ain't* is an issue about status, not grammar. We don't hear *ain't,* nor do we hear regionalisms like *I might could go* and *the car needs fixed,* in formal speeches or on the nightly news because they are not part of Grammar 1, what has come to be called "standard English."

Modern linguists may find the word *standard* objectionable when applied to a particular dialect, given that every dialect is standard within its own speech community. To label Roberts' Grammar 1 as standard may seem to imply that others are somehow inferior, or substandard. Here, however, we are using *standard* as the label for the majority dialect—or, perhaps more accurately, the status dialect—the one that is used in newscasts, in formal business transactions, in courtrooms, in all sorts of public discourse. If the network newscasters and the president of the United States and your teachers began to use *ain't* on a regular basis, its status too would soon change.

LANGUAGE VARIETY

All of us have a wide range of language varieties available to us. The words we choose and the way in which we say them are determined to a great extent by the speech situation. The way we speak with friends at the pizza parlor is quite different from the conversation we carry on at a formal banquet. "Is it correct?" is probably the wrong question to ask about a particular word or phrase. A more accurate question would be "Is it correct for this situation?" or "Is it appropriate?"

In the written language, too, what is appropriate or effective in one situation may be inappropriate or ineffective in another. The language you use in letters to your family and friends is noticeably different from the language you use when applying for a job. Even the writing you do in school varies, depending on the situation. The language of the personal essay you write for your composition class has an informality that would be inappropriate for a business report or a history research paper. As with speech, the purpose and the audience make all the difference.

Edited American English is the version of our language that has come to be the standard for written public discourse—for newspapers and books and for most of the writing you do in school and on the job. It is the version of our language that this book describes, the written version of the status dialect as it has evolved through the centuries and continues to evolve.

What we think of as the "rules" of Edited American English have come to us from many sources: Some are the judgments of long-ago printers; others come from early grammarians who looked to Latin for guidance. Most grammar books and dictionaries now and in the past describe—and sometimes prescribe—the version of English used by influential writers and speakers of their day. Today we don't hear those writers and speakers say "I don't have no money" and "He don't like me" and "I ain't going"—at least not in their public discourse. They say, instead, "I don't have any money" and "He doesn't like me" and "I'm not going," so these are the forms that get included in modern grammar books and usage manuals as the standard.

LANGUAGE CHANGE

Another important aspect of our language that is closely related to the issue of correctness and standards is language change. Change is inevitable in a living organism like language. The change is obvious, of course, when we compare the English of Shakespeare or the King James Bible to our modern version. But we certainly don't have to go back that far to see differences. The following passages are from two different translations of *Pinocchio,* the Italian children's book written in the 1880s by Carlo Collodi. The two versions were published almost sixty years apart. You'll have no trouble distinguishing the translation of 1925 from the one published in 1983:

1a. Fancy the happiness of Pinocchio on finding himself free!

1b. Imagine Pinocchio's joy when he felt himself free.

2a. Gallop on, gallop on, my pretty steed.

2b. Gallop, gallop, little horse.

3a. But whom shall I ask?

3b. But who can I possibly ask?

4a. Woe betide the lazy fellow.

4b. Woe to those who yield to idleness.

5a. Hasten, Pinocchio.

5b. Hurry, Pinocchio.

6a. Without adding another word, the marionette bade the good Fairy good-by.

6b. Without adding another word, the puppet said good-bye to his good fairy.

In both cases the translators are writing the English version of 1880 Italian, so the language is not necessarily conversational 1925 or 1983 English. In spite of that constraint, we can recognize—as you've probably figured out—that the first item in each pair is the 1925 translation. Those sentences include words that we simply don't have occasion to use anymore, words that would sound out of place today in a conversation, or even in a fairy tale: *betide, hasten, bade.* The language of 1925 is simply not our language. In truth, the language of 1983 is not our language either. We can see and hear change happening all around us, especially if we consider the new words required for such fields as medicine, space science, and E-commerce.

Investigating Language   **1.2**

The difference between the two translations in the first pair of *Pinocchio* sentences is connected to the word *fancy,* a word that is still common today. Why did the 1983 translator use *imagine* instead? What has happened to *fancy* in the intervening decades?

The third pair involves a difference in grammar rather than vocabulary, the change from *whom* to *who.* What do you suppose today's language critics would have to say about the 1983 translation?

The last pair includes a spelling change. Check the dictionary to see which is "correct"—or is *correct* the right word? The dictionary includes many words that have more than one spelling. How do you know which one to use?

Finally, provide examples to demonstrate the accuracy of the assertion that the language of 1983 is not our language.

LANGUAGE IN THE CLASSROOM

How about the classroom? Should teachers call attention to the dialect differences in their students' speech? Should teachers "correct" them? These are questions that the National Council of Teachers of English has addressed in a document called "Students' Right to Their Own Language." The NCTE has taken the position that teachers should respect the dialects of their students. But teachers also have an obligation to teach students to read and write standard English, the language of public discourse and of the workplace that those students are preparing to join. There are ways of doing so without making students feel that the language spoken in their home, the language produced by their own internal grammar rules, is somehow inferior. Certainly one way is to study language differences in an objective, nonjudgmental way, to discuss individual and regional and ethnic differences. The community, the schoolyard, even the individual classroom can serve as the laboratory for examining language in an objective way.

In 1994 the NCTE passed a resolution that encourages the integration of language awareness into classroom instruction and teacher preparation programs. Language awareness includes examining how language varies in a range of social and cultural settings; how people's attitudes towards language vary across cultures, classes, genders, and generations; how oral and written language affects listeners and readers; how "correctness" in language reflects social, political, and economic values; and how first and second languages are acquired. Language awareness also includes the teaching of grammar from a descriptive, rather than a prescriptive, perspective.

CHAPTER *1*
Key Terms

Correctness	Nonstandard dialect
Dialect	Prescriptivism
Edited American English	Regionalisms
Grammar rules	Structuralism
Grammatical	Transformational grammar
Language change	Ungrammatical
Language variety	Usage rules

For Further Reading on Topics in This Chapter

Baron, Dennis E. *Grammar and Good Taste: Reforming the American Language.* New Haven: Yale University Press, 1982.

Haussamen, Brock. *Revising the Rules: Traditional Grammar and Modern Linguistics.* 2nd ed. Dubuque, IA: Kendall-Hunt, 1997.

Hunter, Susan, and Ray Wallace, eds. *The Place of Grammar in Writing Instruction: Past, Present, Future.* Portsmouth, NH: Boynton/Cook, 1995.

Joos, Martin. *The Five Clocks.* New York: Harcourt Brace Jovanovich, 1967.

Kutz, Eleanor. *Language and Literacy: Studying Discourse in Communities and Classrooms.* Portsmouth, NH: Boynton/Cook, 1997.

Pinker, Steven. *The Language Instinct.* New York: William Morrow, 1994.

Wolfram, Walt. *Dialects and American English.* Washington, DC: Center for Applied Linguistics, 1991.

CLASSROOM APPLICATIONS

1. Do you use words or phrases that your parents and others of their generation do not? As a class project, compile your own Dictionary of Slang. Each contribution should include synonyms and context, as dictionary entries generally do. Check a current dictionary. Are your entries already labeled as slang?

Share the list with the older generation. Which expressions do they recognize? What terms did they use to express the same or similar ideas when they were your age? What other slang expressions did they use? What has happened to them? Have any of them become part of our everyday vocabulary? Are any now labeled as slang in the dictionary?

2. The origin of many stock phrases in our language are lost in history. Perhaps you can figure out, or find out, where these phrases came from:

acid test	fall guy
against the grain	greenhorn
bank teller	pass the buck
bring home the bacon	rank and file
by and large	sleep like a top

You may not find the origins of these phrases in the dictionary, so check the reference section of your library for specialized usage dictionaries.

The Grammar of Basic Sentences

Y ou might have been surprised to learn, when you read the introduction to Part I, that you're already an expert in grammar—and have been since before you started school. Indeed, you're such an expert that you can generate completely original sentences with those internal grammar rules of yours, sentences that have never before been spoken or written. Here's one to get you started:

> At this very moment, I, [Insert your name], am reading page 15 of the sixth edition of *Understanding English Grammar.*

Surely the occasion for that sentence has never happened before; you can be quite sure that it's original. Perhaps even more surprising is the fact that the number of such sentences you can produce is infinite.

When you study the grammar of your native language, then, you are studying a subject you already "know"; so rather than learning grammar, you will be "learning about" grammar. If you're not a native speaker, you will probably be learning both grammar and "about" grammar; the mix will depend on your background and experience. It's important that you understand what you are bringing to this course—even though you may have forgotten all those "parts of speech" labels you once consciously learned. The unconscious, or subconscious, knowledge that you have can help you if you will let it. The discussions and the exercises are designed to help you put your intuition to work, to help you bring to a conscious level and use that grammar expertise of yours.

We will begin the study of sentence grammar, the subject known as syntax, by examining basic sentence patterns, the underlying framework of sentences, looking for both their common and their distinguishing features. A conscious knowledge of the basic patterns will provide a foundation for understanding the sentence expansions and variations that come later. In Chapter 3 we will examine the expanded verb, the system of auxiliaries that makes our verbs so versatile. In Chapter 4 we will look at the ways we have of transforming our basic sentence for a variety of purposes.

CHAPTER 2

Sentence Patterns

CHAPTER PREVIEW

We will begin the study of sentence structure, known as **syntax**, by examining ten sentence patterns. These ten patterns, or formulas, represent the underlying skeletal structure of nearly all of our sentences. Your understanding of the patterns will give you a solid framework for understanding the expanded sentences in the chapters that follow. So take your time as you study them; notice what they have in common; recognize what makes them different.

Each of the ten patterns is introduced with a traditional diagram of its basic structure, a visual aid to help you picture the pattern and the relationship of its parts. On page 51 all ten patterns and their diagrams are shown together as a kind of summary of the chapter. It is a page you will find yourself referring to frequently as you work with sentences throughout the book.

As with every subject you study, the discussion of sentence structure requires a special vocabulary—in this case, a language for discussing language. For the most part, that language uses the terms of traditional grammar, many of which may already be familiar to you. To review some of those terms, and to introduce a few new ones, we will begin the chapter with a short overview of our grammar vocabulary.

WORDS AND PHRASES: AN OVERVIEW

We will begin our overview of terminology with **noun** and **verb**, our two largest word categories; then we will put them into structures with labels that may be new to you, the **noun phrase** and the **verb phrase**.

It's not surprising that we think about nouns and verbs together because noun-plus-verb describes our simplest kind of sentence:

> Cats fight.
>
> Mary laughed.

Nouns and verbs are two of our four **form classes**; the other two are **adjectives** and **adverbs**. These four word categories constitute over 99 percent of the vocabulary of English.

You may be familiar with the traditional definition of a noun, such as *cats* or *Mary*, a definition based on meaning: the name of a person, place, or thing. Verbs, too, are traditionally defined according to meaning: words denoting action, being, or state of being. However, the structural grammarians, who introduced the sentence patterns you will study in this chapter, defined the word categories (also called the "parts of speech") somewhat differently, using the characteristic of word form to define nouns and verbs and adjectives and adverbs—hence the term "form classes." This is the approach we follow in this book.

Each of the four form classes has, or can have, particular endings that identify it. Our sample sentences illustrate one such ending for nouns and one for verbs: the **plural** marker, *-s,* on the noun *cat;* the **past tense** marker, *-ed,* on the verb *laugh.* As you'll see, we can use these "formal" characteristics as criteria in our definitions of "noun" and "verb."

Nouns. The plural *-s* is one of two noun endings that we call **inflections**; the other noun inflection is the **possessive case** ending, the apostrophe-plus-*s* (or, in the case of most plural nouns, just the apostrophe). Most nouns will fit into the following framework:[1]

SINGULAR	PLURAL	SINGULAR POSSESSIVE	PLURAL POSSESSIVE
cat	cats	cat's	cats'
horse	horses	horse's	horses'

We have now demonstrated the formal characteristics that define nouns:

---

[1] In words where the plural form has no *-s,* as in the case of a few irregular plural nouns such as *men* and *women,* both possessive forms, singular and plural, take the apostrophe-plus-*s:*

man	men	man's	men's
woman	women	woman's	women's

A noun is a word that can be made plural and/or possessive.

We can enhance this definition by looking at the role the noun fills in the noun phrase.

Noun Phrases. The term **noun phrase** may be new to you, although you're probably familiar with the word **phrase,** which traditionally refers to any group of words that functions as a unit within the sentence. But sometimes a single word will function as a unit by itself, as in our two earlier examples, where *Cats* and *Mary* function as subjects in their sentences. For this reason, we are going to alter that traditional definition of *phrase* to include single words:

> *A phrase is a word or group of words that functions as a unit within the sentence.*

A phrase will always have a head, or **headword;** it will often have modifiers of the headword. As you might expect, the headword of the noun phrase is a noun. Most noun phrases (NPs) also include a noun signaler, or marker, called a **determiner.** Here are three NPs you have seen in this chapter, with their headwords underlined and their determiners shown in italics:

> *the* <u>sentence</u>
>
> *a* solid <u>framework</u>
>
> *the* traditional <u>definition</u>

As the examples illustrate, the headword may be preceded by a modifier. The most common modifier in preheadword position is the adjective, such as *solid* and *traditional.* In Chapter 6 we will take up other structures that function the way adjectives function, as modifier of nouns.

As you may have noticed in the examples, the opening determiners are the **articles** *a* and *the.* While they are our most common determiners, you'll also discover, as you begin to examine sentences, that other word groups also signal noun phrases. For example, the function of possessive nouns and possessive pronouns is almost always that of determiner:

> *Bill's* girlfriend
>
> *their* apartment

Another common word category in the determiner slot is the **demonstrative pronoun** (*this, that, these, those*):

> *this* old house
>
> *these* sentence patterns

Because noun phrases can be single words, as we saw in our earlier examples *(Cats fight; Mary laughs)*, it follows that not all noun phrases will have determiners. Plural nouns *(cats)* and proper nouns *(Mary)* are among the most common that appear without a noun signaler.

In spite of these exceptions, however, it is accurate to say that most noun phrases do begin with determiners. Likewise, it's accurate to say that whenever you encounter a determiner you know you are at the beginning of a noun phrase. In other words, articles *(a, an, the)* and certain other words, such as possessive nouns and pronouns, tell you that a noun headword is coming.

We can now identify three defining characteristics of nouns:

> *A noun is a word that can be made plural and/or possessive; it occupies the headword position in the noun phrase; it is usually signaled by a determiner.*

In the study of syntax, which you are now undertaking, you can't help but notice the prevalence of noun phrases and their signalers, the determiners.

Verbs. When the dictionary identifies a word as a verb, it lists three forms: the **base form** *(laugh)*, the **past tense** *(laughed)*, and the **past participle** *(laughed)*. These three forms are traditionally referred to as the verb's "three principal parts." Because laugh is a **regular verb**, the past tense and the past participle are both formed with the inflectional ending *-ed;* it will be useful for this discussion to compare the forms of *laugh* with those of an **irregular verb** to illustrate the difference:

Base form (also called **present tense**):	laugh	eat
3rd person singular (*-s* form):	laughs	eats
Past tense (*-ed* form):	laughed	ate
Past participle (*-en* form):	laughed	eaten
Present participle (*-ing* form):	laughing	eating

All verbs have these five forms (although the dictionary neglects to mention two of them). The verb *be,* our only verb with more than five, has eight forms: *be, am, are, is, was, were, been, being.*

The sentences you will examine in the discussion of sentence patterns later in this chapter use only the simple present or past tenses—that is, the forms that take no **auxiliaries,** or **helping verbs.** However, in Chapter 3 you will study the verb in its many forms and learn how it patterns with auxiliaries.

The point to be made here is that in using your knowledge of verb inflections you can use the criterion of form to define *verb,* just as you did with *noun:*

A verb is a word that can be used in present and past tenses; it has both an -s form and an -ing form.

Verb Phrases. As you would expect, the headword of a verb phrase, or VP, is the verb; the other components, if any, will depend in part on the kind of verb—for example, whether it is **transitive** *(The cat chased the mouse)* or **intransitive** *(Cats fight).* In most sentences, the verb phrase will include **adverbials** *(Mary laughed loudly),* as you will learn when you study the sentence patterns. You will be studying verb phrases in detail in this chapter because it is the variations in the verb phrases, the sentence **predicates,** that differentiate the ten sentence patterns.

As we saw with the noun phrase, it is also possible for a verb phrase to be complete with only the headword. Our earlier examples—*Cats fight; Mary laughed*—illustrate instances of single-word noun phrases, which are fairly common in most written work, as well as single-word verb phrases, which are not. In fact, single-word verb phrases as predicates are very rare. So far in this chapter, none of the verb phrases in the text come close to the brevity of those two sample sentences.

Adjectives and Adverbs. You will also encounter the other two form classes, adjectives and adverbs, in your study of the sentence patterns. Like nouns and verbs, they can usually be recognized by their form and/or by their position in the sentence.

The inflectional endings that identify adjectives and some adverbs are the **comparative degree** ending, *-er,* and the **superlative,** *-est:*

> big
>
> bigger
>
> biggest

When the word has two or more syllables, the comparative and superlative markers are generally *more* and *most,* rather than the suffixes:

beautiful	quickly
more beautiful	more quickly
most beautiful	most quickly

Another test of whether a word is an adjective or adverb, as opposed to noun or verb, is its ability to pattern with a **qualifier,** such as *very:*

> very beautiful
>
> very quickly

You'll notice that these tests (the inflectional endings and *very*) can help you differentiate adjectives and adverbs from the other two form classes, but they do not help you distinguish the two word classes from each other. However, there is one test that will help you classify a word as an adjective. Only an adjective will fit into both blanks of this "adjective test frame":

The _____ NOUN is very _____.

For example,

The diligent student is very diligent.

The ordinary house is very ordinary.

Because these sentences are grammatical (although perhaps not sentences you'd ever be likely to use), we have shown that the words *diligent* and *ordinary* are adjectives.[2]

There is one test of form that we use to help in identifying adverbs: the *-ly* ending. This suffix differs from the inflectional endings that help us identify nouns and verbs. You'll recall that a noun inflection is a suffix added to a noun to alter its meaning (for example, from singular to plural); however, the word remains a noun. In contrast, the *-ly* ending that makes adverbs so visible is actually added to adjectives to turn them into adverbs:

Adjective				**Adverb**
quick	+	ly	=	quickly
pleasant	+	ly	=	pleasantly
sleepy	+	ly	=	sleepily

Rather than inflectional, the *-ly* is a **derivational** suffix: It enables us to *derive* adverbs from adjectives. Incidentally, the *-ly* means "like" (quickly = quick-like; sleepily = sleepy-like). Because we have so many adjectives that can morph into adverbs in this way—many thousands, in fact—we are not often mistaken when we assume that an *-ly* word is an adverb.

In addition to these "adverbs of manner," as the *-ly* adverbs are called, we have a selection of others that have no clue of form; among them are *then, now, soon, here, there, afterwards, often.* Often the best way to identify an adverb is by the kind of information it supplies to the sentence—information of time, place, manner, frequency, and the like—and also by its

---

[2] A small number of adjectives will not fit the test frame because they do not pattern with *very,* or because they do not work in one of those two adjective slots (e.g., *former, medical*). In other words, the test frame can positively identify a word as an adjective; however, a word that does not fit cannot be ruled out of the adjective class. These subclasses of adjectives are described on pages 258–259.

place and its movability in the sentence. You will be reminded of these qualities in the discussion of sentence patterns.

Prepositional Phrases. Before going on to sentence patterns, let's take a quick look at the **prepositional phrase,** a two-part structure consisting of a **preposition** followed by an object, which is usually a noun phrase. Prepositions are among the most common words in our language. In fact, the paragraph you are now reading includes nine different prepositions: *before, to, at, of, by, among, in, throughout,* and *as.* Prepositional phrases show up throughout our sentences, sometimes as part of a noun phrase and sometimes as a modifier of the verb.

In a noun phrase, the prepositional phrase adds a detail or makes clear the identity of the noun, which it follows in the postheadword position:

> the identity <u>of the noun</u>
> my friends <u>from Lafayette</u>
> the road <u>to Iowa City</u>
> a unit <u>within the sentence</u>

When a prepositional phrase modifies a noun, it is functioning like an adjective, so we refer to its function as **adjectival.**

As a verb modifier, the prepositional phrase adds information that tells when, where, why, how, how often, to what extent, and so on:

> show up <u>throughout our sentences</u> (where)
> swims <u>in the afternoon</u> (when)
> exercised <u>for their health</u> (why)
> watched <u>with horror</u> (how)
> studied <u>for an hour</u> (how long)

Here the prepositional phrases are functioning as adverbs do, as modifiers of the verb, so we refer to their function as **adverbial.**

Unlike the form classes, prepositions cannot be distinguished by their form; that is, they have no endings that identify them, as nouns and verbs often have. Prepositions are one of the word classes called **structure classes.** Other structure classes include determiners, auxiliaries, qualifiers (such as *very,* which you saw in the discussion of adjectives and adverbs), and **conjunctions** (connecting words like *and, or,* and *but*).

As you study the various structures in the sentence patterns, you'll come to recognize a preposition through its role as the headword of a prepositional phrase. And you'll find that those prepositional phrases are functioning either adjectivally, as modifiers of nouns—as we have seen, in the postheadword position of noun phrases—or adverbially, as modifiers of verbs, a role that is examined in the discussion of sentence patterns.

Because prepositional phrases are such common structures in our language, you might find it helpful to review the lists of **simple** and **phrasal prepositions** in Chapter 12. You'll find them on pages 278 and 279–280.

SENTENCE STRUCTURE

To understand grammar is to understand sentence structure—and vice versa: To understand sentence structure is to understand grammar. You began the study of sentence structure in the previous section when you studied the noun phrase and verb phrase and learned to recognize them by their form. In this section we will extend the discussion of form to that of whole sentences.

The study of sentences may at first seem like a formidable, if not impossible, task when you consider that the potential number of sentences a speaker can produce is infinite. But of course it's not impossible. What makes it possible is the systematic nature of sentence structure and the limited number of elements that make up sentences. So despite the infinite possibilities, the number of basic sentence forms, or patterns, is decidedly finite—in fact, the total is very small: Ten sentence patterns account for the underlying skeletal structure of almost all the possible grammatical sentences in English. And the sentences in all those patterns share a great many common elements.

The first step in understanding the skeletal structure of the patterns is to recognize the two parts they all have in common, the **subject** and the **predicate:**

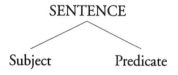

The subject of the sentence, as its name suggests, is generally what the sentence is about—its topic. The predicate is what is said about the subject.

The terms *subject* and *predicate* refer to sentence functions, or roles. But we can also describe those sentence functions in terms of form:

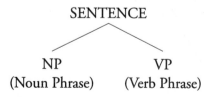

In other words, the subject slot is generally filled by a noun phrase, the predicate slot by a verb phrase. In later chapters we will see sentences in which structures other than noun phrases fill the subject slot; however, the predicate slot is *always* filled by a verb phrase.

Given your knowledge of noun and verb phrases—as well as your intuition— you should have no trouble recognizing the two parts of the following sentences. You'll notice right away that the first word of the subject noun phrase is a determiner.

> The county commissioners passed a new ordinance.
>
> The mayor's husband spoke against the ordinance.
>
> The mayor was upset with her husband.
>
> Some residents of the community spoke for the ordinance.
>
> The merchants in town are unhappy.
>
> This new law prohibits billboards on major highways.

Exercise 1

1. As a quick review of noun phrases, identify the headwords of the subject noun phrases in the six sentences just listed:

Commissioners   *husband*   *mayor*

residents   *merchants*   *law*

2. Find two postheadword modifiers in those six noun phrases:

of the community   *in town*

In form, those two modifiers are *prep. phrases* .

Note: Answers to the exercises are provided, beginning on page 383.

You were probably able to identify the subject noun phrases of the sentences and their headwords without difficulty, given your knowledge of noun phrases, as well as your intuitive knowledge of language. A good way to check that knowledge and to make use of your intuition is to substitute a **pronoun** for the noun phrase:

They	passed a new ordinance.
He	spoke against the ordinance.
She	was upset with her husband.
They	spoke for the ordinance.

They   are unhappy.

It   prohibits billboards on major highways.

As you see, the pronoun stands in for the entire noun phrase, not just the noun headword. Making that substitution, which you do automatically in speech, can help you recognize the boundaries of a noun phrase. In these revised sentences, where a pronoun now functions as the subject, you can easily see the line between the two sentence parts, the subject and the predicate.

Recognition of this subject–predicate relationship, the common element in all of our sentences, is the first step in the study of sentence structure. Equally important for the classification of sentences into sentence patterns is the concept of the verb as the central, pivotal slot in the sentence. Notice that in the following list of the ten patterns, the subjects are identical: *The students.* The ten categories are determined by variations in the predicates, variations in the verb headword and in the structures following the verb. So although we call these basic forms *sentence* patterns, a more accurate label might be *predicate* patterns.

SENTENCE

NP   VP
(Subject)   (Predicate)

	NP (Subject)	VP (Predicate)
I.	The students	are upstairs.
II.	The students	are diligent.
III.	The students	are scholars.
IV.	The students	seem diligent.
V.	The students	became scholars.
VI.	The students	rested.
VII.	The students	studied their assignment.
VIII.	The students	gave the professor their homework.
IX.	The students	consider the teacher intelligent.
X.	The students	consider the course a challenge.

THE SENTENCE SLOTS

One way to think about a sentence is to picture it as a series of slots. In the following chart, where all the slots are labeled, you'll see that the first one in every pattern is the subject, and the second—the first slot in the predicate—is the **predicating verb.**

Because the variations among the sentence patterns are in the predicates, we group the ten patterns according to their verb types: the *be* **patterns,** the **linking verb** patterns, the **intransitive verb** pattern, and the **transitive verb** patterns. You'll notice that the number of slots in the predicate varies: Six of the patterns have two, but Pattern VI has only one slot, and three of the transitive patterns, VIII to X, each have three. The label in parentheses names the function, the role, that the slot performs in the sentence.

The subscript numbers you see in some of the patterns show the relationship between noun phrases: Identical numbers—such as those in Patterns III and V, where both numbers are 1—mean that the two noun phrases have the same referent; different numbers—such as those in Pattern VII, where the numbers are 1 and 2—denote different referents. **Referent** means the thing (or person, event, concept, and so on) that the noun or noun phrase stands for. You'll come to understand noun phrase referents in the dicussions of the separate patterns.

This list of patterns, with each slot labeled according to its form and to its role in the sentence, may look formidable at the moment. But don't worry—and don't try to memorize all this detail. It will fall into place as you come to understand the separate patterns.

The **be** *Patterns*

I	**NP**	*be*	**ADV/TP**
	(subject)	(predicating verb)	(adverbial of time or place)
	The students	*are*	*upstairs*
II	**NP**	*be*	**ADJ**
	(subj)	(pred vb)	(subject complement)
	The students	*are*	*diligent*
III	**NP$_1$**	*be*	**NP$_1$**
	(subj)	(pred vb)	(subj comp)
	The students	*are*	*scholars*

continued

The Linking Verb Patterns

IV	NP	linking verb	ADJ	
	(subj)	(pred vb)	(subj comp)	
	The students	*seem*	*diligent*	
V	NP$_1$	lnk verb	NP$_1$	
	(subj)	(pred vb)	(subj comp)	
	The students	*became*	*scholars*	

The Intransitive Verb Pattern

VI	NP	intransitive verb	
	(subj)	(pred vb)	
	The students	*rested*	

The Transitive Verb Patterns

VII	NP$_1$	transitive verb	NP$_2$	
	(subj)	(pred vb)	(direct object)	
	The students	*studied*	*their assignment*	
VIII	NP$_1$	trans verb	NP$_2$	NP$_3$
	(subj)	(pred vb)	(indirect object)	(dir obj)
	The students	*gave*	*the professor*	*their homework*
IX	NP$_1$	trans verb	NP$_2$	ADJ
	(subj)	(pred vb)	(dir obj)	(obj comp)
	The students	*consider*	*the teacher*	*intelligent*
X	NP$_1$	trans verb	NP$_2$	NP$_2$
	(subj)	(pred vb)	(dir obj)	(obj comp)
	The students	*consider*	*the course*	*a challenge*

THE *BE* PATTERNS

The first three formulas state that when a form of *be* serves as the main, or predicating, verb, an adverbial of time or place (Pattern I), or an adjectival (Pattern II), or a noun phrase (Pattern III) will follow it. The one exception to this rule—and, by the way, we can think of the sentence patterns as descriptions of the rules that our internal computer is programmed to follow—is a statement simply affirming existence, such as "I am." Aside from this exception, Patterns I through III describe all the sentences in which a form of *be* is the predicating verb. (Other one-word forms of *be* are *am, is, are, was, were, being,* and *been;* the expanded forms, described in Chapter 3, include *have been, was being, might be,* and *will be.*)

Pattern I: NP *be* ADV/TP

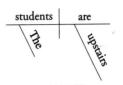

The students are upstairs.

The teacher is here.

The last performance was yesterday.

The ADV in the formula stands for adverbial, a modifier of the verb. The ADV that follows *be* is, with certain exceptions, limited to when and where information, so in the formula for Pattern I we identify the slot as ADV/TP, meaning "adverbial of time or place."[3] In the sample sentences *upstairs* and *here* designate place; *yesterday* designates time. The diagram of Pattern I shows the adverb below the verb, which is where all adverbials are diagrammed.

In the following Pattern I sentences, the adverbials of time and place are prepositional phrases in form:

The next performance is on Monday.

The students are in the library.

The diagram for the adverbial prepositional phrase is a two-part framework with a slanted line for the preposition and a horizontal line for the object:

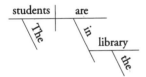   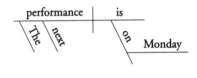

Notice that the object of the preposition is a noun phrase, so it is diagrammed just as the subject noun phrase is—with the headword on the horizontal line and the determiner below it.

Pattern II: NP *be* ADJ

| students | are | \ diligent |

The students are diligent.

The price of gasoline is ridiculous.

The play was very dull.

[3.] See Question 4 at the end of this chapter for examples of these exceptions.

In this pattern the complement that follows *be* is an adjectival. In the language of traditional grammar, this slot is the **subject complement,** which both completes the verb and modifies or describes the subject.[4] The word *complement* refers to a "completer" of the verb. On the diagram the subject complement follows a diagonal line that slants toward the subject to show their relationship.

In the three sample sentences the subject complements are adjectives in form, as they usually are, but sometimes a prepositional phrase will fill the slot. These are set phrases, or idiomatic expressions, that name an attribute of the subject:

You are <u>out of your mind.</u>

Kim is <u>in a bad mood</u>.

Although these sentences may look like those you saw in Pattern I, you can figure out that they belong in Pattern II because you can usually think of an adjective, a single descriptive word, that could substitute for the phrase:

You are <u>crazy</u>.

Kim is <u>cranky</u>.

You can also rule out Pattern I because "out of your mind" and "in a bad mood" do not supply information of time or place.

The diagram for the prepositional phrase in a complement position has the same two-part framework we saw before:

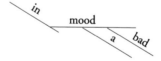

We attach that frame to the main line by means of a pedestal. In this way the structure is immediately identifiable in terms of both form (prepositional phrase) and function (subject complement):

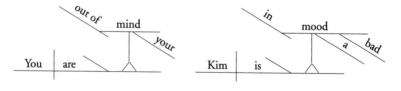

---

[4] More specifically, the traditional label for the subject complement in Pattern II (and IV) is **predicate adjective;** the traditional label for the NP in Pattern III (and V) is **predicate nominative.** We will use the more general term *subject complement* for both adjectives and noun phrases.

PATTERN III: NP₁ *be* NP₁

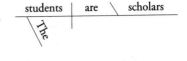

The students are scholars.

Professor Mendez is my math teacher.

The tournament was an exciting event.

The NP, of course, fills the subject slot in all of the patterns; in Pattern III a noun phrase following *be* fills the subject complement slot as well. The numbers that mark the NPs indicate that the two noun phrases have the same referent. For example, when we say "Professor Mendez is my math teacher," the two NPs, "Professor Mendez" and "my math teacher," refer to the same person. The subject complement renames the subject; *be,* the main verb, acts as an "equal sign," connecting the subject with its complement.

Exercise 2

Draw vertical lines to isolate the slots in the following sentences; identify each slot according to its form and function, as the example shows. Then identify the sentence pattern.

Example:

This vacation	has been	wonderful. (Pattern II)
NP	*be*	Adj
subject	pred vb	subj comp

1. Brian's problem is serious. (Pattern __II__)
2. The workers are on the roof. (Pattern __I__)
3. The excitement of the fans is really contagious. (Pattern __II__)
4. Brevity is the soul of wit. [Shakespeare] (Pattern __III__)
5. The final exam was at four o'clock. (Pattern __I__)
6. The kids are very silly. (Pattern __II__)
7. The Wongs were quiet neighbors. (Pattern __III__)
8. Those joggers are out of shape. (Pattern __II__)
9. The basketball team is on a roll. (Pattern __II__)

10. A foolish consistency is the hobgoblin of little minds. [Ralph
    Waldo Emerson] (Pattern __lll__)

Now do a traditional diagram of each sentence, like those you have seen
next to the patterns. (See pages 52–55 for notes on the diagrams.)

THE LINKING VERB PATTERNS

The term *linking verb* applies to all verbs other than *be* completed by a
subject complement—an adjectival or a noun phrase that describes, char-
acterizes, or identifies the subject. Although many grammar books include
be among the linking verbs, we have separated it from the linking verb category in order to emphasize its special qualities—variations of both form
and function that other verbs do not have. However, it is certainly accurate
to think of Patterns II and III as the "linking *be*."

PATTERN IV: NP V-lnk ADJ

The students seem diligent.

I grew sleepy.

The soup tastes salty.

In these sentences an adjectival fills the subject complement slot; it
describes or names an attribute of the subject, just as in Pattern II. In many
cases, a form of *be* can be substituted for the Pattern IV linking verb with
a minimal change in meaning: *I grew sleepy* and *I was sleepy* are certainly
close in meaning. On the other hand, sentences with *be* and *seem* could
have significant differences in meaning.

Pattern IV is a common category for verbs of the senses; besides *taste,*
the verbs *smell, feel, sound,* and *look* often link an adjective to the subject.

The soup smells good.

The dog looks sick.

Again, as with Pattern II, an adjectival prepositional phrase sometimes fills
the subject complement slot:

The piano sounds out of tune.

The fighter seems out of shape.

A complete list of all the verbs that pattern with subject complements
would be fairly short. Besides *seem* and the verbs of the senses, others on
the list are *appear, become, get, prove, remain,* and *turn.* But just because the
list is short, don't try to memorize it. All of these verbs, with the possible

exception of *seem,* hold membership in other verb classes too—transitive or intransitive or both. The way to recognize linking verbs is to understand the role of the subject complement, to recognize the form of the structure following the verb and its relationship to the subject.

PATTERN V: NP₁ V-lnk NP₁

The students became scholars.

My uncle remained a bachelor.

| students | became | scholars |

In this pattern a noun phrase fills the subject complement slot following the linking verb. As the formula shows, the two noun phrases have the same referent, just as they do in Pattern III. We should note, too, that very few linking verbs will fit in Pattern V; most of them take only adjectivals, not noun phrases, as subject complements. The two verbs used in the examples, *become* and *remain,* are the most common. On rare occasions *seem* also takes a noun phrase rather than its usual adjective:

That seemed a good idea.

He seemed a nice person.

But in the case of these sentences, a prepositional phrase with the preposition *like* is more common:

That seemed like a good idea.

He seemed like a nice person.

The subject complement here is an adjectival prepositional phrase, so these two sentences with *like* are Pattern IV.

Again, we should remember that the most common link between two noun phrases with the same referent is *be* (Pattern III). And often the substitution of *be* for the linking verb in Pattern V makes little difference in meaning:

The students became scholars. (Pattern V)

The students are scholars. (Pattern III)

Exercise **3**

Draw vertical lines to identify the sentence slots, as in Exercise 2. Then label them according to their form and function. Identify the sentence pattern. Diagram each sentence.

1. The baby looks healthy.

2. Our new neighbors became our best friends.

3. The piano sounds out of tune.

4. Ryan looks like his older brother.

5. You look a mess!

6. That spaghetti smells wonderful.

7. Your idea seems sensible.

8. Cyberspace remains a complete mystery.

THE OPTIONAL SLOTS

Before looking at the last five patterns, we will examine an **optional slot,** the adverbial slot, which can appear in every sentence pattern. It is useful to think of the two or three or four slots in the basic patterns as sentence "requirements," the elements needed for sentence completeness. But it's obvious that most sentences include information beyond the basic requirements—words or phrases that answer such questions as *where, when, why, how,* and *how often.* Because sentences are grammatical without them, we consider the elements filling these adverbial slots as "optional." You'll recall that in the case of Pattern I, however, the ADV/TP slot is required. But a Pattern I sentence can include optional adverbials, too, along with its required time and/or place adverbial:

The fans were in line (*where?*) for tickets to the play-offs (*why?*).

The plane was on the runway (*where?*) for an hour (*how long?*).

All ten sentence patterns can include optional adverbials, which come at the beginning or end of the sentence or even in the middle. And a sentence can have any number of adverbials, providing information about time, place, manner, reason, and the like.

I stopped <u>at the deli</u> (*where?*) <u>for some bagels</u> (*why?*). (Pattern VI)

<u>On Saturday night</u> (*when?*) the library was almost deserted.
   (Pattern II)

Mario <u>suddenly</u> (*how?*) hit the brakes. (Pattern VII)

Our most common adverbials are simple adverbs (*suddenly, quickly, here, soon, always, sometimes*) and prepositional phrases (*at the deli, on Saturday night, for some bagels*). In Chapter 5 you will study other forms that add adverbial information.

No matter where they occur in the sentence, all adverbials are diagrammed as modifiers of the verb; the adverbs go on diagonal lines and prepositional phrases on a two-part line below the verb:

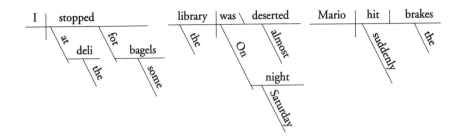

Adverbs can be modified with words like *very*, known as **qualifiers.**

She walked very fast.

A qualified adverb is called an "adverb phrase."

THE INTRANSITIVE VERB PATTERN

PATTERN VI: NP V-int

The students rested.

Mary laughed.

The visitors from El Paso arrived.

This formula describes the pattern of intransitive verb sentences. An **intransitive verb** has no complement—no noun phrase or adjectival—in the slot following the verb. Such skeletal sentences, however, are rare in both speech and writing; most Pattern VI sentences contain more than the simple subject and verb. You're likely to find adverbial information added:

The students rested <u>after their long trip</u>.

Mary laughed <u>loudly</u>.

The visitors from El Paso <u>finally</u> arrived <u>at the airport</u>.

You may have noticed that the diagram of this pattern looks a great deal like that of Pattern I, with no complement following the verb on the main line. But there is a difference: The adverbial in Pattern I is not optional; it is required. Another important difference between Patterns I and VI is in the kind of adverbials the sentences include. Pattern I nearly always has a structure that tells where or when. The optional adverbials of Pattern VI, however, are not restricted to time and place information; they can answer other questions, such as *why* or *how* or *how long*. We can say, "John *slept* soundly" or "John *slept* for an hour" (Pattern VI), but we cannot say, "John *was* soundly" or "John *was* for an hour."

Exceptions to the Intransitive Pattern. Unlike the linking verb patterns, with their handful of verbs, the intransitive category has thousands of members. And among them are a few verbs that require an adverbial to make them complete (much like the required adverbial in Pattern I). For example, the following sentences would be ungrammatical without the adverbial:

> My best friend resides in Northridge.
>
> The boys sneaked past the watchman.
>
> She glanced at her watch.

Reside and *sneak* and *glance* are intransitive verbs, but without the adverbial they are obviously incomplete. We could provide a new sentence pattern for this category of intransitive verbs, but since the number is so small, we will simply consider them exceptions to the usual Pattern VI formula.

Exercise *4*

Prepositional phrases can be adverbial (modifying verbs) or adjectival (modifying nouns). In isolation, however, the two look exactly alike. You need context in order to identify the function.

Here are two sentences with identical prepositional phrases—identical in **form** only:

  1. The puppy <u>on the porch</u> is sleeping.
  2. The puppy is sleeping <u>on the porch</u>.

In sentence (1) the phrase "on the porch" tells "which puppy"; in (2) it tells where the puppy is sleeping. Of course the position in each case also provides a good clue. In (1) it's part of the subject noun phrase. If we substituted the pronoun *she,* it would take the place of the whole NP—"the puppy on the porch."

  She is sleeping

In (2), "on the porch" fills the optional adverbial slot.

  In this exercise you are to identify each prepositional phrase in the following sentences as either adjectival or adverbial. Underline each one, then indicate the noun or verb it modifies.

Example:

The children <u>in the park</u> are playing <u>on the swing</u>.
         ADJ   ADV

1. The rug in the dining room is dirty.
2. On sunny days we lounge on the lawn between classes.
3. The break between classes seems very short on sunny days.
4. At the diner on Water Street, we chatted aimlessly until midnight.
5. Daylilies grow wild in our backyard.
6. In 1638 a young philanthropist of Puritan background became the founder of the oldest university in the United States.
7. The name of that young man was John Harvard.
8. My cousin from Iowa City works for a family with seven children.

For added practice with sentence patterns I through VI, rewrite each of those sentences without their adverbial and adjectival modifiers to clarify the underlying skeletal patterns; then identify the patterns by number.

Intransitive Phrasal Verbs. **Phrasal verbs** are common structures in English. They consist of a verb combined with a preposition-like word, known as a **particle**; together they form an **idiom**. The term *idiom* refers to a combination of words whose meaning cannot be predicted from the meaning of its parts; it is a set expression that acts as a unit. In the following sentence, the meaning of the underlined phrasal verb is not the meaning of *up* added to the meaning of *made:*

    We <u>made up</u>.

Rather, *made up* means "reconciled our differences."

In the following sentence, however, *up* is not part of a phrasal verb:

    We jumped up.

Here *up* is simply an adverb modifying *jumped.* The meaning of *jumped up* is the meaning of the adverb *up* added to *jumped.* The two diagrams demonstrate the difference:

Another way to demonstrate the properties of verbs such as *made up* and *jumped up* is to test variations of the sentences for parallel results. For example, adverbs can often be shifted to opening position without a change in meaning:

Up we jumped.

But in applying this movability test to the verb *made up,* we produce an ungrammatical sentence:

*Up we made.

Here are some other Pattern VI sentences with phrasal verbs. Note that the first two include adverbial prepositional phrases. You'll discover that all five fail the movability test, just as *made up* did.

We <u>turned in</u> at midnight.

The union finally <u>gave in</u> to the company demands.

Tony will <u>pull through</u>.

My favorite slippers <u>wore out</u>.

The party <u>broke up</u>.

Another test you can apply is that of meaning. In each case the phrasal verb has a special meaning that is different from the combined meaning of its parts: Here *gave in* means "capitulated"; *pull through* means "recover"; *broke up* means "ended." This meaning test is often the clearest indication that the word following the verb is indeed a particle producing a phrasal verb.

Exercise **5**

Before diagramming these sentences, decide whether the word following the verb is an *adverb* or a *particle* or a *preposition*. Try both the movability test and the meaning test to help you determine the slot boundaries. Then diagram the sentences.

1. The car turned in a complete circle.
2. The boys turned in at midnight.
3. The baby turned over by himself.
4. The students turned around in their seats.
5. A big crowd turned out for the parade.
6. The fighter passed out in the first round.
7. He came to after thirty seconds.
8. Susan came to the party late.

9. Zane Grey once lived on Catalina Island.

10. His stories live on in our mythology of the Old West.

THE TRANSITIVE VERB PATTERNS

Unlike intransitive verbs, all **transitive verbs** take one or more complements. The last four formulas classify transitive verbs according to the kinds and number of complements they take. All transitive verbs have one complement in common: the **direct object.** Pattern VII, which has only that one complement, can be thought of as the basic transitive verb pattern.

PATTERN VII: NP$_1$ V-tr NP$_2$

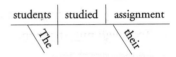

The students studied their
assignment.

The lead-off batter hit a home run.

That car needs four new tires.

In these sentences the noun phrase following the verb, the **direct object,** has a referent different from that of the subject, as indicated by the different numbers in the formula. Traditionally, we think of the transitive verb as an action word: Its subject is considered the doer and its object the receiver of the action. In many Pattern VII sentences this meaning-based definition applies fairly accurately. In our Pattern VII sample sentences, for instance, we can think of *their assignment* as the receiver of the action *studied* and *a home run* as a receiver of the action *hit.* But sometimes the idea of *receiver of the action* doesn't apply at all:

Our team won the game.

We enjoyed the game.

It hardly seems accurate to say that *game* "receives the action." And in

Red spots covered her neck and face.

the verb indicates a condition rather than an action. So although it is true that many transitive verbs are action words and many direct objects are receivers, this meaning-based way of analyzing the sentence doesn't always work.

We can also think of the direct object as the answer to a *what* or *whom* question:

The students studied (*what?*) geometry.

Devon helped (*whom?*) her little brother.

However, the question will not differentiate transitive verbs from linking verbs; the subject complements in Patterns III and V also tell *what*:

> Pat is a doctor. (Pat is *what?*)
>
> Pat became a doctor. (Pat became *what?*)

The one method of distinguishing transitive verbs that works almost every time is the recognition that the two noun phrases have different referents. We don't have to know that *study* and *hit* and *need* are transitive verbs in order to classify the sentences as Pattern VII; we simply recognize that the two noun phrases, the one before the verb and the one following, do not refer to the same thing. Then we know that the second noun phrase is the direct object.

An exception occurs when the direct object is either a **reflexive pronoun** (John cut *himself*) or a **reciprocal pronoun** (John and Mary love *each other*). In sentences with reflexive and reciprocal pronouns, the two NPs, the subject and the direct object, have the same referent, so the numbers 1 and 2 in the formula are inaccurate. In terms of the referents of the NPs, these sentences actually resemble Pattern V, the linking verb pattern. But clearly the purpose and sense of the verbs—*cut* and *love* in the case of these examples—are not like those of the linking verbs. We include these exceptions, where the difference is not in the verbs, in Pattern VII, simply recognizing that when the direct object is a reciprocal or reflexive pronoun the referent numbers are inaccurate.

Transitive Phrasal Verbs.   Many of the idiomatic phrasal verbs belong to the transitive verb category, and like other transitive verbs they take direct objects. Compare the meaning of *came by* in the following sentences:

> He came by his fortune in an unusual way.
>
> He came by the office in a big hurry.

In the first sentence, *came by* means "acquired"; in the second, *by the office* is a prepositional phrase that modifies the intransitive verb *came*, telling where:

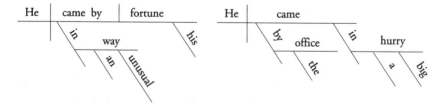

You can also demonstrate the difference between these two sentences by transforming them:

By which office did he come?

*By which fortune did he come?

It is clear that *by* functions differently in the two sentences.

The transitive phrasal verbs include both two- and three-word strings:

I don't <u>go in for</u> horse racing.   _____

I won't <u>put up with</u> your nonsense.   _____

The dog suddenly <u>turned on</u> its trainer.   _____

The principal <u>passed out</u> the new regulations.   _____

I finally <u>found out</u> the truth.   _____

You can test these as you did the intransitive phrasal verbs, by finding a single word that has the same general meaning. On the blank lines write the one-word substitutes.

Exercise   6

Identify the form and function of the sentence slots; then identify the sentence pattern. (Remember to be on the lookout for phrasal verbs.) Diagram each sentence.

1. The boys prepared a terrific spaghetti dinner.
2. An old jalopy turned into our driveway.
3. The ugly duckling turned into a beautiful swan.
4. The fog comes on little cat feet. [Carl Sandburg]
5. On Sundays the neighbor across the hall walks his dog at 6:00 A.M.
6. Betsy often jogs with her dog.
7. After two months the teachers called off their strike.
8. The whole gang reminisced at our class reunion about the good old days.
9. My best friend from high school arrived on Friday for the weekend.
10. The mass of men lead lives of quiet desperation. [Thoreau]

PATTERN VIII: NP$_1$ V-tr NP$_2$ NP$_3$

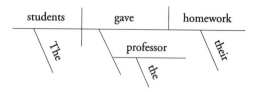

The students gave the professor their homework.

The judges awarded Mary the prize.

The clerk handed me the wrong package.

In this pattern, *two* noun phrase complements follow the verb. Again, the three different subscript numbers on the three NPs indicate that the three noun phrases all have different referents. (When the referents are the same, the numbers are the same, as in Patterns III and V.) The first slot following the verb is the indirect object; the second is the direct object. Even though both Patterns VII and VIII use transitive verbs, they are easily distinguished, since Pattern VII has only one NP following the verb and Pattern VIII has two.

We traditionally define **indirect object** as the recipient or beneficiary of the direct object or as the person to whom or for whom the action is performed. In most cases this definition applies accurately. A Pattern VIII verb—and this is a limited group—usually has a meaning like "give," and the indirect object usually names a person who is the receiver of whatever the subject, NP$_1$, gives. As with Pattern VII, however, the most accurate way to distinguish this pattern is simply to recognize that all three noun phrases have different referents: In the first sample sentence, *the students, the professor,* and *their homework* all refer to different people or things. Incidentally, in the third Pattern VIII sample sentence, a pronoun rather than a noun phrase fills the indirect object slot.

An important characteristic of the Pattern VIII sentence is the option we have of shifting the indirect object to a position following the direct object, where it will be the object of a preposition:

The students gave their homework <u>to the professor</u>.

The judges awarded the prize <u>to Mary</u>.

The clerk handed the wrong package <u>to me</u>.

With some Pattern VIII verbs the preposition will be *for* rather than *to:*

Jim's father bought him a new car.

Jim's father bought a new car <u>for him</u>.

When the direct object is a pronoun rather than a noun phrase, the shift is required; without the prepositional phrase, the sentence would be ungrammatical:

The students gave it to the professor.

*The students gave the professor it.

Jim's father bought it for him.

*Jim's father bought him it.

You'll notice that the shift will not alter the diagram—except for the added word. The indirect object is diagrammed as if it were the object in an adverbial prepositional phrase—even when there is no preposition:

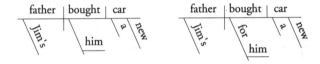

Shifting of the indirect object from the slot following the verb to that of object of the preposition does not mean that the sentence pattern changes: It is still Pattern VIII. Remember that the sentence patterns represent verb categories. Pattern VIII covers the "give" group of verbs, those that include both a direct object and a "recipient" of that object. In other words, there are two possible slots for that recipient, the indirect object, in the Pattern VIII sentence.[5]

In most Pattern VIII sentences, all three NPs have different referents, represented by the numbers 1, 2, and 3. But when the indirect object is a reflexive or reciprocal pronoun (*myself, themselves, each other*, etc.), its referent is identical to that of the subject:

Jill gave *herself* a haircut.

We gave *each other* identical Hanukkah gifts.

---

[5]Some traditional grammar textbooks maintain that when the recipient is shifted to the object position in a prepositional phrase it loses its status as indirect object. However, given our classification of sentence patterns based on verb categories, it seems logical to recognize both versions of the sentence as Pattern VIII and thus retain the label "indirect object" for the recipient in both positions.

Exercise 7

Identify the form and function of the sentence slots. Identify the sentence patterns and diagram the sentences.

Note: Remember that Pattern VIII is the first sentence pattern you have studied in which *two* required slots follow the verb. In most cases they can be thought of as *someone* (the indirect object) and *something* (the direct object). Remember, too, that all of the sentence patterns can include optional slots—i.e., adverbial information (where, when, how, why)—in addition to their required slots.

1. Jessica made her new boyfriend some cookies. V\\\
2. I made an A on my research paper. V\\
   NP   NP   prep phrase
3. For lunch Manny made himself a humongous sandwich.
4. The kids made up a story about Pokemon monsters.
5. The teacher wrote a lot of comments in the margins.
6. My advisor wrote a letter of recommendation for me.
7. I wrote down the assignment very carefully.
8. My roommate always writes in her diary after dinner.

PATTERN IX: NP₁ V-tr NP₂ ADJ

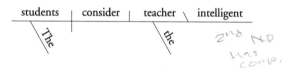

The students consider the teacher intelligent.

The teacher made the test easy.

The boys painted their hockey sticks blue.

In this pattern the direct object, NP₂, is followed by a second complement, an adjective that modifies or describes the direct object; this is the **object complement.** The relationship between the direct object and the object complement is the same as the relationship between the subject and the subject complement in Patterns II and IV. In Patterns II and IV the subject complement describes the subject; in Pattern IX the object complement describes the direct object. We could say, in fact,

The teacher is intelligent.

The test is easy.

The hockey sticks are blue.

The function of the object complement is twofold: (1) It completes the meaning of the verb; and (2) it describes the direct object.

When we remove the object complement from a Pattern IX sentence, we are sometimes left with a grammatical and meaningful sentence: "The boys painted their hockey sticks." (This is now Pattern VII.) However, most Pattern IX sentences require the object complement; the meaning of the first two examples under the Pattern IX formula would change without it:

> The students consider the teacher.

> The teacher made the test.

Pattern IX is a small class, with relatively few verbs, most of which appear equally often in Pattern VII, where they take the direct object only. Other verbs commonly found in this pattern are *prefer, like,* and *find.* Some Pattern IX verbs, such as *consider* and *make,* also commonly appear in Pattern X.

PATTERN X: NP$_1$ V-tr NP$_2$ NP$_2$

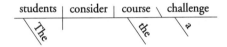

> The students consider the course a challenge.

> The students elected Emma chairperson.

> They named their dog Sandy.

Just as both adjectives and noun phrases can be subject complements, both adjectives and noun phrases also serve as object complements. In Pattern X the object complement is a noun phrase, one with the same referent as the direct object, as indicated by the numbers in the formula. Its twofold purpose is much the same as that of the adjectival object complement in Pattern IX: (1) It completes the meaning of the verb; and (2) it renames the direct object. And, again, we can compare the relationship of the two noun phrases to that of the subject and subject complement in Pattern III:

> The course is a challenge.

> Emma is the chairperson.

In fact, the possibility of actually inserting the words *to be* between the direct object and the following slot can serve as a test for Patterns IX and X. That is, if *to be* is possible, then what follows is an object complement. Which of the following sentences will pass the "to be" test?

> Taro finds his job easy.
>
> Taro found his job easily.
>
> Pam found her job the hard way.
>
> Pam finds her job a challenge.

If you have decided that the first and last sentences in the list could include *to be*, you have identified object complements. The other two, you'll discover, end with adverbials that tell "how" about the verb.

Sometimes the object complement is signaled by *as*, which we call an **expletive:**

> We elected Tom *as* our secretary.
>
> We refer to him *as* "Mr. Secretary."
>
> I know him *as* a good friend.

In some cases, the *as* is optional; in other cases, it is required. With the verbs *refer to* and *know,* for example, we cannot add the object complement without *as:*

> *We refer to him "Mr. Secretary."
>
> *I know her a good friend.

The expletive is diagrammed just before the object complement but above the line:

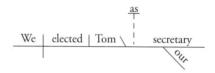

This use of *as* is discussed further on pages 286–287.

COMPOUND STRUCTURES

Every slot in the sentence patterns can be expanded in many ways, as you'll learn in the chapters to come. We'll introduce one common expansion here—that of **coordination,** turning a single structure into a compound structure. Coordination is accomplished with another of the structure classes, the **conjunctions,** the most common of which are the **coordinat-**

ing conjunctions *and, or,* and *but.* The **correlative conjunctions** are two-part connectors*: both–and, not only–but also, either–or,* and *neither–nor.*

Every slot in the sentence patterns can be filled by a compound structure:

Cats *and* dogs fight. (compound subject)

They *either* drove *or* took the bus. (compound predicate)

The teacher was tough *but* fair. (compound subject complement)

We drove over the river and through the woods. (compound adverbial prepositional phrase)

I finished both my biology project and my history paper. (compound direct object)

To diagram compound structures, we simply double the line and connect the two parts with a dotted line. The conjunction goes on the dotted line.

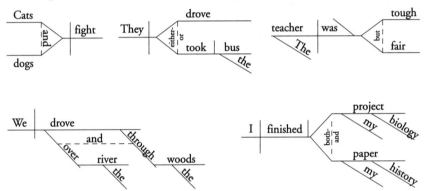

In Chapter 9 we will take up the coordination of full sentences.

Exercise 8

First identify the sentence slots according to their form and function to help you identify sentence patterns. Then diagram the sentences. (Note: The list includes sentences representing all four verb classes: *be,* linking, intransitive, and transitive.)

1. The kids on our block and their dogs drive my mother crazy. \⅄

2. She calls them a menace to the neighborhood. ✕

3. On Friday the weather suddenly turned cold and blustery. |⅃

4. Yesterday Luis bought himself an expensive leather coat at Nordstrom. ⅃|\\

5. England's soccer fans have a reputation for wild behavior.

6. My boss at the pizza parlor promised me a raise.

7. Hector's party broke up at midnight.

8. The Green Party chose Ralph Nader as its candidate in 2000.

9. Joe cut himself a huge piece of cake.

10. Alaska became the forty-ninth state in 1959.

11. According to the latest census, Wyoming is our least populous state.

12. Some people consider Minnesota's winters excessively long.

13. Our team plays Indiana in the Holiday Invitational Tournament on Saturday night.

14. I ordered you a large Coke and a cheeseburger with onions.

15. Professor Moore assigned the class six chapters for Monday.

EXCEPTIONS TO THE TEN SENTENCE PATTERNS

The ten sentence patterns described here represent the skeletal structure of most English sentences—at least 95 percent, if not more. However, some sentences can be thought of as exceptions to a particular pattern. For example, certain intransitive verbs, such as *reside, sneak,* and *glance,* would be ungrammatical without an adverbial—as we saw on page 36. Certain transitive verbs also differ from the majority because they require adverbials to be complete:

We *placed* an ad in the paper.

Joe *put* the groceries away.

To be accurate, the formulas for these sentences would have to include ADV as a requirement, not just an optional slot. However, because the number of these exceptions is small, we will simply include them as variations of Pattern VI or Pattern VII.

Another group of verbs, sometimes called "midverbs," include characteristics of both transitive and intransitive verbs: They require a complement, as transitive verbs do, but the complement differs from mainstream direct objects. For example, rather than telling "what" or "whom," the complements following the verbs *weigh* and *cost* provide information of amount, or measure; they have almost an adverbial sense:

The roast weighs five pounds.

The roast cost twenty dollars.

Even though *weigh* and *cost* are different from the exceptional intransitive and transitive verbs cited earlier (which take straightforward adverbials of place), we will consider these uses of *weigh* and *cost* as Pattern VI, rather than add a new sentence pattern, recognizing that for them too the "optional slot" is not optional.

IMPERATIVE SENTENCES (COMMANDS)

We have described sentences as two-part structures consisting of a subject and a predicate. However, in the case of **imperative sentences,** or **commands,** the subject is unstated, although clearly understood:

SENTENCE

Subject   Predicate

(you)   Help!
(you)   Take your time.
(you)   Sit down.

Commands are fairly common in casual speech. They are not as common in writing, although you've seen them several times in this chapter, in the directions for the exercises:

Draw vertical lines to identify the sentence slots.

Diagram each sentence.

In the diagram of the imperative sentence, the understood subject (you) is shown in parentheses:

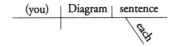

PUNCTUATION AND THE SENTENCE PATTERNS

There is an easy punctuation lesson to be learned from the sentence patterns with their two or three or four slots:

DO NOT PUT SINGLE COMMAS BETWEEN THE REQUIRED SLOTS.

That is, never separate

- the subject from the verb.
- the verb from the direct object.
- the direct object from the object complement.
- the indirect object from the direct object.
- the verb from the subject complement.

For example, in this sentence there is no place for commas:

All of the discussion groups I took part in during Orientation
Week were extremely helpful for the incoming freshmen.

Even though the noun phrases that fill the slots may be long, the slots are never separated by commas. A pause for breath does not signal a comma. Sometimes punctuation is called for *within* a noun phrase slot, but even then the rule applies: no single commas between the required slots.

The one exception to this rule occurs when the direct object is a direct quotation following a verb like *say*. Here the punctuation convention calls for a comma before the quoted words:

He said, "I love you."

DIAGRAMMING THE SENTENCE PATTERNS

The traditional sentence diagram is a visual aid to help you learn the patterns, to understand their common features, and to distinguish their differences. On page 51, where all ten diagrams are shown together, you can see the relationships among them. For example, the two linking verb patterns closely resemble the two *be* patterns, II and III, above them. Likewise, the intransitive verb pattern, VI, placed at the left of the page, looks exactly like the main line of Pattern I. Finally, the slanted line that separates the subject complement from the verb in the *be* and linking verb patterns, II through V, depicts a relationship similar to that of the object complement and object in Patterns IX and X, which are also separated by a slanted line. You might find it useful to label the slots on the diagrams according to their functions (subject, subject complement, direct object, indirect object, object complement).

The be *Patterns*

I. NP *be* ADV/TP

II. NP *be* ADJ

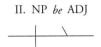

III. NP₁ *be* NP₁

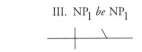

The Linking Verb Patterns

IV. NP V-lnk ADJ

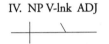

V. NP₁ V-lnk NP₁

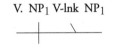

The Intransitive Verb Pattern

VI. NP V-int

The Transitive Verb Patterns

VII. NP₁ V-tr NP₂

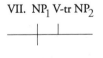

VIII. NP₁ V-tr NP₂ NP₃

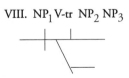

IX. NP₁ V-tr NP₂ ADJ

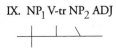

X. NP₁ V-tr NP₂ NP₂

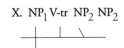

NOTES ON THE DIAGRAMS

Except for a few modifications, this method of diagramming follows the Reed and Kellogg system, which dates back to the late nineteenth century and traditional school grammar. The diagram provides you with a visual framework for organizing details of the sentence patterns, recognizing their similarities and differences, and understanding the relationship of their parts. Doing the diagram forces you to account for every structure in the sentence.

The diagram is not perfect by any means. One major drawback is that it does not maintain word order. And there are a number of sentence structures that it does not represent accurately. But for the most part, for most of our sentences, the diagram provides a valuable visual aid.

The Main Line. The positions on the main horizontal line of the diagram represent the slots in the sentence pattern formulas. Only two required slots are not included on the main line: the adverbial (see Pattern I) and the indirect object (see Pattern VIII). The vertical line that bisects the main line separates the subject and the predicate, showing the binary nature of the sentence. The other vertical and diagonal lines stop at the horizontal line:

The Noun Phrase. The noun phrases we have used so far are fairly simple; in Chapter 6 we will identify a wide variety of structures that can modify and expand the noun. But now we will simply recognize the feature that all noun phrases have in common—the noun head, or headword. This is the single word that fills the various NP slots of the diagrams; it always occupies a horizontal line. The modifiers slant down from the noun headword:

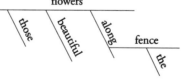

Qualifiers of adjectives are placed on diagonal lines attached to and parallel with the adjective:

The Verb Phrase.

1. The verb and its auxiliaries go on the main line. In the case of negative verbs, the *not* is usually placed on a diagonal line below the verb. If if is contracted, it can remain attached to the verb:

2. The subject complement follows a diagonal line. The line slants toward the subject to show their relationship:

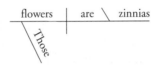

3. The direct object always follows a vertical line:

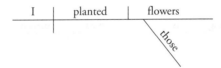

Note that only Patterns VII through X have this vertical line following the verb: the only patterns with a direct object.

4. The object complement is set off from the direct object by a line that slants toward the object:

5. The indirect object is placed below the verb. We can understand the logic of this treatment of the indirect object when we realize that it can be expressed by a prepositional phrase without changing the meaning or the pattern of the sentence. Both of these sentences are Pattern VIII:

The students gave <u>the teacher</u> an apple.

The students gave an apple <u>to the teacher</u>.

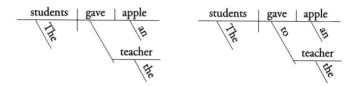

6. Adverbs are placed on slanted lines below the verb; they are modifiers of the verb:

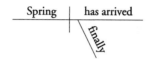

7. Like the qualifiers of adjectives, qualifiers of adverbs are placed on diagonal lines attached to the adverb:

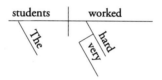

The Prepositional Phrase. The preposition is placed on a diagonal line, its object on a horizontal line attached to it. The prepositional phrase slants down from the noun or verb it modifies. When the prepositional phrase fills the subject complement slot, it is attached to the main line by means of a pedestal:

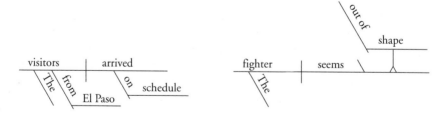

Compound Structures. The two (or more) parts of a compound structure are connected by a dotted line, which holds the conjunction. If a modifier applies to both (or all) parts of the compound structure, it is attached to a line common to them:

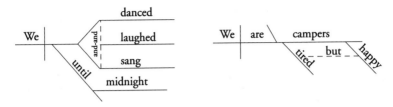

The two clauses of a compound sentence are connected with a dotted line from verb to verb, with the conjunction on a solid line between the two:

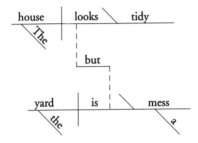

Punctuation. There are no punctuation marks of any kind in the diagram, other than apostrophes.

CHAPTER 2

Key Terms

In this chapter you've been introduced to the basic vocabulary of sentence grammar. Even though this list of key terms may look formidable, some of the terms are already familiar, and those that are new will become more familiar as you continue the study of sentences. You'll discover too that the patterns and their diagrams, as shown on page 51, provide a framework for helping you organize many of these concepts.

Adjectival	Article
Adjective	*Be* patterns
Adverb	Command
Adverbial	Comparative degree

Complement

Compound structure

Coordinating conjunction

Correlative conjunction

Demonstrative pronoun

Determiner

Direct object

Headword

Imperative sentence

Indirect object

Intransitive verb

Linking verb

Noun

Noun phrase

Object complement

Optional slot

Particle

Past tense

Phrasal verb

Phrase

Plural

Possessive case

Predicate

Predicating verb

Preposition

Prepositional phrase

Pronoun

Qualifier

Reciprocal pronoun

Referent

Reflexive pronoun

Sentence pattern

Subject

Subject complement

Superlative degree

Transitive verb

Verb

Verb phrase

Sentences
for PRACTICE

Identify the form and function of the sentence slots; identify the sentence pattern; diagram.

1. My uncle recently moved to Arizona for his health. VI

2. The cherry trees in Washington, D.C., were a gift from the Japanese government in 1912. III

3. After the picnic the teacher rounded up the students for the long bus ride. VII

4. Both the asparagus and the strawberries in our garden grow fast during June. VI

5. Our grocer calls asparagus the Rolls Royce of vegetables. X

6. In 2000 scientists announced important breakthroughs in research on the human genome. VII

7. Some people find modern art very depressing.

8. According to the afternoon paper, the police looked into the sources of the reporter's information.

9. Our art class was at the museum and the botanical gardens on Tuesday afternoon.

10. Jeff pleaded innocent.

11. Barbara and Dennis now telecommute from Washington to their jobs in New Jersey.

12. On Saturday night we left the waitress a generous tip for her splendid service.

13. Kristi became the Webmistress for a new dot-com company.

14. Yesterday my landlord was in a state of panic.

15. According to the latest UN statistics, Norway is now the world's largest exporter of seafood.

QUESTIONS
?
for DISCUSSION

1. Here are some pairs of sentences that look alike. Think about their sentence patterns; label the form and function of their slots and discuss the problems you encounter; diagram the sentences to demonstrate their differences.

   > The teacher made the test hard.
   >
   > The batter hit the ball hard.
   >
   > My husband made me a chocolate cake.
   >
   > My husband made me a happy woman.
   >
   > We set off through the woods at dawn.
   >
   > We set off the firecrackers at dawn.

2. The following sentences are either Pattern I or Pattern II; in other words, the prepositional phrases following *be* are either adverbial or adjectival. What test can you use to distinguish between them?

   > The mechanic is under the car.
   >
   > The mechanic is under the weather.
   >
   > The teacher is in a bad mood.
   >
   > The teacher is in the cafeteria.

3. Very few verbs are restricted to a single category. Verbs like *taste* and *feel* commonly act as linking verbs, but they can fit into other classes as well. Identify the patterns of the following sentences:

> The cook tasted the soup.
>
> The soup tasted good.

> I felt the kitten's fur.
>
> The fur feels soft.

> The farmers in Iowa grow a lot of wheat.
>
> The wheat grows fast in July.
>
> We grew weary in the hot sun.

> She appeared tired.
>
> Black clouds appeared suddenly on the horizon.

4. Some sentences in English are not represented by one of the ten patterns described in this chapter. Among those that don't fit very well are certain sentences with *be* as the main verb:

> The book is about black holes.
>
> The potato salad is for the picnic.
>
> I am from San Francisco.
>
> I am in favor of the amendment.
>
> The misunderstanding was over a scheduling conflict.
>
> Pat and Jen are among the most popular students in our class.

The prepositional phrases in these sentences are different from those we saw in Patterns I and II. How would you characterize the difference? A paraphrase of the sentence might help you to determine a possible pattern. And in the following *be* sentences, the noun phrase in subject complement position is different from those we saw in Pattern III. Do these sentences belong in Pattern III? If not, where do they belong?

> My shoes are the wrong color.
>
> This new wallpaper is an odd pattern.

In what way does the following sentence change our understanding of the *be* patterns?

> The time is now.

5. People commonly say "I feel badly" when discussing their physical or mental condition. Using your understanding of sentence patterns, explain why this is sometimes considered an ungrammatical sentence. Assuming that "I feel badly" is indeed questionable, how do you explain the acceptance of "I feel strongly about that"?

6. What is unusual about the following sentence? Think about the sentence pattern:

    The waitress served me my coffee black.

7. We have seen sentences in which prepositional phrases function as subject complements. Can they be object complements as well?

8. A sentence is **ambiguous** when it has more than one possible meaning. You can illustrate the two meanings of the following sentences by diagramming each in two different ways. Think about sentence patterns and the referents of the noun phrases.

    Herbert found his new bride a good cook.

    Rosa called her mother.

CLASSROOM APPLICATIONS

The following can be organized as either oral or written activities, perhaps as timed group competitions:

1. Write four sentences about summer (winter, fall, spring) in which each sentence uses a different verb category: *be*, linking, intransitive, and transitive.

2. Write ten sentences about your favorite sport or hobby, using all ten patterns.

3. Drawing on your own internal dictionary, write down as many two-word (verb + particle) idioms as you can, using the particles *up, down, in, out, on, off,* and *over*. Here are some verbs to get you started, but don't limit yourself to these: *break, take, look, run.* (Note: The resulting idioms will include both nouns and verbs—e.g., *[the] break-in, [to] break up.*)

CHAPTER
3

Expanding the Main Verb

CHAPTER PREVIEW

In Chapter 2 we applied the term *form classes* to nouns, verbs, adjectives, and adverbs, the content words of the language, all of which have endings, or forms, that help us identify them. This chapter examines verbs, the most systematic of the four form classes. In this examination of verbs and their auxiliaries, you will be introduced to the discovery method of the transformational linguists, whose goal is to understand how our internal rules generate, or produce, grammatical sentences—or, in this case, grammatical verb strings.

We will analyze the underlying rules that enable us to come up with the wide variety of auxiliary + verb combinations that we use every day. This analysis of our verb expertise, in fact, probably illustrates better than any other part of the grammar what we mean by the word *system*.

THE FIVE VERB FORMS

Before analyzing the system for adding auxiliaries, we will review the five forms that all of our verbs have so that we can conveniently discuss them, using labels that reflect our emphasis on form rather than meaning. Here again are the two verbs we looked at in Chapter 2, one regular and one irregular:

	Regular	Irregular
base form (present tense)	laugh	eat
-*s* form (3rd person, present, singular)	laughs	eats
-*ed* form (past tense)	laughed	ate
-*ing* form (present participle)	laughing	eating
-*en* form (past participle)	laughed	eaten

Most of our verbs—all except 150 or so—are regular, as are all the new verbs that we acquire. For example, here are two recent acquisitions:

I <u>faxed</u> a letter to you yesterday.

I have <u>e-mailed</u> the invitations to our reunion.

As the verb *laugh* and these two new ones illustrate, regular verbs are those in which the past tense and the past participle are formed by adding the **suffix** -*ed* (or, in a few cases, -*t*) to the base form. Among the irregular verbs, there are many patterns of irregularity, but the deviations from regular verbs show up only in these two forms, the past and the past participle. All verbs, without exception, have regular -*s* and -*ing* forms. (This might be the only rule in our grammar without an exception!)

In our discussion of verbs, we will use the label -*ed* to denote the past tense form and -*en* to denote the past participle form. The past of regular verbs provides the -*ed* label; the past participle of irregular verbs like *eat* (as well as our most common verb, *be*, and about fifteen others, including *drive, give, break,* and *speak)* provides the label for the past participle, which we call the -*en* form. This means that the -*en* form of *laugh* is *laughed;* the -*ed* form of *eat* is *ate.*

Anyone familiar with a foreign language will appreciate the simplicity of our small set of only five verb forms. Instead of adding auxiliaries to express differences as we do in English, a speaker of French or Spanish must add a different suffix to the verb. French verbs, for instance, have more than seventy different forms to express variations in person, number, tense, and mood.

A speaker of English uses only two different forms *(eat, eats)* to express the present tense in first, second, and third **person**, both singular and plural; the speaker of French uses five:

	Singular	Plural
1st person	I eat *(je mange)*	we eat *(nous mangeons)*
2nd person	you eat *(tu manges)*	you eat *(vous mangez)*
3rd person	he eats *(il mange)*	they eat *(ils mangent)*

The speaker of English uses only one form *(ate)* to express the simple past tense in all three persons, both singular and plural. Again, the French speaker uses five, all different from the first set. In fact, for the various tenses and moods, the speaker of French uses fourteen such sets, or conjugations, all with different verb endings.

The only English verb with more than five forms is *be,* the most irregular of our irregular verbs. It is also the only verb with a separate form for the **infinitive,** or base *(be);* it is the only one with three forms for present tense *(am, is, are)* and two for *past (was, were);* and of course it has an *-en* form *(been)* and an *-ing (being)*—eight forms in all. In addition to its status as a main verb, *be* also serves as an auxiliary in our verb-expansion rule and as the auxiliary that turns the active voice to passive, as you will learn in this chapter.

Exercise 9

Fill the blanks with the four additional forms of the verbs listed on the left. If you have a problem figuring out the *-ed* form, simply use it in a sentence with *yesterday:* "Yesterday I _____." If you have trouble figuring out the *-en* form, use it in a sentence with *have:* "I have _____."

BASE	-*s* FORM	-*ed* FORM	-*ing* FORM	-*en* FORM
1. have	_____	_____	_____	_____
2. do	_____	_____	_____	_____
3. say	_____	_____	_____	_____
4. make	_____	_____	_____	_____
5. go	_____	_____	_____	_____
6. take	_____	_____	_____	_____
7. come	_____	_____	_____	_____
8. see	_____	_____	_____	_____
9. get	_____	_____	_____	_____
10. move	_____	_____	_____	_____
11. prove	_____	_____	_____	_____
12. put	_____	_____	_____	_____
13. think	_____	_____	_____	_____
14. beat	_____	_____	_____	_____
15. meet	_____	_____	_____	_____

The first nine verbs in this exercise, along with *be,* make up a list of the ten most frequently used verbs in English.

Q. What do these ten have in common?

A. They are all irregular!

AUXILIARY–VERB COMBINATIONS

You learned in Chapter 2 that the predicating verb is the central, or pivotal, slot in the sentence. It is the verb that determines the slots that follow. The predicating verbs we have used in sentence examples so far have been one-word forms, the simple present or past tense, such as *are, were, studied, became, consider.* In our everyday speech and writing, of course, we are just as likely to use expanded forms that include one or more **auxiliaries**, also called **helping verbs:**

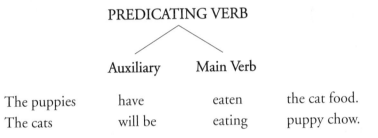

PREDICATING VERB

Auxiliary   Main Verb

| The puppies | have | eaten | the cat food. |
| The cats | will be | eating | puppy chow. |

As this branching diagram shows, we are using the term *predicating verb* as a label for the entire string that fills the verb slot in the sentence patterns, including auxiliaries and the main verb.

To discover how our auxiliary system works, we will examine a dozen sentences, all of which have a form of *eat* as the main verb, beginning with the two we have just seen:

1. The puppies <u>have eaten</u> the cat food.
2. The cats <u>will be eating</u> puppy chow.
3. I <u>eat</u> an apple every day.
4. I <u>ate</u> one this morning.
5. My sister <u>eats</u> a banana every day.
6. I <u>should eat</u> bananas for their potassium.
7. I <u>am eating</u> healthy these days.
8. We <u>were eating</u> popcorn throughout the movie.
9. We <u>may eat</u> out on Saturday night.
10. I <u>had eaten</u> all the chips by the time the guests arrived.
11. I <u>could have eaten</u> even more.
12. We <u>have been eating</u> junk food all evening.

What is the system underlying these one- and two- and three-word verb strings? How many more variations are there? If we were going to write a computer program to generate all the possible variations, what rules and restrictions would have to be included?

To answer these questions, we will make some observations about the verb strings in our twelve sentences:

1. The base form, *eat*, is used both by itself [3] and with *should* [6] and *may* [9].

2. the *-ed* and *-s* forms of *eat* [4 and 5] are used only by themselves, never with an auxiliary word.

3. An *-en* form, *eaten* or *been*, is used after a form of *have: have* [1, 11, and 12] and *had* [10].

4. The *-ing* form, *eating*, is used after a form of *be: be* [2], *am* [7], *were* [8], and *been* [12].

5. A form of *eat*, the main verb (MV), is always the last word in the string.

We will represent these last three observations by means of a formula:

(have + -en) (be + -ing) MV

In Chapter 2, you'll recall, the parentheses in the sentence pattern formulas mean "optional." The same is true here. Both *have* and *be* are optional auxiliaries: A grammatical verb string does not require either or both of them. As the formula indicates, however, when we do choose *have* as an auxiliary, we are also choosing *-en*; that is, the *-en* suffix will attach itself to the following word. And when we choose *be*, the *-ing* suffix will attach itself to the following word. In the formula the main verb is shown without parentheses because it is not optional; it is always a component of the predicating verb.

We can derive two further observations from the twelve sentences:

6. Besides *have* and *be*, the sentences illustrate another kind of auxiliary—*will* [2], *should* [6], *may* [9], and *could* [11], called **modal auxiliaries (M)**.

7. When a modal is selected, it is always first in line.

Now we can add another element, (M), to the formula:

(M) (have + -en) (be + -ing) MV

The formula reads as follows:

- In generating a verb string, we can use a modal auxiliary if we choose; when we do, it comes first.

- We can also choose the auxiliary *have;* when we do, an *-en* form follows it.
- We can also choose the auxiliary *be;* when we do, an *-ing* form follows.
- When we use more than one auxiliary, they appear in the order given: modal, *have, be.*
- The last word in the string is the main verb.

To demonstrate how the formula works, let's look at the verbs in three of our twelve *eat* sentences:

Sentence 1: **The puppies <u>have eaten</u> the cat food.**

Here we passed up (M) and chose *have* + *-en* as the auxiliary. The *-en* will be attached to the following word:

$$\text{have + -en + eat} \; = \; have\ eaten$$

Sentence 2: **The cats <u>will be eating</u> puppy chow.**

This time we chose M, the modal auxiliary *will;* we skipped (have + -en) and chose *be* + *-ing:*

$$\text{will + be + -ing + eat} \; = \; will\ be\ eating$$

Sentence 12: **We <u>have been eating</u> junk food all evening.**

In this sentence we skipped (M) and chose both *have* + *-en* and *be* + *-ing:*

$$\text{have + -en + be + -ing + eat} \; = \; have\ been\ eating$$

So far we have a simple but powerful formula, capable of generating a great many variations of the verb. But something is missing. How did we generate *were eating* in sentence [8] and *had eaten* in sentence [10]? What is different about them? The difference is **tense**, which refers to time: *had* and *were* are past tense, the *-ed* forms of *have* and *be.* This means we have to add one more component to the formula: T, for tense. Among the five forms of the verb, you will recall, the present and past forms are the only tenses, so in the formula T will represent either present or past tense.

Here, then, is the complete formula for what is known as the **verb-expansion rule:**

T (M) (have + -en) (be + -ing) MV

You might find the branching diagram helpful for visualizing the rule:

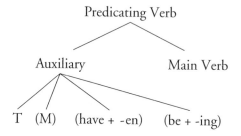

The branching diagram illustrates the predicating verb as a two-part structure: an auxiliary and a main verb. Those two parts are obvious in a sentence such as

> We *had eaten* by the time you arrived.

or

> I *was eating* when you arrived.

Sometimes the two parts of the predicating verbs are not as obvious:

> He *eats* too fast.

> Beth already *ate*.

Look again at the formula, and remember that parentheses mean "optional." The components of the verb that are shown without parentheses are required.

In sentences with *eats* and *ate,* then, what does the auxiliary consist of?

Look again at the second observation we made on page 64 about our list of twelve sentences: "The *-ed* and *-s* forms of *eat* are used only by themselves, never with an auxiliary word." It's clear then that the auxiliary component of the verbs in sentences with *ate* or *eats* is simply T.

THE MODAL AUXILIARIES

We have six major modals in English, four of which have different forms for present and past:

Present	*Past*
will	would
shall	should
can	could
may	might

Two modals have no past form:

must

ought to

Although we call these forms present and past, that meaning is not really accurate in present-day English. For example, in "I may eat" (present), the act of eating is not going on; in "I might eat" (past) the act of eating is not over; in fact, in both cases it may never happen.

Only in a few instances do the modals indicate actual time. In the company of a time adverbial, *can* and *could* will designate present or past:

This morning the groundhog <u>can</u> see his shadow.

Yesterday the groundhog <u>could</u> see his shadow.

However, because we want to emphasize the concept of the predicating verb as a "tensed verb," we will recognize that the position following T carries the tense marker, no matter what occupies that position, whether a modal, the auxiliary *have*, the auxiliary *be,* or the main verb.

The modals differ from the auxiliaries *have* and *be*, both of which can fill the role of main verb in addition to their auxiliary role. The modals never fill the main verb slot, nor do they have all five forms that verbs have.[1] They are so named because they affect what is called the mood of the verb. **Mood** refers to the manner in which a verb is expressed, such as a fact, a desire, a possibility, or a command. **Indicative mood** refers to a sentence dealing with a fact or a question about a fact. The modals convey conditions of probability, possibility, obligation, or necessity: *I may eat; I could eat; I should eat; I must eat.* These are known as the **conditional mood.** We

---

[1]Sometimes modals appear without verbs in elliptical clauses, where the main verb is understood but not expressed:

Who'll cook the spaghetti? I *will.*

May I join you? Yes, you *may.*

should note also that the modals *will* and *shall* produce what traditional grammarians call the future tense: *will eat* and *shall eat*. (Future time is also commonly expressed with *be* + *ing* + *go*—"I'm going to eat soon"— and with present tense and an adverbial—"The bus leaves at noon.")

Exercise 10

A. What is the expanded verb that each of the following strings will produce? (Assume in each case that the subject is Fred.)

Example:

   past + have + -en + help = *had helped*

1. pres + have + -en + work
2. past + be + -ing + work
3. pres + will + be + -ing + play
4. past + be + -ing + be
5. pres + be + -ing + have
6. past + shall + have + -en + have
7. past + have + -en + have
8. past + can + have + -en + be
9. pres + may + have + -en + be + -ing + try
10. past + may + have + -en + be + -ing + be

B. Identify the components of the predicating verb in each of the following sentences. Your answers will look like the strings given in Part A.

Example:

   Mike was having a bad day = *past* + *be* + *-ing* + *have*

1. The students were studying in the library.
   Past + be + -ing + study
2. I have finally found my lost scarf. [Note: Adverbs, such as *finally*, should not appear in your verb string.]
   present + have + -en
3. I lost it on the first day of classes.
   past + lose
4. Mickey has been skipping classes lately.
   present + have + -en + be + -ing + skip
5. He could be in big trouble.
   past + can + be
6. My hard drive crashed yesterday.
   past + crash
7. Joanie certainly seems happy in her new apartment.
   present + seems

8. She will probably be having a party this weekend.
9. My roommate may be graduating after only three years.
10. I should have studied harder for this test.

THE SUBJUNCTIVE MOOD

You may also be familiar with the **subjunctive mood**. Unlike the conditional mood, the subjunctive does not involve modal auxiliaries. Rather, it is simply a variation of the verb that we use in special circumstances:

1. In *that* clauses after verbs conveying a strong suggestion or recommendation, we use the base form of the verb:

> We suggested that Mary go with us.
>
> Kathy insisted that Bill consult the doctor.
>
> I move that the meeting be adjourned.

Even for third-person singular subjects, which would normally take the *-s* form, we use the base form in these clauses: Mary *go;* Bill *consult;* the meeting *be.* Other verbs that commonly take clauses in the subjunctive mood are *command, demand, ask, require, order, recommend,* and *propose.* A subjunctive *that* clause also follows certain nouns and adjectives related to commands and suggestions:

> The suggestion that Bill see the doctor was a good one.
>
> It is advisable that he get a thorough checkup.

2. In *if* clauses that express a wish or a condition contrary to fact, we use *were* as the standard form of *be,* no matter what the subject:

> If I were you, I'd be careful.
>
> If Joe weren't so lazy, he'd probably be a millionaire.

The use of *was* is also fairly common in sentences like the second example:

> If Joe was here, he'd agree with me.

In writing, however, the subjunctive *were* is the standard form.

USING THE VERB FORMS

Following are examples of our most common verb forms; their traditional labels are shown in parentheses.[2]

Base form and -s form (SIMPLE PRESENT)

I <u>live</u> in Omaha.

The news <u>comes on</u> at six.   *Historical, habitual*

Milton's poetry <u>speaks</u> to everyone.   *or timeless present*

I <u>understand</u> your position.   *Present point in time*

Pres + be + -ing + MV (PRESENT PROGRESSIVE)

I <u>am working</u> at Wal-Mart.   *Present action of*

John <u>is taking</u> philosophy this term.   *limited duration*

Note that both of these present forms can indicate future time with the addition of an appropriate adverbial:

The bus <u>leaves</u> *at seven.*

We'<u>re having</u> pizza *tonight.*

Past + MV (SIMPLE PAST)

I <u>moved</u> to Omaha last March.

A virus <u>erased</u> all of my data.   *Specific point in time*

Note that with an appropriate adverbial, this form can indicate a period of time in the past:

I <u>studied</u> Spanish *for three years in high school.*

Past + be + - ing + MV (PAST PROGRESSIVE)

A baby <u>was crying</u> during the   *Past action of limited*

    entire ceremony this morning.   *duration (often to show*

I <u>was trying</u> to sleep last night dur-   *one particular action dur-*

    ing the party, but it was no use.   *ing a larger span of time).*

---

[2] These traditional labels are called tenses. However, given our use of *tense* in the verb-expansion rule—that is, our restriction of T to present and past—we will adopt the linguist's term **aspect** in reference to the verb strings that are expanded with the perfect (*have + -en*) and progressive (*be + -ing*) auxiliaries. For more about the description of tense and aspect, see Brock Haussamen, *Revising the Rules: Traditional Grammar and Modern Linguistics,* 2nd ed. (Dubuque, IA: Kendall/Hunt, 1997).

Pres + have + - en + MV (PRESENT PERFECT)

The leaves <u>have turned</u> yellow already.

I <u>have finished</u> my work.

I <u>have memorized</u> several of Frost's poems.

A completed action extending from a point in the past to either the present or the near present or occurring at an unspecified past time.

Past + have + - en + MV (PAST PERFECT)

The hikers <u>had used up</u> all their water, when finally they found a hidden spring.

The students <u>had finished</u> only the first page of the test by the time the bell rang.

Past action completed before another action in the past.

Pres + have + - en + be + - ing + MV (PRESENT PERFECT PROGRESSIVE)

The authorities <u>have been looking</u> for the arson suspect since last Sunday.

Past action continuing into the present.

Past + have + -en + be + - ing + MV (PAST PERFECT PROGRESSIVE)

The authorities <u>had been looking</u> for the suspect even before the fire broke out.

Continuing past action completed before another action in the past.

EXCEPTIONS TO THE RULE

The verb-expansion rule is simple, but it is powerful. With it we can expand the verb slot in all the sentence patterns to express a great many variations in meaning. Given the variety of modals we have, which we can use with or without *have + -en* and *be + -ing*, the number of possible variations adds up to fifty or more for most verbs. However, we rarely use all the possibilities for any given verb. Our system restricts the use of some, and others we simply have no occasion for.

Although we may say,

He seems grumpy.

and

They have remained friends.

We would probably never say,

*He is seeming grumpy.

or

*They have been remaining friends.

Most of the exceptions involve the restriction of *be* + *-ing* with certain linking verbs, with *be* as main verb, and with a small number of transitive verbs that refer to mental processes, such as *prefer, know,* and *like,* or states, such as *own, resemble,* and *weigh.* The restriction also applies to Pattern I (NP *be* ADV/TP) sentences, where *be* + *-ing* never appears as an auxiliary:

The students are upstairs.

*The students are being upstairs.

The bus will be here soon.

*The bus is being here soon.

If English is your mother tongue, these rules are part of your internal grammar; they're not rules you think about at all when you speak or write. However, if you are not a native speaker of English, if you're still learning some of the nuances of the language, you might want to pay special attention to this *be* + *-ing* restriction.

✗THE STAND-IN AUXILIARY *DO*

You may have noticed that one common auxiliary does not appear in our verb-expansion rule (even though it appears in this sentence)—the auxiliary *do,* along with its *-s* and *-ed* forms, *does* and *did.* Why have we left those forms out of the discussion of auxiliaries? Don't they belong in our list, as modals perhaps or as alternatives to *have* + *-en* and *be* + *-ing?*

No, they don't. Even though most grammar books include the forms of *do* in their auxiliary lists along with modals and *have* and *be,* they don't really belong there. Their role in the predicating verb is very different from that of the others. They belong in a list by themselves.

Consider which of the following sentences sound grammatical to you and which do not:

1. Boris may not work today.

2. Boris worked not yesterday.

3. Amy is not living here.

4. Amy lives not here.

5. Amy is not here.

You may have noticed that all five sentences, including the two that are ungrammatical, have something in common: They are all negative. And it's that negative marker *not* that makes 2 and 4 ungrammatical. Without it, there would be no problem.

Boris worked yesterday.

Amy lives here.

What do the other three have that those two don't? 1 and 3 have auxiliaries; 5 has a form of *be* as the main verb. In order to make 2 and 4 grammatical, we have to add an auxiliary. Here's where *do* comes into our grammar:

Boris didn't work yesterday.

Amy doesn't live here.

When an auxiliary is required for a sentence variation, including negative sentences and questions, and there is no auxiliary, then *do* comes to the rescue—it stands in as a kind of dummy auxiliary. Linguists sometimes call this operation **do support.**

Earlier in this chapter we posed the following question: If we were going to write a computer program to generate all the possible verb strings in our language, what rules and restrictions would have to be included? In answering that question, we came up with our systematic verb-expansion rule. But somewhere in that computer program in our heads, there's also a footnote of sorts: It says that if the predicating verb is not a form of *be* or if it does not include an auxiliary, then, before we can add *not*, we must call on our trusty "stand-in" auxiliary *do.* In other words, the negative marker needs an auxiliary or *be* to attach itself to. Just as the tense marker, T, attaches itself to the first word it comes to in the verb string, the negative marker attaches itself to the first auxiliary—and if there isn't one, it calls up *do.*

The purpose of this discussion of *do* is twofold: (1) to help you understand the distinction between *do* and the other auxiliaries; (2) to help you appreciate how your grammar expertise automatically calls on *do* whenever you need an auxiliary.

In the next chapter we will examine two other circumstances that call for the stand-in auxiliary *do:* questions and emphatic sentences.

THE PASSIVE VOICE

Changing Active Voice to Passive. In the sentences we have examined so far, the subject serves as **agent** or actor, the performer of the action that the verb describes, while the direct object receives the action or is acted upon. We call this an active relationship: the **active voice.** In the transitive verb patterns (VII–X), the opposite relationship, the **passive**

voice, is also an option. Let's look at a Pattern VII sentence as it shifts from active voice to passive:

The boys ate the pizza.   The pizza was eaten by the boys.

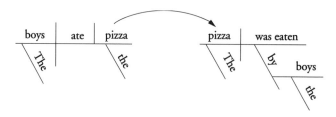

The passive transformation involves three steps, all of which are fairly easy to see in this example:

1. The original direct object (*the pizza*) becomes the subject.

2. *be* + *-en* is added to the active verb.

3. The original subject becomes the object of the preposition *by.* This third step is optional; many, if not most, passive sentences do not include the *by* phrase.

To understand the primary distinction between active and passive voice, it's important to recognize what happens to the subject–verb relationship in the transformation. Unlike the active sentence, where the subject performs the action, the subject of the passive sentence does nothing. It is still the receiver of the action, just as it was when it was in object position. So even though the object shifts to the subject slot, its meaning relationship to the verb remains the same. For example, in our sample sentence, "the pizza" is still being acted upon, still receiving the action of the verb. It's still getting eaten! The passive sentence simply relates that action from a different perspective.

In addition to that passive relationship between subject and verb, there's another feature that marks passive sentences even more clearly: the *be* auxiliary followed by the *-en* form of the verb, as described in Step 2. It's accurate to think of the verb-expansion rule we've been studying in this chapter as the *active* verb rule:

Active: T (M) (have + -en) (be + -ing) MV

According to our rule, if we use *be* as an auxiliary, the main verb will be the *-ing* form. For example,

past + be + -ing + eat = *was (or were) eating*

Step 2 in the passive transformation adds *be* + *-en* to the rule:

Passive: T (M) (have + -en) (be + -ing) **be + -en** MV

As mentioned previously, only sentences with transitive verbs—and thus with direct objects—can be transformed into the passive voice, so this passive version of the verb-expansion rule applies only to sentence patterns VII through X.

In our sentence about the pizza (*The boys ate the pizza*), we have taken the active verb, which is

$$\text{past + eat} = \text{ate}$$

and have added *be + -en:*

$$\text{past + be + -en + eat} = \text{was eaten}$$

What will happen to the passive verb if our original (active) sentence includes *be + -ing?*

$$\text{past + be + -ing + eat} = \text{[The boys] were eating [the pizza].}$$

The passive, with its added *be + en*, will now include two *be* auxiliaries in the verb string:

$$\text{past + be + -ing + be + -en + eat} = \text{[The pizza] was being eaten.}$$

Whenever you see two forms of *be* as auxiliaries, you can be sure the sentence is passive.

Sentences with irregular verbs like *eat*—that is, those in which the *-en* form is actually *-en (give, take, choose, break, speak)*—are fairly easy to recognize when they're in the passive voice:

A gift <u>was given</u> to the outgoing secretary.

The class picture <u>will be taken</u> by a professional photographer.

The winner <u>has been chosen</u> by a faculty committee.

The clue that these verbs are in the passive voice, not the active, is the *be* that precedes that *-en* main verb. (You'll recall from the verb-expansion rule that when the *-en* main verb is produced by the active rule, the auxiliary word that pairs up with it is *have*, not *be.*)

In sentences with regular verbs, however, the *-ed* and *-en* forms look identical. Both are written with the *-ed* suffix:

1. Yesterday I <u>studied</u> for my statistics test all day.
2. I <u>have studied</u> statistics every day this week.

How do we decide if *studied* is the *-ed* (past) or the *-en* (past participle)? Remember that the verb-expansion rule has two requirements: Tense (present or past) and Main Verb. This means that in sentence 1, *studied* has to include Tense, since there's no auxiliary word:

$$\text{past} + \text{study} \;=\; \text{studied}$$

It's clear that in sentence 1, *studied* is the *-ed* form. In 2, the Tense has attached itself to *have*, the first word in the string, not to *study*, so it's clear that *studied* is not the *-ed* form; it acquired its ending elsewhere:

$$\text{pres} + \text{have} + \text{-en} + \text{study}$$

The verb *studied* in sentence 2, then, is the *-en* form.

Now let's look at two more sentences with regular verbs to figure out if they are active or passive:

3. Scientific advances in medicine <u>have changed</u> our lives.
4. Insulin <u>was discovered</u> in 1921.

We know from the previous discussion of *studied* that the main verbs in sentences 3 and 4 cannot be the *-ed* (past) form, since both have auxiliaries that carry the tense: present (*have*) in 3; past (*was*) in 4. Therefore, both *changed* and *discovered* are *-en* forms. And what do we know about *-en* forms? First, we know that our active rule produces the *-en* form in the company of *have,* as we saw in 2; so, clearly, *have changed* is active. We also know that in order to make a verb passive we add *be* + *-en* to the active verb string. So in 4, both the absence of *have* and the presence of *be* tell us that *was discovered* is passive.

Here, then, are four rules about verbs that we can extract from our active and passive verb-expansion rules. Think of these as helpful "rules of thumb" that will heighten your awareness of verbs:

Rule 1: A verb without an auxiliary is always active.

Rule 2: When the main verb ends in *-ing,* it is active.

Rule 3: If an *-en* main verb is preceded by a form of *have,* it is active.

Rule 4: If an *-en* main verb is preceded by a form of *be,* it is passive.

Now apply these rules of thumb as you identify the voice of the following sentences as either active (A) or passive (P). In the parentheses, write the number of the rule that helped you decide.

I have eaten too much again. A or P (   )

Amy's car was stolen during the night. A or P (   )

I finally finished my homework. A or P (   )

We were studying for the exam. A or P (   )

These are not rules to memorize. They are simply ways of helping you use your awareness of auxiliaries as you analyze sentences. Remember that the difference between the active and passive verbs is the *be* + *-en* component that we add to the active to form the passive.

(*Note*: This discussion should make clear that the words *past* and *passive* are not related: *past* refers to tense; *passive* to voice. A verb in the passive voice can be either present or past tense.)

The Transitive-Passive Relationship. The ties between the transitive verb and the passive voice are so strong—there are so few exceptions—that we can almost define "transitive verb" in terms of this relationship. In other words, a transitive verb is a verb that can undergo the passive transformation. There are a few exceptions, including *have,* one of our most common verbs. In only a few colloquial expressions does *have* appear in the passive voice: "A good time was had by all," "I've been had." But in most cases *have* sentences cannot be transformed:

I had a cold.

*A cold was had by me.

Juan has a new car.

*A new car is had by Juan.

Other verbs that fit Pattern VII but are rarely transformed into passive are *lack* ("He lacks skill in debate") and *resemble* ("Mary resembles her mother"). Linguists sometimes classify these as "midverbs" and assign them to a separate sentence pattern. But on the basis of form (NP$_1$ V NP$_2$), we will classify these sentences as Pattern VII and simply look on them as exceptions to the passive rule.

Exercise  **11**

Transform the following active sentences into the passive voice, retaining the same verb tense and aspect:

1. My roommate wrote the lead article in today's *Collegian*.
2. Bach composed some of our most intricate fugues.
3. My brother-in-law builds the most expensive houses in town.
4. He is building that expensive apartment complex on Allen Street.
5. The county commissioners will discuss a new tax collection system at their next meeting.
6. Heavy thunderstorms have knocked down power lines in three counties.
7. People on neighboring farms could see the fire.
8. A hidden microphone was recording our conversation.
9. An advisor should have approved your plan of study.
10. Brightly colored posters decorate the classroom.

Changing Passive Voice to Active. To transform a passive sentence into active voice, you need to perform three operations that essentially undo the three steps that produce the passive voice:

1. First, identify the agent, or actor—the doer of the verbal action. If the agent is named, you'll find it following the preposition *by*. If it's not there, just make one up—"someone" or, in the third example, "the company":

> Our proposal has been approved by the president. [Agent: the president]

> Dr. Stevens was appointed chair of the grievance committee. [Agent: someone]

> All employees are given a year-end bonus. [Agent: the company]

2. Next, delete *be* + *-en* from the verb string:

> **has been approved** = pres + have + -en + b̶e̶ + -e̶n̶ + approve

> **was appointed** = past + b̶e̶ + -e̶n̶ + appoint

> **are given** = pres + b̶e̶ + -e̶n̶ + give

3. Rewrite the sentence with the agent in subject position, the revised verb in place, and the passive subject shifted to the object slot following the verb:

> The president has approved our proposal.
>
> Someone appointed Dr. Stevens chair of the grievance committee.
>
> The company gives all employees a year-end bonus.

With a "give" verb, as the last example illustrates, the passive subject may have to be shifted to the indirect object slot. Note too that the verb must agree with its new subject, so you add -s to the verb *give*. And as the first example illustrates, if the passive has auxiliaries other than *be* + *-en*, the active will retain them:

> has been approved → has approved

Exercise \12\

Change these passive sentences to the active voice. Remember that in some cases the agent may be missing, so you will have to supply a subject for the active, such as "someone." Identify the sentence patterns for the active sentences you have produced.

1. The football team was led onto the field by the cheerleading squad.
2. The cheerleaders are chosen by a committee in the spring.
3. The new reporters had been warned by the managing editor about late submissions.
4. Several apartments in our building have been burglarized recently.
5. A shipment of fresh lobsters should be delivered soon.
6. Dental floss was manufactured for the first time in 1882.
7. The abortion question is being discussed around the country.
8. Gabrielle must have been granted an extension on her loan payment.
9. The play was called a smashing success.
10. The poison has been rendered harmless.

Investigating Language **3.2**

One way to think about the tricky verbs *lie* and *lay* is in terms of their sentence patterns: One is intransitive (Pattern VI) and one is transitive

(Pattern VII). Read the following information adapted from *Webster's Ninth New Collegiate Dictionary*, then fill in the blanks with their various forms.

lie/ (intran) **lay**/; **lain**/; **lying** 1 a. to be or to stay at rest in a horizontal position; be prostrate: REST, RECLINE (~motionless) (~asleep) b. to assume a horizontal position—often used with *down.*

lay/ (tran) **laid**/; **laid**/; **laying** 1: to beat or strike down with force 2 a: to put or set down b: to place for rest or sleep; esp: BURY 3: to bring forth and deposit (an egg).

BASE	-*s* FORM	-*ed* FORM	-*ing* FORM	-*en* FORM
1. lie	_____	_____	_____	_____
2. lay	_____	_____	_____	_____

Now identify the verbs in the following sentences as transitive or intransitive and indicate the base form of the verb: Is it *lie* or *lay*?

1. I should lay the papers in neat piles on the table. _____

2. The cat has never lain so still before. _____

3. The tiles were laid neatly in a row. _____

4. Yesterday he lay very still. _____

5. I laid the baby on the bed for her nap. _____

6. I lay on the beach for two hours yesterday. _____

If you are accustomed to hearing people say "I'm going to lay down for a nap" or commanding their dogs to "lay down," you may think that the last sentence in the list sounds wrong. It's not unusual to hear people say "I laid on the beach." In fact, it is so common that at the end of the definition for *lay*, just quoted, the dictionary includes *lie* as an intransitive synonym—and labels it "nonstandard." In other words, when you say "lay down," you are using *lay* as a synonym for the intransitive *lie*. (If your dog responds only to standard usage, you'll have to say "lie down.") The reason for the common nonstandard usage becomes clear when you examine the five forms of the two verbs: Both sets include *lay.*

The confusion arising with two other pairs of tricky verbs—*rise/raise* and *sit/set*—can be resolved in the same way as with *lie/lay*, that is, in terms of their sentence pattern category. The dictionary will identify them as transitive or intransitive and list their -*ed*, -*en*, and -*ing* forms.

Diagramming the Passive. You have probably noticed that the diagram of the passive Pattern VII sentence looks exactly like the diagram of a Pattern VI:

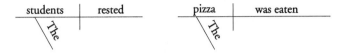

But don't make the mistake of thinking that the sentence pattern has changed: It has not. "The pizza was eaten" is a Pattern VII sentence, a *passive* Pattern VII. With the passive transformation rule, we have added a new dimension to the job of identifying sentence patterns. We now have to ask, "Is it active or passive?" Your four rules of thumb will help you answer that question.

The other three transitive verb patterns can also undergo the passive transformation. In most Pattern VIII sentences, the indirect object serves as the subject of the passive:

PATTERN VIII:

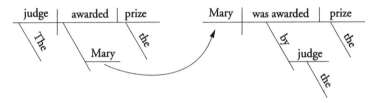

In this pattern, where we have two objects following the verb—both an indirect and a direct—we retain the direct object in the passive transformation. Traditional grammarians refer to this as the **retained object**. Another possibility in Pattern VIII is to use the direct object as the subject of the passive, as we do in Pattern VII, and then retain the indirect object:

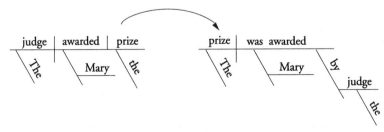

The resulting sentence has a somewhat formal or old-fashioned sound: "The prize was awarded Mary." A more common version includes the preposition *to:* "The prize was awarded to Mary."

In the active voice of Patterns IX and X again two complements, the direct object and the object complement, follow the verb; but in these two patterns only the direct object can serve as the subject of the passive transformation:

PATTERN IX:

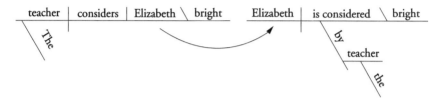

PATTERN X:

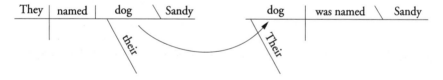

The diagrams of these passive sentences look like those of the linking verb patterns, where a subject complement describes or renames the subject. The relationship of the direct object and the object complement remains exactly what it was in the active voice; so when the object becomes the subject, it follows that the object complement becomes the subject complement. How, then, do we distinguish these passives from Patterns IV and V—especially when the agentive *by* phrase does not occur?

Elizabeth is considered bright.

Their dog was named Sandy.

Remember your four rules of thumb: When a form of *be* appears as an auxiliary without *-ing* following, the verb is passive. And because only transitive verbs can undergo the passive transformation, *is considered* and *was named* cannot be linking verbs.

You might find it useful to add these passive diagram frames below their active versions on page 51.

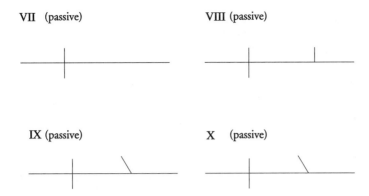

VII (passive)   VIII (passive)

IX (passive)   X (passive)

The purposes and rhetorical effects of the passive voice are discussed in Chapter 14, "Rhetorical Grammar," beginning on page 323.

THE VERB SYSTEM OF AFRICAN AMERICAN VERNACULAR ENGLISH

One of the most noticeable differences between Edited American English (EAE) and African American Vernacular English (AAVE) occurs with the verb-expansion rule.[3] In this chapter we have seen how *have* and *be* function systematically as auxiliaries to designate the perfect (*Mary has worked*) and the progressive (*Mary is working*) forms of the verb. We have also noted that *do* kicks in for questions (*Did Mary eat?*), negative sentences (*Mary didn't eat*), and emphasis (*Mary did eat*) when no other auxiliary is available.

The AAVE system calls for these same auxiliaries, but combines them in different ways. Here is a partial list of AAVE verb strings along with the EAE equivalent for each:

1. He eat. (present) "He is eating."
2. He be eating. (habitual) "He is usually eating."
3. He been eating. (remote past) "He has been eating for a long time."
4. He been ate. (remote past) "He ate a long time ago."
5. He done ate. (completive) "He has already eaten."
6. He been done ate. (remote past completive) "He finished eating a long time ago."
7. He had done ate. (completive) "He had already eaten."

---

[3] This description is adapted from an article by Lisa Green: "Study of Verb Classes in African American English," *Linguistics and Education* 7 (1994): 65–81.

We would need more data, of course, to come up with an accurate verb-expansion rule for AAVE. However, we can recognize certain regular features of the system from this small sample:

1. The auxiliary *done* appears in all the "completive" forms. Note that the adverb *already* or the verb *finished* is required to express the EAE equivalent.

2. The auxiliary *been* (pronounced "bin" and spoken with strong stress) carries the meaning of "remote" time. The EAE equivalent requires "a long time" or "a long time ago" to make this remote past distinction.

In terms of form, the fact that the auxiliary *done* appears in the string with other auxiliaries clearly sets this system apart from EAE, where *do* is not part of the verb-expansion rule, but, as mentioned earlier, occurs only as a stand-in auxiliary. (It should be noted that in AAVE a form of *do* also kicks in for some questions and negatives, as in EAE.) Another distinguishing feature of AAVE is the "habitual" *be,* shown in the second example. It includes the meaning "usually" or "habitually," whereas in EAE the adverb must be supplied.

It should be obvious from this brief description that the verb forms of AAVE, although different from those of EAE, are generated by a highly systematized set of rules. This recognition should also illustrate an important lesson that the linguists have contributed to language education: that all dialects of English are equally grammatical.

CHAPTER 3
Key Terms

Active voice	Modal auxiliary
African American Vernacular English	Negative sentence
Agent	Passive voice
Auxiliary	Person
Conditional mood	Regular verb
Do support	Stand-in auxiliary
Indicative mood	Subjunctive mood
Infinitive	Tense
Irregular verb	Verb-expansion rule
Main verb	

Sentences
for PRACTICE

Identify the components of the main verb in each of the following sentences. Your answers will be in the form of verb strings, such as those given in Exercise 10.

1. The press has recently labeled our new senator a radical on domestic issues.

2. During the campaign everyone was calling him reactionary.

3. The teacher should have given the class more information about the exam.

4. According to the students, their teacher was being downright secretive.

5. In Florida the Coast Guard is now confiscating the boats of drug runners.

6. Some sports reporters have called Oriole Park in Baltimore the architecture of nostalgia.

7. The president may soon name three women to top posts in the Department of State.

8. Our company will try a new vacation schedule in the summer.

9. All the workers are taking their two-week vacations at the same time.

10. Pat has been jogging regularly for six years.

11. Until last week, Mario had never told me his middle name.

12. Many large firms are now hiring liberal arts majors for management positions.

13. Employers value them for their analytical ability.

14. The suspect's alibi may have been a lie.

15. I should have been studying on a regular basis throughout the semester.

16. People are constantly teasing me about my southern accent.

17. Apparently they have never heard a southern accent around here before.

18. Writers have produced almost 2,500 works about the *Bounty* mutiny during the past 200 years.

Decide which of these sentences can be transformed into the passive voice, and then do so. Identifying their sentence patterns will help you in making that decision. Remember that to form a passive verb you must add *be* + *-en* to the active verb string. Remember also that the active and passive versions of the sentence have different subjects.

1. "I've already ate" is a fairly common nonstandard usage in our country. Explain how it deviates from the standard usage described by the verb-expansion rule. Compare it with "I've already tried"; can you discover a logical reason for the nonstandard usage? Does that particular nonstandard form ever occur with regular verbs?

2. The verb *get* shows up quite regularly with other verbs. Identify the patterns of these sentences, all of which include a form of *get:*

    They got married in July.

    The window got broken.

    I get tired at basketball games.

    The cookies always get eaten before they get cold.

    I got there too late.

    Should we alter the passive rule to account for any of these sentences? How does "The window was broken" differ from "The window got broken"?

3. The difference between two such sentences as

    He is tall.   *and*   He is silly.

    is obviously in the adjective that fills the subject complement slot. We cannot say

    *He is being tall.

    but we can say

    He is being silly.

    so there must be a fundamental difference between the two adjectives.

The contrast is between **stative** and **dynamic** qualities—the one describing a state, usually permanent, and the other a changing quality. What is there about *be + -ing* that makes this restriction seem logical? Can you think of other stative adjectives (other than *tall*) that are restricted from the subject complement slot with *be + -ing?*

Perhaps a better way of describing the contrast between *silly* and *tall*—between silliness and height—concerns the presence or absence of volition, the power of choice. Which of the following adjectives describe characteristics that are willed: *young, tough, nice, red, absorbent, reckless, round?* Can these adjectives serve as subject complements with *be + -ing?*

4. Consider further restrictions on *be + -ing:*

   *Mary is resembling her mother.

   *The blue dress is fitting you.

   Can we speak of dynamic and stative or willed and nonwilled qualities of verbs as well as of adjectives? Consider the following verbs: *assume, suit, equal, enjoy, desire, agree with, mean, know, contain, lack, like.* Do any of these have restrictions? Why?

5. Do nouns carry such distinctions, too? Try the following nouns in the subject complement slot of Pattern III: *a doctor, a nuisance, a hero, a nice person, a gentleman, a hard worker, a construction worker.* Here is the slot: "He is being _____ ." Can all of them be used with *be + -ing?* What conclusions can you draw about NPs? Does volition, or the power of choice, make a difference?

6. In the following sentences, what does *'s* stand for?

   He's had enough.

   Mary's not here.

   She's already gone.

   She's already left.

   He's finished.

   Now consider the following sentences:

   Are you done?

   Mike is already gone.

   In what way do they appear to violate our verb-expansion rule?

7. We usually think of contractions (*doesn't, shouldn't, I'll, he'd,* etc.) as optional, informal variations of verbs. And we generally think of them as forms that are best avoided in formal writing. Consider the following sentences in this light. Are the foregoing assumptions true?

Can't you come with me?

Doesn't the sunset look beatuiful this evening?

Hasn't everyone tried to conserve energy?

Are you sure he'll try hard enough to win?

I'm very hungry.

8. You can demonstrate the ambiguity of the following negative sentences by adding two possible follow-up sentences to each:

I'm not taking Math 10 because it's so easy.

He did not kill his wife because he loved her.

9. The following aphorism is ambiguous too:

No news is good news.

Restate the sentence in two ways to demonstrate its two meanings.

CLASSROOM APPLICATIONS

1. Examine the following headlines, copied from a daily newspaper. You'll notice that some have incomplete verb phrases. Rewrite the headlines to complete the incomplete verbs, then identify their sentence patterns. (Note: You'll have to pay attention to voice—active or passive—in identifying the patterns.)

Dissidents form action committee. (Pattern _____)

Hurricane kills seven. (Pattern _____)

Six found guilty of extortion. (Pattern _____)

Team vies for championship. (Pattern _____)

Battle of Verdun remembered in ceremony. (Pattern _____)

Candidates ready for runoff election. (Pattern _____)

New city planner named. (Pattern _____)

Woman injured in crash. (Pattern _____)

Fulbright scholarships awarded to two. (Pattern _____)

Check the headlines of your local paper. Which patterns do you find? Do you find any difference in the patterns used for sports headlines and those heading general news?

2. About fifty years ago, David Bourland, a semanticist, invented a writing system that he labeled "E-prime," a version of English without the verb *be*. He rejected all of its forms (*be, am, is, are, was, were, been, being*), including its use as

both the main verb and auxiliary and its use in contractions (*I'm, it's, there's, we're,* etc.). As Bourland and others have noted, *be* outdistances all other verbs in frequency of use—and overuse. In fact, your own writing teachers may have advised you to look for alternatives to some of the *be* sentences in your essays.

To practice your E-prime skills, turn to Chapter 1 and find the first paragraph of the section titled "The Question of Standards" on page 8. You'll discover six forms of *be* in the first four sentences. Rewrite those sentences without *be.* Remember that when you eliminate *be,* you also eliminate the passive voice and all main verbs in the *-ing* form.

Some E-prime users also take pride in speaking without *be.* As a class exercise, see if you can avoid all forms of *be* in your next class discussion.

You'll find further information about E-prime in Cullen Murphy's article "'To Be' in Their Bonnets," *Atlantic* (February 1992).

(Note: Unlike the paragraph in Chapter 1 referred to, these two Classroom Applications contain no instances of *be* in a predicating verb, either as an auxiliary or as the main verb.)

Transforming the Basic Patterns

CHAPTER PREVIEW

The ten sentence-pattern formulas described in Chapter 2 represent the underlying framework of almost all the sentences we speak and write. For example, underlying the sentence you just read, the first one in this paragraph, is a basic Pattern VII sentence:

The formulas	represent	the framework.
NP_1	V-tr	NP_2

The two NP slots have been expanded with a variety of phrases and clauses, but the underlying subject and verb and direct object are there, in order, just as the formula describes them; you can pick out the basic skeleton with little trouble.

But it's not always so easy. We don't always use straightforward statements (**declarative sentences**) like that one; sometimes we alter the word order to ask questions (**interrogative sentences**); sometimes we suppress the subject and give commands (**imperative sentences**); sometimes we shift the object or complement before the subject for special emphasis (**exclamatory sentences**):

Interrogative:	Have you ever found those books you lost?
	Where do you think you lost them?
Imperative:	Find those books.
Exclamatory:	What a helpful librarian we have!

The ten sentence-pattern formulas describe basic declarative sentences; all ten patterns can undergo the transformations that turn them into these other three sentence types. In this chapter we will look briefly at the three

90

alternatives; we will also take up two other transformations that, like the passive voice, alter the word order and emphasis of certain basic sentences: the *there* transformation and the cleft sentence.

INTERROGATIVE SENTENCES

One of the first lessons in the study of a foreign language is how to turn statements into questions. In our native language, of course, we begin asking questions automatically, without lessons, at an early age. A child's questions develop along with statements in stages, beginning with one- and two-word strings—"Why? Where go?"—progressing in a short time to more complicated constructions—"Can I go with Daddy? Where is Daddy going?"

The two questions about Daddy, although they look similar, represent two basic kinds of questions we have in English: the **yes/no question** and the *wh*-question, or interrogative-word question. Both kinds of questions are transformations of basic sentences in which one or more elements are shifted from their usual sentence positions.

In the yes/no question, we shift the auxiliary—or the first auxiliary, if there is more than one—to the beginning of the sentence:

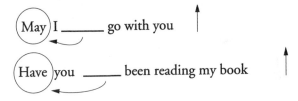

For most speakers of English, the yes/no question is also signaled by rising intonation at the end, as indicated by the arrow (and indicated in writing by the question mark).[1] The yes/no question, as its label suggests, permits "yes" and "no" as appropriate answers, although other answers are also possible:

---

[1] One of the dialect distinctions in parts of central Pennsylvania (and perhaps in other parts of the country as well) is the absence of this rising intonation. For many speakers who are natives of the area, yes/no questions have the same intonation pattern as statements and *wh*-questions:

May I go with
you

Q: May I go with you?   A: We'll see.

Q: Have you been reading my book?   A: Do you mind?

We diagram the question as we would the statement underlying it. Because the diagram includes no marks of punctuation, our only clue to its original question form is the capitalized auxiliary:

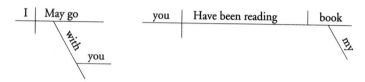

The *wh*-question is somewhat more complicated than the yes/no question in that it involves two movement operations. It begins with a question word, or **interrogative,** that elicits specific information, such as *why, where, when, who, what,* and *how.* In the question about Daddy, the information asked for, represented by the interrogative word, fills the optional adverbial slot in a Pattern VI sentence:

<u>Where</u> is Daddy going?

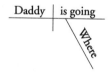

The interrogative can also fill an NP slot:

<u>What</u> have you been reading?

Some interrogatives act as determiners:

<u>Whose</u> car are you taking?

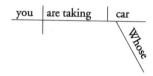

<u>Which</u> brand is cheapest?

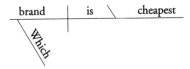

As the preceding examples show, the slots of the basic sentence pattern of a question will be out of order because the interrogative word always comes first, no matter what grammatical function it has. However, when the information being elicited is a *who* or *what* that fills the subject slot, then normal word order is maintained:

<u>Who</u>	broke	the window?
<u>What</u>	is making	that noise?
NP$_1$	V-tr	NP$_2$

The other difference between the *wh*-question and the statement is the shifted first auxiliary:

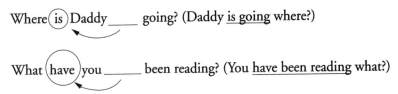

Where (is) Daddy _____ going? (Daddy <u>is going</u> where?)

What (have) you _____ been reading? (You <u>have been reading</u> what?)

Again, this shift will not occur when the interrogative fills the subject slot:

<u>What</u> is happening in there?

<u>Who</u> has been eating my porridge?

Investigating Language **4.1**

When *who* functions as the subject, it is in the **subjective case.** Sometimes, however, *who* occupies the role of object, as direct object or object of a preposition. Those functions call for a different case: the **objective** *whom.*

To whom shall we send invitations?

Whom did you invite?

You may be thinking that both of these *whom* sentences sound formal—if not downright stuffy. In fact, you probably don't hear them very often, if at all. You're more likely to hear and to say,

Who shall we send invitations to?

Who did you invite?

Why do you suppose *who* sounds better, or more natural, in those two questions?

Although the two versions with *who* may be common in speech, in formal writing you'll want to pay attention to case—and use *whom* for direct objects, indirect objects, and objects of prepositions. *Who* is used only for subjects and subject complements.

Examine the role of the *who* or *whom* in the following sentences. (It may help you to picture a diagram.) Change the case if it is nonstandard; if necessary, rewrite the sentence to make it sound natural.

Who should we choose as vice-president?

Whom shall I say is calling?

(Note: You'll read more about *who* and *whom* in Chapter 6, where they function as relative pronouns and in Chapter 7, where interrogatives introduce dependent clauses. The concept of case is discussed further in Chapter 13, "Pronouns.")

THE STAND-IN AUXILIARY

So far the system of transforming statements into questions seems fairly simple; certainly we should be able to program a computer to replace a sentence slot with the appropriate interrogative word and to shift the first auxiliary. But a complication arises in sentences that require the auxiliary shift when there is no auxiliary. As you might suspect, it's time to call once again on our stand-in auxiliary *do,* just as we do for negative sentences that have no auxiliary.

Consider the possible questions contained in the following statement:

Denny polishes his car every week.

There are no complications with a *who* question, where the word order remains the same:

Who polishes his car every week?

But a yes/no question or one that asks *what* or *how often* or *why* introduces *do* support into the process:

Does Denny polish his car every week?

What does Denny polish every week?

How often does Denny polish his car?

Why does Denny polish his car every week?

If the underlying sentence had been in the past tense instead of the present, we would have used *did:*

Denny <u>polished</u> his car last week.

<u>Did</u> Denny polish his car last week?

Like the other auxiliaries, *do* carries the tense, so the past tense has shifted from the verb *polished* to the auxiliary *do.*

As we saw in the case of negative sentences, *do* support does not apply to sentences with *be* as the main verb, even when there is no auxiliary; the *be* itself does the shifting:

The teacher is at her desk → Is the teacher at her desk?

The pizza was expensive → Was the pizza expensive?

The students are scholars → Are the students scholars?

EMPHATIC SENTENCES

The stand-in *do* also applies to emphatic sentences. When we want to put special emphasis on a sentence, we normally shift the main point of loudness, the main stress, to the auxiliary:

Denny is polishing his car. → He IS polishing his car.

I'm going home tomorrow. → I AM going home tomorow.

He's reading your book. → He IS reading your book.

But in the absence of an auxiliary, a form of *do* can be added to carry the stress:

He polishes his car every week → He DOES polish his car every week.

He polished his car yesterday → He DID polish his car yesterday.

When *do* support is applied to a verb in the past tense, such as *polished,* the *do* will carry the past marker, as it does in negative statements and questions. Note that the resulting emphatic verb is *did polish;* the main verb is the base form, *polish.*

In its role as a stand-in auxiliary, *do* has no effect on meaning. It merely acts as kind of operator that enables us to add emphasis to sentences not containing auxiliaries or *be* and to transform them into negatives and questions. The emphatic *do* is much more common in speech than in expository prose.

IMPERATIVE SENTENCES

Imperative sentences, or **commands**, take the base form of the verb without auxiliaries:

> Be careful.
>
> Help yourself.
>
> Kiss me again.
>
> Tell me a story.

Note that the example with *be* demonstrates that the verbs of imperative sentences differ from those of other sentences in having no tense.

In most imperative sentences the subject is the understood *you*, the personal pronoun that refers to the person or persons being addressed. Although commands can be made from all the sentence patterns, there are some verbs that rarely produce them: *resemble, lack, seem*. These are among the **stative** verbs generally—verbs that refer to a state rather than an action; and many are the same verbs that are not expanded with *be* + *-ing*, which we saw in Chapter 3 as exceptions to the verb-expansion rule. (See also Discussion Questions 3 and 4 on pages 86–87.)

Investigating Language   *4.2*

Notice that the simple commands in the foregoing list are positive; another command that most of us use fairly often is the negative kind: "Don't do this" and "Don't do that." Here are some more examples:

> Don't be silly.
>
> Don't do anything I wouldn't do.
>
> Don't forget to take out the garbage.

You'll notice that they all have the auxiliary *do*. Why is that?
And here's another with *do:*

> Do be careful.

That one isn't negative: Why does it need *do?*

In answering these *why* questions, consider what you know about the form of the verb in commands and what you know about our use of the stand-in auxiliary.

In the imperative sentences we have seen so far, the subject is the understood *you* and the verb is the base form. As you probably discovered in thinking about negative commands, it's because we use the base alone, with neither tense nor an auxiliary word, that we need to add *do* when we make the command negative or emphatic. Those are two circumstances that require auxiliary words.

There are exceptions to the general rule about the understood *you:* Sometimes the *you* is not understood, it is stated:

>
> You behave yourself.
>
> Now don't you forget to write.
>
> You do the best you can.

And sometimes the subject is not the second person *you.* In the following sentences, it is third person:

>
> Somebody help Julie with the dishes.
>
> Don't anybody move.

You've probably learned about the concept of **person** in your composition and literature classes in connection with point of view. In this book you'll study it in connection with personal pronouns in Chapter 13.

You might want to look over that discussion just to understand better the principle underlying imperative sentences and to recognize the subtleties of these exceptions to the standard "you" command.

EXCLAMATORY SENTENCES

We usually think of the **exclamatory sentence**, or exclamation, as any sentence spoken with heightened emotion, written with an exclamation point:

>
> I hate purple!
>
> Take that cat out of here this minute!
>
> Don't anybody move!

But in terms of form, the first sentence immediately preceding is *declarative,* a straightforward statement, and the other two are *imperative.* In contrast, what we call the exclamatory transformation includes a shift in word order that focuses special attention on a complement:

>
> What a helpful librarian we have!
>
> How very peaceful the countryside is!
>
> What a hard-working president we elected!

The *what* or *how* that introduces the emphasized element is added to the underlying sentence pattern:

>
> We have a helpful librarian. (Pattern VII)
>
> The countryside is very peaceful. (Pattern II)
>
> We elected a hard-working president. (Pattern VII)

The exclamation mark signals the reader that the sentence (or sentence fragment, in some cases) is expressing excitement or emotion that goes beyond standard intonation. In reading such sentences aloud, we use both higher pitch and louder stress. Whether or not a sentence includes the actual transformation—with the shift of the complement and the addition of *what* or *how*—we recognize the exclamation by its intonation pattern and its signal of the exclamation mark. To understand the significance of that mark to the written language, read the following pairs aloud and listen to your voice:

Have you ever seen such a mess?

Have you ever seen such a mess!

Is this rain ever going to stop?

Is this rain ever going to stop!

The written language, of course, cannot convey the subtleties of the meaning that the spoken language can, although punctuation certainly helps. In the following section we'll see some other tools that writers have to control the reader's intonation.

Exercise *13*

Diagram the following sentences, each of which has undergone one or more of the transformations that you have learned about: passive, interrogative, negative, imperative, and exclamatory. You'll find it useful to identify the sentence patterns.

1. Where have all the flowers gone?
2. Cut everyone a piece of that delicious cake.
3. Call me Ishmael. [Herman Melville]
4. Should the students be allowed into the gym before eight on the night of the dance?
5. How far that little candle throws his beams. [Shakespeare]
6. Don't be deceived by the flattery of strangers.
7. What a jerk I am sometimes!
8. Give my regards to Broadway. [George M. Cohan]

OTHER SENTENCE TRANSFORMATIONS

The sentence types we have just seen—interrogative, imperative, and exclamatory—are variations of the basic declarative sentence that apply with few exceptions to all ten sentence patterns. In Chapter 3 we studied the passive voice, the result of a transformation that applies to the transitive verb patterns. We will now look briefly at two other fairly common transformations that alter word order for purposes of emphasis in certain kinds of sentences.

The *There* Transformation. Like the exclamatory sentence, the ***there* transformation** includes an introductory word that plays no grammatical role in the basic sentence pattern. It also includes a shift in word order: The unstressed *there*, known as an **expletive**, introduces the sentence; the subject of the sentence follows *be:*

There's a fly in my soup.

There is an error message on the computer screen.

To diagram a *there* transformation, we must identify the underlying pattern. As the diagram shows, *there* has no grammatical function in the basic sentence:

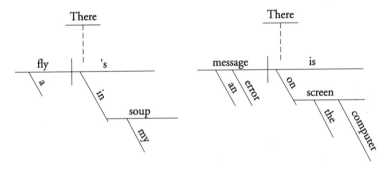

When we use the *there* transformation, we are taking advantage of the natural rhythm of language. In general, our language is a series of valleys and peaks, a fairly regular pattern of unstressed and stressed syllables:

Sentences usually begin with an unstressed valley. And more often than not, that first, unstressed slot is the subject. But the *there* transformation changes that usual word order: When the unstressed *there* fills the opening slot, it delays the subject until that first peak position of stress.

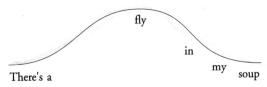

The *there* transformation applies when the subject of the sentence is indefinite: "*a* fly" or "*an* error message" rather than "*the* fly" or "*the* error message." The **indefinite article** is a signal that the subject of the *there* transformation is new information; we use the **definite article**, *the*, for old, or known, information. We might have occasion to say,

There's that fly that knows good soup.

if a particular fly under discussion lands in the soup. But clearly this is a known fly, so this is not the unstressed *there*. The stress it carries marks it as an adverb providing information of place (it's called the "locative" adverb, from the word *location*). The same is true of

There's that error message I told you about.

In these sentences with definite subjects, we have simply shifted the order of the basic sentence pattern, as we sometimes do to emphasize adverbials:

Here's your book.

Right off the end of the pier plunged the getaway car.

The expletive *there* is always unstressed; the adverb *there*, when it opens a sentence, is nearly always stressed, providing an exception to the normal rhythm pattern of that opening unstressed valley we just saw. The adverb *there*, besides providing information of place, often acts as a kind of pointer. For example, read the following pair of sentences aloud and notice the difference in meaning and stress of the two *there*s:

There's a piece of the jigsaw puzzle missing.

There it is, on the floor.

You can almost see the finger pointing in the case of the second *there*.

In addition to the indefinite subject, the *there* transformation usually has a form of *be* either as the main verb or, in the case of the transitive and intransitive patterns, as an auxiliary. Pattern I (NP be ADV/TP) is the most common pattern we transform with *there*; Patterns II and III, in which *be* acts as a linking verb, will not accept the *there* transformation.

The form of *be* will, of course, depend on the tense and on the number of the subject, whether singular or plural:

There <u>were</u> <u>some problems</u> with the heat in our new apartment.

There <u>has been a problem</u> with the plumbing, too.

But an exception to the general rule of **subject–verb** agreement occurs with the *there* transformation. A compound subject, which we usually treat as plural, may take the *-s* form of *be* under some circumstances:

There <u>was</u> some great blocking and some fine running and passing in Saturday's game.

In this sentence "there were" would be awkward, even though the subject is compound.

The *there* transformation without a form of *be* is also possible, but such sentences are not very common:

> There came from the alley a low moaning sound.

> There followed a series of unexplained phenomena.

> There remains an unanswered question.

Listen to the difference between these sentences and those with *be*. These have a tight, controlled quality about them. Notice also that when a verb other than *be* follows *there* it shares the stress with the subject.

You will read more about the rhythm of sentences and about the *there* transformation as a tool for the writer in Chapter 14.

Exercise 14

Identify the function of *there* in the following sentences. Is it the expletive or is it the locative adverb? Also identify the sentence patterns.

1. There's often a flock of blackbirds lining the telephone wire in our neighborhood.
2. There they are now.
3. There's nothing to do tonight.
4. There's always TV to watch.
5. There's Henry across the street.
6. There he goes.
7. Isn't there a spelling checker on your word processor?
8. There but for the grace of God go I.

The Cleft Sentence. Another sentence variation that provides a way to shift the focus of attention is the cleft transformation, so called because it divides a clause into two parts: It cleaves it. The **cleft sentence** allows a writer to accomplish by means of word order what a speaker can do by varying the point of main stress or loudness. The following variations show how a speaker can change the focus or meaning of a sentence simply by putting stress on different words, that is, by saying certain words louder:

> MARY wrecked her motorcycle in Phoenix during the Christmas break. (It wasn't Diane who did it.)

> Mary wrecked her MOTORCYCLE in Phoenix during the Christmas break. (Not her car.)

Mary wrecked her motorcycle in PHOENIX during the Christmas break. (Not in Albuquerque.)

Mary wrecked her motorcycle in Phoenix during the CHRIST-MAS break. (Not Thanksgiving.)

Because the conventions of writing do not include capital letters for words that should get main stress, as shown in the preceding sentences, the writer's intended emphasis may not always be clear. The cleft transformation solves the problem. In one kind of cleft sentence the main subject is *it* with a form of *be* as the main verb. In reading the following sentences aloud, you'll notice that you automatically stress the word or phrase following *was:*

It was <u>Mary</u> who wrecked her motorcycle in Phoenix during the Christmas break.

It was <u>her motorcycle</u> that Mary wrecked in Phoenix during the Christmas break.

It was <u>in Phoenix</u> that Mary wrecked her motorcycle during the Christmas break.

It was <u>during the Christmas break</u> that Mary wrecked her motorcycle.

Another kind of cleft sentence uses a *what* clause in subject position. Note that the added *was* separates the original sentence into two parts:

Mary wrecked her motorcycle.

What Mary wrecked <u>was</u> her motorcycle.

Sometimes *what* shifts the original verb phrase into subject position. Again, a form of *be* is added as the main verb:

A branch in the road <u>caused the accident</u>.

<u>What caused the accident</u> was a branch in the road.

Thick fog <u>reduced the visibility to zero</u>.

<u>What reduced the visibility to zero</u> was the thick fog.

You'll notice in both the *it* and *what* clefts that the sentence pattern of the main clause has changed, a change that does not occur with the other transformations.

The cleft transformations produce sentences that are quite complicated structurally, with clauses filling certain slots in the patterns, so we will not be concerned here with their diagrams. In Chapter 14 the cleft transformations are discussed in terms of their rhetorical effects.

CHAPTER 4
Key Terms

Case	*It* cleft
Cleft sentence	Objective case
Command	Person
Declarative sentence	Stand-in auxiliary
Do support	Subjective case
Emphatic sentence	Subject–verb agreement
Exclamatory sentence	*There* transformation
Expletive *there*	*Wh*-question
Imperative sentence	*What* cleft
Interrogative sentence	Yes/no question

Sentences
for PRACTICE

Using the transformations you have studied in this chapter (interrogative, imperative, exclamatory, "there," and cleft), write as many variations of the following sentences as you can.

1. Hundreds of angry women were protesting the candidate's position on abortion at yesterday's political rally in the student union.

2. Myrtle's special marinated mushrooms added a festive touch to the salad.

3. A big family is moving into the apartment upstairs next week.

4. A strange man was lurking suspiciously on the neighbor's front porch last night.

5. The encroachment of civilization on wilderness areas bothers a great many environmentalists.

6. Athletes from many countries set new records at the 2000 Olympic Games in Australia.

7. A month of unseasonably warm weather almost ruined the ski season last winter.

8. An old stone bridge near our home is a popular subject for local photographers.

9. Several gangs of kids in the neighborhood are cleaning up the empty lot on the corner.

10. Computer viruses are becoming a serious problem.

QUESTIONS
?
for DISCUSSION

1. Do we ever need the stand-in auxiliary *do* for a passive sentence? Why or why not?

2. How many transformations has the following sentence undergone? *Don't be fooled!* What is unusual about the sentence? (Hint: Remember Question 1.)

3. Why do the following sentences from Shakespeare and the King James Bible sound strange to our twenty-first-century ears? What particular change that has taken place in the language do these sentences illustrate?

   Let not your heart be troubled.

   Know you where you are?

   Wherefore weep you?

   Revolt our subjects?

   What means this shouting?

4. In Chapter 2 we looked briefly at sentence variations that help us distinguish verb–particle combinations (phrasal verbs) from verb–adverb combinations:

   We jumped up → Up we jumped.

   We made up → *Up we made.

   The cleft transformation, introduced in this chapter, can also be useful in identifying properties of verbs:

   He came by the office in a big hurry.

   He came by his fortune in an unusual manner.

   Where he came was by the office.

   *Where he came was by his fortune.

Joe turned on the bridge and looked around.
Joe turned on the light and looked around.

It was on the bridge that Joe turned and looked around.
*It was on the light that Joe turned and looked around.

Here are some other pairs that look alike. Use transformations to demonstrate their differences:

The student looked up the word.
The teacher looked up the hall.

Sharon called up the stairs.
Karen called up the club members.

An old jalopy turned into the driveway.
Cinderella's coach turned into a pumpkin.

CLASSROOM APPLICATIONS

1. In this chapter we looked briefly at our system for turning sentences into questions, a process that sometimes requires *do*. The tag question is another method for turning statements into questions:

   John is washing his car, <u>isn't he</u>?
   Perry should wash his too, <u>shouldn't he</u>?

   Add the tags that turn the following statements into questions:

   Harold has finally stopped smoking, _____?
   The students are not studying Latin, _____?
   Bev finished her book on schedule, _____?
   Tim and Joe are good carpenters, _____?
   Kris is a good carpenter, too, _____?
   She builds beautiful cabinets, _____?

   Now look at the system you followed for adding these questions. How many steps are involved? Imagine writing a computer program so that it, too, could generate tag questions. What are the steps you would have to include?

> Here are three more tags to supply:
>
> Harold should stop smoking, _____ ?
>
> Harold ought to stop smoking, _____ ?
>
> Harold may stop smoking soon, _____ ?

Take a poll among your friends to get their responses to these three. Do all the respondents agree? Do they follow the procedure you described in the first set? What do these tags tell you about the changing nature of the language?

2. Add tag questions to the following sentences:

> There's a good movie on TV tonight, _____ ?
>
> There were a lot of students absent today, _____ ?

Now explain why some linguists prefer to call *there* the subject of the sentence rather than an expletive. Give other evidence to support or refute that position.

Expanding the Sentence

In this section we will take up three methods of expanding sentences: modification, noun phrase substitution, and coordination. You first learned about modification in Chapter 2, when you added adverbs to verb phrases and adjectives to noun phrases and prepositional phrases to both. In Chapters 5 and 6 you'll see other structures, as well as these, that function as adverbials and adjectivals. In Chapter 7 you'll see verb phrases and clauses that fill noun phrase slots; in Chapter 8, modifiers of the sentence as a whole; and in Chapter 9, the expansion of the sentence and its parts by means of coordination.

FORM AND FUNCTION

One way to organize all of these new details of sentence structure is to think in terms of form and function. The labels designating **form** that you have learned include the names of word classes such as noun, verb, adjective, adverb, preposition, and conjunction; the various phrases you have come to recognize—noun phrase, verb phrase, prepositional phrase—are also form designations. We recognize, and can label, the form of a structure like *the puppy* as a noun phrase and *on the porch* as a prepositional phrase on the basis of their forms. That is, we need not see these structures in sentences in order to recognize their forms. Until we give those structures a context, however, we have no way of discussing their **functions.** In Chapter 2, you'll recall, we saw a prepositional phrase functioning in two ways, as both an adjectival and an adverbial:

The puppy <u>on the porch</u> is sleeping.

The puppy is sleeping <u>on the porch</u>.

Only when it's in a larger structure can we discuss a word or a phrase in terms of both form and function. In the chapters that follow, the sentence expansions include verb phrases and clauses functioning as adverbials and adjectivals and nominals.

The following outline will be helpful to you in understanding the two-sided analysis of form and function and in organizing the details of sentence expansions.

Form	*Function*
Word	*Adverbial*
noun	modifier of (*verb*)
verb	
adjective	*Adjectival*
adverb	subject complement
	object complement
Phrase	modifier of (*noun*)
noun phrase	
verb phrase	*Nominal*
gerund	subject
infinitive	subject complement
participle	direct object
prepositional phrase	indirect object
	object complement
Clause	object of preposition
independent sentence	appositive
nominal clause	
adverbial (subordinate) clause	*Sentence Modifier*
adjectival (relative) clause	

You'll discover that all of the general functions listed on the right—adverbial, adjectival, nominal, and sentence modifier—can be carried out by all of the general forms listed on the left—words, phrases, and clauses. As an illustration of this principle, turn to the table of contents and read the headings for Chapter 5. You will see that the chapter title names and defines a function: "Modifiers of the Verb: Adverbials." The major subheadings name the five forms that carry out that function: Adverbs, Prepositional Phrases, Noun Phrases, Verb Phrases, and Clauses.

In this section of the book we will again use the sentence diagram to illustrate the various ways of expanding sentences, first with adverbials, then with adjectivals, nominals, and coordinated structures. The sentences are beginning to get long and complex, it's true; however, if you remember to consider the two-sided analysis of form and function, the diagrams will enhance your understanding. Each of the various forms we have discussed—noun phrase, prepositional phrase, verb phrase, clause—has a particular diagram, no matter what its function in the sentence. For example, a prepositional phrase is always diagrammed as a two-part structure, with the preposition on the diagonal line and the object of the preposition on the attached horizontal line; a noun phrase is always diagrammed with the headword on the horizontal line and its modifiers attached below it.

Always begin your analysis of a sentence by identifying the underlying pattern, one of the ten basic sentences you diagrammed in Chapter 2. Then analyze each of the slots to see how it has been expanded. If you take these expansions one step at a time, asking yourself questions about form and function, you'll come to understand the system that produces the sentences of your language.

In these five chapters on sentence expansion, you will be building on your knowledge of the basic sentence patterns. It might be a good idea at this point to revisit Chapter 2, to review the sentence patterns and their slots.

CHAPTER
5

Modifiers of the Verb: Adverbials

CHAPTER PREVIEW

In this chapter you will learn about five different structures that function as adverbials—in other words, that do the job that adverbs generally do. If you have studied traditional grammar, you may recall the definition of adverb as "a word that modifies a verb, an adjective, or another adverb." However, when the structural grammarians looked at English objectively, they challenged that definition, recognizing that modifiers of adjectives and adverbs form a separate group from those that modify verbs: They are words, like *very,* that intensify or qualify adjectives (*very nice*) and adverbs (*very quickly*), but do not necessarily modify verbs (**very walked, *walked very*). The structuralists also emphasized that the term *adverb* refers to a word class with particular characteristics, not to the function of "verb modifier." It's true, of course, that adverbs modify verbs: That's their main function in our language. But it's also true that there are other words and word groups that can, and commonly do, modify verbs. This chapter will introduce you to all of the forms that function as verb modifiers—that is, as adverbials.

Although only one of the sentence patterns has an adverbial in a required slot—Pattern I: NP *be* ADV/TP—the symbol for an optional adverbial, (ADV), could be added to all ten formulas. Adverbial information—structures telling where, when, why, how, and so on—is common in every sentence pattern. And no sentence is limited to a single adverbial. In the following sentence, each of the underlined structures—

an adverb, a prepositional phrase, and a clause—adds adverbial information to the verb *gasped*:

> The audience gasped <u>nervously</u> <u>throughout the theater</u> <u>when the magician thrust his sword into the box.</u>
>
> The audience gasped (*How?*) nervously.
>
> The audience gasped (*Where?*) throughout the theater.
>
> The audience gasped (*When?*) when the magician thrust his sword into the box.

Even though all the adverbials in the preceding sentence follow the verb, there is really no fixed slot for most adverbials; in fact, movability is one of their most telling characteristics, and, for the writer, one of the most useful. In the preceding sentence, for example, there are several possibilities for ordering the three adverbials:

> When the magician thrust his sword into the box, the audience nervously gasped throughout the theater.
>
> Throughout the theater the audience gasped nervously when the magician thrust his sword into the box.

The position may depend on the writer's emphasis, on the rhythm of the sentence, or simply on the desire for sentence variety.

But no matter what positions the adverbials occupy—whether at the beginning, middle, or end of the sentence—the traditional diagram will show them as modifiers of the verb:

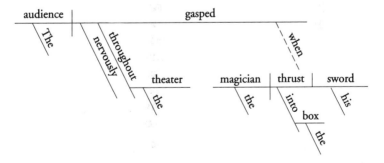

Even though the diagram shows the modifiers in the order that they appear in the sentence, an exact reading of the diagram may still not be possible. For instance, this one does not show whether *nervously* comes before or after *gasped*. But because the purpose of diagramming is to illustrate visually the relationship of the various parts of the sentence, an exact left-to-right reading of the diagram is not necessarily important.

The preceding sample sentence includes structures of three different forms functioning adverbially: an adverb, a prepositional phrase, and a clause. Other structures that provide adverbial information are noun phrases and verb phrases. In this chapter we will take up each of these forms in its role as adverbial.

ADVERBS

The words we recognize as adverbs most readily are the adverbs of **manner**—the *-ly* words, such as *nervously, quietly,* and *suddenly.* These adverbs, derived from adjectives, usually tell "how" or "in what manner" about verbs:

They gasped nervously	=	in a nervous manner
They talked quietly	=	in a quiet manner
It stopped suddenly	=	in a sudden manner

The manner adverbs are probably the most movable of all the adverbials; they can appear before or after the verb, as well as at the beginning or end of the sentence:

Suddenly the wind shifted.

The wind suddenly shifted.

The wind shifted suddenly.

Notice that all three versions of the sentence are diagrammed the same; the only clue to word order is capitalization:

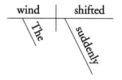

A single-word adverb can even come within the verb string, between the auxiliary word and the main verb:

The roof was suddenly blown off by a strong gust of wind.

Or between auxiliaries:

I have actually been working on my term project.

In all positions the manner adverbs can be marked by qualifiers, words such as *very, quite, so,* and *rather:*

Quite suddenly the crowd grew restless.

The old woman crooned very softly.

The airline employees handled our luggage rather carelessly.

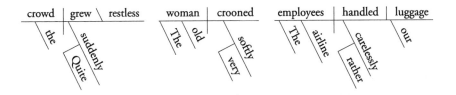

Like the adjectives they are derived from, these adverbs can be made comparative and superlative with *more* and *most*:

More suddenly than the police expected, the crowd grew restless.

The sails flapped more and more furiously as the wind grew stronger.

Besides the *-ly* adverbs, many other single-word adverbs provide information of time, place, frequency, and the like: *now, then, nowadays, today, often, always, sometimes, seldom, never, here, there, everywhere*, and many others.

I still jog here sometimes.

Nowadays I seldom swim.

Some of these, like the manner adverbs, can be compared and qualified:

I should jog more often.

Nowadays Judd and Betty jog quite often.

Although movability is a characteristic of all single-word adverbs, the various subclasses are bound by certain restrictions as to order. For example, in the following sentence, the adverbials of place and time cannot be reversed:

I am going there now.

*I am going now there.

Now I am going there.

*There I am going now.

The rules governing the order and movement of adverbs are quite complex, but as native speakers we are unaware of that complexity; our linguistic computers are programmed to follow the rules automatically.

Investigating Language **5.1**

The adverbs of frequency, such as those in these six sentences, are among our most movable. In terms of meaning, some are positive and some negative.

1. My friends and I have pizza <u>frequently</u>.
2. <u>Occasionally</u> I order mushrooms.
3. <u>Sometimes</u> I order extra cheese.
4. <u>Seldom</u> do I order hot sausage.
5. <u>Never</u> will I order anchovies.
6. I <u>rarely</u> finish the whole thing.

The movability of these adverbs enables us to change the emphasis in subtle ways. Interestingly, however, the six adverbs in this list don't always behave alike. Notice what has happened in sentences 4 and 5: How do the auxiliaries in those two differ? What rule goes into effect with these "negative" adverbs? What will happen to sentence 6 when you attempt a shift to the opening position?

PREPOSITIONAL PHRASES

The **prepositional phrase** is our most common structure of modification, appearing regularly as a modifier of both nouns and verbs, as we have seen in our sample sentences throughout the chapters.

Prepositional Phrase

Preposition	Object
throughout	the theater
during	the Christmas break
along	the shore
in	our backyard
for	my sake
according to	the weather report
by	yourself
instead of	taking the elevator
over	the rainbow
because of	his stubborn streak
outside	the office building
without	your cooperation

As you learned in Chapter 2, the diagram for the adverbial prepositional phrase is always attached to the verb:

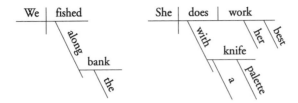

Some prepositional phrases have modifiers that qualify or intensify them, just as adjectives and adverbs do:

He arrived <u>shortly</u> before noon.

The house was built <u>directly</u> over the water.

In the diagram the modifier will be attached to the preposition:

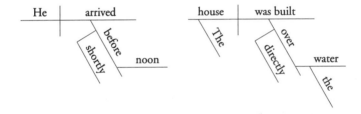

Sentences often have more than one adverbial prepositional phrase:

We hiked <u>in the woods</u> <u>for several hours</u> <u>on Saturday</u>.

And like adverbs, adverbial prepositional phrases can occupy several positions, with those referring to time often more movable than those referring to place, especially when both appear in the same sentence:

<u>For several hours</u> <u>on Saturday</u> we hiked <u>in the woods</u>.

<u>On Saturday</u> we hiked <u>in the woods</u> <u>for several hours</u>.

We are less likely to say:

<u>In the woods</u> we hiked <u>on Saturday</u> <u>for several hours</u>.

In general, an adverbial with main focus will occupy a slot at or near the end of the sentence. But no matter where in the sentence they appear—whether at the beginning, the middle, or the end—in the diagram the adverbial prepositional phrases will be attached to the verb:

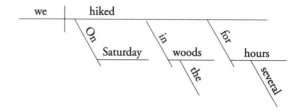

Diagram the following sentences, paying particular attention to the adverbials. Your first step should be to identify the sentence pattern.

1. In winter we burn wood for our heat.
2. We can heat our house very efficiently in cold weather because of its good insulation.
3. My roommate just went to the store for a loaf of bread.
4. She'll be here in a minute.
5. In an interview on *CNN*, the chairman of the Federal Reserve discussed his views on both fiscal and monetary policy.
6. E-mail systems throughout the world are being constantly invaded by viruses.
7. During an election year, the environment inevitably becomes big news.
8. Man is by nature a political animal. [Aristotle]

Because prepositional phrases can modify both verbs and nouns, ambiguity is fairly common. The prepositional phrase in the following sentence, for example, could be interpreted as meaning either "with whom" or "which problems":

They discussed their problems <u>with the teacher</u>.

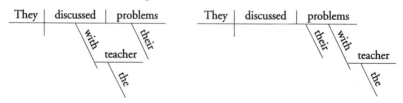

In speech, meaning is rarely a problem, and when it is, the listener can ask for clarification. But the solitary reader has no one to ask, "What do you mean?" or "How's that again?" So the writer has an obligation to make such questions unnecessary. Understanding when modifiers are ambiguous is important for writers; avoiding ambiguity is a requirement of clear writing.

Exercise 16

Rewrite each of the following sentences in two ways to show its two possible meanings.

1. I'm going to wax the car in the garage.
2. We watched the game on the porch.
3. I hid from the neighbors upstairs.
4. Fred tripped his teammate with the bat.
5. Susan washed the stones she found in the river.

NOUNS AND NOUN PHRASES

Nouns and noun phrases that function adverbially form a fairly short list designating time, place, manner, and quantity. Here are some of them:

We walked home. _____

I'm leaving Monday morning. _____

I'm going your way. _____

Every day he studied two hours. _____

I travel a great deal. _____

We are flying tourist class. _____

I sent the package airmail. _____

The Boy Scouts hiked single file down the trail. _____

He arrived this evening. _____

These noun phrases may look suspiciously like direct objects or subject complements, but if you remember to think about the kind of information that adverbials contribute to the sentence, you should have no trouble in recognizing them as adverbials. In the blank following each sentence, write the adverbial question that the noun phrase answers.

These noun phrases work like prepositional phrases—like prepositional phrases with missing prepositions. The traditional grammarian labels them **adverbial objectives** and diagrams them as though they were the objects in prepositional phrases:

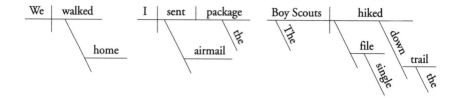

In some of these sentences the preposition is optional: (*on*) Monday morning, (*for*) two hours, (*by*) airmail, (*in*) single file. This method of diagramming the adverbial noun phrase acknowledges both its *form*—a noun headword on a horizontal line with or without modifiers—and its *function*—a modifier of the verb.

Investigating Language   5.2

In Chapter 2, when you first studied the sentence patterns, you were advised to think in terms of the referents of the NPs in determining the sentence patterns. For example, you can distinguish Pattern V,

Carmen became a doctor [NP$_1$ V NP$_1$]

from Pattern VII,

Carmen called a doctor [NP$_1$ V NP$_2$]

by recognizing the relationship that the two NPs have to each other. That is, when the NP that follows the verb has a referent different from that of the subject, you can assume that it's a direct object and that the verb is transitive:

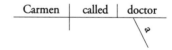

In Chapter 3, you learned about another test for determining if a verb is transitive: Can you make the sentence passive? Can you say "A doctor was called (by Carmen)"? In this case, the answer is yes. This means that the verb is transitive and the sentence is Pattern VII.

Now we come to a complication of sorts—sentences that look like Pattern VII:

We arrived home.

I work Sundays.

In both cases the verb is followed by an NP with a referent different from that of the subject. What test can you apply to show that *arrived* and *work* are not transitive verbs?

Here's a pair that might fool you. How can you show that they belong to different patterns? What tests can you apply?

Terry is flying the plane.

Terry is flying first class.

You'll want to bear in mind the kind of information that adverbials and direct objects contribute, the kinds of questions that they answer.

Exercise 17

Underline the adverbials in the following sentences and identify their forms. Then identify the sentence patterns. In making your judgments, you'll want to think about the kind of information that each slot contributes to the sentence.

1. Pete is working nights this week.
2. I was awake the whole night.
3. I'll see you soon.
4. This morning Pam threw away the leftover spaghetti.
5. George will do dishes next time.
6. I love weekends.
7. Bill works weekends.
8. At the first sign of winter the birds flew south.

VERB PHRASES

Infinitives. The most common form of the verb in an adverbial role is the infinitive, the base form of the verb with *to:*

Mom cashed a check <u>to give Jody her allowance</u>.

I went home early <u>to relax before the party</u>.

Jennifer took on two paper routes <u>to earn money for camp</u>.

Remember that the infinitives—*to give, to relax,* and *to earn*—are not simply verbs with *to;* they are entire verb phrases, complete with complements and modifiers.

Underlying the first infinitive phrase is a Pattern VIII sentence:
Mom gave Jody her allowance.

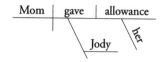

When we turn that predicate into an infinitive, the relationship of the complements and the verb stays the same, as the diagram of the infinitive shows. We have a Pattern VIII infinitive, an adverbial that tells why, in a Pattern VII sentence:

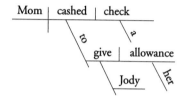

At first glance you may confuse the infinitive with a prepositional phrase, such as *to school* or *to the store; to* appears in both constructions, and the traditional diagrams are similar. But there is an important difference in form: In the prepositional phrase, a noun phrase follows *to;* in the infinitive, a verb phrase follows *to.*

Underlying the *relax* infinitive phrase is a Pattern VI sentence:
I relaxed before the party.

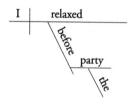

Underlying the *earn* phrase is a Pattern VII sentence:
Jennifer earned money for camp.

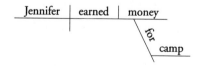

The Pattern VI sentence is now a Pattern VI infinitive phrase; the Pattern VII sentence is now a Pattern VII infinitive phrase. The *relax* phrase has been added to a Pattern VI sentence (*I went home early*), the *earn* phrase to a Pattern VII (*Jennifer took on two paper routes*):

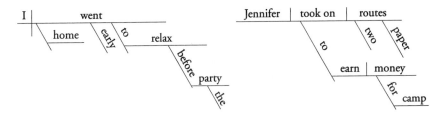

Note, too, that the subjects of the sentences are also the subjects of the infinitives.

In the first and third sentences, where the infinitive phrases follow nouns, *check* and *routes*, they may appear to modify those nouns. The clue that says otherwise is the meaning "in order to" that underlies almost all adverbial infinitives; they answer the question *why:*

> Mom cashed a check <u>in order to give Jody her allowance</u>.
>
> I went home early <u>in order to relax before the party</u>.
>
> Jennifer took on two paper routes <u>in order to earn money for camp</u>.

In fact, we often include *in order*, especially in introductory position:

> <u>In order to earn money for camp</u>, Jennifer took on two paper routes.

In diagramming the expanded version, you can treat it like a phrasal preposition, with "in order to" on the diagonal line.

There are exceptions. Occasionally an infinitive functions adverbially without the meaning of "in order to," but such sentences are uncommon in speech:

> The detective glanced out the window only <u>to see</u> the suspect slip around the corner.
>
> I arrived at the auditorium only <u>to find</u> every seat taken.

These infinitives have an almost main-verb rather than adverbial quality. We could, and probably would, more often say:

> The detective glanced out the window <u>and saw</u> the suspect slip around the corner.
>
> I arrived at the auditorium <u>and found</u> every seat taken.

Other exceptions, which are fairly common idioms, occur with the verbs *come* and *live*. Here too the infinitive has main-verb status:

> I've <u>come to believe</u> in UFOs.
>
> I've <u>come to understand</u> your point of view.
>
> You'll <u>live to regret</u> that remark.

Dangling Infinitives. We noted that the subject of the sentence is also the subject of the adverbial infinitive. When this is not the case, the infinitive is said to "dangle." In the following sentences, the infinitive phrases have no stated subject:

> <u>To keep farm machinery in good repair</u>, a regular maintenance schedule is necessary.
>
> For decades the Superstition Mountains in Arizona have been explored in order <u>to find the fabled Lost Dutchman Mine</u>.

Certainly the problem with these sentences is not a problem of communication; the reader is not likely to misinterpret their meaning. But in both cases a kind of fuzziness exists that can be cleared up with the addition of a subject for the infinitive:

> <u>A farmer</u> needs a regular maintenance schedule <u>to keep the farm machinery in good repair</u>.
>
> For decades <u>people</u> [or <u>adventurers</u> or <u>prospectors</u>] have explored the Superstition Mountains in Arizona <u>to find the fabled Lost Dutchman Mine</u>.

Participles. When -*ing* verbs function as adverbials and adjectivals, they are called **participles**. Although we have traditionally thought of the participle as an adjectival (and that is certainly its more common role), some participles and **participial phrases** clearly have an adverbial function, providing information of time, place, reason, and manner, as other adverbials do:

> My uncle made a fortune <u>selling real estate</u>. (*How?*)
>
> The kids came <u>running out of the house</u>. (*How? Where?*)
>
> Betsy went <u>swimming</u> (*Where?*)

The participial phrase is diagrammed on a diagonal line that bends to become horizontal, so that it accommodates any complements or modifiers the participle may have:

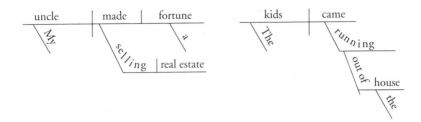

Some participial phrases have characteristics of both adverbials and adjectivals:

<u>Standing near a huge puddle</u>, Jan got thoroughly splashed.

Here the opening verb phrase could be expanded into either a *who* clause (Jan, *who was standing near a huge puddle*, got thoroughly splashed) or a *while* clause (*While she was standing near a huge puddle*, Jan got thoroughly spashed). The *who* clause is adjectival, as you will learn in Chapter 6; the *while* clause, as you will see in the next section of this chapter, is adverbial. The sentence would be correctly analyzed either way.

Exercise 18

Underline all the adverbial modifiers in the following sentences. Identify the sentence pattern of the main clause and any of the adverbial verb phrases. After doing that analysis, you should have no trouble diagramming the sentences.

1. Our cat often jumps up on the roof to reach the attic window.
2. Sometimes she even climbs the ladder to get there.
3. Last night my computer blinked ominously during an electrical storm.
4. I immediately turned it off.
5. We went to the mall last Saturday to check out the big sales.
6. Afterwards we stayed home to watch the playoff game with Uncle Dick.

CLAUSES

What is a **clause**? When is a clause adverbial?

The label *clause* denotes a form: a group of words with a subject and a predicate. The ten sentence patterns described in Chapter 2 have this form. The branching diagram, you'll recall, illustrates the two parts:

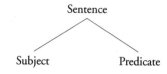

In other words, the ten sentence patterns are essentially clause patterns.

From the standpoint of mechanical conventions, we can define **sentence** as a word or group of words that begins with a capital letter and ends with a period or other terminal punctuation. A more complete definition would read as follows:

> A *sentence* is a word or group of words based on one or more subject–predicate, or clause, patterns; the written sentence begins with a capital letter and ends with terminal punctuation.

This definition eliminates "Wow!" and "The very idea!" and "Rats!" as sentences, but it includes commands, such as "Help!" with its underlying subject–predicate "You help me." All sentences, then, are clauses, *but not all clauses are sentences.*

At the opening of this chapter we saw a *when* clause in the sentence about the magician:

> The audience gasped nervously throughout the theater <u>when the magician thrust his sword into the box</u>.

Without the word *when,* this clause would be a complete sentence. The subordinator *when,* however, turns it into a **dependent clause**—in this case, a dependent clause functioning as an adverbial.

The term *dependent clause,* in contrast to **independent clause,** refers to any clause that is not itself a complete sentence. In later chapters we will see other dependent clauses, some that function as adjectivals, modifying nouns, and others as nominals, filling NP slots. In traditional terms, any sentence that includes a dependent clause of any kind is known as a **complex sentence.** A sentence with two or more independent clauses is a **compound sentence.** And one with a dependent clause and more than one independent clause is called **compound-complex.**

Another set of contrasting labels traditionally given to clauses (in addition to *independent* and *dependent*) is *main* and *subordinate.* It's accurate to say that the terms *main clause* and *independent clause* are synonymous—and, in fact, are used interchangeably. With their counterparts, however, there is a difference: *Dependent* and *subordinate* are not generally used interchangeably.

The term *subordinate clause* is often restricted to those dependent clauses that are introduced by subordinating conjunctions—words like *since* and *if* and *because* and *when.* That definition rules out the nominal clauses, which are introduced by expletives and interrogatives. It also rules out the adjectival clauses, which are introduced by relative pronouns and relative adverbs. We will see these other dependent clauses in the next two chapters.

The most common subordinators that introduce adverbial clauses are *after, because, before, since, so, until, when,* and *while.* Here in the adverbial chapter you will see examples of clauses that answer such adverbial questions as *when* and *why,* as you'll see in the following sentences:

You should eat some breakfast <u>before you take that exam.</u>

Pay close attention to your e-mail <u>because a virus could be lurking there.</u>

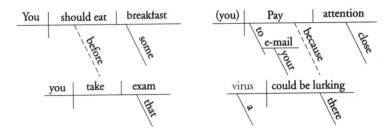

At first glance these sentence diagrams may look complicated, but as you can see, they are simply two sentence patterns connected by the subordinator that introduces the adverbial clause.

Exercise 19

Diagram the sentences, paying particular attention to all the sentence patterns, those of adverbial verb phrases and clauses, as well as of main clauses. Remember, too, that any adverbial that includes a verb (as clauses and verb phrases do) can also include other adverbials.

1. We will be visiting Yellowstone Park this summer, when we drive across the country in our new SUV.
2. Last year we stayed at Silver Falls State Park for three days during our vacation in Oregon.
3. Whenever our dog sees lightning or hears thunder, he scratches frantically at the door to get our attention.
4. Is Mike really moving to Memphis to look for a job after he graduates?
5. I never take the subway home at night because my family worries about me.
6. After our building was burglarized twice in one month, we searched the ads to find a new apartment.

PUNCTUATION OF ADVERBIALS

You may have noticed in the examples that some opening adverbials are set off by commas and some are not. Their punctuation is sometimes a matter of choice, especially in the case of phrases. Generally a short prepositional phrase or noun phrase or an adverb will not be set off:

> Saturday morning we all pitched in and cleaned the garage.
>
> By noon we were exhausted.
>
> Hastily they gathered their books and left the room.

With longer prepositional phrases there is a choice:

> At the top of the hill the hikers sat down to rest.
>
> At the end of a long and exhausting morning, we all collapsed.

When the end of the adverbial slot is not readily apparent, the comma will be needed to prevent misreading:

> During the winter, vacation days are especially welcome.
>
> In the middle of the night, winds from the north brought subzero temperatures and the end of Indian summer.

The two opening adverbial structures that are *always* set off by commas are verb phrases and clauses—no matter what their length:

> To earn money for camp, Jennifer took on two paper routes.
>
> To succeed, you'll need self-discipline.
>
> When the speech finally ended, the audience broke into applause.

When an adverbial interrupts the verb phrase for a special effect, it will be set off by commas:

> I finally bought, on my birthday, a brand new car.
>
> The stranger asked me, quite openly, for my credit card number.

When the opening phrase is parenthetical—more clearly a comment on the whole sentence than a straightforward adverbial—then a comma is called for:

> According to all the polls, the incumbent was expected to win.
>
> On the other hand, not everyone was surprised at the outcome of the election.
>
> Luckily, no one was hurt.

The punctuation of sentence modifiers is discussed in Chapter 8.

Investigating Language *5.3*

It's not at all unusual for inexperienced writers to punctuate subordinate clauses as complete sentences. It's probably the most common sentence fragment that teachers encounter.

> The children have been quite bored this summer. Because the swimming pool has been closed since July.

> Although we had a lot of rain last spring. Apparently the drought is not over yet.

Given what you know about sentence slots, can you explain why writers would make that mistake? In the second example, what's the difference between *although* and *apparently*?

If you listen carefully to the intonation of subordinate clauses and complete sentences, you will hear the difference. Read the clauses aloud:

> because you were here

> since Joe went away

> if he knows the truth

Now read them without the subordinator:

> You were here.

> Joe went away.

> He knows the truth.

You can probably hear the pitch of your voice dropping at the end of the last three. In the set with subordinators, your pitch would normally stay more level on the last word. (Even if you didn't read them with that contrast, you probably could do so to illustrate the difference.)

There's another way of reading that first group: as if they were answers to questions. In fact, such sentence fragments are common in conversation:

> Q. Why did you come back?   A. Because you were here.

> Q. How long have you lived alone?   A. Since Joe went away.

> Q. Will Mike ever forgive you?   A. If he knows the truth.

Does this reading help explain why writers make punctuation errors? What can a writing teacher do to help students understand and correct their punctuation?

CHAPTER 5
Key Terms

Adverb

Adverbial

Adverbial clause

Adverbial infinitive

Adverbial noun phrase

Adverbial participle

Adverbial prepositional phrase

Ambiguity

Clause

Dangling infinitive

Dependent clause

Independent clause

Infinitive

Main clause

Movability

Participle

Participial phrase

Prepositional phrase

Sentence

Sentence fragment

Subordinate clause

Subordinating conjunction

Sentences
for PRACTICE

Underline the adverbials in the following sentences and identify their forms. For additional practice, identify the sentence patterns and diagram the sentences. Remember also to identify the sentence patterns of the adverbial verb phrases and clauses.

1. By the end of the fifth inning, the playoff game had already become boring.

2. When the fall foliage shows its colors in New England, thousands of tourists go there to enjoy nature's astonishing display.

3. On Halloween night the neighborhood children rang every doorbell on the block to fill their bags with goodies.

4. The recent decline on Wall Street may have occurred because many new dot-com companies lost their investors' money and then lost the investors.

5. According to the *Wall Street Journal,* the deficit is considered our most serious domestic problem.

6. When both Mark McGwire and Sammy Sosa were chasing Roger Maris's home run record in 1998, the baseball season got really exciting.

7. The myth of the "sugar high" may finally be laid to rest by a new scientific study, according to a report in the *Los Angeles Times*.

8. Because of a lyme disease outbreak in several counties, fewer hunters applied for licenses in the fall of 2001.

9. Cowards die many times before their death. [Shakespeare]

10. Be silent always when you doubt your sense. [Alexander Pope]

11. Diane must take nineteen credits to graduate this semester.

12. Susan plans to stay home on Friday to fix a special gourmet dinner for her roommates.

13. During the month of December there will be dozens of holiday specials on television.

14. Where were you when I needed a shove to get my car to the garage for repairs?

15. Never in the field of human conflict was so much owed by so many to so few. [Winston Churchill]

QUESTIONS
?
for DISCUSSION

1. How would you analyze the following sentences, which were spoken in a television interview by an attorney whose client had been accused of murder:

   > You're not talking a traffic ticket here. You're talking somebody's life.

   In considering the sentence patterns and the referents of the noun phrases, you might think that *talking* is a transitive verb. Is it?

2. How do you account for the difference in meaning of the following sentences? Why is "in the mountains" so important?

   > After his retirement, Professor Jones lived for six months in the mountains.

   > After his retirement, Professor Jones lived for six months.

3. As you know, single-word adverbs are often movable, producing

a number of variations in a sentence. How many acceptable variations can you produce by adding the adverb *frequently* to the following sentence?

I have had colds this year.

Are there any slots in the sentence where *frequently* is clearly unacceptable?

4. Recently a banner was hung across a city's main street to recognize the local bus company's ten years of service to the community. On it was printed the company's name, followed by the verb phrase "serving our community" and, in bold print, these three words:

SAFELY   ECONOMICALLY   FRIENDLY

What suggestion could you have made to the banner committee if they had asked for your advice?

CLASSROOM APPLICATIONS

1. Compose a cinquain (pronounced "sin-cane")—a five-line poem in which the number of syllables increases with each line— about an action or feeling; in other words, your topic is a verb. For the five lines, use the five forms of adverbials you studied in this chapter: adverb, prepositional phrase, noun phrase, verb phrase, and clause—preferably in that order. The title of your poem will be the verb (or, possibly, a verb + direct object or a verb + subject complement) that you're expanding with the five adverbials. Here is an example:

Waiting

Here

For you

One last time

To plead my case

Because you promised to listen

Here are some possible titles for you to try: Sleeping, Studying Grammar, Worrying, Playing Soccer, Feeling Special, Making Friends, Skiing, Thinking.

2. Shifting the position of certain adverbs—such as *only, almost, simply,* and *merely*—can alter the meaning in a sentence. The following sentences differ in meaning because of the different locations of *only:*

> Only Rupert crammed for the final exam. [Others did not cram.]
>
> Rupert only crammed for the final exam. [He didn't prepare in any other way.]
>
> Rupert crammed for the final exam only. [He didn't cram for quizzes or other tests.]

Shift the position of *only* in the following sentence; you should be able to put it in five different places.

Adults may swim in the lake after 4 P.M.

Explain how each location alters the meaning.

CHAPTER 6

Modifiers of the Noun: Adjectivals

CHAPTER PREVIEW

The traditional definition of *adjective* is "a word that modifies a noun."
Like the word *adverb*, however, *adjective* refers to a word class with particular characteristics, not to a grammatical function. That traditional
definition, then, turns out to be a definition not of *adjective* but rather of
adjectival, the topic of this chapter. By now you've probably come to realize that the adjective is only one of many structures that modify nouns.
(You've been seeing adjectival prepositional phrases since Chapter 2.) In
addition to adjectives and prepositional phrases, you'll learn that verb
phrases and clauses—and even other nouns—also modify nouns.
Because of their frequency in the sentence and the variety of structures
we use to expand them, noun phrases provide a remarkable range of
possibilities for putting ideas into words. In this chapter the description
of noun modification provides further evidence that our grammar is
highly systematic.

As you know, a noun phrase occupies at least one slot in every sentence pattern—that of subject. In six of the ten patterns, noun phrases
occupy one or more slots in the predicate as well: direct object, indirect
object, subject complement, and object complement; the noun phrase
also serves as the object of the preposition. Most of the NPs used in the
sample sentences have been simple two-word phrases: *the students, a
scholar, an apple, their homework.* But in the sentences we actually speak
and write, the noun phrases are frequently expanded with modifiers—not

only with adjectives, the basic noun modifier, but with other nouns and noun phrases, with prepositional phrases, verb phrases, and clauses.

We live next door to <u>an *orange* house</u>. (adjective)

My sister lives in <u>a *brick* house</u>. (noun)

<u>The house *on the corner*</u> is new. (prepositional phrase)

<u>That house *covered with ivy*</u> looks haunted. (verb phrase)

This is <u>the house *that Jack built*</u>. (clause)

We can think of the noun phrase as a series of slots (in much the same way as we looked at the expanded verb), with the determiner and noun headword as the required slots and the modifiers before and after the headword as optional:

NOUN

NP = <u>Det</u>   (__)   (__)   <u>HEAD-</u>   (__)   (__)   (__)
WORD

THE HEADWORD

Filling the headword slot in the noun phrase is, of course, the noun, the word signaled by the determiner. (In the previous list, the word *house* fills the headword slot of the underlined noun phrases.) Traditional grammarians define noun as "the name of a person, place, or thing"—a definition based on meaning. That definition works in a limited way. But a better way to identify nouns, as you learned in Chapter 2, is to put your innate language ability to work: Is the word signaled by a determiner—or could it be? Can you make it plural? Also, an understanding of the system of pre- and postnoun modifiers in the noun phrase will make the identification of the noun headword an easy matter.

Recognition of the headword of the noun phrase can also help in preventing problems of subject–verb agreement. Such problems can arise when a postheadword modifier includes a noun itself:

*The stack of instruction <u>forms</u> were misplaced.

*The complicated instructions on the new income tax <u>form</u> really confuses me.

With just a few exceptions, it is the number, either singular or plural, of the headword in the subject noun phrase that dictates the form of the verb in the present tense. In the preceding sentences, the writer has used the wrong noun in making the verb selection. *Stack* and *instructions* are the headwords; *forms* and *form* are simply parts of postnoun modifiers.

> The stack was misplaced.

> The stack of instruction forms was misplaced.

> The instructions really confuse me.

> The complicated instructions on the new income tax form really confuse me.

The exceptions to this system involve noun phrases with certain **collective nouns** and pronouns in which the modifier rather than the headword determines the verb:

> A bunch of my friends are coming over for dinner.
>
> Some of the cookies are missing.
>
> Some of the cake is missing.

This topic, along with other details of determiners, is discussed further in the "Determiner" section of Chapter 12.

THE PRENOUN MODIFIERS

The Determiner. The *determiner,* one of the structure classes, is the word class that signals nouns. This class includes *articles, possessive nouns, possessive pronouns, demonstrative pronouns,* and *numbers,* as well as a variety of other common words. When you see one of these words, you can be fairly sure you're at the beginning of a noun phrase.

The native speaker rarely thinks about determiners; they are automatic in speech. But for the writer, the determiner's role is something to think about. For example, as the first word of the noun phrase, and thus frequently the first word of the sentence and even of the paragraph, the determiner can provide a bridge, or transition, between ideas. The selection of that bridge can make subtle but important differences in emphasis:

> This attempt at reconciliation proved futile.
>
> The attempt at reconciliation. . .
>
> Their attempt. . .
>
> One such attempt. . .

<u>All their</u> attempts. . .

<u>Those</u> attempts. . .

In selecting determiners, writers have the opportunity not only to make such distinctions but also to help their readers move easily from one idea to the next in a meaningful way.

Some nouns, of course, are used without determiners: proper nouns (*John, Berkeley*), noncountable nouns (*salt, water*), abstract nouns (*justice, grief*), and sometimes plural count nouns (*apples, students*). You will read more about these categories in Chapter 11.

Adjectives and Nouns. These two word classes generally fill the slots between the determiner and the headword. When the noun phrase includes both an adjective and a noun as modifiers, they appear in that order; they cannot be reversed:

DETERMINER	ADJECTIVE	NOUN	HEADWORD
the	ugly		house
the		brick	house
our	little	neighbor	boy
an	ancient	marble	bathtub
that	nervous	test	pilot
Bill's	new	kitchen	table

[handwritten annotations in left margin: "possessive pronoun" pointing to "our"; "Article" pointing to "an"; "demonstrative" pointing to "that"; "possessive N." pointing to "Bill's"]

We do not say, "Bill's kitchen new table" or "Our neighbor little boy."

The adjective slot frequently includes more than one adjective; all of them modify the headword:

the funny brown monkey

the little old man

You'll notice that there are no commas in the preceding noun phrases, even though there are several modifiers before the noun. But sometimes commas are called for. A good rule of thumb is to use a comma if it is possible to insert *and* between the modifiers. We would not talk about "a little and old man" or "a funny and brown monkey." However, we would say "a strange and wonderful experience," so in using these two adjectives without *and*, we would use a comma:

a strange, wonderful experience

That comma represents juncture in speech—a pause and slight upward shift in pitch. Read the following pair of sentences aloud and listen to the difference in your voice:

> On the table stood a little black suitcase.
>
> On the table stood an ugly, misshapen suitcase.

In general, the system calls for a comma between two adjectives when they are of the same class, for instance, when they are both abstract qualities such as "strange" and "wonderful" or "ugly" and "misshapen." However, in the earlier example—*funny brown monkey*—the adjectives *funny* and *brown* are not alike: "funny" is an abstract, changeable quality; "brown" is a concrete, permanent quality.

The adjective can also be qualified or intensified:

the extremely bright young lady

a really important career decision

In this situation we often have occasion to use a hyphen to make the relationship clear:

> a half-baked idea
>
> a Spanish-speaking community
>
> a bases-loaded home run

Hyphens are especially common when the modifier in the adjective slot is a participle (the *-ing* or *-en* verb), as in the previous examples: *baked, speaking,* and *loaded* are participles. And because participles are verbs, they are also commonly modified by adverbs:

> a well-developed paragraph
>
> the fast-moving train
>
> this highly publicized event
>
> a carefully conceived plan

The hyphen rule here is fairly straightforward: The *-ly* adverbs (such as *highly, carefully, really,* and *extremely*) do not take hyphens; other adverbs (such as *well* and *fast*) do take hyphens.

Other classes of words also need hyphens when the first modifier applies not to the headword but to the second modifier:

high-technology industries

two-word verbs

all-around athletes

free-form sculpture

In these modifiers, if the hyphen were eliminated, the reader would not necessarily know that *two* does not apply to *verbs*, nor *all* to *athletes*, nor *free* to *sculpture*.

Another occasion for hyphens in the preheadword position occurs when we use a complete phrase in the adjective slot:

an off-the-wall idea

the end-of-the-term party

a middle-of-the-road policy

my back-to-back exams

When a phrasal modifier fills the subject complement or an ending adverbial slot in the sentence pattern, however, the hyphens are generally omitted:

Our party will be <u>at the end of the term</u>.

My exams during finals week are <u>back to back</u>.

In certain idioms they would probably be retained:

Her idea seemed off-the-wall to me.

The policy he subscribes to is strictly middle-of-the-road.

The position in the sentence can also affect the earlier hyphenated examples:

The paragraph was well developed.

The industry did research in high technology.

In the diagram of the noun phrase, no matter where in the sentence it appears and no matter how many modifiers it includes, the headword is on a horizontal line with the determiner, adjective(s), and modifying noun(s) slanting down from it:

When the modifiers themselves have modifiers, either qualifiers or other nouns, the diagram will make that clear:

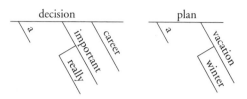

When the determiner is a possessive noun, it may have a determiner of its own: my daughter's car, the car's electrical system:

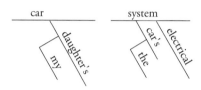

As the diagrams illustrate, the whole phrases "my daughter" and "the car" have been made possessive. You can show that *my daughter's* and *the car's* constitute a single modifier of the headword by substituting a possessive pronoun: *her* car, *its* electrical system.

Exercise 20

A. Label the determiner (D) and headword (H) in each underlined noun phrase in the following paragraph. Identify the form (adjective, noun, participle) of any modifiers that fill the slots between the determiner and headword.

Born in England, Joshua Abraham Norton migrated to San Francisco in 1849, where he became <u>a highly successful land speculator</u>. By 1853, he was worth an estimated quarter of a million dollars—a wealthy man, even by <u>today's standards</u>. But when he attempted to corner the market on rice, he lost <u>his entire fortune</u>. <u>This financial disaster</u> affected his mind, and on September 17, 1859, he sent to <u>a local newspaper</u> an announcement that he had been chosen the Emperor of the United States. The city was amused and accepted <u>their newly discovered eccentric</u>; he ate without paying in restaurants, and theaters reserved special seats for him. Wearing <u>an old blue military uniform</u> with epaulets and a hat with feathers, he attended <u>every public function and meeting</u>. <u>A large upholstered chair</u> was always reserved for him in <u>the state legislature</u>. Norton even issued <u>his own imperial bonds</u>, <u>each note</u> granting the bearer <u>the face value</u> plus seven percent interest at maturity, apparently in 1900. But

Emperor Norton died on January 8, 1880, on his way to <u>a scientific conference</u>. <u>His lavish funeral</u> was attended by a reported thirty thousand people.

B. Underline the determiner and headword of each noun phrase in the following sentences. Identify the form of any modifiers that fill slots between them. Punctuate the noun phrases with commas and hyphens, if necessary.

1. The department's personnel committee met in the main office this morning.
2. Our whole family is impressed with the new Sunday brunch menu at the cafeteria.
3. Serena's daughter found an expensive-looking copper-colored bracelet in the subway station.
4. The bicycle safety commission will discuss the new regulations at their regular meeting this noon.
5. Her lovely, gracious manner was apparent from the start.
6. Any mother could easily perform the job of several air traffic controllers.
7. The rising interest rates should be a serious concern for every cost-conscious citizen.

THE POSTNOUN MODIFIERS

The postheadword position in the noun phrase may contain modifiers of many forms; when there is more than one, they appear in this order:

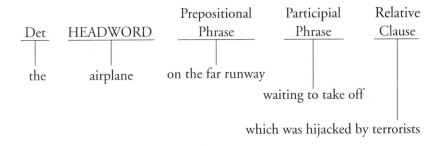

In this section we will look at all of these structures that follow the headword, beginning with the most common postnoun modifier, the prepositional phrase.

Prepositional Phrases. The adjectival prepositional phrase, which modifies a noun, is in form identical to the adverbial prepositional phrase described in Chapter 5. In its adjectival role the prepositional phrase identifies the noun headword in relation to time, place, direction, purpose, origin, and the like:

The *house* on the corner is new.

The security *guard* in our building knows every tenant personally.

I have always admired the lovely *houses* along Sparks Street.

The *meeting* during our lunch hour was a waste of time.

Jack is a *man* of many talents.

An adjectival prepositional phrase helps to identify a noun or pronoun by answering the questions "Which one?" or "What kind of?" Which house is new? The one *on the corner.* Jack is what kind of man? One *of many talents.*

Because the prepositional phrase itself includes a noun phrase, the adjectival prepositional phrase demonstrates the recursiveness of the language—the embedding of one structure in another of the same kind. Such recursiveness occurs in many parts of the sentence: a sentence within a sentence, a noun phrase within a noun phrase, a verb phrase within a verb phrase. In the case of the adjectival prepositional phrase, we nearly always have a noun phrase within a noun phrase. And we needn't stop with one embedding; we could continue branching that NP at the bottom of the diagram with another Det + N + PP, which would produce yet another NP:

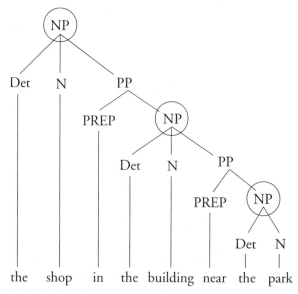

Such strings, though fairly common, especially at the end of the sentence, are sometimes open to ambiguity:

> My sister manages the flower shop in the new brick building near the park on Center Street.

Our linguistic computer most readily associates a modifier with the nearest possible referent:

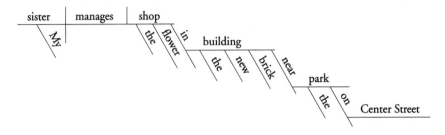

If a different meaning is intended—if, for example, it is the building rather than the park that is on Center Street—the writer must make that clear: "the flower shop in the brick building on Center Street that is near the park."

Exercise 21

Underline the adjectival prepositional phrases in the following sentences. If any of them are ambiguous, rewrite them to clear up the ambiguity.

1. A young man with a cast on his left foot hobbled down the street.
2. I will meet you in the lobby of the museum near the visitors' information booth.
3. The party after the game at Bob's house must have been a riot.
4. The threat of computer viruses is causing concern among scientists.
5. The computer world is being threatened by an enemy from within.
6. The textbook for my science course was written by a Nobel laureate from Stanford.
7. Politicians in the United States must raise large sums of money to get elected.
8. The candidates with the weakest qualifications usually have the most complaints about the selection process.

Relative Clauses. Like the adverbial clause that modifies verbs, the **relative clause** (also called the **adjectival clause**) is a dependent clause. In its adjectival function, the relative clause identifies the noun or pronoun it modifies— and almost always appears immediately after that noun or pronoun:

> The arrow <u>that has left the bow</u> never returns.

> Relatives are persons <u>who live too near and visit too often</u>.

Like adjectival prepositional phrases, relative clauses answer the questions "Which one?" or "What kind of?" Which arrow? The one *that has left the bow*. What kind of persons? Those *who live too near and visit too often*.

In form, a relative clause is a sentence pattern, complete with a subject and a predicate. The only difference between a relative clause and a complete sentence is the introductory word, the relative pronoun (*who, whose, whom, which,* or *that*). Like other pronouns, the relative pronoun has an **antecedent**, the noun that it refers to and replaces. The traditional diagram clearly shows the relationship of the clause to the noun it modifies:

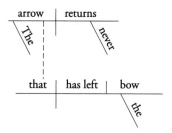

Three features of the relative pronoun will help you to recognize the relative clause: (1) The relative pronoun renames the headword of the noun phrase in which it appears; in our example, *arrow* is the antecedent of *that*. (2) The relative pronoun fills a sentence slot in its own clause; in the example, *that* is in the subject slot. And (3) the relative pronoun introduces the clause, no matter what slot it fills.

Let's look at another example of a relative clause introduced by *that*, perhaps our most common relative pronoun:

> This is the house *that Jack built.*

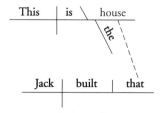

The diagram illustrates those three features of relative pronouns: (1) The antecedent of *that* is *house,* the word it is attached to in the diagram;

(2) *that* fills a slot in the clause; and (3) *that* opens its clause, even though it functions as the direct object in the clause.

In referring to people, we generally use *who* rather than *that*; and when it functions as an object in its clause, the form we use is *whom*, the objective case:

> A man <u>whom I knew in the army</u> phoned me this morning.

> The clerk at the post office, <u>to whom I complained about our mail service</u>, was very patient with me.

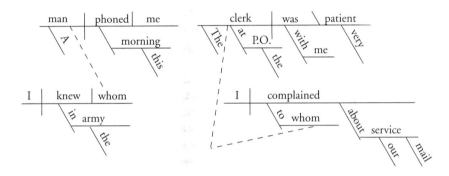

Notice in the second preceding example that *whom* is the object of a preposition. You may have noticed that the preposition, not the relative pronoun, is the first word in the relative clause. This is the only instance where the relative is not the immediate clause opener—that is, when the relative pronoun is the object of a preposition.

The following sentence illustrates the **possessive case** of *who*. Like other possessive pronouns (such as *my, his, their*), *whose* functions as a determiner in its clause:

> The student <u>whose notes I borrowed</u> was absent today.

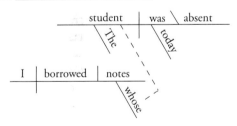

The dotted line connects the pronoun to its antecedent, *the student*; in other words, "whose notes" means "the student's notes."

Another common relative pronoun is *which*:

> *Huckleberry Finn,* <u>which we read in high school</u>, is a classic <u>that often causes controversy</u>.

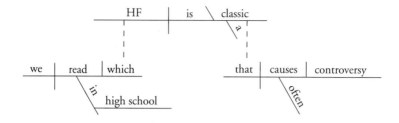

You'll read more about *which* later in the chapter, in connection with punctuation.

The following example illustrates an important feature of sentences in which the relative pronoun *that* is the direct object in its clause:

> You can choose a color <u>that you like</u>.

You will note that this sentence would be equally grammatical without *that:*

> You can choose a color you like.

The relative *that* is often deleted, but the deletion is possible only when the pronoun functions as an object in its clause, not when it acts as the subject.

The objective case relative, *whom,* like the relative *that,* can often be deleted too:

> A woman [whom] my mother knew in high school has invited me to dinner.

Even though the *whom* is deleted, it will have a place on the diagram; it is "understood." The deleted word can be shown in brackets, or it can be replaced by an x:

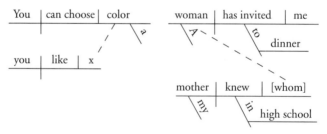

Exercise 22

Underline the relative clauses in the following sentences. Identify (1) the noun that the clause modifies; (2) the role of the relative in its clause; and (3) the sentence pattern of the clause.

1. A rattlesnake that doesn't bite teaches you nothing. [Jessamyn West]

2. Jacqueline Kennedy Onassis, who died in 1994, was a figure of mystery.

3. Come with me to the concert that the jazz club is sponsoring.

4. The gift she gave the bride and groom attracted a lot of attention.

5. A weed is a plant whose virtues have not been discovered. [Ralph Waldo Emerson]

6. What do you say about a couple of kids who have everything but good sense?

7. Terry received congratulations from people whom she had not seen in years.

8. I skimmed the last article, in which the connection between automobile exhaust and acid rain is explained.

9. The shed, which was damp and drafty, at least provided shelter from the rain.

10. This is the cat that killed the rat that ate the malt that lay in the house that Jack built.

Note: Your teacher may also want you to diagram these sentences. Having analyzed the clauses, you've done most of the work already!

All the relative pronouns fill slots in the clauses that nouns normally fill. However, some adjectival clauses are introduced not by relative pronouns but by the **relative adverbs** *where, when,* and *why.* In these clauses the relative replaces an adverbial structure in its clause. The relative adverb *where* introduces clauses that modify nouns of place:

Newsworthy events rarely happen in the small *town* <u>where I was born.</u>

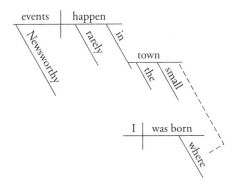

Note in the diagram that the relative adverb *where* modifies the verb *was born* in its own clause; however, the clause itself is adjectival, modifying *town.*

When clauses modify nouns of time:

> I will be nervous until next *Tuesday,* <u>when results of the audition will be posted.</u>

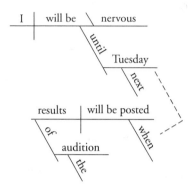

Why clauses modify the noun *reason:*

> I understand the *reason* <u>why Margo got the lead in the spring play.</u>

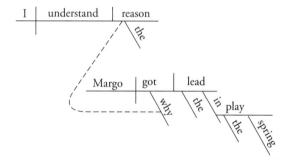

Where, when, and *why* clauses are often equally acceptable, and sometimes smoother, without the relative:

> I understand the reason <u>Margo got the lead.</u>

> I will be nervous until the day <u>the results are posted.</u>

Participial Phrases. You'll recall that the formula describing the noun phrase includes three postheadword modifiers:

			(1)	(2)	(3)
			Prepositional	Participial	Relative
<u>Det</u>	<u>Adj</u>	<u>Noun</u> <u>HEADWORD</u>	<u>Phrase</u>	<u>Phrase</u>	<u>Clause</u>

You've been seeing the prepositional phrase as an adjectival since Chapter 2:

the neighbors <u>from Korea</u>

the president's announcement <u>about the meeting</u>

And in the previous section you studied the relative clause:

the man <u>who lives across the street</u>.

If we change the form of the verb in the relative clause by adding *be* + *-ing*,

the man <u>who is living across the street</u>,

we can easily demonstrate that the adjectival **participial phrase** is essentially a reduced relative clause:

the man <u>living across the street</u>.

This noun phrase, with its participial phrase as a modifier, will fit in any nominal slot of the sentence:

I know <u>the man living across the street</u>. (direct object)

<u>The man living across the street</u> seems very nice. (subject)

I often visit with <u>the man living across the street</u>. (object of the preposition)

Like the other adjectivals, in the diagram the participial phrase is attached below the noun. As we saw in the case of adverbials, the participial phrase begins on a diagonal line, which then bends to become a horizontal line. The horizontal line will accommodate any complements and/or modifiers the participle may have:

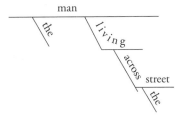

You'll notice that the diagram of the participial phrase looks exactly like the predicate of the sentence (or relative clause) that underlies it:

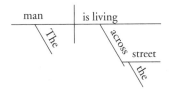

The clause—and the participial phrase—are Pattern VI.

Here are two further examples of participial phrases, the first a transitive verb, the second a linking verb:

The students <u>taking the SAT</u> look nervous.

Do you recognize those boys <u>acting so foolish</u>?

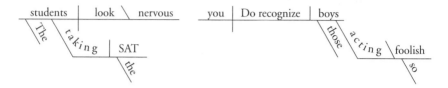

Note that the participles are diagrammed exactly like the predicates of the sentences that underlie them:

Again, you will recognize that the participial phrases are reduced versions of clauses:

The students <u>who are taking the SAT</u> look nervous.

Do you recognize the boys <u>who are acting so foolish</u>?

The only difference between the verb in the clause and the verb in the participial phrase is the presence or absence of the auxiliary *be* and tense.

As the examples illustrate, transitive participles will have direct objects (taking *the SAT*), and linking-verb participles will have subject complements (acting *so foolish*). And all participles, just like verbs in all the sentence patterns, may be modified by adverbials of various forms.

In the following sentence, we have added the adverbial noun phrase *this morning*:

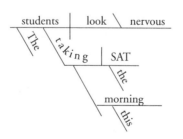

Here are three key points that will help you understand participles:

1. Verbs from all four classes—*be,* linking, intransitive, and transitive—can function as participles.

2. The noun phrases in all the NP slots can include participles (or participial phrases) as modifiers: direct objects, subject complements, object complements, indirect objects, objects of prepositions, as well as subjects.

3. The noun that the participle modifies is its subject; that is, the relationship between the headword of the noun phrase in which the participle is embedded and the participle itself is a subject–verb relationship. In the diagram, the participle is connected to its own subject.

Exercise 23

Turn each of the following sentences into a noun phrase that includes a participial phrase as a postnoun modifier. Use the noun phrase in a sentence.

Example:

Two dogs are fighting over the bone.

Sentence:

I recognize *those two dogs fighting over the bone.*

1. An expensive sports car is standing in the driveway.
2. The baby is sleeping upstairs in the crib.
3. The fans are lining up at the ticket office.
4. The students are searching the Internet.
5. The fullback was charging through the line.
6. The teachers are walking the picket line.

Prenoun Participles. When a participle is a verb alone, with no complements or phrasal modifiers, it will usually occupy the adjective slot in preheadword position:

Our <u>snoring</u> visitor kept the household awake.

The <u>barking</u> dog across the street drives us crazy.

A <u>rolling</u> stone gathers no moss.

These preheadword participles are diagrammed just as the others are:

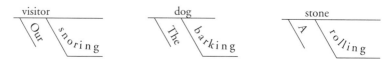

In this position, an adverb sometimes modifies the participle:

Our <u>loudly snoring</u> visitor kept the household awake.

The <u>peacefully sleeping</u> baby was a joy to watch.

Passive Participles.   The participles we have seen so far are the *-ing* form of the verb (traditionally called the present participle); as you would expect, the clauses underlying them are also in the active voice. Another common form of the adjectival participle is the *-en* form. This form, which is traditionally called the past participle, might be more accurately called the "passive participle."

The houses <u>designed by Frank Lloyd Wright</u> are national treasures.

The car <u>being driven by the front runner</u> has developed engine trouble.

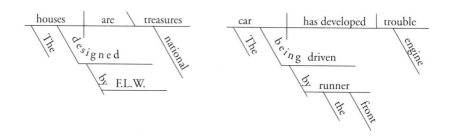

Like the *-ing* participles, the *-en* participles are also reduced clauses:

The houses <u>that were designed by Frank Lloyd Wright</u> are national treasures.

That car <u>that is being driven by the front runner</u> has developed engine trouble.

Both of these underlying relative clauses are in the passive voice. (Note that in the last example, the active voice version of the verb includes *be* + *-ing*: *is driving*. When *be* + *-en* is added to make it passive, the resulting verb has two forms of *be* as auxiliaries: *is being driven*.)

Remember, we produce a passive sentence by adding *be* + *-en* to the verb, so a passive verb is always the *-en* form. When we turn such sentences into participles, they will automatically have the *-en* form.

Exercise **24**

Underline the participles in the following sentences; identify their sentence patterns. Diagram.

1. The award given every year to the outstanding volunteer has been announced.
2. Being a philosopher, she can propose a problem for every solution.
3. He has all the gall of a shoplifter returning an item for a refund.
4. The hostess gave the departing guests some leftover food for their pets.
5. Finding the price reasonable, they rented the apartment on the spot.
6. Congress shall make no law abridging the freedom of speech or of the press.
7. They planned the class picnic for Saturday, hoping for good weather.
8. The university will not fund research involving genetic manipulation.
9. The special computer workshops held on campus last weekend were designed for students majoring in business.
10. The teachers' union has finally approved the last two disputed sections of the contract offered by the school district.

The Participle as Object Complement. You'll recall from Chapter 2 that two of the required slots in the sentence patterns, two functions, are filled by adjectivals: the subject complement slot in Patterns II and IV and the object complement slot in Pattern IX. In most cases, these slots are filled by adjectives:

The teacher seems angry. (subject complement)

We found the teacher unreasonable. (object complement)

We did see some examples, however, of prepositional phrases as subject complements:

The teacher was in a bad mood this morning.

The piano sounds out of tune.

We could easily come up with prepositional phrases as object complements as well:

> We found the teacher <u>in a bad mood</u> this morning.
>
> I consider your behavior <u>out of line</u>.

The object complement slot can also be filled by a participle:

> I could feel my heart <u>beating faster</u>.

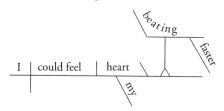

Again, we make use of the pedestal in the diagram to place the participle's characteristic bent line in the object complement slot on the main line.

What this diagram says is that "my heart beating faster" is not a single noun phrase; it is two separate structures. You can test this conclusion by substituting a pronoun for the direct object:

> I could feel <u>it</u> beating faster.

Clearly there are two slots following the verb, both of which are required for the sense of the sentence.

The distinction between the participle as object complement—a separate slot—and the participle as a modifier in the direct object slot may be subtle:

> The police found the murdered witness.
>
> The police found the witness murdered.

Again, you can determine the number of slots following the verb by substituting pronouns:

> The police found him.
>
> The police found him murdered.

A fairly reliable way to determine if the sentence has an object complement is to insert *to be:*

> I could feel my heart *to be* beating faster.
>
> The police found him *to be* murdered.

The resulting sentences may not be the most natural way of expressing the object complement, but they are certainly grammatical.

Movable Participles. We can think of the postheadword slot in the noun phrase as the "home base" of the participle, as it is of the relative clause. But unlike the clause, the participial phrase can be shifted to the beginning of the sentence when it modifies the subject:

> <u>Built by Frank Lloyd Wright in 1936</u>, the Kauffman house at Fallingwater is one of Western Pennsylvania's most valued architectural treasures.

> <u>Carrying heavy packs on their backs</u>, the hikers were exhausted when they reached the summit of Black Butte.

The participial phrase that modifies the subject can also be shifted to the end of the sentence if the sentence is fairly short:

> The students cheered noisily for the basketball team, <u>standing up throughout the game</u>.

No matter where it appears in the sentence, the adjectival participial phrase is attached in the diagram to its own subject, the headword of the noun phrases in which it appears:

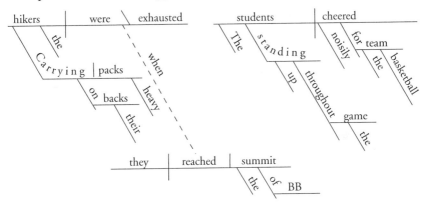

Dangling Participles. The introductory participial phrase provides a good way to add variety to sentences, to get away from the standard subject opener. But it carries an important restriction:

> The participle can open the sentence only when its subject is also the subject of the sentence and is located in regular subject position. Otherwise, the participle dangles.

This restriction applies to both adverbial and adjectival participles. A dangling participle, in other words, is a verb in search of a subject:

> *Having found the rent reasonable, the apartment turned out to be perfect.

(It was not the apartment that found the rent reasonable!)

> *Standing nervously on the platform, a barrage of ripe tomatoes suddenly pelted the candidate.

(The tomatoes weren't standing on the platform!)

A common source of the dangling participle is the sentence with a "delayed subject." Two common delayers are the *there* transformation and the anticipatory *it:*

> *Having moved the patio furniture into the garage, there was no longer room for the car.
>
> *Knowing how much work I had to do yesterday, it was good of you to come and help.

In the last sentence the subject of the participle, *you,* is there, but it appears in the predicate rather than in the usual subject position. As readers and listeners, we process sentences with certain built-in expectations. We expect the subject of an introductory verb to be the first logical noun or pronoun.

Incidentally, moving a participle to the end of the sentence will not solve the problem if the subject has been omitted. Even there, we expect the subject of the sentence to be the subject of the participle as well:

> *There was no longer room for the car, having moved the patio furniture into the garage.

Often the most efficient way to revise such sentences is to expand the participial phrase into a complete clause:

> <u>After we moved the patio furniture into the garage</u>, there was no longer room for the car.
>
> It was good of you to come and help yesterday <u>when you learned how much work I had to do.</u>

Another common source of the dangling participle is the passive sentence:

> *Having worked hard since 6:00 A.M., the project was completed before noon.

Here the problem arises because the passive transformation has deleted the agent, which is also the subject of the participle. Transforming the sentence into the active voice will solve the problem:

> Having worked hard since 6:00 A.M., *we* completed the project before noon.

Exercise 25

Rewrite the following sentences to eliminate the dangling participles.

1. Needing considerable repair, my parents were able to buy the house for little money.
2. Installing a new program, all other applications should be turned off.
3. Having misunderstood the assignment, my paper got a low grade.
4. Covered with the grime of centuries, the archeologists could not decipher the inscription.
5. Searching for change in her purse, the bus left without her.
6. Having spent four hours on the operating table, a double bypass was performed on the patient's severely blocked arteries.
7. Once considered only an average player, Chris's game has improved greatly in the last three months.
8. Breaking in through the window of the girls' dormitory, the dean of men surprised several members of the football team.
9. Pickled, I'll eat anything.
10. Seen from miles away, you might mistake the mountain for a cloud.

PUNCTUATION OF CLAUSES AND PARTICIPLES

The question regarding punctuation of clauses and participles is the question of **restrictive** versus **nonrestrictive modifiers**. Put simply, the question is "Should I set off the phrase or clause with commas?"

In answering this question, the writer must think about the referent of the noun being modified. Is it clear to the reader? In the case of a singular noun, is there only one possible person (or place or thing, etc.) to which the noun can refer? In the case of plurals, are the limits understood? If there is only one, the modifier cannot restrict the noun's meaning any further: The modifier is therefore nonrestrictive and will be set off by commas. It might be useful to think of these commas as parentheses and the modifier as optional; if it's optional, we can assume it's not needed to make the referent of the noun clear.

If the referent of the noun is not clear to the reader—if there is more than one possible referent or if the limits are not known—the purpose of the modifier is quite different: to restrict the meaning of the noun. Thus the modifier in this case is restrictive and is not set off by commas. You may find the terms *defining* and *commenting* easier to understand than *restrictive* and *nonrestrictive*.[1] Does the modifier define (restrict) the noun or does it merely comment on (not restrict) it?

Notice the difference in the punctuation of the following pair of sentences:

> The football players wearing shiny orange helmets stood out in the crowd.

> The football players, wearing shiny orange helmets, stood out in the crowd.

In the first sentence the purpose of the participial phrase is to define *which* football players stood out in the crowd. We could illustrate the situation by depicting a crowd of football players on the field, some of whom are wearing *shiny orange helmets;* they are noticeable—they *stand out in the crowd* of football players—because the others are wearing drab, dark helmets or perhaps no helmets at all. In the second sentence the modifier merely comments on the players—it does not define them. An illustration of this situation might show a group of orange-helmeted football players signing autographs in a crowd of children; those players would stand out in that crowd with or without orange helmets. The modifier does *not* tell *which* football players stood out in the crowd; they *all* did. (And, incidentally, they were all wearing orange helmets.)

Context, of course, will make a difference. What does the reader already know? For example, out of context the clause in the following sentence appears to be restrictive:

> The president <u>who was elected in 1932</u> faced problems that would have overwhelmed the average man.

Ordinarily we would say that the noun phrase *the president* has many possible referents; the *who* clause is needed to make the referent clear; it defines and restricts *the president* to a particular man, the one elected in 1932. But what if the reader already knows the referent?

> Franklin Delano Roosevelt took office at a time when the outlook for the nation was bleak indeed. The president, <u>who was elected in 1932</u>, faced decisions that would have overwhelmed the average man.

In this context the clause is simply commenting; the referent of the noun phrase *the president* is already defined by the time the reader gets to it. Many times, however, context alone is an insufficient determinant; only

---

[1.]These terms are used by Francis Christensen in *Notes Toward a New Rhetoric* (New York: Harper & Row, 1967), pp. 95 ff.

the writer knows if the clause defines or comments. The reader can only take the writer's word—or punctuation—at face value:

> The rain began with the first drumbeat. Only the band members <u>who were wearing rain gear</u> stayed reasonably dry. Everyone else at the parade, spectators and marchers alike, got wet.

Without commas the clause restricts the meaning of the noun phrase *the band members*; it defines those band members who stayed dry. With commas the clause suggests that all the band members were wearing rain gear.

Francis Christensen emphasizes that the writer must also be aware of what the reader might infer from the restrictive clause or phrase. "When the modifier is restrictive, the sentence makes one statement and implies its opposite; and what it implies is just as important as what it states."[2] In other words, in the preceding sentence the clause *who were wearing rain gear* implies that some band members were *not* wearing rain gear and did *not* stay reasonably dry. In the case of the football players, the modifier in the first sentence, the one with the restrictive participial phrase, suggests the presence of football players who were *not* wearing shiny orange helmets and did *not* stand out in the crowd. That implication is built into the restrictive modifier. If such an opposite statement is not true, the writer must be careful to avoid giving the reader the wrong impression. In writing the sentence with commas, the writer would no longer be identifying or defining a *subgroup* of dry band members or football players; with commas, the clauses become comments about the *entire group*.

So in reaching a decision about commas, the writer must take into account (1) what the reader knows (Is the referent clear without this information?) and (2) what the reader will infer if the modifier is restrictive.

Avoiding Comma Errors. The writer who uses commas at every pause in the sentence probably uses too many commas. In speech we often pause between the subject and the verb or between the verb and the direct object—that is, between the slots in the sentence pattern; but in writing we never separate these slots with commas. A simple pause, then, does not signal a comma. The pause that signals a comma usually includes a change in pitch.

Reading a sentence aloud as you would normally speak can be useful in identifying such changes. If you wanted to distinguish the dry band members from the wet ones, for example, you would probably speak the sentence with the loudest stress on *rain,* with secondary stress on *dry*:

The band members wearing rain gear stayed dry.

---

2. Christensen, p. 98.

The line indicates the normal pitch or **intonation** contour, showing rising pitch over the loudest syllable and falling pitch at the end. The intonation contour of the sentence with a nonrestrictive modifier is quite different:

The band members, wearing rain gear, stayed dry.

The nonrestrictive modifier has an intonation contour separate from that of the main sentence, so that this sentence has three main stress points. In reading the second sentence aloud, you'll especially notice a difference in the stress you give to *band;* it is longer and louder than it is in the other version, with its single intonation contour. And if you listen carefully to the words *members* and *gear,* you'll detect a slight rise in pitch at the very end of the words. That is the pitch rise that is often signaled by a comma.

Actually this sentence probably sounds strange when you hear yourself say it; it has an unnatural, stilted quality. That quality occurs because we rarely speak in sentences with nonrestrictive modifiers in postnoun position. This is an important difference between speaking and writing. In making punctuation decisions about such modifiers, the writer can take advantage of this difference by reading the sentence aloud.

In the case of participial phrases that modify the subject, the writer has another useful test: Can the modifier be shifted to the beginning or end of the sentence? If that shift does not change the meaning, the modifier is nonrestrictive. The restrictive participial phrase will remain within the noun phrase, whereas the nonrestrictive phrase can introduce the sentence and sometimes follow it:

<u>Wearing rain gear</u>, the band members stayed reasonably dry.

In the case of the relative clause, the relative pronoun provides some clues for punctuation:

1. The adjectival *that* clause is always restrictive; it is never set off by commas.

2. The *which* clause is generally nonrestrictive; it is set off by commas. You can test a *which* clause by substituting *that*: If it works, the clause is restrictive and should not have commas, and if not, it is nonrestrictive. NOTE: There is an exception to this general rule about *that* in restrictive and *which* in nonrestrictive clauses: Only *which* functions as the object of a preposition; *that* does not. So the relative in that position will be *which* whether the clause is restrictive or nonrestrictive:

    I probably won't get either of the jobs for which I applied.

    Pat got a terrific new job, for which I also applied.

3. If the relative can be deleted, the clause is restrictive:

> The bus (that) I ride to work is always late.

> The woman (whom) I work with is always early.

The next two rules apply to both clauses and phrases:

4. After any proper noun the modifier will be nonrestrictive.

> Herbert Hoover, elected president in 1928, was the first president born west of the Mississippi River.

5. After any common noun that has only one possible referent the modifier will be nonrestrictive:

> My youngest sister, who lives in Oregon, is much more domestic than I.

> The highest mountain in the world, which resisted the efforts of climbers until 1953, looks truly forbidding from the air.

Exercise 26

Identify the postheadword modifiers in the following sentences as restrictive or nonrestrictive by adding commas if needed.

1. Samuel Johnson who published his famous dictionary in 1755 defined a lexicographer as "a harmless drudge."

2. The town where I was born which has a population of 3,000 offers very little in the way of entertainment for teenagers.

3. No one could identify the man standing in the hotel window.

4. Naphtha which is highly flammable is no longer used in dry cleaning.

5. As director of personnel you must often make decisions that are painful to you and your employees.

6. Any book printed before 1501 is called an incunabulum which literally means "swaddling clothes."

7. The hurricane bearing down on Florida frightened the residents who live along the coast.

8. My Aunt Hazel who is an expert shopper spends several hours planning her purchases.

9. Con men can always find people who are trusting, greedy, and foolish.

10. Ozzie Smith leaping high in the air speared the line drive that would have won the game.

MULTIPLE MODIFIERS

So far most of the sentences used to illustrate adjectivals have had a single postheadword modifier, either a clause or a phrase. But we often have more than one such modifier, and when we do, the order in which they appear is well defined: prepositional phrase, participial phrase, relative clause:

the security guard [in our building] [who checks out the visitors]

the woman [from London] [staying with the Renfords]

the DC-10 [on the far runway] [being prepared for takeoff] [which was hijacked by a group of terrorists]

In a traditional diagram, all the noun modifiers in both pre- and post-position are attached to the headword:

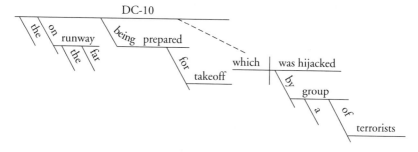

A change in the order of modifiers would change the meaning:

the DC-10 being prepared for takeoff, which was hijacked by a group of terrorists on the far runway

Here the prepositional phrase no longer specifies *which* DC-10; it has become an adverbial modifier in the relative clause, modifying *was hijacked*. In this version *DC-10* has only two postheadword modifiers, not three:

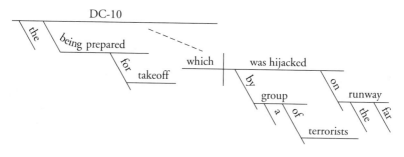

Just as ambiguity may result from a string of prepositional phrases, these multiple modifiers, too, are sometimes open to more than one interpretation:

the driver of the bus standing on the corner

a friend of my sister who lives in Tampa

In context these noun phrases may or may not be clear to the reader. In any case, the ambiguity is easily avoided:

the driver of the bus who was standing on the corner

the driver of the bus parked at the corner

my sister's friend from Tampa

my sister in Tampa's friend (or, my sister in Tampa has a friend who...)

OTHER POSTNOUN MODIFIERS

Infinitives. The infinitive—the base form of the verb preceded by *to*—can serve as a modifier in the postheadword. As a verb, it will have all the attributes of verbs, including complements and modifiers, depending on its underlying sentence pattern:

the way <u>to be helpful</u>

the time <u>to start</u>

the party after the play <u>to honor the director</u>

the best place in San Francisco <u>to eat seafood</u>

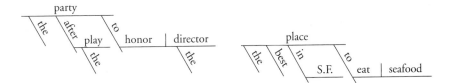

As the last two examples illustrate, the infinitive can be separated from the headword by another modifier. These examples also illustrate another common feature of the adjectival infinitive: Its subject may not be the noun it modifies; its subject is frequently just understood—the object in an understood prepositional phrase:

That was a nice thing [for you] to do.

Fisherman's Wharf is not necessarily the best place in San Francisco [for one] to eat seafood.

Noun Phrases. Nouns or noun phrases of time and place can follow the headword:

> the party <u>last night</u>
> the ride <u>home</u>

These adjectival noun phrases are diagrammed just as the adverbial noun phrases are—on horizontal lines:

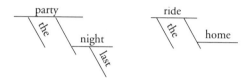

Adjectives. Qualified adjectives and compound adjectives, which usually occupy the preheadword position, can follow the headword if they are set off by commas:

> the neighbors, <u>usually quiet</u>
> the neighborhood, <u>quiet and peaceful</u>

Like the nonrestrictive participles, these nonrestrictive adjectives can also introduce the sentence when they modify the subject:

> <u>Usually quiet</u>, the neighbors upstairs are having a regular brawl tonight.
> <u>Quiet and peaceful</u>, the neighborhood slept while the cat burglars made their rounds.

Adverbs. Even adverbs can occupy the postheadword position in the noun phrase:

> That was my idea <u>exactly</u>.
> The people <u>here</u> have no idea of conditions <u>there</u>.

Exercise **27**

Identify all the postnoun modifiers in the following sentences and label them by form. A sentence may contain more than one postnoun modifier.

  1. Curling is a game in which players slide circular, handle-topped granite stones across the ice toward a target.

2. The sport, which originated in Scotland and the Netherlands, combines the skills of bowling and shuffleboard with the strategies of billiards and chess.

3. It is played on an ice rink that is 42 yards long and 10 yards wide, in teams of four players to a side.

4. Each player propels two stones toward a target that is 38 yards away.

5. Curling stones are made from a very special granite called Blue Hone, which is known for its toughness and resiliency.

6. Players "deliver" their stones with a twist of the wrist, imparting the curling action for which the game is named.

7. The third and fourth players on a team look for ways to knock the opponents' stones out of bounds.

8. An important piece of curling equipment is the broom, used by players to melt the ice slightly in the path of a teammate's stone.

9. The winning team is the one whose stones are closest to the center of the target; for each stone that is closer, one point is scored.

10. The sport is extremely popular in Canada, where there are more than a million curlers, who play both at local clubs and on a thriving cash circuit.

Investigating Language 6.1

Grammarians and language experts have been discussing the question of when and whether to use *who* or *whom* for well over two hundred years, with citations that stretch from Shakespeare to the 1996 presidential campaign:

Who wouldst thou strike?   (*The Two Gentlemen of Verona*, 1595)

Consider who the King your father sends,

To whom he sends, and what's his embassy.   (*Love's Labour's Lost*, 1595)

It all boils down to who do you trust.   (Bob Dole, 1996)

Who do you trust to select the [pizza] toppings?   (Bill Clinton, 1996)

In all four of these examples, the pronoun *who* functions as the direct object in its clause. Countless grammar books, dating as far back as 1762, maintain that *who* is incorrect in that position, that *whom* is called for. Why? Because in Latin grammar, the direct object slot requires the objective case, not the nominative (or subjective). But William Safire, in his *New York Times* column "On Language" (June 30, 1996), contends that

> at the beginning of a sentence, *whom* comes across as an affectation. In politics, formality went out with neckties, and what is comfortable to the listener's ear is to be preferred in address.

Safire agrees with many linguists who recognize that *who* is natural in speech at the beginning of a sentence or clause and that *whom* is natural only after a preposition:

> To whom shall I mail the check?

If the preposition comes at the end of the sentence, however, we will probably hear *who* in speech:

> Who shall I mail the check to?

The written language is a different issue. A writer can usually find a way to avoid both the affectation of *whom* and the "ungrammatical" *who* when the objective case is called for:

> Where shall I mail the check?
>
> Who should receive the check?

Another usage issue connected with substitutes for *whom* concerns the use of *that* when referring to people:

> A woman that I knew in high school has invited me to lunch.

Most handbooks consider this use of *that* unacceptable for formal writing, prescribing the use of *who* when referring to people. In this sentence, the correct form would be the awkward *whom*. Here the obvious solution is to delete the pronoun:

> A woman I knew in high school has invited me to lunch.

But when the clause is set off by commas, the pronoun cannot be deleted:

> Jane Barnard, whom I knew in high school, has invited me to lunch.

Can you find a way to revise this sentence in order to avoid this awkward use of *whom?*

CHAPTER 6
Key Terms

Adjectival	Nonrestrictive modifier
Adjectival clause	Participial phrase
Adjectival infinitive	Participle
Adjectival prepositional phrase	Passive participle
Adjective	Possessive case
Antecedent	Postheadword modifier
Case	Preheadword modifier
Dangling participle	Relative adverb
Demonstrative pronoun	Relative clause
Determiner	Relative pronoun
Headword	Restrictive modifier
Intonation	

Sentences
for PRACTICE

Draw vertical lines between the slots of the sentence patterns. Mark the headword of each NP with an X, the determiner with a D; underline the pre- and postheadword modifiers; then label each according to its form. Circle any pronouns that fill NP slots.

For further practice, identify the sentence patterns and diagram the sentences. Remember that all verb phrases and clauses functioning as adverbials and adjectivals also have identifiable sentence patterns.

1. The clown, acting silly to entertain the children, was not very funny.
2. The initials engraved inside my ring are BFJ.
3. My neighbor's husband, who is a strong union man, would not cross the picket line that the clerical workers organized at the mill where he is a foreman.
4. The company's reorganization plan, voted down last week, called for the removal of all incumbent officers.

5. At midnight Cinderella's beautiful coach, in which she had been driven to the ball, suddenly became a pumpkin again.

6. History is something that never happened, written by someone who wasn't there.

7. The old gentleman in Union Square, whom I met last week, sits all day near the fountain, playing solitaire and poker on his laptop.

8. The play's the thing wherein I'll catch the conscience of the king. [Shakespeare]

9. Uneasy lies the head that wears the crown. [Shakespeare]

10. Calling Pearl Harbor Day a day that would live in infamy, President Roosevelt asked Congress for a declaration of war.

11. Having been a police officer in downtown Nashville for thirty years, my neighbor grew restless and bored after he retired from the force.

12. The town in Missouri where I lived until I reached my fifteenth birthday is in the foothills of the beautiful Ozarks.

13. Beauty in things exists in the mind which contemplates them. [David Hume]

14. The newly formed commission on gender equity could not meet on a day when Professor Lang was out of town.

15. That tall man standing in the corner who smiled when I waved at him is my roommate from college.

QUESTIONS
?
for DISCUSSION

1. Generate a noun phrase according to each of the following formulas:
   A. det + adj + HEADWORD + participial phrase
   B. det + adj + noun + HEADWORD + clause
   C. det + adj + HEADWORD + prep phrase + part phrase
   D. det + noun + HEADWORD + part phrase + clause

   Use your NPs in sentences as follows:

   Use A as the direct object of a Pattern VII sentence.

   Use B as the object of a preposition.

   Use C as an indirect object.

   Use D as the direct object in a relative clause.

2. In our description of the noun phrase we saw that the headword slot is filled by a word that is a noun in form. Would you consider these underlined noun phrases as exceptions to the rule?

   The rich are different from other people.

   I was late for our meeting.

   You clean the upstairs, and I'll do the downstairs.

3. Explain the source of the ambiguity in the following sentence:

   My brother is considered the area's best foreign car mechanic.

4. In this chapter we discussed the recursive quality of the noun phrase—that is, the embedding of one noun phrase in another. Give a sentence in which a relative clause is embedded in another relative clause; give another in which a participle is embedded in another participial phrase; another with a participle in a relative clause; another with a relative clause in a participial phrase.

5. We quoted Francis Christensen as saying that restrictive modifiers make one statement and imply the opposite. What opposite statements can you infer from the following?

   All the students with an average of 90 or higher will be excused from the final.

   The flight controllers who saw the strange lights in the sky became firm believers in UFOs.

   The customers who witnessed the fight were called to testify.

   How would the meaning of these sentences change if the postnoun modifiers were set off by commas?

6. What is the source of the ambiguity in the following sentences?

   Tony buried the knife he found in the cellar.

   Fred tripped his teammate with the baseball bat.

   Diagram each in two ways to show its two possible meanings.

7. Speech can convey meaning that writing cannot. Read the following sentence in two ways to show two different meanings:

   The affluent Japanese travel all over in America.

   Now write the sentence in two ways to show the difference.

8. Both of the following sentences include an adjectival infinitive as a modifier of *decision*; and in both, the expletive *as* introduces an

object complement. But there's an important difference between them. Diagram both sentences to illustrate the difference.

> The Jaycees are hailing the decision to admit women as a landmark.

> The Jaycees are hailing the decision to admit women as members.

9. In *The Book of Lists* (Morrow, 1977), David Wallechinsky, Irving Wallace, and Amy Wallace describe a comma "that cost the government two million dollars before Congress could rectify the error." Here's the expensive sentence:

> All foreign fruit, plants are free from duty.

The clerk who wrote the rule was supposed to use a hyphen instead of a comma. Explain the difference.

CLASSROOM APPLICATIONS

1. There are very few, if any, nouns that cannot function as modifiers of other nouns. Here's a vocabulary exercise to test this statement. Begin with a common noun, such as *light* or *tree* or *house*. Use it as a modifier; then use the noun you modified as a modifier. See how long you can keep the chain going—perhaps around the room at least once. For example,

> *tree farm, farm building, building code, code word, word game, game player, player piano, piano bench, bench warmer, warmer oven, oven light. . .*

If you get stuck, you can go back and change a word to start a new path.

2. The term "sentence combining" refers to a popular method of teaching sentence structure in which writers learn to combine short sentences in various ways. This method is based on the work of the transformational linguists, who hold that every modifier in the noun phrase is actually a basic sentence. For example, this sentence,

The silly, awkward clown is entertaining the children,

combines three basic sentences:

The clown is entertaining the children.

The clown is silly.

The clown is awkward.

There are other ways in which these same three sentences could be combined:

The silly clown entertaining the children is awkward.

The awkward clown who is entertaining the children is silly.

Silly and awkward, the clown is entertaining the children.

The clown, silly and awkward, is entertaining the children.

The children are being entertained by the silly, awkward clown.

While entertaining the children, the clown was silly and awkward.

The awkward clown was being silly as he entertained the children.

Using your knowledge of both adverbial and adjectival modifiers, combine the following groups of sentences in as many ways as you can. (Try for at least a dozen!)

Becky stood before the magistrate.

Becky felt nervous.

The dancers kept time to the raucous music.

The dancers wore strange costumes.

The dancers acted crazy.

The young man waited for the train.

The train was very late.

The young man looked impatient.

The young man paced back and forth on the station platform.

The Noun Phrase Functions:
Nominals

CHAPTER PREVIEW

In the previous two chapters you saw how the simple sentence patterns can be expanded by adding optional modifiers of various kinds—words, phrases, and clauses that function as adverbials and adjectivals. In this chapter you will learn how the NP slots can be expanded by using structures other than noun phrases. We begin this chapter by reviewing the various roles that NPs play in our basic sentence patterns, including an optional NP slot called the **appositive**. Then we examine in detail how to fill these same slots with verb phrases and dependent clauses instead of noun phrases.

THE NOMINAL SLOTS

You have already learned that the terms *adverbial* and *adjectival* denote functions. An *adverbial* is any form—any word, phrase, or clause—that does what an adverb does—that is, modify a verb. *Adjectival* refers to any structure that does what an adjective usually does—modify a noun. But you'll notice that we have not used the parallel *-al* term for noun, **nominal,** until now. Up to this point, all of the required slots in the sentence patterns, such as subject and direct object, have been filled with noun phrases (and sometimes with pronouns, which stand in for NPs). We did this mainly for simplicity. But now that we're going to study other forms that fill the required sentence slots, it's time to introduce the term *nominal.*

All of those NP slots you learned about in Chapter 2 are actually nominal slots. Adverbials and adjectivals have only one function each—to modify a verb or modify a noun. But nominals perform a variety of functions, most of which are required to produce a complete grammatical sentence. As you'll recall, NPs fill a number of different slots in the basic sentence patterns:

Subject: <u>My best buddy</u> lives in Iowa.

Direct object: I visited <u>my best buddy</u> last Christmas.

Indirect object: I sent <u>my best buddy</u> a card for his birthday.

Subject complement: The town's new mayor is <u>my best buddy</u>.

Object complement: I consider Rich <u>my best buddy</u>.

Object of a preposition: The town has a lot of respect for <u>my best buddy</u>.

As you will see, these slots can be filled with forms other than NPs—namely, verb phrases and dependent clauses. But before we get to those other forms, let's look at one more nominal function, one that does not show up in the sentence patterns—an optional nominal slot called the **appositive.**

APPOSITIVES

An appositive is a nominal companion, a structure (usually an NP) that adds information to a sentence by renaming another nominal. It is sometimes called "a noun in apposition."

My best buddy, <u>Rich</u>, lives in Iowa.

The prosecutor cross-examined the next witness, <u>the victim's ex-husband</u>.

You can easily understand the optional nature of the appositive: These sentences would be grammatical without the added information. On the diagram the appositive occupies a place right next to the noun, or other nominal structure, that it renames:

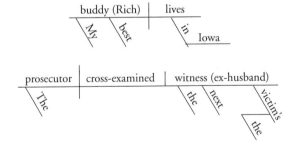

If the appositive renames the subject, it can be used to introduce the sentence:

<u>An ex-Marine who once played professional football,</u> the prosecutor was an intimidating presence in the courtroom.

No matter where the appositive is placed, in the diagram it is shown in the same slot as the nominal it renames:

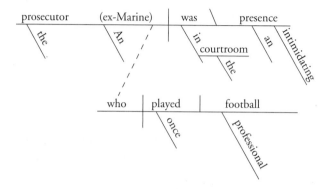

Punctuation of Appositives. The distinction between restrictive and nonrestrictive modifiers, which you learned in connection with participial phrases and relative clauses, also applies to appositives. When the appositive defines (restricts) the meaning of the nominal it renames, no commas are needed. An altered version of the first example will illustrate the distinction:

My buddy Rich lives in Iowa.

In the earlier example, the added name simply comments:

My best buddy, Rich, lives in Iowa.

The adjective *best* makes all the difference. *My best buddy* obviously refers to one specific person, just as *my only buddy* would. *My buddy*, however, has a general reference; the added name makes the referent of the noun phrase specific, actually defining the phrase *my buddy*. You can hear the contrast when you read the two sentences aloud.

Exercise **28**

Underline the noun phrases that are functioning as appositives. Remember, an appositive noun phrase has the same referent as the nominal it renames.

1. Folk songs, simple ballads sung to guitar music, became very popular in the 1960s.
2. One of the best-known folk singers of that period was Arlo Guthrie, son of the legendary songwriter Woody Guthrie.

3. An offbeat film about illegal trash dumping, "Alice's Restaurant" was inspired by Arlo's song of the same name.
4. The theme of many Arlo Guthrie songs, the search for personal freedom, is still appealing today.
5. Gillian Welch, a contemporary folk singer and songwriter, combines simple ballad-like melodies with topical lyrics in two very popular CDs, *Revival* and *Hell Among the Yearlings.*
6. I went to the concert with my friend Casey, who is Gillian Welch's biggest fan.

In Chapter 14, we take up the use of colons and dashes in connection with appositives. And in the following sections of this chapter, we include appositives in forms other than noun phrases—verb phrases and clauses.

NOUN PHRASE SUBSTITUTES

Three other structures can perform the grammatical functions that noun phrases generally perform: the gerund phrase, the infinitive phrase, and the nominal clause. Our study of these nominal forms—these substitutes for NPs—will focus on their five primary functions: subject, direct object, subject complement, object of a preposition, and appositive.

GERUNDS

In Chapter 3 you saw the *-ing* form of the verb combined with a *be* auxiliary functioning as the predicating, or tensed, verb:

The children <u>are running</u> through the woods.

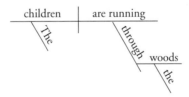

Here the diagram clearly shows the sentence as Pattern VI, with the intransitive verb *are running* modified by an adverbial prepositional phrase.

In the previous chapter you saw the *-ing* verb functioning as a noun modifier, called the participle; and you'll recall that the noun the participle modifies is also the participle's subject:

The children <u>running through the woods</u> look happy.

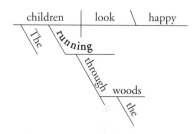

In this chapter we are using the same *-ing* verb as a nominal, filling a slot that a noun phrase usually fills. In this function, it is called a **gerund:**

<u>Running through the woods</u> is the children's favorite activity.

We can think of gerunds as names. But rather than naming persons, places, things, and events, as nouns generally do, gerunds name actions or behaviors or states of mind or states of being. And because they are verbs in form, gerunds will also include all the complements and modifiers that tensed verbs include. In our gerund example, *running* is modified by an adverbial prepositional phrase, *through the woods*, just as it was as a main verb: *The children are running through the woods.*

Even though sentences with gerunds in the NP slots may look more complicated than those you've seen before, the system for analyzing them is the same. You do that by identifying the sentence pattern. The first step is to locate the predicating verb. No matter what structure fills the subject slot, you can determine where it ends by substituting a pronoun, such as *something* or *it*:

Running through the woods is the children's favorite activity.

In other words,

<u>It</u> is the children's favorite activity.

Now you've identified the predicating verb, *is*, a form of *be*. Next you'll see that a noun phrase (*the children's favorite activity*) follows, so you know the sentence is Pattern III.

The next step is to identify the form of the structure filling that "it" slot. You can recognize "Running through the woods" as a gerund because it begins with an *-ing* verb form. (You can usually identify the form of a structure by looking at the first word.)

In diagramming the gerund when it fills a slot in the main clause, we simply attach the phrase to the main line by means of a pedestal, just as we did in Chapter 2 when a prepositional phrase filled the subject complement slot. The line for the gerund itself has a small step at the left, which identifies the *-ing* verb as a gerund:

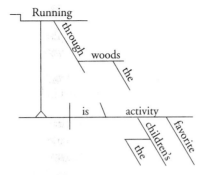

Following are examples of other NP slots occupied by gerund phrases.

Direct object: Both adults and teenagers enjoy playing computer games.

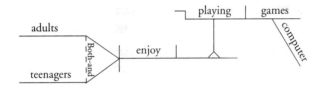

Subject complement: My favorite pastime is playing computer games.

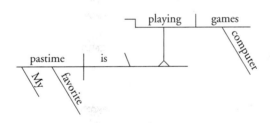

Object of a preposition: I work off a lot of tension by playing computer games.

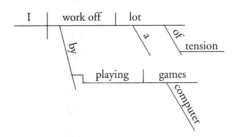

Appositive: My favorite pastime, playing computer games, is inexpensive but time-consuming.

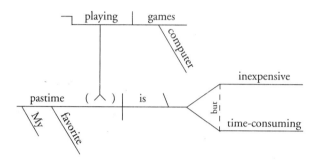

The Pattern of the Gerund. In these sentences with the gerund phrase *playing computer games,* the gerund *playing* has a direct object (*playing* what?), so we can identify the underlying sentence, with its one slot following the verb, as Pattern VII:

X is playing computer games.

The predicating verb in every pattern has the potential for becoming a gerund phrase when it is turned into the *-ing* form :

Pattern III: My little brother <u>is a pest</u>. *(being a pest)*

Pattern VIII: Tony <u>gave the landlord a bad time</u>. *(giving the landlord a bad time)*

Pattern IX: We <u>painted the bathroom orange</u>. *(painting the bathroom orange)*

In the following sentences, those *-ing* verb phrases have become gerunds filling NP slots:

My little brother enjoys <u>being a pest</u>. (direct object)

After <u>giving the landlord a bad time</u>, Tony regretted his behavior. (object of a preposition)

Our bright idea, <u>painting the bathroom orange</u>, was a decorating disaster. (appositive)

It's important to note that just because the function of the verb phrase changes—from predicating verb to nominal—its sentence pattern does not. The three gerunds remain Patterns III, VIII, and IX, respectively.

Exercise **29**

A. Identify the gerund phrases in the following sentences, and indicate the function (subject, direct object, subject complement, object of a preposition, appositive) that each one performs in its sentence. Also identify the sentence patterns of the main clause and of the gerund phrase. Diagram the sentences.

1. Flying a supersonic jet has been Sally's dream since childhood.
2. The coach enjoys playing practical jokes on his players.
3. The speaker began by telling a few jokes.
4. My hardest accomplishment last semester was staying awake in my eight o'clock class.
5. Leaving the scene of the accident was not a good idea.
6. Two witnesses reported seeing the suspect near the entrance of the bank.
7. Michelle Kwan trained hard to achieve her objective, winning a fourth World Championship.
8. The cost of going to college has risen dramatically in the last ten years.
9. Thinking a problem through requires time, solitude, and concentration.
10. For many generations the primary goal of women in our culture was being a good wife and homemaker.

B. Compose sentences that include the following verb phrases as gerunds. Try to use each gerund phrase in at least two different functions.

taking grammar tests   giving people a helping hand

being punctual   lying on the beach

Investigating Language   **7.1**

Compare these pairs of sentences:

Her job was selling computers in a discount store.

She was selling computers in a discount store.

My brother is getting into trouble again.

My problem is getting into law school.

How do the patterns of the two sentences in each pair differ? What are the predicating verbs? Which ones contain gerunds? How would the diagrams for each be different? Marking off the sentence slots with vertical lines will help to show the differences in the sentence patterns. You can also try substituting pronouns to help you see where the NP slots begin and end.

The Subject of the Gerund. The subject of the gerund—that is, the person or agent performing the action expressed in the gerund—is usually not stated. It is often the same as the subject of the sentence, as in item 2 in Exercise 29, where "coach" is the subject of both "enjoys" (the main verb) and "playing" (the gerund). Sometimes the subject can be inferred from another word in the sentence, as in item 4, where "my" indicates who had trouble "staying awake." The subject of the gerund will usually be left unstated when it names a general, rather than a particular, action or behavior, as in items 8 and 9 in Exercise 29.

But sometimes the subject can be expressed in the gerund phrase itself. When it is, it will often be in the possessive case:

> <u>His drinking</u> is excessive.
>
> I objected to <u>Jeremy's receiving a scholarship</u>.
>
> <u>Your complaining about the work</u> will not make it any easier.

Although the possessive case may sometimes sound excessively formal or even incorrect, it is the form considered standard in formal writing.

In the diagram, the subject of the gerund is diagrammed like a determiner and attached to the step on the left:

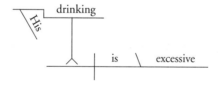

Dangling Gerunds. Read the following sentences. What is the problem with them?

> Upon seeing the stop sign, the car screeched to a halt.
>
> By proofreading my papers, my grades improved greatly.
>
> The ingredients should be assembled before starting to bake a cake.

You probably recognized that these sentences aren't strictly logical; they suggest that the car saw the stop sign, the grades proofread the papers, and the ingredients baked the cake. We call that problem the "dangling gerund," a problem that occurs when the subject of the gerund is not stated or clearly implied. These sentences have the same fuzzy quality that dangling participles have.

Dangling gerunds usually turn up when the gerund serves as the object in an opening or closing prepositional phrase. To clear up a dangling gerund, you can revise the sentence in one of two ways:

1. Make sure that the subject of the main clause is also the subject of the gerund:

> Upon seeing the stop sign, I brought the car to a screeching halt.
>
> By proofreading my papers, I improved my grades greatly.

2. Turn the prepositional phrase with the gerund into an adverbial clause:

> Assemble the ingredients before you start to bake a cake.

Exercise 30

Improve the following sentences by providing a clear subject for the gerund.

1. After finishing the decorations, the ballroom looked beautiful.
2. Your revising time will be reduced by following a few helpful pointers.
3. In making a career decision, your counselor will be a big help.
4. By signing this waiver, no claims against the owner can be made.
5. Our backpacks got really heavy after hiking up that steep mountain trail.

INFINITIVES

Another form of the verb that functions as a nominal is the **infinitive phrase**—the base form of the verb with *to*. Like the gerund, the nominal infinitive names an action or behavior or state of being. In fact, the infinitive closely parallels the gerund and is often an alternative to it:

> Gerund: <u>Remaining neutral on this issue</u> is unconscionable.

> Nominal infinitive: <u>To remain neutral on this issue</u> is unconscionable.

You have already seen infinitives functioning as modifiers of verbs (Chapter 5, Adverbials) and as modifiers of nouns (Chapter 6, Adjectivals).

In this chapter you will see the nominal infinitive functioning as subject, direct object, subject complement, and appositive:

> *Subject:* <u>To be a successful farmer these days</u> requires stamina and perseverance.
>
> *Direct object:* My cousin wants <u>to be a successful farmer</u>.
>
> *Subject complement:* My cousin's ambition is <u>to be a successful farmer</u>.
>
> *Appositive:* My cousin's ambition, <u>to be a successful farmer</u>, requires stamina and perseverance.

As with gerunds, you can substitute a pronoun to help you decide what nominal slot the infinitive phrase fills:

> <u>Something</u> requires stamina and perseverance.
>
> My cousin wants <u>something</u>.
>
> My cousin's ambition is <u>this</u>.

Infinitives, like gerunds, are verb forms; they may include complements and/or adverbial modifiers. As you learned in the discussion of adverbial infinitives in Chapter 5, infinitive phrases can be derived from all the sentence patterns. Our "farmer" infinitive is Pattern III. In the first example it fills the subject slot in a Pattern VII sentence:

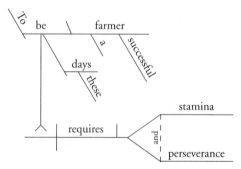

In the diagram, the infinitive phrase, like the gerund, is connected to the main line with a pedestal. The infinitive itself is on a two-part line exactly like that of a prepositional phrase. (It's easy to tell the difference, however: In the infinitive phrase, *to* is followed by a verb, not by a noun phrase.)

In the following sentence, a Pattern VII infinitive phrase functions as an appositive:

> My job, to hand out the diplomas, was a last-minute assignment.

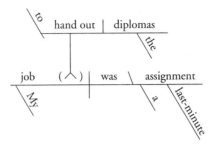

The action expressed in the infinitive phrase renames the subject, *My job;* it tells what the job is.

Exercise *31*

Identify the sentence pattern of each infinitive phrase and the function that the infinitive phrase plays in the sentence. Diagram the sentences.

1. Ruth plans to give her father a necktie for Christmas.
2. To side with the truth is noble.
3. Our only hope is to beg for mercy.
4. To walk across campus alone at night could be dangerous.
5. Both candidates desperately want to become president.
6. Winston Churchill had a rule never to take strong drink before lunch.
7. My friend Renato likes to shock people with his outrageous political views.
8. My first fixed and unbending principle is to be flexible at all times. [Everett Dirksen]
9. The worst solitude is to be destitute of sincere friendship. [Francis Bacon]
10. To know him is to love him.

The Subject of the Infinitive. In most of the infinitive sentences we have seen so far, the subject of the tensed verb is also the subject of the infinitive. For example, in item 7 of the previous exercise, "My friend Renato likes to shock people with his outrageous political views," *friend* is the subject of both *likes* and *to shock.* But when an infinitive has a general meaning, the sentence may not include that infinitive's actual subject, especially if the infinitive occupies the subject slot:

> <u>To listen to k.d. lang</u> is pure delight.

In some cases, however, the subject of the infinitive will be expressed in a prepositional phrase:

> <u>For Conchita to win this match</u> would be a miracle.

> <u>For the district attorney to take part in this discussion</u> is a conflict of interest.

Conchita and *district attorney* are the subjects of the infinitives *to win* and *to take part.*

Prepositional phrases with embedded infinitives also occur in the direct object position after verbs like *hope, like, want,* and *prefer:*

> Conchita's fans would like <u>for her to win this match</u>.

> We are hoping <u>for our legislature to make a wise decision about school taxes</u>.

In the diagram for these sentences, the vertical line between the object of the preposition and the infinitive indicates the subject–verb boundary:

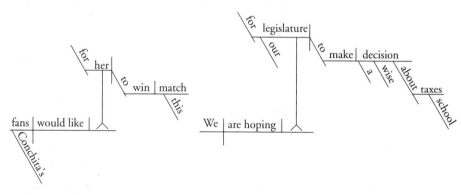

Some verbs that can appear in such sentences are also grammatical without the preposition *for:*

> Conchita's fans would like her to win this match.

In these examples we have treated the infinitive and its subject as a single unit filling the direct object slot:

> Conchita's fans would like <u>something</u>.

> We are hoping <u>something</u>.

But in the following sentence, there are two slots:

We asked <u>the uninvited guests</u> <u>to leave the party</u>.

In this sentence, we have both a "somebody" and a "something" following the verb; so rather than analyze the sentence as Pattern VII, we would explain it as Pattern VIII, with the "someone" as an indirect object:

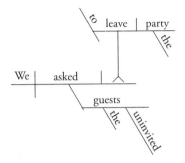

You might argue that the verb *asked* is not a "give" verb, as most Pattern VIII verbs are, and that *uninvited guests* isn't really a "recipient," as most indirect objects are. However, the two slots clearly have different referents, so the Pattern VIII formula, with its NP_2 and NP_3, seems to fit. We can also transform the sentence into passive voice to show that *to leave* occupies a separate slot from *the uninvited guests:*

The uninvited guests were asked to leave the party.

Exercise 32

Underline the nominal verb phrases—gerunds and infinitives—in the following sentences; include any subjects of gerunds and infinitives that might be expressed within the phrase. Then identify the function of each nominal verb phrase. Finally, diagram the sentences. Be sure to think about sentences patterns.

1. The best thing would be for you to tell the truth.
2. By remaining silent, you are merely making the situation worse.
3. To ignore the judge's order would be foolhardy.
4. Ms. Graham chose to welcome the new investor into the company.
5. This invitation thwarted his latest plan, to buy up a controlling number of stocks.
6. Raising the company's national profile was the new owner's long-term goal.
7. Our composition teacher wants us to write three drafts of every assignment.

8. I appreciate your proofreading this final version for me.

9. The class finally persuaded the instructor to extend the deadline.

10. The baby's crying upset the rest of the passengers.

NOMINAL CLAUSES

In the preceding sections you have seen examples of verb phrases—gerunds and infinitives—filling NP slots. In this section you will see that **nominal clauses** can do so as well:

>   I understand <u>that several students have launched a protest</u>.

>   I wonder <u>what prompted their action</u>.

These nominal clauses (also called "noun clauses") are further examples of dependent clauses, just as adverbial and adjectival clauses are; they do not function as complete sentences, as independent clauses do.

The trick of substituting a pronoun to determine the boundaries of the NP slot is especially useful when the nominal slot it filled by a clause, as in the two previous examples:

>   I understand <u>something</u>.

>   I wonder <u>something</u>.

The pronoun substitutes for the entire nominal slot.

These two examples also illustrate the two kinds of introductory words that signal nominal clauses: the **expletive** *that* and **interrogative** words such as *what*. The diagrams will show a basic difference between them:

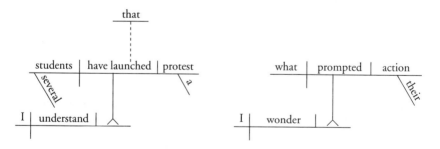

The interrogative *what* fills a grammatical role in the clause it introduces—in this case, that of subject; the expletive does not.

(*Diagramming note:* The pedestal can be attached to the nominal clause wherever it is convenient to do so. The expletive is placed above the clause it introduces and attached with a broken line, again wherever convenient.)

The Expletive *That*. The term *expletive* refers to a sentence element that plays no grammatical role itself; it's an added element that enables us to manipulate a structure for reasons of emphasis and the like. The expletive *that* makes it possible to embed one sentence as a nominal in another sentence. In the previous example, the Pattern VII sentence "Several students have launched a protest" becomes the direct object in another Pattern VII sentence. The diagram illustrates the added-on quality of the expletive.

The expletive *that* can turn any declarative sentence into a nominal clause:

The guests from El Paso will arrive soon.	→	I hope that the guests from El Paso will arrive soon.
The common cold is caused by a virus.	→	That the common cold is caused by a virus has been clearly established by science.

When the *that* clause fills the direct object slot, as in the first example, the sentence may be grammatical without the expletive:

I hope the guests from El Paso will arrive soon.

When the clause is in the subject position, however, the expletive is required:

*The common cold is caused by a virus has been clearly established by science.

Nominal *that* clauses can also function as subject complements and appositives, as the following examples illustrate:

Subject complement: Your assumption is <u>that interest rates will remain relatively low</u>.

Appositive: The reviewer's criticism, <u>that the characters lack conviction</u>, is fully justified.

Exercise **33**

Create a nominal *that* clause to fill the following slots. Identify the function of the clause that you've added.

1. You should know _____.

2. _____ makes everyone angry.

3. My parents are expecting _____.

4. _____ has not occurred to them.

5. The truth is _____.

6. The fact _____ disturbs me.

Nominal clauses that begin with the expletive *that* should not be confused with adjectival clauses that begin with the relative pronoun *that*. Compare the following examples:

Nominal clause: I know <u>that I reminded you about the deadline</u>.

Adjectival clause: You ignored the reminders <u>that I gave you</u>.

Because the expletive *that* plays no grammatical role in its clause, the nominal clause will be a complete sentence without the *that: I reminded you about the deadline.* But the relative pronoun *that* does have a role to play within its clause; if you remove it, the remaining words won't be a complete sentence: **I gave you.*

You can also distinguish between *that* clauses by replacing the *that* with *which.* If the clause is adjectival, the sentence will still be grammatical:

You ignored the reminders <u>which I gave you</u>.

But if you substitute *which* for the expletive *that* in a nominal clause, the result will be clearly ungrammatical:

*I know which I reminded you about the deadline.

Here are some more sentences with clauses introduced by *that.* Decide which clauses are nominal (introduced by an expletive) and which are adjectival (introduced by a relative pronoun):

The color that you chose for the walls doesn't match the rug.

_____

Milton suspects that someone has been using his computer.

_____

The books that I need for chemistry class are expensive. _____

I suppose that the books that I need for art history will be expensive too. _____, _____

The idea that I need your help is absurd. _____

The idea that you proposed to the committee is a brilliant one.

_____

He gave her a look that you could have poured on a waffle. [Ring Lardner] _____

You can check your answers by doing a diagram to make sure that you've identified the *that* correctly.

Interrogatives. One of the sample sentences we saw earlier included a nominal clause introduced by the interrogative *what:*

I wonder <u>what prompted their action</u>.

Other **interrogatives**, or question words, that introduce nominal clauses are *who, whose, whom, which, where, when, why*, and *how*. Unlike the expletive, the interrogative always plays a grammatical role in its own clause. In the previous example, *what* functions as the subject of *prompted*. In the following sentence, *what* is the direct object in its clause:

I wonder <u>what the students are demanding</u>.

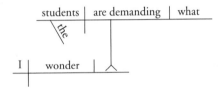

In both of these examples, the *what* clause functions as the direct object. Another common function of nominal clauses introduced by interrogatives is that of subject, as shown in the next two examples:

<u>*Where* you are going</u> is no business of mine.

Where is an interrogative adverb, so it acts as an adverb in its clause. The interrogative pronoun *who* will be the subject in its own clause:

<u>*Who* will be at the party</u> remains a mystery.

Who can also be the subject complement in its clause. Here the clause fills the direct object slot:

I don't know <u>*who* that stranger is</u>.

In the following sentences *which* and *what* function as determiners in their clauses; both clauses fill the direct object slot:

I wonder <u>*which* brand of yogurt has the least fat</u>.

I can't decide <u>*what* brand I should buy</u>.

Nominal clauses introduced by interrogatives can also function as objects of prepositions and as appositives:

> *Object of a preposition:* Clarice knows a lot about <u>how computers work</u>.

> *Appositive:* The dean's question, <u>why the students didn't object sooner</u>, has not been answered.

Exercise 34

Both *when* and *where* hold membership in two word classes. As **subordinators** they introduce adverbial clauses; as **interrogatives** they introduce nominal clauses. Identify the function of the *where* and *when* clauses in the following sentences. Are they adverbial or nominal? If the clause is nominal, identify the NP slot it fills. Also identify the sentence patterns of both the independent and dependent clauses.   *if can substitute something → nominal*

1. Julie could not remember where she had left her keys.
2. Rob lost his keys when he misplaced his backpack.   *D.O.*
3. When I get in late, my roommate gets upset.   *ADVERBIAL*
4. When I get home is my own business.   *ADVERBIAL* / *SUBJECT*
5. The starship *Enterprise* ventures where explorers have never gone before.   *ADVERBIAL*
6. When you decide where we are having dinner, give me a call.   *nominal D.O.*
7. I learn by going where I have to go. [Theodore Roethke]   *ADVERBIAL*
8. They have finally decided where the wedding will be held.
9. When I am an old woman, I shall wear purple. [Jenny Joseph]
10. The police asked where we were when the accident occurred.

Exercise 35

Underline the nominal clause in each of the following sentences. Then identify its function in the sentence: What NP slot does it fill? Diagram the sentences.

1. Until yesterday I never realized how awesome a redwood tree could be.
2. The main complaint about his presentation was that it was too short.
3. What Carlos said about his cousin is unfair and inaccurate.
4. Our psychology teacher is writing a book about why people fear intimacy.

5. My sister told her children that they could have a dog.
6. Who invented calculus is a matter of some dispute.
7. We could not tell which twin was Elaine.
8. Everyone wondered when the play would end.
9. I wish he would explain his explanation. [Lord Byron]
10. The decision that they should replay the point upset both contestants.

Punctuation of Nominal Clauses. As many of the previous examples and exercise items illustrate, sentences with nominal clauses can get fairly long. But with one exception, the punctuation of these sentences remains exactly the same as the punctuation of the basic sentence: no single commas between the sentence pattern slots. The exception occurs when the direct object is a direct quotation. The standard convention calls for a comma between a verb like *say* or *reply* and the quotation:

He said, "I will meet you at the gym at five o'clock."

In this sentence the quoted passage is essentially a nominal clause in direct object position.

Exercise 36

Underline the nominal clauses, gerund phrases, and nominal infinitives in the following sentences. Identify the function that each of them performs in its sentence.

1. You can't lose weight by clipping a diet out of a magazine.
2. To search for the causes of lower SAT scores would be an exercise in conjecture.
3. The neighbors never suspected that we had a pet boa constrictor in our house.
4. The guest speaker's E-mail message informed us when he would arrive.
5. The airlines are planning to raise their fares.
6. Several airlines announced recently that they are planning to raise their fares.
7. A major cause of highway accidents is falling asleep at the wheel.
8. Why the Backstreet Boys are so popular is a mystery to many people.
9. The knowledge that the semester is almost over makes me happy.

10. The instructor asked us to make copies of our poems for everyone in class.

11. We should concern ourselves with how higher tuition will affect future enrollments.

12. When I saw the questions that were on the exam, I realized I had studied the wrong chapters.

NOMINALS AS DELAYED SUBJECTS

We have seen nominal clauses that fill the subject slot, some of which have a formal quality more characteristic of writing than speech; in fact, such sentences are uncommon in speech:

> That the common cold is caused by a virus has been clearly established.

> That Sherry left school so suddenly was a shock to us all.

In conversation we are more likely to delay the information in that opening clause, substituting for the subject what is called the **anticipatory *it***:

> It has been clearly established that the common cold is caused by a virus.

> It was a shock to us all that Sherry left school so suddenly.

The infinitive phrase as subject can also be delayed in this way:

> To play computer games   →   It is fun to play computer
>   is fun.   games.

> To remain neutral on this   →   It is unconscionable to remain
>   issue is unconscionable.   neutral on this issue.

The anticipatory *it* allows us to change the stress of the sentence, in much the same way that we saw with the cleft sentence in the discussion of sentence transformations in Chapter 4 (pages 101–102). This use of *it* as a tool for writers is discussed in Chapter 14 (pages 318–320).

CHAPTER 7

Key Terms

Anticipatory *it*	Delayed subject
Appositive	Dependent clause
Clause	Direct quotation
Dangling gerund	Expletive *that*

Gerund

Independent clause

Infinitive

Interrogative

Nominal

Nominal clause

Nominal verb phrase

Objective case

Subjective case

Subordinator

Tensed verb

Sentences
for PRACTICE

Draw vertical lines to show the sentence slots. Label the form of the structure that occupies each slot. Identify the sentence pattern for each verb phrase and clause. Diagram the sentences.

1. I wonder what Jeff's problem is.

2. I think that I know what the solution to Jeff's problem is.

3. Chondra said that she would call me today when she got back home.

4. Speaking on television last week, the president announced that he will propose a tax cut during this session of Congress.

5. Where you will be in ten years is a question you probably think about sometimes.

6. The defendant's claim that he was kidnapped by aliens did not impress the jury.

7. I know how men in exile feed on dreams. [Aeschylus]

8. The hen is an egg's way of producing another egg.

9. My roommate, who will graduate this month, wonders why finding a job in his field, business management, is so difficult.

10. I haven't figured out which Shakespeare play is my favorite.

11. According to the U.S. Customs Service, smuggling birds from the Caribbean has become a big business.

12. Our biological rhythms play a crucial role in determining how alert we feel.

13. I remember hearing from my grandmother about how the Great Depression affected her family.

14. The rule that we follow in this organization is that debate should be internal.

15. It is often very difficult to let your children make their own decisions.

QUESTIONS
?
for DISCUSSION

1. Why is the appositive set off with commas in the second of these two sentences?

    Mark's brother George coaches basketball in Indiana.

    Mark's brother, George, coaches basketball in Indiana.

    Which sentence tells you that Mark has only one brother? Which sentence implies that Mark has more than one brother? Why does the following sentence need commas?

    The senator's husband, Reuben, accompanied her to Washington.

2. Consider the differences in meaning in these two pairs of sentences. How do you account for these differences? Do the differences involve different sentence patterns?

    Mel stopped to talk to Walt.

    Mel stopped talking to Walt.

    Mel started talking to Walt.

    Mel started to talk to Walt.

3. Show by a diagram how the following two sentences are different. Identify their sentence patterns.

    I went to work.

    I want to work.

4. What is the source of the ambiguity in the following sentence?

    I disapprove of her smoking.

    If the smoker were male instead of female, how would the sentence be stated? Would it still be ambiguous?

5. What are two possible meanings of the following ambiguous sentence?

    The shooting of the hunters was a wanton act.

    In what way is the traditional diagram inadequate to account for that ambiguity?

6. One of the most common roles for nominals is as object of the preposition. In the following sentences, identify the form of that object in the underlined prepositional phrases.

> This afternoon I took a nap <u>after exercising</u>.
>
> <u>Before starting my exercise program</u>, I had a thorough physical examination.
>
> <u>Until recently</u>, I did very little exercise.
>
> <u>After my physical</u>, I began doing calisthenics gradually.
>
> <u>From then on</u>, I began to be careful about my diet, too.
>
> <u>For the truly obese</u>, strenuous exercise can be dangerous.

7. In Chapter 3 we examined the passive voice of predicating verbs. Can gerunds and infinitives be passive?

8. The traditional grammarian would label the *who* clause in this famous line by Shakespeare an adjectival clause. Why? Why is it not nominal? How would you as a twenty-first-century speaker word this statement?

> Who steals my purse steals trash.

CLASSROOM APPLICATIONS

The following can be organized as either oral or written activities, perhaps as timed group competitions:

1. The fact that verb phrases and clauses can fill NP slots gives the language great embedding capabilities. For example, a gerund phrase could easily fill the direct object slot in a nominal clause. Picture the diagram:

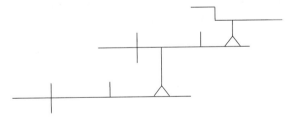

Here's a six-word sentence that would fit:
I know that Joe enjoys swimming.

Now try two other patterns:

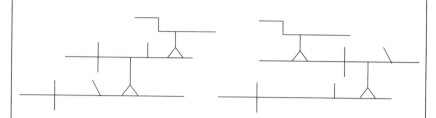

(Hint: Bear in mind that the expletive *that* can turn almost any sentence into a nominal clause. Now write a sentence with a gerund in the position shown—as subject or direct object; then turn that sentence into a nominal clause. In the first example, the sentence "Joe enjoys swimming" has been embedded as the direct object following the verb *know*.)

2. This time your task is the opposite of #1: Write a sentence in which a nominal clause is embedded in a gerund phrase.

3. Write a sentence in which an adjectival clause is embedded in a nominal clause.

4. Write a sentence in which an adverbial infinitive phrase is embedded in a gerund phrase.

5. Write a sentence in which a gerund phrase is embedded in an adverbial clause.

Note: These exercises can be organized for group or individual competition in the class. To add to the challenge, the topic of the sentences can be specified: Write about baseball, summer, winter sports, health, rap music, competition, the election campaign, movies, etc. And, of course, other specific directions could be included: Use a nominal *who* clause; use the passive voice; include two prepositional phrases; include an indirect object, etc.

Sentence Modifiers

CHAPTER PREVIEW

The modifiers and nominals you studied in the three preceding chapters add information that expands units within the sentence: adverbials (Chapter 5), adjectivals (Chapter 6); and noun phrase substitutes (Chapter 7). The structures you will study in this chapter, however, have no clear connection to a particular sentence slot; instead, the information they add relates to the sentence as a whole.

Some of the structures identified here as sentence modifiers are often treated as adverbials. For example, most descriptions of grammar, including traditional grammar, treat all subordinate clauses as verb modifiers. Certainly, the line between the two functions—adverbial and sentence modifier—does become fuzzy at times.

In general this chapter serves as a way of gathering into one place those parts of our grammar that share an "outsider" quality, that lie outside the boundaries of the main sentence. To identify such a quality, however, is not to judge the importance of a structure in terms of meaning. It's true that sentences may be grammatical without a vocative, interjection, absolute phrase, sentence appositive, or the other independent structure described here. That fact does not lessen the impact that such a structure may have on the meaning or intent of the sentence, nor its impact on or connection to the larger text.

One difference from the preceding chapters that you'll notice in this one is the absence of traditional diagrams. As you know, the purpose of the diagram is to illustrate the relationship among all the sentence parts. The diagrams of the other modifiers, the adverbials and adjectivals, show them attached to the verb or noun they modify. The traditional Reed and Kellogg diagrams of these "outsider" structures do not adequately illustrate their connection to the sentence as a whole.

===

Like the modifiers of nouns and verbs, modifiers of the sentence as a whole also come in the form of single words, phrases, and clauses. Because most of the single-word modifiers are adverbs in form, you may be tempted to label them adverbials. However, as the following pair of sentences illustrates, there is a clear contrast in meaning between (1) the adverb as adverbial and (2) the adverb as **sentence modifier**:

1. He did not explain the situation <u>clearly</u>.
2. <u>Clearly</u>, he did not explain the situation.

In this case, there are a number of tests you can apply to verify the difference. For example, the adverb in sentence 1 can be moved to the preverb position:

He did not clearly explain the situation.

We probably wouldn't make the same change in 2, but if we did, we would have to include the commas, to retain the parenthetical meaning:

He did not, clearly, explain the situation.

The commas would also stay if we moved the sentence modifier to the end:

He did not explain the situation, clearly.

The substitution of close synonyms would also clarify the difference:

Obviously, he did not explain the situation.

*He did not explain the situation obviously.

He did not explain the situation very well.

*Very well, he did not explain the situation.

Not all single-word sentence modifiers are as easy to demonstrate as this one, where a clear contrast in meaning exists between *clearly* in its two roles. But most sentence modifiers do have this same parenthetical quality:

<u>Invariably</u>, the dress or pair of shoes I like best is the one with the highest price tag.

<u>Luckily</u>, the van didn't get a scratch when it hit the ditch.

<u>Undoubtedly</u>, we will see interest rates gradually rise.

The book you want is out of print, <u>unfortunately</u>.

But not all sentence modifiers are separated by commas:

> <u>Perhaps</u> the entire starting lineup ought to be replaced.

Here it is fairly clear that *perhaps* raises a question about the idea of the sentence as a whole. If it were moved to a position within the sentence, it would probably be set off by commas:

> The entire starting lineup, <u>perhaps</u>, ought to be replaced.

So the absence of a comma after an introductory modifier does not rule it out as a sentence modifier; but neither does the presence of a comma rule it in. As we saw in the earlier chapters on noun and verb modifiers, both adjectivals and adverbials can sometimes be shifted to the opening position. That shift does not in itself make them sentence modifiers. For example, in the following sentences the introductory phrases are adjectival, modifiers of the subject:

> <u>Hot and tired</u>, we loaded the camping gear into the station wagon for the long trip home.

> <u>Limping noticeably</u>, the runner rounded third base and managed to beat the throw at home plate.

Verb modifiers in introductory position are somewhat more open to interpretation as sentence modifiers, because adverbials do tend to add information that relates to the whole idea. In Chapter 5 we classified phrases like the following as modifiers of the verb, although admittedly the designation is somewhat arbitrary; a case could be made for such modifiers to be classified as sentence modifiers rather than adverbials:

> <u>To polish his skills for his trip to Las Vegas</u>, Tim plays poker every night.

> <u>Almost every Monday morning</u>, I make a vow to start counting calories.

> <u>On a day like today</u>, I prefer to stay in bed.

The less clearly a modifier is related to a particular part of the sentence, the more clearly we can classify it as a modifier of the sentence as a whole. English has many idiomatic expressions—unvarying formulas that have an independent or parenthetical quality—that are clearly sentence modifiers. Unlike the previous three adverbial examples, the introductory modifiers in the following sentences are not added for information such as *when* or *where* or *why:*

> <u>Frankly</u>, I didn't expect sailing to be so much work.

> <u>To our amazement</u>, the driver of the Corvette walked away from the accident.

> To my regret, I've never seen the Grand Canyon.
>
> Speaking of the weather, let's decide on the place for our picnic.
>
> To tell the truth, I have never read *Silas Marner*.

Besides the adverb, these examples include two prepositional phrases, a participial phrase, and an infinitive phrase.

You might think that the last two sentence modifiers in the list, which are verb phrases in form, look suspiciously like the danglers that we have seen in earlier discussions of gerunds and infinitives and participles. But it's probably accurate to say that, in contrast to those earlier examples, *speaking of the weather* and *to tell the truth* have achieved the status of independent idiomatic expressions, or set phrases.

NOUNS OF DIRECT ADDRESS: THE VOCATIVES

Another structure set off by a comma is the noun or noun phrase of direct address, known as a **vocative**:

> Ladies and gentlemen, please be seated.
>
> Jennifer, your date is here.

Although the vocative is not a modifier in the same sense that other structures are, in that it does not modify the meaning of the sentence, it does have a relationship to the sentence as a whole. And like other modifiers, it can come at the beginning, middle, or end of the sentence:

> We certainly hope, my dear friends, that you will visit again soon.
>
> I promise you won't see me here in court again, your honor.
>
> Tell us, Mr. President, how your new tax plan will benefit the economy.

The purpose of the vocative, as the term "direct address" implies, is to direct the writer's or speaker's message to a particular person or group. (In most cases it's the speaker's message: This structure is much more common in speech than in writing.) And, as the foregoing examples illustrate, the vocative can express the attitude of the writer or speaker and reflect the tone, whether formal or informal, serious or light, familiar or distant. In that sense, certainly, the vocative is a "sentence modifier": It can affect the meaning of the words.

INTERJECTIONS

The **interjection**—usually a single word or short phrase—can also be considered as a modifier of the sentence as a whole:

> Oh, don't frighten me like that!
>
> Wow! That's not what I expected.

The traditional view of grammar treats the interjection as one of the eight parts of speech, probably because there is no other way to categorize such "nonwords" as *oh* and *ah* and *wow* and *ouch*. However, many words that we recognize as nouns and verbs are also used as exclamatory sentence modifiers of this kind:

> <u>Heavens</u>, I don't know what to say.
>
> <u>Good grief</u>! Don't confuse me with the facts!
>
> <u>My word</u>! This will never do.

Like the vocatives, interjections are much more likely to occur in speech than in writing (other than written dialogue).

It might seem logical to consider these actual words as interjections, the same as we treat *oh* and *wow;* however, we do not put all such "interjections" into a single parts-of-speech class, as the traditional grammarians do. Such a classification distorts the principle on which we make judgments about word categories. Except for *oh* and *ah* and *whew* and a few others, we recognize interjections strictly by their exclamatory, or emotional, function in the sentence. It's true, of course, that the familiar definitions given to the traditional eight parts of speech are not necessarily consistent in their criteria; for example, nouns and verbs are defined according to their meaning (as names and as actions) and adjectives and adverbs by their function (as modifiers). Nevertheless, out of all eight traditional "parts of speech," only the interjection category is denoted strictly by sentence function, rather than as a word type; that is, the other seven traditional parts of speech (noun, verb, adjective, adverb, pronoun, preposition, and conjunction) are names of word classes. It is for this reason that the interjection is not included in our inventory of structure words, described in Chapter 12, but, rather, is included here as one kind of sentence modifier.

Exercise 37

Underline any sentence modifiers in the following sentences.

1. <u>Amazingly</u>, the money held out until the end of the month.
2. The twins look amazingly alike. *adv.*
3. <u>Well</u>, I plan to stay, myself.
4. <u>Myself</u>, I plan to stay well. *n o u*
5. <u>Strangely</u>, he seemed to look right through me.
6. I thought he looked at me strangely. *adv.*
7. <u>Without a doubt</u> our team will win the league championship.
8. We will <u>no doubt</u> win the league championship.

9. I told my friend I was not interested in her scheme.   none

10. I told you, my friend, that I am not interested.

SUBORDINATE CLAUSES

In Chapter 5 we looked at the adverbial clauses, recognizing that they, too, often seem to relate to the sentence as a whole rather than to the verb specifically. Those introduced by *where, when, before,* and *after* seem to be the most "adverbial" of all in that they convey information of time and place about the verb; but certainly we could make an equal case for classifying even these as sentence modifiers. **Subordinate clauses** introduced by such subordinators as *if, since, as,* and *although* seem even more clearly to modify the idea of the whole sentence, because the subordinator explains the relationship of one idea to another:

> *If* you promise to be there, I'll go to Sue's party.
>
> I'll go with you, *although* I would rather stay home.

The phrasal subordinators, too, may relate one complete clause to another:

> *Provided that* the moving van arrives on schedule, we'll be ready to leave by three o'clock.
>
> All the members of the city council, *as far as* I know, voted in favor of the new dog ordinance.

(See page 283 for a list of the simple and phrasal subordinators.)

Some of the interrogatives and **indefinite relative pronouns** introduce conditional clauses that are clearly sentence modifiers:

> *Whatever* decision you eventually make, I'll support you.
>
> *Whichever* route we take, there's no way we'll get there on time in this traffic.
>
> *No matter how much* overtime I work, my paycheck never seems to stretch far enough.

The subjunctive *if* clauses that we saw in Chapter 3 can also join this list of clauses that say something about the sentence as a whole:

> If I were you, I'd skip the party.

Punctuation of Subordinate Clauses. In opening position the subordinate clause is always set off by a comma; in closing position, punctuation is related to meaning. As a general rule, when the idea in the main clause is conditional upon or dependent upon the idea in the subordinate clause, there is no comma. For example, the idea of the main clause—the opening clause—in the following sentence will be realized only if the idea in the subordinate clause is carried out; thus here the main clause depends on the *if* clause:

I'll go to Sue's party *if you promise to be there.*

But in the next sentence the subordinate clause does not affect the fulfillment of the main clause:

I'm going to the party that Sue's giving on Saturday night, *even though I know I'll be bored.*

The distinction between these two functions is comparable to the restrictive/nonrestrictive distinction we examined in connection with adjectivals in Chapter 6. If the subordinate clause "defines" the situation, it will not be set off from the main clause; if it simply "comments," it will take the comma.

In general *even though* and *although* are preceded by commas; *if* is not. The point to be made here is that the subordinator relates the idea in its clause to the idea in the main clause, so the subordinate clause clearly functions as a modifier of the sentence as a whole—even though it is not preceded by a comma. But in opening position, the clause is always followed by a comma. The use of the comma with final subordinate clauses is probably one of the least standardized of our punctuation rules. The final criteria must be readability and clarity for the reader.

Exercise 38

Add commas to the following sentences, if necessary.

1. We left the party as soon as we politely could.
2. Jim agreed to leave the party early and go bowling with us, although he was having a good time.
3. When the storm is over, we can head for home.
4. We might as well put on the coffee, since we're going to be here for another hour.
5. I know that Jerry and I will never be able to afford that much money for rent, even, if it does include utilities.
6. I won't be able to stay in this apartment if the rent goes any higher.
7. I won't be able to stay in this apartment, even if the rent stays the same.
8. If you can't stand the heat, get out of the kitchen. [Harry Truman]

Elliptical Clauses. Many subordinate clauses are **elliptical**—that is, certain understood words are left out:

> <u>While</u> [we were] <u>waiting for the guests to arrive</u>, we ate all the good hors d'oeuvres ourselves.
>
> <u>When</u> [I am] <u>in doubt about the weather</u>, I always carry an umbrella.

As a reader, you have no problem understanding either of those elliptical clauses: In both cases the missing words, the subject of the elliptical clause, show up as the subject of the main clause.

What would happen if that understood subject did not show up? The result would be a fuzzy sentence, similar to those we have seen with dangling participles and gerunds and infinitives. Like the opening verb phrase, the elliptical element sets up certain expectations in the reader; it's the writer's job to fulfill those expectations. Consider what you expect in the main clause following these elliptical openers:

> *<u>When late for work</u>, the subway is better than the bus.
>
> *<u>If kept too long in hot weather</u>, mold will grow on the bread.
>
> *<u>While driving to the game on Saturday</u>, an accident tied up traffic for over an hour.

As with many of the dangling structures we have seen, the message of the sentence may be clear; but there's simply no reason for a writer to set up a situation in which the reader must make the connections—and must do so in a conscious way. Those connections are the writer's job.

In some cases only the elliptical version is grammatical:

> I'm a week older <u>than Bob</u>.
>
> My sister isn't <u>as tall as I</u>.

>   *or*

> I'm a week older <u>than Bob is</u>.
>
> My sister isn't as tall <u>as I am</u>.

We would never include the entire clause:

> *I'm a week older <u>than Bob is old</u>.
>
> *My sister isn't as tall <u>as I am tall</u>.

In both of these examples, we are comparing an attribute of the subjects of the two clauses. But the ellipses in such comparisons can produce ambiguity when the main clause has more than one possible noun phrase for the subordinate clause to be compared with:

> The Packers beat the Patriots worse <u>than the Panthers</u>.
>
> Joe likes Mary better <u>than Pat</u>.

In these sentences we don't know whether the comparison is between subjects or objects because we don't know what has been left out. We don't know whether

The Packers beat the
Patriots worse <u>than</u> }

the Packers beat the Panthers.
or
the Panthers beat the Patriots.

Joe likes Mary better <u>than</u> }

Joe likes Pat.
or
Pat likes Mary.

The comparison in the clauses with *as . . . as* can become a problem when an alternative comparison is added. Here is how such comparisons should read:

Our team is <u>as good as</u>, or <u>better than</u>, the Wildcats.

But sometimes the writer (or speaker) omits the second *as:*

*Our team is as good, or better than, the Wildcats.

*My sister is just as strong, or stronger than, you.

These omissions do not result in ambiguity, but the sentences clearly have a grammatical problem—an incomplete comparison.

Incidentally, these clauses of comparison are actually modifying adjectives—*older, tall, worse, better, good,* and *strong*—the qualities that are being compared, rather than modifying the sentence as a whole. We are discussing them here with the sentence modifiers because of the shared elliptical feature.

Exercise 39

A. Rewrite the three sentences on page 202 to include a subject in the elliptical clause. You may have to make changes in the main clause as well.

1. When late for work, the subway is better than the bus.

2. If kept too long in hot weather, mold will grow on the bread.

3. While driving to the game on Saturday, an accident tied up traffic for over an hour.

B. Now rewrite the following sentences, supplying the words missing in the elliptical clauses. Are the sentences clear?

1. I picked up a Midwestern accent while living in Omaha.

2. My accent is not as noticeable as Carlo's.

3. Holmes hit Ali harder than Norton.

4. If necessary, strain the juice before adding the sugar.

5. While waiting at the train station in Lewistown, there was no place to sit.

6. If handed in late, your grade will be lowered 10 percent.

7. Love goes toward love, as schoolboys from their books.
   But love from love, toward school with heavy looks.
   [Shakespeare]

8. The weather in Little Rock is not as humid as New Orleans.

ABSOLUTE PHRASES

The **absolute phrase** (also known as the *nominative absolute*) is a structure independent from the main sentence; in form the absolute phrase is a noun phrase that includes a postnoun modifier. The modifier is commonly an *-en* or *-ing* participle or participial phrase, but it can also be a prepositional phrase, an adjective phrase, or a noun phrase. The absolute phrase introduces an idea related to the sentence as a whole, not to any one of its parts:

Our car having developed engine trouble, we stopped for the night at a roadside rest area.

The weather being warm and clear, we decided to have a picnic.

Victory assured, the fans stood and cheered during the last five minutes of the game.

Absolute phrases are of two kinds—with different purposes and different effects. (Moreover, both are structures generally used in writing, rather than in speech.) The preceding sentences illustrate the first kind: the absolute that explains a cause or condition. In the first sentence, the absolute phrase could be rewritten as a *because, when,* or *since* clause:

When our car developed engine trouble,

or

Since our car developed engine trouble,   } we stopped for the night. . . .

or

Because our car developed engine trouble,

The absolute construction allows the writer to include the information without the explicitness that the complete clause requires. In other words, the absolute phrase can be thought of as containing all the meanings in the three versions shown here rather than any one of them.

In the following sentence the idea in the *because* clause could be interpreted as the only reason for the picnic:

> Because the weather was warm and clear, we decided to have a picnic.

The absolute construction, on the other hand, leaves open the possibility of other reasons for the picnic:

> The weather being warm and clear, we decided to have a picnic.

It also suggests simply an attendant condition rather than a cause.

In the second kind of absolute phrase, illustrated by the sentences following, a prepositional phrase (*above his head*), adjective phrase (*alert to every passing footstep*), or noun phrase (*a dripping mess*), as well as a participle (*trembling*), may serve as the postnoun modifier. This second kind of absolute adds a detail or point of focus to the idea stated in the main clause:

> Julie tried to fit the key into the rusty lock, her hands trembling.
>
> The old hound stood guard faithfully, his ears alert to every passing footstep.
>
> Hands above his head, the suspect advanced cautiously toward the uniformed officers.
>
> Her hair a dripping mess, she dashed in out of the rain.

This technique of focusing on a detail allows the writer to move the reader in for a close-up view, just as a filmmaker uses the camera. The absolute phrase is especially effective in writing description. Notice how the authors of the following passages use the main clause of the sentence as the wide lens and the absolute phrase as the close-up:

> There was no bus in sight and Julian, his hands still jammed in his pockets and his head thrust forward, scowled down the empty street.
>
> FLANNERY O'CONNOR, *Everything That Rises Must Converge*

> The man stood laughing, his weapons at his hips.
>
> STEPHEN CRANE, *The Bride Comes to Yellow Sky*

> To his right the valley continued in its sleepy beauty, mute and understated, its wildest autumn colors blunted by the distance, placid as a water color by an artist who mixed all his colors with brown.
>
> JOYCE CAROL OATES, *The Secret Marriage*

APPOSITIVES

You'll recall that one of the nominals described in Chapter 7 is the appositive, a structure that in form is often a noun phrase:

> Our visitor, <u>a grey-haired lady of indeterminate age</u>, surprised us all when she joined in the volleyball game.

In this example, the appositive renames the subject of the sentence. But sometimes we use a noun phrase to rename or, more accurately, to encapsulate the idea in the sentence as a whole. We call these structures sentence appositives:

> He waved his pink right hand in circles, <u>his favorite gesture</u>.
>
> JOHN FOWLES, *The Magus*

We often use a dash to set off the sentence appositive:

> The musical opened to rave reviews and standing-room-only crowds—<u>a smashing success</u>.

> A pair of cardinals has set up housekeeping in our pine tree—<u>an unexpected but welcome event</u>.

Like the absolutes, which are also noun phrases in form, these sentence appositives are related to the sentence as a whole, but their purpose is quite different: They simply label, or restate, the idea of the main clause; they do not introduce a new, subordinate idea, as both kinds of absolute phrases do.

The rhetorical effects of sentence appositives are discussed further in Chapter 14.

Exercise 40

Underline any absolute phrases in the following sentences. Is the modifier of the headword an adjective, a prepositional phrase, a noun phrase, or a participle?

1. The cat lay by the fire, purring contentedly, her tail moving from side to side like a metronome.

2. Chuck and Margie kicked their way through the fallen leaves, their arms draped across each other's shoulders.

3. The rain having persisted for over an hour, the game was officially stopped in the sixth inning.

4. Michelle lounged in front of the fire, her book open on the floor, her eyes intent on the flames.

5. He saw the city spread below like a glittering golden ocean, the streets tiny ribbons of light, the planet curving away at the edges, the sky a purple hollow extending into infinity. [Anne Tyler]

6. Then the boy was moving, his bunched shirt and the hard, bony hand between his shoulder-blades, his toes just touching the floor, across the room and into the other one, past the sisters sitting with spread heavy thighs in the two chairs over the cold hearth, and to where his mother and aunt sat side by side on the bed, the aunt's arms about his mother's shoulders. [William Faulkner]

RELATIVE CLAUSES

Most relative clauses are modifiers of nouns, and most are introduced by a relative pronoun that refers to that noun:

> Joe's car, <u>which he bought just last week</u>, looks like a gas guzzler to me.

In this sentence the antecedent of *which* is the noun *car;* the noun is modified by the clause.

But in some sentences *which* refers not to a particular noun but to a whole idea; it has what we call *broad reference*. In the following sentence, the antecedent of *which* is the idea of the entire main clause:

> Joe bought a gas guzzler, <u>which surprised me</u>.

All such broad-reference clauses are introduced by *which*, never by *who* or *that*, and all are nonrestrictive—that is, they are set off by commas:

> Tom cleaned up the garage without being asked, <u>which made me suspect that he wanted to borrow the car</u>.

> This summer's heat wave in the Midwest devastated the corn crop, <u>which probably means higher meat prices for next year</u>.

Many writers try to avoid the broad-reference relative clause, instead using *which* only in the adjectival clause to refer to a specific noun. In inexperienced hands the broad-reference *which* clause often has the vagueness associated with dangling modifiers:

> I broke out in a rash, <u>which really bothered me</u>.

In this sentence the referent of *which* is unclear; *which* could refer to either the *rash* or the *breaking out*. There are a number of alternatives in which the meaning is clear:

> Breaking out in a rash really bothered me.

> The rash I got last week really bothered me.

Even though they are not particularly vague, the earlier examples, too, can be revised in ways that avoid the broad-reference *which:*

> When Tom cleaned up the garage without being asked, I suspected that he wanted to borrow the car.
>
> Tom's cleaning up the garage without being asked made me suspect that he wanted to borrow the car.
>
> This summer's heat wave in the Midwest, which devastated the corn crop, probably means higher meat prices for next year.

Exercise   *41*

Rewrite the following sentences to eliminate the broad-reference *which.*

1. I had to clean the basement this morning, which wasn't very much fun.

2. Otis didn't want to stay for the second half of the game, which surprised me.

3. The president criticized the Congress rather severely in his press conference, which some observers considered quite inappropriate.

4. The first snowstorm of the season in Denver was both early and severe, which was not what the weather service had predicted.

5. We're having company for dinner three times this week, which probably means hot dogs for the rest of the month.

CHAPTER 8
Key Terms

Absolute phrase

Broad-reference clause

Direct address

Elliptical clause

Idiomatic expression

Independent modifier

Interjection

Relative clause

Sentence appositive

Sentence modifier

Subordinate clause

Vocative

Sentences
for PRACTICE

Draw vertical lines to set off sentence modifiers; identify them by form. If the sentence modifier is, or includes, a verb phrase or clause, identify its sentence pattern.

1. My brother will finish basic training next month if everything goes smoothly.

2. Last week stock prices scored surprisingly strong gains as Wall Street experienced one of the busiest periods in the market's history.

3. If you don't mind, I want to be alone.

4. Speaking of travel, would you like to go to Seattle next week to see the Seahawks play?

5. Incidentally, you forgot to pay me for your share of the expenses.

6. The weather being so beautiful last Sunday, we decided to go to Silver Creek Falls for a picnic.

7. The invitations having been sent, we started planning the menu for Maria's birthday party.

8. Jennifer stayed in bed all day, her fever getting worse instead of better.

9. If bread is kept too long in hot weather, mold will begin to grow on it.

10. The giant redwoods loomed majestically, their branches filling the sky above us.

11. It is impossible to enjoy idling thoroughly unless one has plenty of work to do. [Jerome K. Jerome]

12. Luckily, Sunday was a nice day, so we didn't miss our weekly hike.

13. Freddie suggested we take a taxi instead of the subway—a splendid idea.

14. Old Town was festive, indeed—the stores decorated with bright-colored banners, the air alive with music, the streets crowded with people.

15. If I can stop one heart from breaking, I shall not live in vain. [Emily Dickinson]

QUESTIONS
?
for DISCUSSION

1. Many of the simple and phrasal subordinators listed on page 283 introduce clauses that could be interpreted as either sentence modifiers or verb modifiers. How would you classify the underlined clauses in the following sentences—as sentence modifiers or as verb modifiers? Why?

> I'll return your book <u>as soon as I finish it</u>.
>
> He'll lend me the money <u>provided that I use it for tuition</u>.
>
> The dog looked at me <u>as if he wanted to tell me something important</u>.
>
> Nero fiddled <u>while Rome burned</u>.

2. The following sentences are both illogical and ungrammatical. What is the source of the problem?

> The summer temperatures in the Santa Clara Valley are much higher than San Francisco.
>
> The Pirates' stolen-base record is better than the Cardinals.

3. The following sentence is less elliptical than those you just read, but it's equally fuzzy. What is the source of its problem?

> The people of Atlanta are much friendlier than they are in New York.

4. Consider the pronouns in these elliptical clauses. Are they the correct form? Is it possible that both sentences are correct?

> I think my little sister likes our cat better than me.
>
> I think my little sister likes our cat better than I.

5. A common subject for discussion among people who think about language and usage is the "problem" of *hopefully*. The following sentences are, in fact, avoided by many speakers and writers.

> Hopefully, we will get to the theater before the play starts.
>
> Hopefully, this play will be better than the last one we saw.

Is the adverb *hopefully* used incorrectly in these sentences? Should it be used only as a manner adverb? Or can it function as a sentence modifier? Make a case for both sides of the issue. (In considering *hopefully*, think also about other adverbs as sentence modifiers, such as *clearly*, *luckily*, and *admittedly*.)

6. How do you explain the difference in meaning between the following sentences, which appear so similar on the surface? Discuss the effect of the understood elliptical clause in the second sentence. Are both sentences negative?

   I have never been happy with our living arrangement.

   I have never been happier with our living arrangement.

CLASSROOM APPLICATIONS

1. Combine the following pairs of sentences, reducing one of them to a sentence modifier. Experiment with variations.

Example:

I was lucky. I knew how to swim
<u>Luckily, I knew how to swim</u>.

1. The door was closed. We climbed in the back window.
2. The contract is invalid. That's a fact.
3. The guests departed. We resumed our normal household routine.
4. Consider the circumstances. He was lucky to escape alive.
5. Felice is the best tenor in the choir. That's my opinion.
6. I'll tell you the truth. I don't like your new haircut.
7. She did not complete her thesis. That is unfortunate.
8. The copy machine has been malfunctioning. That was apparent.
9. Our school orchestra is not the best in the world. Everyone is sure of that.
10. It doesn't matter what you say. Graham is going to quit school.

2. One popular technique for teaching writing, which dates back to the schools of Ancient Greece, is known as modeling. Students learn to write by copying the form of sentences, using the same blueprint while supplying new words. For this exercise, you are to model the following sentences, some of which you saw earlier as examples of absolute phrases. Remember the comparison of the absolute to the close-up view; the main clause provides the wide-angle shot.

Example:

The man stood laughing, his weapon at his hips.

Modeled version:

The woman sat smoking, a black poodle in her lap.

1. The man stood laughing, his weapon at his hips. (Stephen Crane)

2. With a breathy shriek the train pulled away, the crowd cheering, waving at the caboose until it was out of sight. (E. Annie Proulx)

3. There was no bus in sight and Julian, his hands still jammed in his pockets and his head thrust forward, scowled down the empty street. (Flannery O'Connor)

4. He smiled to himself as he ran, holding the ball lightly in front of him with his two hands, his knees pumping high, his hips twisting in the almost girlish run of a back in a broken field. (Irwin Shaw)

5. Soon afterwards they retired, Mama in her big oak bed on one side of the room, Emilio and Rosy in their boxes full of straw and sheepskins on the other side of the room. (John Steinbeck)

6. In the pouring rain, following a muddy, almost invisible path, I finally arrived at the station, my shoes leaving puddles with every step, my clothes and satchel waterlogged. (Devon Riley)

CHAPTER 9

Coordination

CHAPTER PREVIEW

Throughout the previous chapters you have been seeing **coordination** within sentences, both in the samples for discussion and in the text itself. In fact, the sentence you just read includes one such structure, a compound prepositional phrase connected by the correlative conjunction *both–and*. We make these connections at every level—word, phrase, and clause; in speech we do so automatically.

In this chapter we will take up several features of compound structures within the sentence, including punctuation, ellipsis, subject–verb agreement, and parallelism. Then we will look at the coordination of whole sentences, with special emphasis on the punctuation conventions that apply to them.

COORDINATION WITHIN THE SENTENCE

Punctuation. A simple punctuation rule applies to nearly all the compound pairs of words, phrases, and clauses that occur within the sentence: We use no comma with the conjunction. Notice in the following examples that no comma appears even when the two parts being joined are fairly long:

> On Homecoming weekend our frat party <u>started at noon *and* lasted until dawn</u>. (compound verb phrase)
>
> I will buy <u>*either* the blue dress with the long sleeves *or* the green print with a matching jacket</u>. (compound noun phrase)
>
> He said <u>that he would get here sooner or later *and* that I shouldn't start the rehearsal without him</u>. (compound dependent clause)

An exception to the rule against commas with compound elements occurs when the conjunction is *but:*

I have visited a lot of big cities, <u>but</u> never Los Angeles.

I worked hard all night, <u>but</u> just couldn't finish my project.

My new white dress is beautiful, <u>but</u> not very practical.

There's a clear disjunction with *but,* resulting, of course, from its meaning: It introduces a contrast. Furthermore, the phrase introduced by *but* could almost be thought of as an elliptical clause, another reason that the comma seems logical:

I worked hard all night, but [I] just couldn't finish my project.

My new white dress is beautiful, but [it is] not very practical.

Another exception to the comma restriction occurs when we want to give special emphasis to the second element in a coordinated pair:

I didn't believe him, and said so.

My new white dress is beautiful, and expensive.

This emphasis will be even stronger with a dash instead of a comma:

I didn't believe him—and said so.

My new white dress is beautiful—and expensive.

We also use commas with a series of three or more elements:

We <u>gossiped, laughed, and sang</u> together at the class reunion, just like old times.

These commas represent the pauses and slight changes of pitch that occur in the production of the series. You can hear the commas in your voice when you compare the two—the series and the pair. Read them aloud:

We gossiped, laughed, and sang.

We laughed and sang.

You probably noticed a leveling of the pitch in reading the pair, a certain smoothness that the series did not have. In the series with conjunctions instead of commas, you'll notice that same leveling:

We gossiped <u>and</u> laughed <u>and</u> sang together at the class reunion, just like old times.

When conjunctions connect all the elements, we use no commas.

In the series of three, some writers—and some publications as a matter of policy—use only one comma, leaving out the **serial comma**, the one immediately before *and:*

We gossiped, laughed <u>and</u> sang together at the class reunion, just like old times.

Perhaps they do so on the assumption that the conjunction substitutes for the comma. But it really does not. In fact, this punctuation misleads the reader in two ways: It implies a closer connection than actually exists between the last two elements of the series, and it ignores the pitch change, however slight, represented by the comma. The main purpose of punctuation, after all, is to represent graphically the meaningful speech signals—pitch, stress (loudness), and juncture (pauses)—that the written language otherwise lacks. That small pitch change represented by the comma can make a difference in emphasis and meaning.

Exercise 42

Punctuate the following sentences.

1. Pete sanded the car on Friday and painted it with undercoating on Saturday.

2. Even though the car's new paint job looks terrific now, I suspect it will be covered with rust and scratches and dents before next winter.

3. I spent a fortune on new tires, shock absorbers, and brake linings for the car last week.

4. The car that my father had back in the 1960s and 1970s, a 1959 Chevy, required very little maintenance and no major repairs during the ten or more years he drove it.

5. I have decided to park my car until gas prices go down and to ride my bicycle instead.

6. I don't suppose I'll ever be able to afford either the down payment or the insurance on a new Corvette, the car of my dreams.

Elliptical Coordinate Structures. Elliptical structures are those in which something has been left out. You'll recall from the discussion in the previous chapter that fuzziness or ambiguity sometimes results when the "understood" element is not, in fact, understood. The same kind of problem can occur with coordinate structures.

One common ellipsis is the elimination of the second determiner in a coordinate noun phrase:

The cat and dog are sleeping on the porch.

A problem can arise when the noun phrase includes modifiers:

Our new cat and dog are sleeping on the porch.

The clear implication of the noun phrase is that both the cat and the dog are new. If that's not the case, then *dog* needs its own determiner:

> Our new cat and our dog are sleeping on the porch.

> *or*

> Our dog and new cat are sleeping on the porch.

Postnoun modifiers can also be the source of ambiguity in coordinate structures:

> Visitors to this area always admire the flower gardens and stately elms on campus.

Without a determiner for *elms*, the reader is justified in inferring that both the flowers and trees are on the campus, although it's certainly possible that the writer had a different intention. The problem of ambiguity is much more blatant when both noun phrases have determiners:

> Visitors to this area always admire the flower gardens and the stately elms on campus.

Now the reader has no way to decide what *on campus* modifies. If only the elms are on campus, the writer can either reverse the two noun phrases or add another modifier so that both locations are clear:

> . . .the stately elms on campus and the flower gardens.

> . . .the flower gardens near City Hall and the stately elms on campus.

Here's a similar problem sentence, one with an ambiguous *by* phrase:

> Penn State's administration building, Old Main, is best known for its presidential portraits and [its] murals by Henry Varnum Poor.

With or without the determiner for *murals,* this sentence is ambiguous. Another problem can occur with numbers as determiners:

> There were six men and women waiting in line.

> There were six dogs and cats on the porch.

> There were six mothers and daughters at the mother-daughter reception.

We don't, of course, know whether the noun phrases include six or twelve people or animals.

There are many possibilities for structural ambiguity, where the reader simply has no way of knowing the writer's intention. Coordinate structures are especially open to misinterpretation. It's the job of the writer to make sure that the meaning is clear.

Subject–Verb Agreement. When nouns or noun phrases in the subject slot are joined by *and* or by the correlative *both–and,* the subject is plural:

> My roommate and his brother are coming to the wedding.

However, the coordinating conjunction *or* and the correlatives *either–or* and *neither–nor* do not have the additive meaning of *and;* with *or* and *nor* the relationship is called disjunctive. In compound subjects with these conjunctions, the verb will be determined by the closer member of the pair:

> Neither the speaker nor the listeners were intimidated by the protestors.
>
> Either the class officers or the faculty advisor makes the final decision.
>
> Do the class officers or the faculty advisor make the final decision?
>
> Does the faculty advisor or the class officers make the final decision?

If the correct sentence sounds incorrect or awkward because of the verb form, you can simply reverse the compound pair:

> Either the faculty advisor or the class officers make the final decision.

When both members of the pair are alike, of course, there is no question:

> Either the president or the vice-president is going to introduce the speaker.
>
> Neither the union members nor the management representatives were willing to compromise.

For most verb forms, you'll recall, there is no decision to be made about subject–verb agreement; the issue arises only when the -*s* form of the verb or auxiliary is involved. In the following sentences, there is no -*s* form:

> Either the class officers or the faculty advisor will make the final decision.
>
> Either the faculty advisor or the class officers will make the final decision.

Another situation that sometimes causes confusion about number—that is, whether the subject is singular or plural—occurs with subjects that include a phrase introduced by *as well as* or *in addition to* or *along with:*

> *The sidewalk, in addition to the driveway, need to be repaired.
>
> *The piano player, as well as the rest of the group, usually join in the singing.
>
> *Mike, along with several friends, often help out at the bakery on weekends.

These additions to the subject are parenthetical; they are not treated as part of the subject. To make the subject compound—to include them—the writer should use a coordinating conjunction, such as *and:*

> The sidewalk <u>and</u> the driveway <u>need</u> to be repaired.
>
> The piano player <u>and</u> the rest of the group usually <u>join</u> in the singing.
>
> Mike <u>and</u> several friends often <u>help</u> out at the bakery on weekends.

Parallel Structure. An important requirement for coordinate structures is that they be **parallel**. A structure is parallel when all the coordinate parts are of the same grammatical form. The conjunctions must join comparable structures, such as pairs of noun phrases or verb phrases or adjectives:

> The <u>short blonde woman</u> *and* <u>her apricot poodle</u> seemed to belong together.
>
> The stew <u>smells delicious</u> *and* <u>tastes even better</u>.
>
> The entire cast gave <u>powerful</u> *and* <u>exciting</u> performances.

Unparallel structures occur most commonly with the correlative conjunctions: *both–and, either–or, neither–nor,* and *not only–but also.* For example, in the following sentence, the two coordinators introduce structures of different forms:

> **Either* <u>they will fly straight home</u> *or* <u>stop overnight in Dubuque</u>.

Being able to picture the diagram can be helpful in preventing such unparallel structures. With the sentence above, you'll discover that the conjunction line would connect a complete sentence (*they will fly straight home*) and a verb phrase (*stop overnight in Dubuque*). Because the two structures are not parallel, the diagram simply won't work.

A diagram of the following sentence won't work either:

> **I'll *either* <u>take a bus</u> *or* <u>a taxi</u>.

The conjunction line would have to connect a verb phrase and a noun phrase; again the two structures are not parallel.

Such problems are easy to correct. It's just a matter of shifting one part of the correlative pair so that both introduce the same kind of construction:

> They will *either* <u>fly straight home</u> *or* <u>stop overnight in Dubuque</u>.
>
> I'll take *either* <u>a bus</u> *or* <u>a taxi</u>.

Further examples of the correlative conjunctions are given in Chapter 12.

Exercise 43

Rewrite the following sentences, paying particular attention to unparallel structures and agreement errors.

1. I can't decide which activity I prefer: to swim at the shore in July, when the sand is warm, or jogging along country roads in October, when the autumn leaves are at their colorful best.

2. I almost never watch television. There is either nothing on that appeals to me or the picture disappears at a crucial moment.

3. I neither enjoy flying across the country nor particularly want to take the train.

4. Either the members of the school board or the superintendent make the final decision.

5. The recipe was either printed wrong, or I misread it.

6. I was unhappy with what he said and the way he said it.

7. The coach announced an extra hour of drill on Saturday and that the practice on Sunday would be canceled.

8. My history class, as well as both English classes, require a term paper.

9. Aunt Rosa has promised to fix her famous lasagna for my birthday dinner and will also bake my favorite cake.

10. For the picnic we brought baskets of chicken and lemonade.

COORDINATING COMPLETE SENTENCES

We have three methods of joining independent clauses to produce **compound sentences**: (1) using coordinating conjunctions; (2) using the semicolon, either with or without conjunctive adverbs; and (3), for limited situations, using the colon.

Conjunctions. The compound sentence with a coordinating conjunction such as *and* shows up at an early stage of the writer's development:

We went to the fair, <u>and</u> we had a good time.

Robby is mean, <u>and</u> I don't like him.

Such sentences can, of course, be effective when they are used sparingly, but they will strike the reader as immature when overused. The compound sentence is most effective when the coordinate ideas have relatively equal importance—when the two ideas contribute equal weight:

> I disapprove of her spending money on lottery tickets, <u>and</u> I told her so.

> The curtain rose to reveal a perfectly bare stage, <u>and</u> a stillness settled over the audience.

> Pete filled the bags with hot roasted peanuts, <u>and</u> I stapled them shut.

Note that the punctuation rule that applies to the compound sentence differs from the rule regarding internal coordinate constructions. Between the sentences in a compound sentence we do use a comma with the conjunction; between the parts of a coordinate structure within the sentence we do not. When the clauses of a compound sentence are quite short and closely connected, however, we sometimes omit the comma. The following sentence, for example, would probably be spoken without the pitch change we associate with commas:

> October came <u>and</u> the tourists left.

The coordinators *and* and *or* can link a series of three or more sentences:

> Pete filled the bags, <u>and</u> I stapled them shut, <u>and</u> Marty packed them in the cartons.

> The kids can wait for me at the pool, <u>or</u> they can go over to the shopping center and catch the bus, <u>or</u> they can even walk home.

In these two sentences, the first conjunction can be replaced by a comma:

> Pete filled the bags, I stapled them shut, <u>and</u> Marty packed them in the cartons.

But usually joins only two clauses:

> Jill wanted me to wait for her, <u>but</u> I refused.

But can introduce the final clause when *and* or *or* joins the first two:

> Pete filled the bags, <u>and</u> I stapled them, <u>but</u> Marty refused to lift a finger.

> The kids can wait for me at the pool, <u>or</u> they can walk to the bus stop, <u>but</u> I really think they ought to walk home.

Semicolons. When a semicolon connects two coordinate clauses, the conjunction can be omitted:

> Pete packed the hot roasted peanuts into bags; I stapled them shut.

> The curtain rose; a stillness settled over the audience.

The semicolon is also used when a **conjunctive adverb** introduces the second clause. Note, too, that the conjunctive adverb is set off by a comma:

> We worked hard for the Consumer Party candidates, ringing door-bells and stuffing envelopes; <u>however</u>, we knew they didn't stand a chance.

> We knew our candidates didn't have a hope of winning; <u>nevertheless</u>, for weeks on end we faithfully rang doorbells and stuffed envelopes.

Of all the adverbial conjunctions, only *yet* and *so* can be used with a comma instead of a semicolon between clauses:

> Several formations of birds were flying northward, <u>so</u> I knew spring was on the way.

> Several formations of birds were flying northward, <u>yet</u> I suspected that winter was far from over.

In both of these sentences, a semicolon could replace the comma, depending on the writer's emphasis. The semicolon would put extra emphasis on the second clause. *So* and *yet* straddle the border between the coordinating conjunctions and the conjunctive adverbs; they are often listed as both. In meaning, *so* is similar to *therefore* and *yet* to *however;* but unlike these conjunctive adverbs, *so* and *yet* always introduce the clause, so in this respect they are perhaps closer to the coordinating conjunctions. Sometimes we use both the conjunction and the adverbial: *and so; but yet.*

Because they are also adverbials, most conjunctive adverbs are movable; they can appear in the middle of the clause or at the end, as well as at the beginning:

> We worked hard for the Consumer Party candidates; we knew, <u>however</u>, they didn't stand a chance.

> *or*

> we knew they didn't stand a chance, <u>however</u>.

These choices are examined further in Chapter 14. Other common conjunctive adverbs are listed on page 283.

Colons. As a sentence connector, the colon is rather specialized. Unlike the semicolon, which connects sentences with the meaning of *and,* the colon makes an announcement of sorts: It means "namely." You're probably familiar with the colon that signals an appositive or a list:

> I'm taking three English courses this semester: advanced grammar, American lit, and Shakespeare.

Here the colon says, "Here it comes, the information I promised." When the colon signals a complete sentence, the message is similar. It promises to complete the idea set up in the first clause:

> We finally made our decision: We would sell the house and move.
>
> Easton, Pennsylvania, is a most colorful city: It's where Crayolas are made.

This use of the colon is discussed in more detail in "The Rhetoric of Punctuation" on page 343.

Diagramming the Compound Sentence. In the diagram a broken line connects the two verbs, with the connector on a solid line approximately halfway between the two clauses:

> Pete filled the bags, and I stapled them shut, but Marty refused to lift a finger.

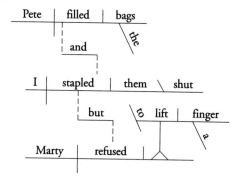

Investigating Language **9.1**

Combine the following groups of sentences into compound sentences, using conjunctions of your choice, including conjunctive adverbs. In each case there are a number of possible ways to combine them, depending on the emphasis.

1. The library closes at noon on Thursdays.
   It is open until 9:00 P.M. on Fridays.

2. The food at the new French restaurant is exceptionally good.
   The prices are exceptionally high.

3. I am going to take piano lessons this fall.
   I may take guitar lessons, too.

4. My first-period students are bright.
   They are wide awake at 8:00 A.M., too.

5. Our trip across Kansas was long and straight and uneventful.
   The trip across Kansas took an entire day.

Now turn your compound sentences into **compound-complex sentences** by adding a dependent clause to each one. The dependent clause can be nominal, adverbial, or adjectival. (You may have to make other changes to accommodate the dependent clauses.)

1. _____

   _____

2. _____

   _____

3. _____

   _____

4. _____

   _____

5. _____

   _____

CHAPTER 9
Key Terms

Colon

Compound sentence

Compound structure

Compound-complex sentence

Conjunction

Conjunctive adverb

Coordinating conjunction

Coordination

Correlative conjunction

Elliptical coordinate structure

Parallel structure

Semicolon

Serial comma

Subject–verb agreement

Sentences
for PRACTICE

Underline the sentence slots that have coordinate structures; circle the conjunctions. For further practice, identify the sentence patterns and diagram the sentences.

1. Despite the economic recovery, many auto workers in Detroit and many steelworkers in Pennsylvania are still unemployed.

2. I lent my son and daughter-in-law a sizable sum of money.

3. They have recently moved to Ohio and will soon be buying a new house.

4. To get your rebate, simply fill out the coupon and mail it to the company's headquarters in Michigan.

5. I have battled beetles and aphids and tent caterpillars for the entire summer.

6. Next month many students and tourists will be going to our nation's capital to visit the historical monuments or perhaps to stroll along the streets and simply enjoy that beautiful city.

7. My friends and I, finding the movie boring, left at intermission and adjourned to our favorite hangout.

8. Hope is the thing with feathers
   That perches in the soul,
   And sings the tune without the words,
   And never stops at all. [Emily Dickinson]

9. Thousands of Americans, united by a deep and urgent concern about the quality of life for themselves and future generations, have given both their money and their time to the environmental movement.

10. The hundreds of separate groups that make up the environmental movement are demonstrating to get the support of their fellow citizens and their legislators.

11. Having found an apartment that was inexpensive, roomy, and close to the subway, we made a split-second decision and rented it on the spot.

12. The woods are lovely, dark, and deep,
    But I have promises to keep,
    And miles to go before I sleep. [Robert Frost]

13. The boom in cosmetic surgery is apparently the result of new, more sophisticated procedures, safer anesthetics, and the desire for self-improvement.

14. Only two knots are required for most fly-fishing situations: a knot for tying on the fly and a knot for joining monofilament.

QUESTIONS
?
for DISCUSSION

1. In the following sentences the coordinate ideas are unparallel in form. Do some seem more acceptable than others? Rank them in order of acceptability. Rewrite those that can be improved.

> Almost every lineman on the squad was overweight and out of condition when the season started.
>
> She volunteered her services at the Senior Citizens' Center frequently and with boundless enthusiasm.
>
> The old man, broke and having no friends to turn to, simply disappeared from the neighborhood.
>
> I have always loved sports of all kinds and jog regularly.

2. Consider the following compound sentences. Are they parallel? Can you find a way to improve them? What is their special problem?

> I fixed three bowls of popcorn for the party, but it was eaten up before most of the guests even got there.
>
> Burglars broke into the art museum last night, and three valuable paintings were stolen.
>
> The television lost its sound last week, but luckily it got fixed before the World Series started.

3. Explain the ambiguity of the prenoun compound modifier in these two sentences.

> Six red and blue banners were hanging from the ceiling.
>
> My uncle sells used cars and motorcylces.

4. Explain why the verbs or auxiliaries in the following sentences would not be the *-s* form even though the subject headwords *crime* and *stamina* are singular.

> Blue collar and white collar crime are on the increase.
>
> Both physical and mental stamina are required for long-distance running.

5. The following passage commonly appears on labels of movie videos:

> This film has been modified from its original version. It has been formatted to fit your screen.

In what way would the meaning change if, instead of the period, a colon followed the first sentence? In what way is the passage ambiguous as written?

CLASSROOM APPLICATIONS

1. Notice how choppy and repetitious the following passage sounds:

> I know very little about laboratory science. I have the impression that conclusions are supposed to be logical. From a given set of circumstances a predictable result should follow. The trouble is that in human behavior it is impossible to isolate a given set of circumstances. It is also impossible to repeat these circumstances. That is true of history, too. Complex human acts cannot be reproduced. They cannot be deliberately initiated. They cannot be counted upon like the phenomena of nature.

Now read the original of that choppy passage (from an article by Barbara Tuchman, "Is History a Guide to the Future?"). Observe how coordination makes it smoother and more concise. (The coordinating conjunctions and transitional expressions have been italicized.)

> I know very little about laboratory science, *but* I have the impression that conclusions are supposed to be logical; *that is,* from a given set of circumstances a predictable result should follow. The trouble is that in human behavior *and* history it is impossible to isolate *or* repeat a given set of circumstances. Complex human acts cannot be *either* reproduced *or* deliberately initiated—*or* counted upon like the phenomena of nature.

Now revise the following passage (a "de-combined" section from Lewis Thomas's *Lives of a Cell*), using coordination to eliminate choppiness and unnecessary repetition:

> The Iks, a nomadic tribe in northern Uganda, have become celebrities. They have also become literary symbols for the ultimate fate of disheartened mankind. They are also symbols of heartless mankind at large. Two disastrous things happened to

them. They were compelled to give up hunting. They had to become farmers on poor hillside soil. Also, an anthropologist detested them. The anthropologist wrote a book about them.

2. The following is a typical sentence combining exercise—a list of sentences to be formed into an effective paragraph. As you can see, these sentences include a great deal of repetition, some of which you can eliminate by using coordination. Experiment with both coordination and modification in combining these ideas.

1. The Anza-Borrego Desert State Park is California's largest state park.

2. The Anza-Borrego encompasses 600,000 acres.

3. The park reaches south to within three miles of the border with Mexico.

4. The Santa Rosa Mountains form the western border of the Anza-Borrego.

5. The Santa Rosa Mountains rise to a height of 8,700 feet.

6. The San Ysidro Mountains form the southwestern border of the Anza-Borrego.

7. The Anza-Borrego holds a rich archaeological heritage.

8. Archaeologists have found evidence of early inhabitants.

9. These early people lived in the Anza-Borrego 6,000 years ago.

10. The technology of these people did not yet include pottery.

11. Their technology did not include the bow and arrow.

12. The Anza-Borrego is rich in fossil remains.

13. The extinct North American camel has been uncovered in the Anza-Borrego.

14. This camel is known as Camelops.

15. The age of the camel fossils is estimated to be 800,000 years.

Words and Word Classes

If you studied traditional grammar in middle school or high school, you may remember learning about the eight "parts of speech": noun, verb, adjective, adverb, pronoun, preposition, conjunction, and interjection. As you may recall from Chapter 1, early grammarians came up with those eight categories in order to make their description of English conform to the word categories of Latin. Scholarly grammarians, however, recognize that the accurate description of a language—any language—requires a framework of its own.

When the structural linguists went about identifying the word categories of English, they did so by examining the language as it is actually used, by reading personal letters and listening to phone conversations. They looked at the words themselves, at their forms, their meanings, and their functions in the sentence, and then established two main categories: the form classes and the structure classes. You will see those two broad categories in Chapters 11 and 12.

In Chapter 2 you learned to distinguish the four form classes—nouns, verb, adjectives, and adverbs—on the basis of their forms. Throughout the chapters you've been introduced to various structure classes. As you studied the sentence patterns and their expansions, you came to recognize the differences between these two broad categories of words. In general, the **form classes** provide the primary lexical content; the **structure classes** explain the grammatical or structural relationships. We can think of the form-class words as the bricks of the language and the structure words as the mortar that holds them together.

Probably the most striking difference between the form classes and the structure classes is characterized by their numbers. Of the half million or more words in our language, the structure words—with some notable exceptions—can be counted in the hundreds. The form classes, however, are large, open classes; new nouns and verbs and adjectives and adverbs regularly enter the language as new technology and new ideas require them. They are sometimes abandoned, too, as the dictionary's "obsolete" and "archaic" labels testify. The structure classes, on the other hand, remain constant—and limited. We have managed with the very same small store of prepositions and conjunctions for generations, with few changes. It's true that we don't hear *whilst* and *betwixt* and *thy* anymore, nor do we see them in contemporary prose and poetry, but most of our structure words are identical to those that Shakespeare and his contemporaries used.

FORM CLASSES	STRUCTURE CLASSES	
Noun	Determiner	Pronoun
Verb	Auxiliary	Conjunction
Adjective	Qualifier	Interrogative
Adverb	Preposition	Expletive
		Particle

An important difference between the classes has to do with form. As their label suggests, the form classes are those that can undergo changes in form—that are, in fact, distinguishable by their form—whereas the structure classes are not. But, as with almost every "rule" of the language, we will encounter exceptions. For example, auxiliaries are among the structure classes, although some of them, because they are verbs, show form variations; *be, have,* and *do,* as you know, can be both auxiliaries and verbs. Some of the pronouns also have variations in form. On the other hand, there are many words in the form classes that have no distinctions in form and do not undergo change—nouns like *chaos,* adjectives like *main,* and adverbs like *there.*

Another complication in our two-part, form/structure division is the inclusion of the determiner and qualifier classes, both of which are more accurately described as *functions,* rather than word classes. The determiner class, as you will see in Chapter 12, includes words from other classes, such as pronouns; the fact that it also includes possessive nouns actually makes it an open class. The qualifier class, too, includes words from other classes, such as adverbs, so that class, also, is open to membership.

Before looking at the classes individually, we need to examine the basic unit of word formation, the morpheme; an understanding of the morpheme is central to the conscious understanding of words. Then we will take up the form classes, the structure classes, and, in a separate chapter, pronouns.

A caveat, a word of caution, is in order here: Don't be intimidated by the amount of detail you find about the word classes in these four chapters.

These are not details for you to memorize—not at all. For the most part, in fact, they are simply descriptions of details you already know, not only from your study of grammar but also from your everyday use of the language, even though you may not have thought consciously about them.

You'll find that these descriptions of words and word classes will be especially useful to you as a reference tool when questions arise in your own writing and sentence analysis. And they will certainly be useful if you are planning a career in teaching.

CHAPTER
10

Morphemes

CHAPTER PREVIEW

In this chapter, in preparation for the study of word classes, you will learn
about morphemes, basic units of meaning that make up words. You'll find
that an understanding of morphemes will help to trigger your unconscious language expertise, as you consciously study the form of words.
You'll learn that nouns, verbs, adjectives, and adverbs have characteristics
that enable you to identify them, not by their meanings but by their forms.

Some of the detail in this chapter may also trigger memories of vocabulary
and dictionary lessons from your early grades. When you study morphemes,
you are actually studying in a conscious way the lexicon in your head—
your internal dictionary. In fact, for this chapter you'll need access to the
other kind of dictionary too—the alphabetical kind that sits on your desk.

When we study sentence patterns and their transformations and expansions, we are studying **syntax.** The structural linguist, however, begins
the study of grammar not with syntax, but with **phonology,** the study of
individual sounds. At the next level, before syntax, comes **morphology,**
the study of **morphemes,** combinations of sounds with meaning.

This definition of *morpheme* may sound to you like the definition of
word. Many morphemes are, in fact, complete words; *head* and *act* and
kind and *walk* (as well as *and*) are words consisting of a single morpheme,
a single meaningful combination of sounds. But others, such as *heads* and
actively and *unkindly* and *walking,* consist of two or more morphemes, each
of which has meaning itself. The success you had years ago in learning to

read and spell was in part dependent on your awareness of the parts of words. For instance, in spelling a word like *actively*, you probably break it into its three morphemes automatically: Its stem, or **base morpheme**, is the verb *act;* the suffix *-ive* turns it into an adjective; and the suffix *-ly* turns the adjective into an adverb. Each of these three morphemes, the base and the two suffixes, has meaning itself; and each appears in other environments (other words) with the same meaning. These are the two primary criteria that we use to identify the morphemes in a word: They have meaning; they appear with the same meaning in other words.

We should also emphasize that *morpheme* and *syllable* are not synonymous—even though the morphemes discussed so far consist of a single syllable. There are, in fact, many two-syllable words in English that are single morphemes: *carrot, college, jolly, merit, over.* Furthermore, many two-morpheme words are single syllables: *acts, walked, dog's.* So even though it may be understandable to think of syllable boundaries as boundaries for morphemes, it is inaccurate to do so.

The individual morphemes in a word are not always quite as obvious as they are in words like *actively.* In the word *reflections*, for example, we can recognize the verb *reflect*, the *-ion* ending that turns it into a noun, and the *-s* that makes it plural: *reflect + ion + s.* But how about the word *reflect?* Is that a single morpheme, or is it two? Are *re* and *flect* separate morphemes? Do they both have meaning? Do they appear in other environments with the same meaning? Certainly there are many words that begin with the prefix *re-: reverse, rebound, refer.* In all these, *re-* means "back," so *re* passes the morpheme test. How about *flect?* We have *inflect* and *deflect.* The dictionary reveals that all three words with *flect* are based on the Latin verb *flectere*, meaning "to bend." So in the word *reflections* we can identify four morphemes: *re + flect + ion + s.*

Incidentally, it's not unusual to need the dictionary to understand the morpheme structure of a word. The meanings of words often change, and their origins become obscure. Take the word *obscure*, for example. How many morphemes does it have, one or two? What does *scure* mean? Does it appear in other words with the same meaning? Is *ob* the same morpheme we find in *observe?* What does it mean? And how about *observe?* Is that the verb *serve?* Such meanderings into the dictionary in search of clues about morphemes can heighten our awareness of words and appreciation of language. And certainly an awareness of morphemes can enhance the understanding of language essential to both reader and writer. When we study etymology or historical linguistics, we begin to understand the intricacies of morphemes, their changes, and their variations. But our interest in morphemes here is a limited one. We will look mainly at those that signal the form classes, that contribute to our understanding of the parts of speech.

BASES AND AFFIXES

All words, as we have seen, are combinations of morphemes, or, in the case of a word like *act* (as well as the eight words preceding it in this sentence), single morphemes. All morphemes are either **bases** (*act*), which we define as the morpheme that gives the word its primary lexical meaning, or **affixes** (*-ive, -ly*); and all affixes are either **prefixes**, those that precede the base (*re-*), or **suffixes**, those that follow it (*-ion*):

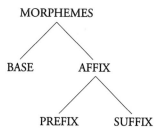

Exercise   **44**

The following four sets of words illustrate some of the relationships of morphemes. In each set find the common base. What does the base mean? Draw vertical lines in the words to show the separate morphemes.

nova	auditor	durable	conceive
renovation	audience	endure	capable
innovate	inaudible	duration	susceptible
novice	auditorium	during	capture
novelist	audio	endurance	intercept

BOUND AND FREE MORPHEMES

One other feature of morphemes concerns their ability to stand alone. Many cannot. For example, the affixes are **bound**, or attached, to another morpheme rather than **free** to stand alone; that's what *affix* means. In the word *actively*, only the first morpheme is free: *-ive* and *-ly* are bound. In *reflections*, even the base is bound; *flect* is not a word that can stand by itself. We call this a bound base. Other examples of words without free morphemes are *concur, conceive, depict, expel*, and many others with these common prefixes. There are also a few affixes that are free, such as *able*, *like*, and *less*. A free morpheme is a word; a bound morpheme is not. The solid arrows in the following diagram represent the most common circumstance, the broken ones the less common:

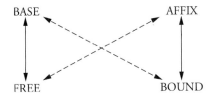

Exercise **45**

Find a word to fit each of the following formulas. Include only the morphemes called for.

Examples:

free + bound = *birds*
bound + free = *rerun*

1. free + bound

2. bound + free

3. free + bound + bound

4. bound + free + bound

5. free + free

6. bound + free + bound + bound

7. bound + bound

8. bound + bound + bound

DERIVATIONAL AND INFLECTIONAL MORPHEMES

Another feature of affixes we want to recognize is their classification as either derivational or inflectional. Although we have several hundred suffixes, distinguishing between the derivational and inflectional ones is easy to do. Only eight are **inflectional**. You'll recognize four of them from the discussion of verbs in Chapter 3.

-s (plural)
-s (possessive) } Noun inflections

-s (3rd-person singular)
-ed (past tense)
-en (past participle)
-ing (present participle) } Verb inflections

-er (comparative)
-est (superlative) } Adjective and adverb inflections

All the other suffixes, as well as all the prefixes, are **derivational**.

As the branching diagram shows, all prefixes are derivational, whereas suffixes are either derivational or inflectional:

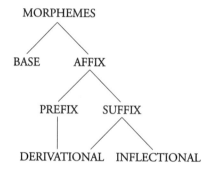

The term *derivational* refers to the change that a word undergoes when a derivational morpheme is added: Either the meaning of the word changes or the class, the part of speech, changes—or both. Take the word *inactivity*, for example. With the derivational morpheme *-ive*, the verb *act* becomes the adjective *active*—that is, we derive one class of word from another. When we add *in-*, the class remains the same—*active* and *inactive* are both adjectives—but the prefix does affect the meaning, as prefixes generally do; in other words, we derive a new meaning. Finally, with the addition of *-ity* the adjective becomes the noun *inactivity*.

The significance, then, of derivational morphemes is this ability they give us to derive new words: *Active* and *inactive* are two different words; so are *active* and *actively;* so are *act* and *action*.

The inflectional affixes also change words, of course, but the changes do not represent new words in the same sense that the changes with derivational morphemes do. It is probably accurate to consider the verb *acting* as simply a variation of *act;* likewise, the inflections we add to nouns—the plural and possessive—produce variations of the singular noun; we think of *dogs* and *dog's* simply as variations of *dog,* rather than as different words.

There are two other attributes of derivational morphemes that distinguish them from the inflectional morphemes:

1. **Derivational morphemes are arbitrary.** Unlike the inflectional morphemes, which apply in a systematic way to all, or at least to a significant number of, the words in a class, the derivational morphemes are quite unsystematic. For example, all verbs—with only two or three exceptions—take the inflectional *-s* and *-ing* endings; and almost all verbs have an *-ed* and *-en* inflection as well. However, there's nothing systematic about the derivational endings that we add to other word classes to form verbs: The adjective *able* becomes a verb with the addition of the prefix *en-* (*enable*); *sweet* takes the suffix *-en* (*sweeten*); *legal* takes *-ize* to become a verb (*legalize*); *active* takes *-ate* (*activate*). For many adjectives, however, we have no derivational morpheme at all for producing verbs; we have no way to turn such adjectives as *big, good, happy,* and *vicious* into verbs. On the other hand, we can derive nouns from these particular adjectives by adding *-ness.* As you might expect, however, *-ness* is not our only noun-forming suffix: Others include *-ity* (*generosity, activity, creativity*); *-acy* (*supremacy, literacy*); *-er* (*singer, helper*); or *-ion, -tion* (*action, preparation*); and *-ment* (*contentment, enlargement*). We have no rules to explain what goes with what, no system to account for these differences; that lack of system is what "arbitrary" means.

2. **Derivational morphemes often change the class of the word.** Most of the time, in fact, that change in class is their very purpose; they produce new words. Inflectional morphemes, on the other hand, never change the class. And, as mentioned earlier, we generally don't even consider the inflected form of a word as a different word.

If all these derivational and inflectional morphemes seem complicated to you, it's probably because you haven't thought about them before. If you're a native speaker, they're really not complicated at all; you use them without even thinking. In fact, there is probably no feature of English that illustrates more clearly the innate ability that native speakers have than this inventory of prefixes and suffixes that gives the language such versatility.

Investigating Language | **10.1**

Consider the following sets:

Verb   A. *X* can dorf; *X* dorfs; *X* is dorfing; *X* has dorfed already.

noun   B. Give me that dorf. No, I mean those dorfs. Where's your dorf's snape?

adj   C. You're pretty dorf, but *X* is dorfer, and *Y* is the dorfest of all.

1. In which set is *dorf* an adjective? What morphological—not syntactic—evidence tells you that?

2. In which set is *dorf* a verb? Again, what morphological evidence tells you that?

3. In which set is *dorf* a noun? Once more, what morphological evidence tells you that?

4. What type of morphemes have you been dealing with in these questions: inflectional or derivational?

5. The traditional definition of *noun* is "the name of a person, place, or thing" and that of *verb* is "a word that denotes action, being, or state of being." Instead of using those criteria of meaning, write your own definitions of *noun* and *verb* that are based on form.

ALLOMORPHS

In Exercise 44 the base morphemes *aud* and *dur* are pronounced and spelled the same in all five words in their lists. However, the morpheme *nov* in that same exercise has two pronunciations; in *nova* and *novelist* the vowels are different, comparable to the difference between *node* and *nod*. In the last group in the exercise, the difference from one word to the next is greater still, with variations in spelling as well as pronunciation. In fact, without the help of a dictionary we would be tempted to label *ceive* and *cap* and *cept* as different morphemes altogether, rather than variations of the same one. Such variations of morphemes, which are extremely common in English, are known as **allomorphs**.

Sometimes the base morphemes have allomorphic variations as the result of suffixes. For example, a word ending in *f* often takes a *v* in the plural:

leaf → leaves   wife → wives   elf → elves

We would call *leav* and *wiv* and *elv* allomorphs of *leaf* and *wife* and *elf.* Here are some other examples in which the pronunciation of the base morpheme changes with the addition of a suffix: *type/typify; please/pleasant; press/pressure; able/ability; oblige/obligation; child/children.* Because these allomorphs of the base are not used without the suffix, we would include them in the category of bound bases.

Prefixes and suffixes, too, undergo such variation; that is, they also have allomorphs. For example, notice the negative prefix we add to these adjectives: *unkind, improper, illegal, irrelevant, ineligible.* All these prefixes mean *not,* so it is probably accurate to consider *im, il, ir,* and *in* as allomorphs of the prefix *un,* the most common among them. At any rate, their sounds are determined by their environment.

Suffixes also have allomorphic variation. Consider, for example, the sound you add to make nouns plural:

cat $\rightarrow$ cats   dog $\rightarrow$ dogs   kiss $\rightarrow$ kisses

Even though the first two are spelled the same, the sounds are different: in *cats* the sound is an *s;* in *dogs,* it's a *z.* And in *kisses,* the *es* represents an unstressed vowel sound followed by *z.*

HOMONYMS

You're probably familiar with **homonyms,** words with different meanings that happen to have the same spelling and the same sound, such as *saw* (the tool) and *saw* (the past tense verb). The concept refers also to morphemes, in some cases to parts of words that sound the same but have different meanings. Prefixes and suffixes, for example, can be homonyms. The *ex* in *exchange* and the *ex* in *ex-husband* have two different meanings: "from" and "former." So do the *er* in *singer* and the *er* in *brighter:* "one who" and "more." In the case of *er,* one is derivational and one is inflectional. And the *s* endings we add to verbs and nouns also have different meanings. All of these are examples of homonyms.

You might find it useful to think of homonyms as simply accidents of language, mere coincidences. It's coincidence that the word *bell* and the bound morpheme *bell* (in *rebellion*) sound and look alike. The dictionary will show they have no connection: The free morpheme *bell* has its origin in the Old English word meaning roar; *rebellion* comes from the Latin word for war. And certainly it's coincidence that the name of the carpenter's tool sounds the same and shares the same spelling as the past tense form of *see.*

A subclass of homonyms, called **homophones,** includes those words with identical sounds in which both meaning and spelling are different: *to, two, too; sale, sail.*

Exercise   **46**

Draw vertical lines in the following words to indicate their morpheme boundaries. Identify each morpheme as follows: *bound* or *free; base* or *affix*. Identify each affix as *derivational* or *inflectional*. You will probably need to consult your dictionary.

i free   preci|sion   un|aware   il|legal
d free candid|ate   money   wealth|y
i free detour|ed   side|walks   televi|sion
d free excess|ive|ly   promo|tion   revise|s

CHAPTER 10

Key Terms

Affix   Homophones

Allomorph   Inflectional suffix

Base morpheme   Morpheme

Bound morpheme   Morphology

Derivational morpheme   Phonology

Free morpheme   Prefix

Homonyms   Suffix

QUESTIONS
?
for DISCUSSION

1. Most morphemes are made up of combinations of sounds. Give some examples of morphemes that are single sounds.

2. Consider how the meaning of a word comes about. Explain the origin of the following words:

ambulance	cohort	fancy	mayhem
budget	daisy	hussy	meal
calculate	dial	infant	money
candidate	easel	lunatic	pilot
cigar	escape	magazine	vaccine

3. In Exercise 45 you came up with words containing various combinations of bound and free morphemes. Which of those sequences do you suppose is a compound word? Define *compound word* on the basis of its morpheme content.

   What do the following compound words have in common: *fingerprint, sourpuss, overland, walkway*? In what way are they different?

4. Consider the difference between derivational and inflectional suffixes. What can you say about their positions when both appear on the same word? Is the rule fairly constant? Is it possible for more than one derivational and/or inflectional suffix to appear on a single word?

5. Which of the following words appear to violate the system that you described in Question 4?

   inflectional   sportsmanship   microscopy   teaspoonsful

6. How can the awareness of morphemes be of help in spelling problem words, such as the following?

entirely	innovate	disappoint
safety	inaudible	roommate
professor	misspell	vineyard

7. Explain the difference between the words "painful" and "pained." Under what circumstances would the following sentences be accurate?

   He had a pained expression on his face.

   He had a painful expression on his face.

   Now think about the difference between "healthy" and "healthful." Would you say that carrots are a healthy food to eat? And what's the difference between "masterly" and "masterful"?

8. Our vocabulary expands in many ways. Sometimes we give new meanings to old words or to their combinations, as in *waterbed, whistle-blower, gridlock,* and *moonshot.* And sometimes we combine

two words into a completely new one: We made *brunch* from *breakfast* and *lunch*. What two words do you suppose were combined in the formation of these: *bash, clash, flare*, and *smash?*

CLASSROOM APPLICATIONS

1. Homophones are words with the same pronunciation but with different spellings and different meanings, like *pear* and *pair* or *haul* and *hall*. In his book *A Chocolate Moose for Dinner*, Fred Gwynne plays with homophones, as you can see from the title. Before eating your dessert of chocolate moose, what would you have for your main course? Stake, perhaps? Plan a complete menu for your meal using (misusing!) homophones.

2. Homophones usually occur in pairs. But sometimes there are three or even four words in English that sound alike but differ in meaning and spelling. See how many trios of homophones you can come up with. (For starters, think of another to go with *pair* and *pear*.)

3. Another tricky class of our words is that of heteronyms—pairs of words that are spelled alike but differ in both meaning and pronunciation: *bass/bass, sewer/sewer, row/row*. See how many others you can come up with; then try to use both in the same sentence.

4. Among the bound bases of our vocabulary, some are combined with the suffix *-logy*, meaning a science. For example, the bound base *herpeto*, which means "to creep," when combined with *-logy* means the scientific study of creatures that crawl and creep—reptiles. When we add *-ist*, we get the title of the scientist who studies reptiles: *herpetologist*.

Use your dictionary to figure out the jobs and the job titles that can be produced from the following bound bases:

socio-

bio-

anthropo-

ethno-

cardio-

eco-

patho-

zoo-

geol-

entomo-

The Form Classes

CHAPTER PREVIEW

As you read in the opening of Part IV, an important difference between traditional and structural grammar is in the classification of words. The structuralists' definitions of the form classes—nouns, verbs, adjectives, and adverbs—make use of the native speaker's inherent language ability. For example, does the word have both -*s* and -*ing* forms? Then it's a verb. Can it be made plural or possessive? Then it's a noun. In traditional grammar, the definition of *noun* (the name of a person, place, or thing) and *verb* (a word showing action) are based on meaning.

The new grammarians also differentiate the word itself from its function in the sentence. In addition to a category such as *adjective*, which names the word class, we need the category *adjectival*, which specifies the function of adjectives. The structuralist defines *adjective* as a member of the class that can be qualified (*very big*) and inflected for the comparative and superlative degrees (*bigger, biggest*). By contrast, the traditional class of *adjective* is defined as "a word that modifies a noun." As a result, in a noun phrase such as "the stone house," both words preceding the headword *house* are labeled as adjectives: They fit that traditional definition.

In this chapter, however, we want to study adjectives—as well as nouns, verbs, and adverbs—in a "formal" way, as classes with certain characteristics of form. We will do so by following up on the study of morphemes, by looking at the derivational and inflectional suffixes that distinguish the four form classes. We will also look at the structure words that signal them.

243

NOUNS

We traditionally define *noun* on the basis of meaning, as the *name* of a person, place, thing, idea, event, or the like, and that definition works fairly well. After all, we've been learning names since we spoke our first words: *mama, daddy, cookie, baby.* The word *noun,* in fact, comes from *nomen,* the Latin word for "name."

We also get a sense of "nounness" from the words that signal nouns—the determiners. A word such as *the, my,* or *an* tells us a noun will follow, although not necessarily as the next word: *the* books, *my* sister, *an* honest opinion. Determiners are simply not used without nouns.

But certainly the most reliable clue for recognizing nouns is form. We can often differentiate the form classes from one another without reference to either meaning or context, simply on the basis of their derivational and inflectional suffixes.

Noun Derivational Suffixes. Each of the four form classes has its own inventory of derivational suffixes. The ending *-ion,* for example, converts the verb *reflect* into a noun, so we call it—or its variations, *-tion, -sion, -cion,* and *-ation* —a noun-forming suffix. A quick check of the dictionary reveals that all the *-ion* words listed on the first few pages are also nouns formed from verbs:

abbreviation	abstraction	accusation
abolition	accommodation	acquisition
abortion	accumulation	action

Some *-ion* words function as both nouns and verbs: *question, partition, mention,* and, yes, *function;* you may be able to think of others. But you will find few, if any, *-ion* words that are not nouns; *-ion* is a reliable signal. Many other derivational suffixes do the same job, that of converting verbs into nouns:

accomplish<u>ment</u>	break<u>age</u>
accept<u>ance</u>	deliver<u>y</u>
arriv<u>al</u>	depart<u>ure</u>
assist<u>ant</u>	teach<u>er</u>

This variety of noun-forming suffixes that we add to verbs—and, incidentally, there are many more than these—illustrates not only our versatility in changing one part of speech to another but also the arbitrary way in which we do so. Why, for example, do we say "delivery" and "deliverance" but not "deliverment"? Why "departure" rather than "departation"? Why "deportation" rather than "deporture"? There are no good answers to such questions.

The same arbitrariness runs through all the word classes. For example, many adjectives become nouns with the addition of *-ness:* pretti*ness,* lazi*ness,* strange*ness,* happi*ness,* helpless*ness.* But there is a long list of other suffixes that do the same job: tru*th,* wis*dom,* just*ice,* partial*ity.* And a number of suffixes simply alter the meaning of the word without changing the class; for example, we derive the abstract noun *boyhood* from the concrete noun *boy.* Other examples of suffixes that produce new meanings include *kingdom, friendship, Spaniard, gardener, terrorism.*

Finally, the nouns *partiality* and *activation* illustrate another feature of derivational suffixes, where a noun-forming suffix is added to a word that already has one or more derivational suffixes:

part + *-ial* = partial + *-ity* = partiality
(*noun*)   (*adj.*)   (*noun*)

act + *-ive* = active + *-ate* = activate + *-ion* = activation
(*verb*)   (*adj.*)   (*verb*)   (*noun*)

This feature also illustrates another difference between derivational and inflectional suffixes. The inflectional suffixes do not add on in this way. With the exception of the plural and possessive morphemes of nouns, which may appear in combination, the form-class words will have only one inflectional suffix, and it will always come at the end of the word, after any derivational suffixes.

Exercise *47*

Transform the following verbs into nouns by adding a derivational suffix. Are there any that have more than one noun form?

1. please   +   _ant_   =   _Pleasant_

2. regulate   +   _ion_   =   _regulation_

3. steal   +   _____   =   _stolen_

4. heal   +   _er_   =   _healer_

5. derive   +   _____   =   _____

6. inflect   +   _ion_   =   _inflection_

7. form   +   _____   =   _____

8. revive   +   _____   =   _____

9. seize   +   *ure* = *Seizure*

10. retire   +   *ment* = *Retirement*

Noun Inflectional Suffixes. The other aspect of form that differentiates the four form classes both from the structure classes and from each other is the set of inflectional morphemes that each form class has, which we saw in Chapter 2. Our nouns have only two grammatical inflections, one indicating **number (plural)** and one indicating **case (possessive)**:

SINGULAR	PLURAL	SINGULAR POSSESSIVE	PLURAL POSSESSIVE
cat	cats	cat's	cats'
dog	dogs	dog's	dogs'
horse	horses	horse's	horses'
mouse	mice	mouse's	mice's

The nouns *cat* and *dog* and *horse* illustrate that in speech we can't always distinguish among inflected forms of nouns: *Cats, cat's,* and *cats'* are all pronounced exactly the same. Only in writing can we differentiate the plural from the possessive and from the plural possessive. In the case of *mouse,* with its irregular plural, we of course make the distinction in speech as well as in writing.

The preceding examples illustrate another point about noun inflections: Sometimes the plural inflection is not a single /s/ or /z/ sound, as in *cats* and *dogs.* It may be two sounds, an entire syllable, complete with vowel, as in *horses.* The sound we add is determined by the final sound of the noun. With words ending in what is called a sibilant sound—usually spelled with *s, z, sh, ch, dge,* or *ge*—we must add a syllable to pronounce the -*s* plural (as well as the possessive): kiss*es,* maz*es,* sash*es,* church*es,* judg*es,* pag*es.*

Exercise 48

The possessive marks are missing from the following noun phrases. Read each one aloud; then punctuate each phrase in two ways to show its two possible meanings.

all my teachers assignments   the horses sore legs
all my teachers assignments   the horses sore legs

my sisters husbands business	my sons problems
my sisters husbands business	my sons problems

Recognizing whether or not the added sound is a complete syllable can be a useful clue in spelling. Spelling the plural and possessive of words that end in an /s/ or /z/ sound is sometimes confusing; they not only sound strange, they tend to look strange when they're written:

Mr. and Mrs. Jones are the Joneses. (*Plural*)

Their cat is the Joneses' cat. (*Possessive*)

To turn *Joneses*, the plural of *Jones*, into the possessive case, we add only the apostrophe because we add no new sound, the usual procedure for possessive plurals: *cats', horses', leaders'*. The possessive of singular nouns ending in *s* can also look strange:

The cats of Ross and Kris are Ross's and Kris's cats.

The nephew of Sis is Sis's nephew.

Here we add the extra syllable when we pronounce the possessive of these words, so we add *'s* when we spell them, the usual procedure for the singular possessive. (We should note that some writers prefer to add only the possessive mark, the apostrophe, even though they add a syllable in speech—Ross' and Kris' and Sis'; both spellings are acceptable.) But when the singular has more than one syllable and more than one /s/ or /z/ sound in the last syllable, we generally do not add a sound, so we do not add an s when we write the possessive:

The followers of Jesus are Jesus' followers.

The laws of Texas are Texas' laws.

A good rule of thumb is this: If the pronunciation does not change when you make a noun possessive, then do not add the *-s* inflection when you spell it; add only the apostrophe. If you're not sure how to pronounce the possessive—whether or not to add a syllable—listen to yourself say the word with that added *-s:* Do you say "the Williams's house" or "the Williams' house"? "Martinez's batting average" or "Martinez' batting average"? If it sounds awkward with the added syllable, then add only the apostrophe. Either choice you make will be "correct."

The plural and possessive inflections provide a test of sorts for "nounness." Can the word be made plural and/or possessive? If so, it's a noun. If not? Well, the possibility for nounness is still there. In applying the inflection test to the nouns in the preceding section, we find that all the words on the *-ion* list can take the plural inflection, but most of them will not take the possessive -*s*. With many nouns the *of* prepositional phrase is more common than the possessive -*s* inflection: In general, the more specific or concrete the sense of the noun, the more likely it is that the inflections will be acceptable.

Exercise   49

Transform the *of* possessive phrase into the inflected noun.

1. The son of Mr. Price is Mr. ___Price's___ son.
2. The daughter of Ms. Hedges is Ms. __Hedge's__ daughter.
3. The computer belonging to James is __James'__ computer.
4. The governor of Massachusetts is __Mass'__ governor.
5. The blanket belonging to Linus is __Linus'__ blanket.
6. The garden of the neighbor is the _____ garden.
7. The garden of the neighbors is the _____ garden.
8. The curls on the head and tail of Miss Piggy are _____ curls.
9. The club the women belong to is the _____ club.
10. The wisdom of Confucius is _____ wisdom.

The Meaning of the Possessive Case.   In the examples we have seen so far, the relationship between the possessive noun and the headword is actually one of possession, or ownership, but such a relationship is not always the case. As the following examples show, the possessive noun can be simply a description:

>   an evening's entertainment
>
>   a bachelor's degree
>
>   today's news

It can also be a measure of value or time:

>   a day's wages
>
>   a moment's notice
>
>   a dollar's worth

It can denote origin:

>   the teacher's suggestion
>
>   Lincoln's Gettysburg Address

Sometimes the actual relationship is unclear, even in context:

> We admired <u>Van Gogh's</u> portrait.

This possessive could refer either to a portrait *of* the artist or to a portrait *by* the artist.

Irregular Plural Inflections. Before leaving the noun inflections, we should note the many instances of irregular plurals, such as *mice*, in our lexicon. Some are old forms of English that have resisted becoming regularized: *foot–feet, tooth–teeth, man–men, child–children, ox–oxen.* A number of animal and fish names are irregular in that they have no inflection for the plural: *sheep, deer, bass, salmon, trout.* A large number of borrowed words have retained their foreign plural inflections: *larva–larvae, criterion–criteria, alumnus–alumni, appendix–appendices.* Incidentally, some of these borrowings are now in the process of acquiring regular plurals. *Appendixes* appears along with *appendices; indexes* and *formulas* are even more common than *indices* and *formulae; stadiums* has all but replaced *stadia. Memorandum* is giving way to the shortened *memo*, along with its regular plural, *memos;* and the added complication of gender in *alumnus–alumni* (masculine) and *alumna–alumnae* (feminine) no doubt encourages the use of the simpler, gender-free—and informal—*alum* and *alums.* The borrowed words ending in -*s*—*analysis–analyses, nucleus–nuclei, hypothesis–hypotheses, stimulus–stimuli*—are less likely to lose their foreign inflections; the addition of -*es* to the singular would be cumbersome.

The irregularity of noun inflections, incidentally, applies only to the plural; the possessive follows the regular rule:

SINGULAR	SINGULAR POSSESSIVE	PLURAL	PLURAL POSSESSIVE
man	man's	men	men's
child	child's	children	children's
deer	deer's	deer	deer's
mouse	mouse's	mice	mice's
larva	larva's	larvae	larvae's

Note that these plural possessives look different from regular plural possessives (*dogs'*), only because for regular plural nouns we don't add an -*s* to make the word possessive; the regular plural already has one.

Plural-Only Forms. Some nouns, even when singular in meaning, are plural in form. One such group refers to things that are in two parts—that are bifurcated, or branching: *scissors, shears, pliers, pants, trousers, slacks,* *shorts, glasses, spectacles.* As subjects of sentences, these nouns present no problems with subject–verb agreement: They take the same verb form as other plural subjects do. Interestingly, even though a pair of shorts is a single garment and a pair of pliers is a single tool, we use the plural pronoun in reference to them:

> I bought a new pair of shorts today; <u>they're</u> navy blue.

> I've lost my pliers; have you seen <u>them</u>?

Other plural nouns that have no singular form include *measles, mumps, means, tidings, clothes,* and *athletics.*

A different situation arises with certain plural-in-form nouns that are sometimes singular in meaning. A noun such as *physics, mathematics,* and *linguistics,* when referring to an academic discipline or course, is treated as singular:

> Physics <u>is</u> my favorite subject.

> Linguistics <u>is</u> the scientific study of language.

But sometimes such nouns as *mathematics* and *statistics* are used with plural meanings:

> The mathematics involved in the experiment <u>are</u> very theoretical.

> The statistics on poverty levels <u>are</u> quite depressing.

These uses also call for plural pronouns.

Collective Nouns. Nouns such as *family, choir, team, majority, minority* —any noun that names a group of individual members—can be treated as either singular or plural, depending on context and meaning:

> The <u>family</u> *have* all gone their separate ways.

> The whole <u>family</u> *is* celebrating the holidays at home this year.

> The <u>majority</u> of our city council members *are* Republicans.

> The <u>majority</u> always *rules.*

Other singular-in-form nouns, such as *remainder, rest,* and *number,* also have a plural meaning in certain contexts; their number depends on their modifiers:

> <u>The remainder of the job applicants</u> *are* waiting outside.

> <u>The rest of the books</u> *are* being donated to the library.

> <u>A number of customers</u> *have* come early.

This system also applies to certain indefinite pronouns, such as *some, all,* and *enough:*

Some of the books *were* missing.

All of the cookies *were* eaten.

Notice what happens to the verb in such sentences when the modifier of the subject headword is singular:

The rest of the map *was* found.

Some of the water *is* polluted.

All of the cake *was* eaten.

The remainder of this chapter *is* especially important.

The pronoun to use in reference to these noun phrases will depend on the meaning, and it will usually be obvious:

They (some of the books) *were* missing.

It (some of the water) *is* polluted.

One special problem occurs with the word *none*, which has its origin in the phrase *not one*. Because of that original meaning, many writers insist that *none* always be singular, as *not one* clearly is. However, a more accurate way to assess its meaning is to recognize *none* as the negative, or opposite, of *all* and to treat it in the same way, with its number (whether singular or plural) determined by the number of the modifier or of the referent:

None of the guests *want* to leave.

None of the cookies *were* left.

None of the cake *was* eaten.

All of the guests *are* staying; none of them *are* leaving.

Semantic Features of Nouns. Nouns can be classified according to certain built-in semantic features that affect their distribution. At an early age we begin this process of classification, recognizing, for example, whether a noun can be counted. We can say "one cookie" or "two cookies"; but a noun like *milk* is not countable. This understanding is evident in our selection of determiners:

I want milk.

I want a cookie.

I want some milk.

Within a few short years our linguistic computers have been programmed to make distinctions like this that we are hardly aware of. The nonnative speaker, on the other hand, must work conscientiously to make such distinctions. The person who says "I need a new luggage" or "I have a lot of homeworks" or "I am looking forward to a peace and quiet this weekend" has not distinguished between **countable** and **noncountable nouns**. Linguists have described these features of our nouns in a hierarchy, each level of which has consequences for selecting determiners and other parts of the sentence:

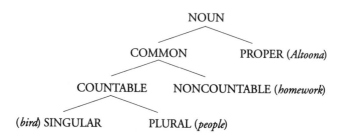

The restrictions built into the word determine its place in the hierarchy; each word carries with it only those features in the higher intersections (or *nodes*) that it is connected with: *Homework* is a noncountable, common noun; *bird* is a singular, countable, common noun. Determiners have related built-in features or restrictions; the determiner *a* (or *an*) includes the features "singular" and "countable," so we are restricted from using it with *homework*. It will signal only those nouns that fit in the lowest, left-hand branch, like *bird*. Some nouns appear in both branches of a node, depending on their meaning. For example, some nouns can be both countable and noncountable:

I had a strange experience yesterday.

I've had experience working with animals.

I baked a cake today.

I'll have some cake.

The term **proper noun** refers to a noun (or noun phrase) with a specific referent: Empire State Building, Grand Canyon, William Shakespeare, London, *The CBS Evening News,* Aunt Mildred, November, Pearl Harbor Day, Thanksgiving. Proper nouns name people, geographic regions and locations, buildings, events, holidays, months, and days of the week; they are usually written with initial capital letters. Although most proper nouns are singular, exceptions occur in the case of mountain ranges and island groups—the Rockies, the Andes, the Falklands—which are plural.

A careful writer would avoid writing sentences like these two:

> *There have been less accidents in the county this year.

> *I have also noticed an increase in the amount of bicycles on the roads.

But there's no problem with these:

> There are fewer students enrolled in the advanced ceramics class this year.

> There is an increase in the number of students enrolled in the beginning course.

Think about where in the noun hierarchy on page 252 you would find *accidents, bicycles,* and *students.* How would a careful writer revise those first two sentences? If you were helping a nonnative speaker revise those sentences, how would you explain the changes?

Would that careful writer avoid any of the following sentences?

> There were less than a dozen accidents in the county this year.

> We had fewer accidents than last year.

> We have less dollars than we need.

> We have less money than we need.

> We have less than ten dollars to last until payday.

You probably gave that nonnative speaker some advice about the use of *less/fewer* and *amount of/number of.* Should you revise your explanation? In what way?

VERBS

The traditional definition of *verb,* like that of *noun,* is based on meaning: a word denoting action, being, or state of being. When we look for the verb in a sentence, we look for the word that tells *what is happening,* and most of the time this method works. But a much more reliable criterion for defining *verb* is that of form. Some verbs have derivational endings that signal that they are verbs; and, with only two or three exceptions, all verbs fit into the verb-expansion rule, the system of adding auxiliaries and inflections described in Chapter 3.

Verb Derivational Affixes. Many of the root words, or bases, that take noun-forming suffixes are verbs to begin with; for example, most of our nouns with -*ion* are formed from verbs. The opposite operation—deriving verbs from other form classes—is less common. We are more likely to turn a noun into a verb without changing its form at all, a process known as **functional shift**—in other words, shifting the function of the word. We *chair* meetings and *table* motions; the carpenter *roofs* the house; the cook *dishes* up the food; the painter *coats* the wall with paint; the gardener *seeds* the lawn and *weeds* the garden; we *butter* the bread, *bread* the chicken—and who among us hasn't *chickened out* at one time or another?

But we also have a few verb-forming affixes that combine with certain nouns and adjectives:

  typ**ify**   dark**en**   activ**ate**   legal**ize**

In addition to these suffixes, the prefixes *en-* and *be-* and *de-* and *dis-* can turn nouns and adjectives into verbs and can alter the meaning of other verbs: *enable, enact, enchant, encounter, encourage, encrust, endear, enforce, enlighten, enthrone, bedevil, bewitch, besmirch, dethrone, derail, disable.* But compared with the large number of derivational morphemes that signal nouns, the inventory of verb-forming affixes is fairly small.

Verb Inflectional Suffixes. The verb-expansion rule describes the system of adding auxiliaries and inflectional suffixes to verbs. So as a clue in identifying the part of speech we call *verb*, the inflectional system is extremely reliable. All verbs, with only one or two exceptions—even those with irregular -*en* and -*ed* forms—have both -*s* and -*ing* forms. This means we can identify a word as a verb simply by noting its -*s* and -*ing* forms. Every verb has the other three forms as well—the base, the -*ed* and the -*en*—but they may not be as recognizable: Verbs such as *hit* and *put,* for instance, show no changes in form from the base (*hit, put*) to the -*ed* form (*hit, put*) to the -*en* form (*hit, put*); others include *cast, hurt, shut, split,* and *spread.* Yet the -*s* and the -*ing* forms are exactly like those of every other verb: *hits, puts, hitting, putting.* The verb inflectional system is so regular, in fact, that we can define *verb* on that basis alone. A word that doesn't have an -*s* or an -*ing* form is simply not a verb.

Investigating Language   *11.2*

It is easy to demonstrate the "verbness" of *ground, water, air,* and *fire,* even though these words may, at first glance, appear to be nouns. First, add the verb inflections. Then write a sentence for each of the four verbs, using the form called for. Remember that the *-en* form will follow the auxiliary *have;* and if you begin your sentence with *yesterday,* you'll automatically use the *-ed* form.

BASE	*-s* FORM	*-ed* FORM	*-ing* FORM	*-en* FORM
1. GROUND	_____	_____	_____	_____
(*-ed*)	_____			
2. WATER	_____	_____	_____	_____
(*-s*)	_____			
3. AIR	_____	_____	_____	_____
(*-ing*)	_____			
4. FIRE	_____	_____	_____	_____
(*-en*)	_____			

Now test the "verbness" of the verbs in the following sentences (*rumor, beware*) by listing their five forms:

It was rumored that Marcus broke his leg.

You should always beware of rumors.

What have you discovered about the reliability of identifying verbs by their inflections? Would a different criterion be more accurate—perhaps one based on the possibility of auxiliaries?

The verbs *rumor* and *beware* are indeed exceptions to the inflectional-suffix rule for identifying verbs. The verb *rumor* is used exclusively in the passive voice, although the dictionary does include the *-ing* form—perhaps used at one time or place in a particular dialect. The verb *beware* is used exclusively with *you*—or, in commands, with the understood *you*. The dictionary lists only the base form for *beware*. But we shouldn't let these two exceptions—and they do appear to be the only two—discourage us from relying on the almost-infallible inflection test for identifying verbs.

ADJECTIVES

In terms of form, adjectives are not as easily identifiable in isolation as are nouns and verbs. Often we need either meaning or context for clues. In

Chapter 2 we made use of a fairly reliable "adjective test" frame, a way to use the context of a sentence to discover if a word is an adjective:

The _____ NOUN is very _____ .

attributive   predicative → , p. 258 *

Only an adjective will fit into both slots. But in some cases the form of the word also provides clues. A number of derivational suffixes signal adjectives.

Adjective Derivational Suffixes. The most reliable derivational suffix identifying a word as an adjective is *-ous;* we know that *gorgeous, famous, porous, courageous,* and *contagious* are adjectives simply on the basis of form. Here are some other adjective-forming suffixes:

merr*y*, funn*y*	child*ish*, redd*ish*
beauti*ful*, wonder*ful*	fragment*ary*, compliment*ary*
terri*fic*, asce*tic*	puni*tive*, ac*tive*
fortun*ate*, temper*ate*	vari*able*, amen*able*

As clues to adjectives, these suffixes are not as reliable as *-ous* because they show up occasionally on other form classes too: hand*ful* (noun), pan*ic* (noun, verb), pun*ish* (verb). But it is safe to say that most words with these endings are adjectives.

Adjective Inflectional Suffixes. The inflectional suffixes that pattern with adjectives are *-er*, the sign of the **comparative degree**, and *-est*, the **superlative**:

Positive:	big	young	smart
Comparative:	bigger	younger	smarter
Superlative:	biggest	youngest	smartest

The *-er* form is used in the comparison of two nouns—that's why this form is called the comparative degree:

Pat is <u>younger</u> than Phyllis.

Phyllis is the <u>smarter</u> of the two.

The comparative degree with *than* can also be followed by a clause rather than a noun phrase:

Pat is younger <u>than I suspected</u>.

The *-est* form, the superlative degree, is used when singling out one of more than two nouns:

Tom was the <u>oldest</u> person in the room.

Of the three candidates, Sarah is the <u>smartest</u>.

For many adjectives the comparative and superlative degrees are not formed with -*er* and -*est* but with *more* and *most*, which we can think of as alternative forms, or allomorphs, of the morphemes -*er* and -*est*. In fact, adjectives of more than one syllable generally pattern with *more* and *most*, with certain exceptions: two-syllable adjectives ending in -*y* or -*ly* (*prettiest, friendlier, lovelier*); some ending in -*le* (*nobler, noblest*), -*ow* (*narrower, narrowest*), and -*er* (*tenderest*).

But *more* and *most* are not exclusive to adjectives either. The -*ly* adverbs, those derived from adjectives, also have comparative and superlative versions: *more quickly, most frequently*. And there are some adjectives, such as *former, main,* and *principal,* that have no comparative and superlative forms.

A small group of words that have comparative and superlative forms can serve as either adjectives or adverbs, so the inflectional test is not completely reliable in identifying a word as an adjective:

early	fast	late	high
earlier	faster	later	higher
earliest	fastest	latest	highest
hard	long	low	deep
harder	longer	lower	deeper
hardest	longest	lowest	deepest

Another word we could add to this list is *near* (*nearer, nearest*), which can serve not only as an adjective and an adverb, but also as a preposition ("Our seats were *near* the fifty-yard line")—the only preposition that takes inflections. In short, the possibility of making a word comparative or superlative is not exclusive to adjectives.

In spite of all these limitations, we have no difficulty distinguishing adjectives in sentences. First, we know the positions they fill in the sentence patterns—as subject and object complements and in noun phrases as prenoun modifiers. And although nouns can also fill all these slots, the differences in the form of nouns and adjectives make it easy to distinguish between them.

On the subject of the comparative and superlative degrees, we should also note that adjectives can be compared in a negative sense with *as, less,* and *least*:

> This picnic is not <u>as enjoyable as</u> I thought it would be.
>
> This picnic is <u>less enjoyable than</u> I thought it would be.
>
> This is the <u>least enjoyable</u> picnic I've ever attended.

We should also note some exceptions to the regular comparative and superlative forms:

good	bad	far	far
better	worse	farther	further
best	worst	farthest	furthest

Exercise **50**

Fill in the blanks with the comparative and superlative degrees of the adjectives listed. Do any of them require *more* and *most?*

POSITIVE	COMPARATIVE	SUPERLATIVE
friendly	_____	_____
helpful	_____	_____
wise	_____	_____
awful	_____	_____
rich	_____	_____
mellow	_____	_____
expensive	_____	_____
valid	_____	_____
pure	_____	_____
able	_____	_____

Subclasses of Adjectives. The adjective test frame, which you saw in Chapter 2 (The _____ **NOUN** is very_____), is useful in identifying adjectives. It is also useful in helping distinguish subclasses of adjectives: those that are limited to the prenoun slot and those that are limited to the complement slots.

Adjectives actually fill three slots in the sentence patterns: as subject complement and object complement (where they are called **predicative adjectives**) and as modifiers in the noun phrase (where they are called **attributive** adjectives). Most adjectives can fill all three slots; the test frame uses two of them: attributive and subject complement.

But a small number will not fill the complement slots. The following adjectives are attributive only: *main, principal, former, mere, potential, atomic, late* (meaning "dead"), and such technical adjectives as *sulfuric* and *hydrochloric*. These do not serve as either subject or object complements in the verb phrase, nor do they take qualifiers, such as *very:*

> He is the former president.
>
> *The president is former.
>
> *My reason is main.
>
> *My main reason is very main.
>
> She is a mere child.
>
> *The child is mere.

Many of the so-called A-adjectives—*ablaze, afraid, aghast, alone, awake*— are predicative only:

> The house was ablaze.
>
> *The ablaze house burned down in an hour.
>
> The children were awake.
>
> *The awake children were noisy.

There are a few others—*fond, ready, ill, well*—that rarely appear in attributive position in reference to animate nouns. We may refer to a "ready wit" but rarely to a "ready person." We may talk about an "ill omen" but rarely an "ill person"; we are more likely to say a "sick person."

Incidentally, not all predicative adjectives take *very*, the sample qualifier in the test frame. We probably wouldn't say "very afraid" or "very awake"; we would be more likely to say "very much afraid" or "very much awake." But these adjectives do combine with other qualifiers: *quite* afraid, *extremely* afraid, *completely* awake, *wide* awake.

A number of adjectives in predicative position appear frequently with complements in the form of phrases or clauses; some adjectives, such as *fond* and *aware*, are rarely used without them:

> The children were <u>afraid that the dog would bite.</u>
>
> The children were <u>aware that the dog would bite.</u>
>
> The dog was <u>fond of biting children.</u>
>
> We were <u>conscious of the problem.</u>
>
> Our team is <u>certain to win.</u>

We call these "complements" rather than, simply, modifiers or qualifiers because they complete the idea expressed by the adjective, in much the same way that direct objects are complements of verbs.

Another subclassification of adjectives relates to their ability to combine with qualifiers. Certain adjectives denote meanings that are **absolute** in nature: *unique, round, square, perfect, single, double.* These can fill both the attributive and predicate slots, but they generally cannot be qualified or compared. We can, of course, say "almost perfect" or "nearly square," but most writers avoid "more perfect" or "very perfect." In the case of *unique,* it has come to mean "rare" or "unusual," in which case "very unique" would be comparable to "very unusual." However, given the historical meaning "one of a kind," the qualified "very unique" makes no sense.

ADVERBS

Of all the form classes, adverbs are the hardest to pin down in terms of both form and position. Many of them have no distinguishing affixes, and except in Pattern I they fill no required slots in the sentence patterns. (We have identified certain verbs in Patterns VI and VII, however—among them, *lay, put, place,* and *set*—that do require adverbials.) The fact that adverbs are often movable is perhaps their most distinguishing characteristic.

The class we are calling "adverb" differs from the class identified as "adverb" in traditional grammar. You'll recall the traditional definition as "a word that modifies a verb, an adjective, or another adverb." This definition includes words that we call "qualifiers," words that intensify or qualify the meaning of adjectives and adverbs: *very* nice, *quite* slow, *rather* quickly. But even when we leave out adjectives and other adverbs from the traditional definition, we are left with a definition of "adverbial"—that is, the definition of a function, not a word class. (Chapter 5 describes many structures—not only adverbs—that function adverbially.) Remember, we are defining the four form classes on the basis of their inflectional and derivational affixes and of the words that signal them—not on the basis of their function in the sentence. You'll read more about the distinction between qualifiers and adverbs in the section on "Qualifiers" in Chapter 12.

Adverb Derivational Suffixes. One common indicator of form we do have is the derivational suffix -*ly*, which we use to derive adverbs of manner from adjectives—adverbs that tell *how* or *in what way* about the verb:

He walked <u>slowly</u>.

She answered <u>correctly</u>.

But -*ly* is not completely reliable as a signaler of adverbs; it also occurs on nouns (*folly*) and on adjectives (*lovely, ugly*). But we are safe in saying that most -*ly* words are adverbs, simply because there are so many adjectives that we can turn into adverbs with this derivational morpheme.

There are some restrictions on this process, however: Not all adjectives can become manner adverbs. These restrictions are related to meaning. Some adjectives describe a state, such as *tall* and *old*, or a fixed or inherent characteristic, such as *Norwegian;* others describe characteristics that change, such as *weak, active,* and *industrious.* Another distinction can be drawn between objective characteristics, such as *tall* and *old*, and subjective ones, such as *nice* and *splendid.* The adjectives that refer to objective or stative or inherent qualities rarely become manner adverbs: *tall, old, fat, young, short, thick, large, flat, round, red.* When they do, they are likely to have a specialized, often metaphorical, meaning: *shortly, hardly, flatly, squarely, widely.*

Besides *-ly*, two other derivational suffixes produce adverbs: *-ward* and *-wise.* Words ending in *-ward* signal direction: *homeward, forward, backward, upward, downward.* Words ending in *-wise*, which indicate manner, include both old usages, such as *otherwise, lengthwise,* and *crosswise,* and new ones that are considered by some writers as unnecessary jargon, such as *budgetwise, weatherwise, moneywise,* and *profitwise.*

Investigating Language | *11.3*

One of our most reliable derivational suffixes is *-ly*. In most cases the message it sends is "adverb of manner": *Quickly* means "in a quick manner," and *slowly* means "in a slow manner." But, as with most rules in our language, there are exceptions to both parts of that message—both the "adverb" part and the "of manner" part.

Consider the *-ly* words in the following sentences. Are they adverbs? Are they adjectives? Could they be nouns or verbs?

1. We're leaving <u>immediately</u> and driving <u>directly</u> to Austin.
2. Bob will be leaving <u>directly</u>.
3. The natives around here are not always <u>friendly</u>.
4. One person I met tried to <u>bully</u> me.
5. He wasn't <u>particularly neighborly</u>.
6. Shedding tears is not considered <u>manly</u>.
7. That is <u>hardly</u> a universal belief, however.
8. My <u>belly</u> aches, but I <u>flatly</u> refuse to stay home.

Use your understanding of form to test these *-ly* words. Remember the inflectional paradigms for nouns and verbs; remember the adjective test frame. And is it possible that *-ly* adverbs have a meaning other than manner? Use your intuition, too!

Adverb Inflectional Suffixes. The comparative and superlative inflections, -*er* and -*est*, combine with adverbs as well as with adjectives, although in a much more limited way. The comparative form of -*ly* adverbs, usually formed by adding *more* rather than -*er*, is fairly common. The superlative degree—*most* suddenly, *most* favorably—is rare in both speech and writing; it invariably calls attention to itself and will often have the main focus of the sentence:

The committee was most favorably impressed with the proposal.

The crime was planned most ingeniously.

In the discussion of adjectives, we listed a few words that serve as both adjectives and adverbs: *early, late, hard, fast, long, high, low, deep*, and *near*. These are simply adverbs made from adjectives without the addition of -*ly*; they are referred to as **flat adverbs**. Except for a few others such as *soon* and *often*, they are the only adverbs that take -*er* and -*est*; most of the -*ly* adverbs take *more* and, occasionally, *most* in forming the comparative and superlative degrees.

A great many adverbs have neither derivational nor inflectional affixes that distinguish them as adverbs. Instead, we recognize them by the information they provide, by their position in the sentence, and often by their movability:

Time:	now, today, nowadays, yesterday
Duration:	already, always, still, yet
Frequency:	often, seldom, never, sometimes, always
Location:	there, here, everywhere, somewhere, elsewhere, upstairs, abroad, outside, nearby
Direction:	away, thence
Concession:	still, yet
Sequence:	afterward, next, then

There are also a number of words without form distinctions that can serve as either prepositions or adverbs: *above, around, behind, below, down, in, inside, out, outside, up.*

Exercise **51**

Fill in the blanks with variations of the words shown on the chart, changing or adding derivational morphemes to change the word class.

	NOUN	VERB	ADJECTIVE	ADVERB
1.	grief	_____	_____	_____
2.	_____	vary	_____	_____

3. _____   _____   _____   ably

4. _____   defend   _____   _____

5. economy   _____   _____   _____

6. _____   _____   pleasant   _____

7. type   _____   _____   _____

8. _____   prohibit   _____   _____

9. _____   _____   _____   critically

10. _____   _____   valid   _____

11. _____   appreciate   _____   _____

12. beauty   _____   _____   _____

13. _____   accept   _____   _____

14. _____   _____   pure   _____

15. *ince*   continue   _____   _____
    tion   *ous*

CHAPTER 11
Key Terms

Absolute adjective

Adjective

Adjective complement

Adjective derivational suffix

Adjective inflectional suffix

Adverb

Adverb derivational suffix

Adverb inflectional suffix

Attributive adjective

Case

Collective noun

Common noun

Comparative degree

Countable noun

Flat adverb

Form classes

Functional shift

Indefinite pronoun

Noncountable noun

Noun

Noun derivational suffix

Noun inflectional suffix

Number	Proper noun
Plural	Superlative degree
Plural-only noun	Verb
Positive degree	Verb derivational suffix
Possessive	Verb inflectional suffix
Predicative adjective	

QUESTIONS
?
for DISCUSSION

1. A government spokesperson recently used the following clauses in a discussion of the economy:

   When we were approaching crunch.

   When push comes to shove.

   What part of speech are *crunch, push,* and *shove?*

2. The traditional Latin term for possessive case is *genitive.* Consider the relationship between the possessive noun and its headword in the following noun phrases:

   the teacher's explanation

   the car's overhaul

   Explain what is meant by *subjective genitive* and *objective genitive.* Now consider the following ambiguous sentence:

   I was disturbed about Tom's punishment.

   What is the source of the ambiguity?

3. We often use verbs adjectivally, as noun modifiers, as you saw in Chapter 6. But many words that look like verbs—that were, in fact, originally verbs—now have the characteristics of adjectives. We have said that we can identify a word as an adjective if it can fit into the adjective test frame (The _____ NOUN is very _____). We also have an inflectional test: Can the word be made comparative and superlative? Using these two tests, identify the underlined words in the following sentences: Are they adjectives or verbs?

Joe took the <u>broken</u> chair to the dump.

That <u>disgusting</u> movie wasn't worth five dollars.

The football rally was <u>exciting</u>.

I feel <u>tired</u>.

Joe was <u>drunk</u> last night.

Many <u>working</u> mothers have problems with day-care.

The <u>decorated</u> tree looks beautiful.

4. Sometimes verbs are used as nouns (gerunds), as you saw in Chapter 7. What test can you apply to the following words to test their part of speech? Are they verbs or nouns?

    The <u>meeting</u> was boring.

    Julie looked lovely at her <u>wedding</u>.

    The committee's <u>finding</u> surprised everyone.

    <u>Jogging</u> is good exercise.

5. Explain the ambiguity of the following sentences in terms of their possible sentence patterns and parts of speech:

    My mother is always entertaining.

    They are frightening people.

6. Shakespeare, as you know, used language in all sorts of original ways. Here are two lines from Romeo and Juliet. What has he done with word classes?

    Thank me no thankings nor proud me no prouds.

    O flesh, flesh, how art thou fishified!

7. The dictionary labels *today* as both an adverb and a noun. Are those labels based on form or function? How should we define *yesterday* and *tomorrow*? Are they also members of both classes? Examine the following passage from *Macbeth* to see how Shakespeare used the words:

    Tomorrow, and tomorrow, and tomorrow
    Creeps in this petty pace from day to day
    To the last syllable of recorded time,
    And all our yesterdays have lighted fools
    The way to dusty death.

8. Here are two lines from Groucho Marx, who also had a way with words:

> Time flies like an arrow.
>
> Fruit flies like a banana.

Use your understanding of both sentence patterns and word classes to explain the joke.

9. In meeting a very tall person, you might ask the question, "How tall are you?" Strangely enough, we would ask the same question of a short person: We don't usually ask, "How *short* are you?" In this pair of adjectives, *tall* is called the unmarked version. Think of other adjectives we use for quantity or size or age or speed: *old/young, big/little, heavy/light, fast/slow.* Does our usage suggest a marked and unmarked version? Under what circumstances would we use the other?

CLASSROOM APPLICATIONS

1. Here's a sentence with a message you may not understand:

> The frabous gricks were brocking my parmy dorfer very botly.

As you see, it's filled with nonsense words. But even though the sentence has no semantic, or dictionary, meaning, it still sounds like English. It has structural meaning. In fact, you can probably figure out the classes of the separate words, as well as the sentence pattern. Identify the derivational and inflectional clues that enable you to do so.

Noun(s):

Verb(s):

Adjective(s):

Adverb(s):

What other clues, in addition to the form of the nonsense words, helped you?

The traditional definitions of *noun* ("the name of a person, place, or thing") and *verb* ("a word showing action") are of no help here. Write new definitions based on the clues you identified.

Noun: _____

Verb: _____

2. Here's another grammatical nonsense sentence for you to interpret:

> Stear, the frabous grick botly brocked my parmy dorfer in the alflit because the dorfer jilked the grick.

First, answer the following questions:

    1. What happened to the dorfer?
    2. Why did it happen?
    3. Who or what did it?
    4. Where did it happen?
    5. Describe the grick and the dorfer.

Now diagram the sentence. Then write a version in which the main clause is in the passive voice. Write a version in which the subordinate clause is passive.

3. Here's an altered version of the sentence in 2:

> Stear, the frabous grick, botly brocked my parmy dorfer in the alflit because the dorfer jilked the grick.

Explain how the addition of one comma changed the syntax. Note that the class of one word has changed in the new version. Which word? Diagram the new version.

4. In his book *Words and Rules: The Ingredients of Language* (Basic Books, 1999), Steven Pinker discusses our ability to form new words with prefixes and suffixes:

> The psychologists Harald Baayen and Antoinette Renouf calculated that every time you open a newspaper you will be faced with at least one word with *un-* that you have never seen before, one with *-ness*, and one with *-ly*: words like *uncorkable, uncheesey, headmistressly, breathcatchingly, pinkness,* and *outdoorsiness.* (p.122)

Check the front page of your daily paper or a current magazine article to test this calculation. See how many such words your class can find, words that do not appear in the dictionary.

CHAPTER 12

The Structure Classes

CHAPTER PREVIEW

In contrast to the large, open form classes, the categories of words known as structure classes are small and, for the most part, closed. Although new words regularly enter the language as nouns and verbs as the need arises for new vocabulary, the structure classes—conjunctions, prepositions, auxiliaries, and the like—remain constant from one generation to the next. As native speakers, we pay little attention to the structure words. Until we notice a nonnative speaker omitting a determiner or using the wrong preposition, we probably don't appreciate the importance of the grammatical sense the structure words contribute.

Part of that grammatical sense comes from the stress–unstress pattern of speech, the rhythm of the language. Most structure words are unstressed: They have the lowest volume, providing valleys between the peaks of loudness that fall on the stressed syllables of the form-class words.

The first three structure classes we will look at are those that signal specific form classes: determiners, the signalers of nouns; auxiliaries, the signalers of verbs; and qualifiers, the signalers of adjectives and adverbs. Then we will look at prepositions and conjunctions, both of which have connective roles; interrogatives, the signalers of questions; expletives, which serve as structural operators of various kinds; and particles.

DETERMINERS

The **determiner** class is one of the structure classes that straddle the line between a word class and a function. On the one hand, our most common determiners, the articles, do indeed constitute a small, closed structure class. At the other end of the spectrum are the possessive nouns, which function as determiners while retaining their membership in the open class "noun." In between are the subclasses of determiners that belong to the closed pronoun class: Demonstrative, possessive, and indefinite pronouns all function as determiners; and, of course, as pronouns they also function as nominals (in fact, "pronominal" would be a more accurate label than "pronoun").

Determiners signal nouns in a variety of ways: They may define the relationship of the noun to the speaker or listener (or reader); they may identify the noun as *specific* or *general;* they may *quantify* it specifically or refer to quantity in general. Because determiners have an important role in the noun phrase, as signalers, we also include them under the umbrella term *adjectival,* as you learned in Chapter 6. Following are the most common classes of determiners, many of which have appeared in our sample sentences:

ARTICLES	POSSESSIVE NOUNS	DEMONSTRATIVE PRONOUNS	NUMBERS
the	John's	this/these	one
a(n)	my son's	that/those	two
	etc.		etc.

POSSESSIVE PRONOUNS		INDEFINITE PRONOUNS			
my	its	several	few	each	all
your	our	little	fewer	every	both
his	their	many	more	either	some
her	whose	much	most	neither	any
		no	enough	less	

We should note that possessive nouns as determiners retain their own determiners: *my daughter's* teacher; *the week's* groceries; *our cat's* fur.

Many of the features of nouns in the hierarchy shown on page 252 affect our selection of determiners. A noun appearing in the lowest, left-hand branch of the diagram, for example—a singular, countable noun—rarely appears without a determiner:

This cookie tastes good.

*Cookie tastes good.

John is my friend.

*John is friend.

There are certain exceptions to this rule. For example, the nouns *town,* *school,* and *car* are singular, countable nouns; nevertheless, in some prepositional phrases they appear without determiners:

> the other side of <u>town</u>
>
> going to <u>school</u>
>
> the best kind of <u>car</u>

These exceptions present no problems for native speakers, of course. We're used to the sometimes arbitrary nature of the determiner:

> We say, "I walked to town," but not "I walked to city."
>
> We say, "I have a cold," but not "I have a flu."
>
> We say, "I attend college," but not "I attend university."
>
> We say, "I'm going into town," but not "I'm going into hospital."

(The British and Australians, incidentally, do "go into hospital," "attend university," and "look out of window.")

The difficulty for the nonnative speaker comes with learning which nouns are countable nouns and which are not. Other complications arise because determiners have built-in restrictions. Some will signal only plural nouns (*these, those, many, few, several*), some only singular nouns (*a, one, each, either, neither, every*), some only noncountables (*much, less*), and others only countables (*few, many, a, one*).

Another fairly regular rule concerns the limitation of determiners with certain noncountable nouns, sometimes called **mass nouns,** such as *luggage, furniture, beer, cake, sugar, rice, coal, steel, water.* When mass nouns are used as noncountable, they cannot be plural, so they do not combine with determiners that have either the "plural" or "countable" feature: *a, one, two, these, several, many.*

> *<u>These furnitures</u> are sturdy.
>
> *<u>Many furnitures</u> are expensive.
>
> *<u>Each furniture</u> has its own charm.

Some determiners have both countable and noncountable features built into them (*this, some, most, all*), so they can combine with both kinds of nouns:

> <u>This furniture</u> is lovely.
>
> <u>This chair</u> is comfortable.
>
> <u>Some furniture</u> is expensive.
>
> <u>Some chairs</u> are expensive.
>
> <u>Most chocolate cake</u> is high in calories.

Most coconut macaroons are delicious.

All polluted water is undrinkable.

Not all rules are necessarily good rules.

The nonnative speaker must consciously learn these features of both nouns and determiners. But a further complication arises when these mass nouns take on countable meanings:

These whole-grain flours are popular now.

The light beers are getting better all the time.

Abstract nouns also present problems for the nonnative speaker because they may appear either with or without determiners:

I have finally regained peace of mind.

I have finally regained my peace of mind.

In some cases the determiner is tied to the presence of a modifier, such as a *that* clause:

*The peace of mind is hard to acquire in these insecure times.

The peace of mind that comes with financial security is my goal.

Even a proper noun may require a determiner when it has certain kinds of modifiers:

The Altoona of my childhood was a railroad town.

And for some inexplicable reason, the article *a* changes the meaning in sentences with *few* and *little*:

I have few friends.	I've had little trouble with my car.
I have a few friends.	I've had a little trouble with my car.

Finally, some determiners are extremely versatile. The **definite article**, *the*, can signal all classes of nouns that can take determiners when the definite meaning is called for—unlike the **indefinite** *a*, which is restricted to countables. The possessives, too—both nouns and pronouns—are wide-ranging, without built-in distribution restrictions.

Exercise **52**

Identify the determiners in the following sentences.

1. My sister doesn't have enough money for her ticket.
2. John's roommate went home for the weekend.
3. Every course I'm taking this term has a midterm exam.

4. Bill spent more money on the week's groceries than he expected to.
5. I spend less time studying now than I did last term.
6. I haven't seen either movie, so I have no preference.

The Expanded Determiner. A determiner is not always a single word. In fact, we can think of the determiner slot itself as a series of slots with optional pre- and postdeterminers. The following formula will account for some fairly common **expanded determiners**, although a description that accounted for all the possibilities would be far more complex. This simplified scheme, however, should help you appreciate the intricacies of the grammar rules built into your linguistic computer.

(predeterminer) + DETERMINER + **(postdeterminer)**

		ORDINAL NUMBERS	CARDINAL NUMBERS
all (of)	the	first	one
both (of)	a	second	two
half (of)	my	etc.	etc.
only	these	next	
especially	etc.	last	
just			
double			

The pre- and postdeterminers are, of course, optional, so they are shown in parentheses in the formula.

In the following sentences, the pre- and postdeterminers are underlined; the determiner is written with capital letters:

All of THE cookies disappeared.

Only MY pretzels disappeared.

THE first ten students in line were chosen.

Only THE next two students complained.

Both (of) THESE students wrote A papers.

Half (of) THE class took part in the demonstration.

I have just ENOUGH gas for the trip.

Another type of expanded determiner is the phrasal quantifier; it can occur with either countable or noncountable nouns:

<u>a lot of</u> classes

<u>a lot of</u> homework

<u>a great many</u> friends

<u>a large number of</u> people

In terms of **subject–verb agreement**, it is the number of the noun—whether singular or plural—that determines the verb: homework *is;* classes (friends, people) *are.*

We also have a large open class of quantifying noun phrases that we use with noncountable nouns; they enable us to count those noncountables:

<u>a quart of</u> milk

<u>a pound of</u> butter

<u>a piece of</u> furniture

<u>a spoonful of</u> sugar

When these noun phrases are subjects, their number is determined by the number of the quantifier: *two quarts* of milk *are; a quart* of milk *is.* We might, in fact, be tempted to call the quantifiers the headwords of these noun phrases, just as we would call *end* and *back* the headwords in the following:

the end of the alley

the back of my hand

The traditional diagram would, in fact, treat these noun phrases and those with the quantifiers in the same way, with the *of* phrase as a modifier of the noun, even though the quantifiers are much more clearly functioning as determiners. The branching diagram demonstrates the structure of these noun phrases much more clearly than the traditional diagram does:

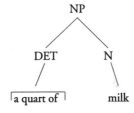

Despite such questions of analysis, however, native speakers know intuitively how to follow these determiner "rules," as complicated and arbitrary as they sometimes are.

AUXILIARIES

Like the determiners and the other structure classes, the **auxiliary** class is limited in membership and closed to new members. Counting the forms of *have* and *be*, the modals, and the forms of *do*, the list of regular auxiliaries numbers around two dozen:

have	be	can	do
has	is	could	does
had	are	will	did
having	am	would	
	was	shall	
	were	should	
	been	may	
	being	might	
		must	
		ought to	

The following modal-like verbs also function as auxiliaries; they are sometimes referred to as semi-auxiliaries.

have to	get	be to
has to	gets	be going to
had to	got	used to

He <u>has to</u> go.	I <u>used to</u> smoke.
She <u>got</u> started.	The bus <u>is to</u> leave at noon.
She <u>got to</u> go.	<u>I'm going</u> to take the bus.

Two other modal-like verbs, *dare* and *need*, commonly appear in negative sentences and in questions:

She <u>need not</u> go.	<u>Dare</u> we go?
I <u>don't dare</u> go.	<u>Need</u> you go?

In function, the auxiliaries are perhaps more intimately connected to verbs than are determiners to nouns, because they alter the verb's meaning in important ways and often determine the form that it takes. Another important difference between the auxiliaries and the other structure classes lies in their systematic distribution. Determiners and qualifiers are somewhat arbitrary in distribution; but with few exceptions every verb can be signaled (preceded) by every auxiliary. The modals *have* and *do* combine with every verb; only *be* is restricted in any way, as we saw in Chapter 3,

where we noted a few verbs, such as *seem*, that rarely appear with *be +
-ing*. This regularity accounts for the relative ease with which nonnative
speakers are able to learn the compound verb forms of English.

Exercise 53

Underline the auxiliaries in the following sentences. Circle the main verb.

1. I have been having problems with my car.
2. I used to use two different brands of motor oil, one for summer
   and one for winter.
3. I should not have eaten those tomatoes.
4. Apparently some people can't even look at tomatoes.
5. Sally will be helping us with the party.
6. Margie has to leave early.
7. The kids are really frustrating me today.
8. The teens can be frustrating years for some adolescents.
9. The gymnasts should continue practicing their balance-beam
   routines.
10. I am keeping my opinions to myself.

QUALIFIERS

As the following lists demonstrate, many words can act as **qualifiers** or
intensifiers to alter the meaning of adjectives and adverbs. (In the adjective test frame the word *very* is used to represent all the possible qualifiers.)
On the diagram the qualifier is attached to the adjective or adverb:

The following list of qualifers can be used with the positive form of
most adjectives, such as *good* and *soft*, and with adverbs of manner, such
as *rapidly:*

very	really	fairly
quite	pretty	mighty
rather	awfully	too

A second group of qualifiers can be used with the comparative degree of adjectives, such as *better* and *nicer,* and with comparative adverbs, such as *sooner, later, nearer,* and *farther:*

still	some	no
even	much	

A number of others have a limited distribution:

<u>right</u> now	<u>just about</u> there
<u>wide</u> awake	<u>almost</u> there
<u>just</u> so	

Many others are used in colloquial expressions:

<u>right</u> nice	<u>darn</u> right
<u>damn</u> sure	<u>real</u> pretty

Some of the adverbs of manner, the *-ly* adverbs, are themselves used as qualifiers with certain adjectives:

<u>dangerously</u> close	<u>politically</u> expedient
<u>particularly</u> harmful	<u>technically</u> possible
<u>absolutely</u> true	<u>especially</u> difficult

Because of the *-ly* adverbs in their ranks, the qualifier class, like that of the determiners, is not a closed class. In fact, the qualifier, like the determiner, can be thought of as both a word class and a sentence function. It has attributes of both.

Investigating Language *12.1*

You may recall that the title of Chapter 5 includes a definition of *adverbial:* "Modifiers of the Verb." The discussion in that chapter takes you through the various forms that modify verbs—adverbs, prepositional phrases, noun phrases, verb phrases, and clauses. Note that the form-class "adverb" is one of five structures that function adverbially.

Now compare that definition with the traditional definition of *adverb*—one you may be familiar with: "a word that modifies a verb, an adjective, or another adverb." This definition clearly includes what we are calling qualifiers—that is, words that modify adjectives and adverbs.

Consider what you have learned about the form classes—nouns, verbs, adjectives, and adverbs; add to that what you know about structures that modify verbs—the adverbials. Then examine the following sentences, two of which are marked as ungrammatical:

Quite slowly the old man climbed the stairs.

*The old man quite climbed the stairs.

The girl is very young.

*The girl will very come over to babysit.

At this point you probably agree that these sentences suggest a difference between adverbs and the qualifiers *quite* and *very* that justifies their membership in separate word classes. Three other words traditionally classified as adverbs in the earlier list of qualifiers are *really, fairly,* and *rather.* Try to come up with sentences that would justify their membership in both classes, adverb and qualifier.

In their relationship to the form classes, the qualifiers are different from the determiners and auxiliaries in that they are optional; all the adjectives and adverbs they modify can appear without them. This is not true of the relationship of nouns and verbs to their signal words: Many nouns cannot appear without a determiner; and two of our verb forms— the *-en* and the *-ing* forms—require auxiliaries to function as the main verb. But like the other structure words, the qualifiers signal the form classes; they provide a useful test to differentiate adjectives and adverbs from other parts of speech.

PREPOSITIONS

The **preposition** (meaning "placed before") is a structure word found in pre-position to—preceding—a noun phrase or other nominal. Prepositions are among our most common words in English; in fact, of our twenty most frequently used words, eight are prepositions: *of, to, in, for, with, on, at,* and *by.*[1] Prepositions can be classified according to form as simple (one-word) or phrasal (multiple-word):

---

[1] This frequency count, based on a collection of 1,014,232 words, is published in Henry Kučera and W. Nelson Francis, *Computational Analysis of Present-Day English* (Providence, RI: Brown University Press, 1967).

Simple Prepositions. The following list includes the most common simple prepositions:

aboard	below	in	since
about	beneath	into	through
above	beside	like	throughout
across	between	near	till
after	beyond	of	to
against	but (except)	off	toward
along	by	on	under
amid	concerning	onto	underneath
among	despite	out	until
around	down	outside	up
as	during	over	upon
at	except	past	with
atop	for	per	within
before	from	regarding	without
behind			

Note that we label these words as prepositions only when they are followed by a nominal—that is, only when they are part of prepositional phrases. In the following sentence, for example, *up* functions as an adverb, not a preposition:

The price of sugar went <u>up</u> again.

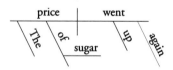

Words like *up* also function as particles in two-word, or phrasal, verbs, such as *hold up:*

A masked gunman <u>held up</u> the liquor store.

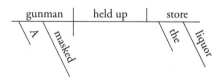

But in the following sentence, *up* is a preposition, part of a prepositional phrase:

We hiked <u>up the steep trail</u>.

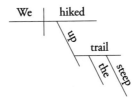

Investigating Language   *12.2*

Speaking of *up*, a "Dear Abby" correspondent sent in the following passage, which he had clipped from the *Reader's Digest* twenty-five years ago:

It's easy to understand UP, meaning toward the sky or toward the top of a list. But when we waken, why do we wake UP? At a meeting, why does a topic come UP? And why are participants said to speak UP? Why are officers UP for election? And why is it UP to the secretary to write UP a report?

The little word is really not needed, but we use it anyway. We brighten UP a room, light UP a cigar, polish UP the silver, lock UP the house and fix UP the old car.

At other times, it has special meanings. People stir UP trouble, line UP for tickets, work UP an appetite, think UP excuses and get tied UP in traffic.

To be dressed is one thing, but to be dressed UP is special. It may be confusing, but a drain must be opened UP because it is stopped UP.

We open UP a store in the morning, and close it UP in the evening. We seem to be all mixed UP about UP.

In order to be UP on the proper use of UP, look UP the word in the dictionary. In one desk dictionary, UP takes UP half a page; and the listed definitions add UP to about 40.

If you are UP to it, you might try building UP a list of the many ways in which UP is used. It may take UP a lot of your time, but if you don't give UP, you may wind UP with a thousand.

Try your hand at writing a similar passage using DOWN or OUT or OFF.

Phrasal Prepositions. Two-word, or **phrasal, prepositions** consist of a simple preposition preceded by a word from another category, such as an adverb, adjective, or conjunction:

according to	as for	but for
ahead of	aside from	contrary to
along with	because of	except for

instead of	out of	thanks to
next to	prior to	up to

Most three-word prepositions consist of preposition + noun + preposition:

by means of	in lieu of
in accordance with	in search of
in back of	in spite of
in case of	on account of
in charge of	on behalf of
in front of	

In a traditional diagram, we usually treat these phrases as we do the simple prepositions:

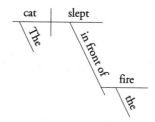

Because *in front of the fire* can also be analyzed as one prepositional phrase embedded in another, we can diagram it another way:

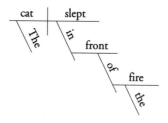

The foregoing lists include the most common, although certainly not all, of the prepositions. We use prepositions automatically, as we do the other structure words, in spite of the sometimes subtle differences in meaning they can express: *below* the stairs, *beneath* the stairs, *under* the stairs, *underneath* the stairs; *in* the room, *inside* the room, *within* the room. As native speakers we understand these distinctions, and, except for a few idioms that sometimes cause problems of usage, we rarely hesitate in selecting the right preposition for the occasion.

Exercise **54**

Identify the prepositions in the following sentences.

1. The Renfords have lived in San Diego since 1985.
2. They like it there because of the climate.
3. I like Minnesota in spite of the cold winters.
4. Prior to 1985, the Renfords lived in Baltimore.
5. According to some economists, the financial health of the Social Security System is in jeopardy.
6. I look on such predictions with skepticism.
7. Except for eggs, which rarely go up in price, the cost of groceries is going out of sight.
8. Thanks to rice and beans, I manage to eat well on my meager income.
9. Between you and me, my grocery money may not hold out until payday.
10. I am finding it hard to live within my budget.

CONJUNCTIONS

We use **conjunctions** to connect words and phrases and clauses within the sentence and to connect the sentences themselves. Within the sentence our most common connectors are the simple *coordinating* conjunctions and the *correlative* conjunctions. For joining sentences we use, in addition, the *subordinating* conjunctions, also called subordinators, and *conjunctive adverbs*. The relative pronouns and relative adverbs also function as connectors, joining relative, or adjectival, clauses to nouns.

Coordinating Conjunctions. We can use a coordinate structure for any slot in the sentence by using a **coordinating conjunction** (*and, or, but, yet, nor, for*):

Riley <u>and</u> Tim worked out on Saturday.

I'll meet you at the ticket window <u>or</u> in the grandstand.

The dessert was simple <u>yet</u> elegant.

Eager to start her new job <u>but</u> sad at the thought of leaving home, Kris packed the car <u>and</u> drove away from the familiar house on Maxwell Avenue.

The coordinating conjunctions also join complete sentences:

> I disapproved of his betting on the horses, <u>and</u> I told him so.
>
> He claims to have won fifty dollars, <u>but</u> I suspect he's exaggerating.
>
> She won't come to the party, <u>nor</u> will she explain why.

Notice that the clause introduced by *nor* requires a subject–auxiliary shift. The coordinating conjunction *for* joins only complete sentences, not structures within the sentence. Even though it is close in meaning to *because,* it differs from the subordinating conjunctions: The *for* clause cannot open the sentence.

Correlative Conjunctions. Like the coordinating conjunctions, the **correlative conjunctions** (*both–and, either–or, neither–nor, not only–but also*) connect both complete sentences and elements within the sentence. Within the sentence *either–or* and *neither–nor* are used alike:

> I will $\begin{Bmatrix} \text{either} \\ \text{neither} \end{Bmatrix}$ meet you in the lobby $\begin{Bmatrix} \text{or} \\ \text{nor} \end{Bmatrix}$ come to your room.

As a connector of sentences, *neither–nor* requires the subject–auxiliary shift; *either–or* does not:

> Neither <u>will I</u> meet you in the lobby, nor <u>will I</u> come to your room.
>
> Either <u>I will</u> meet you in the lobby, or <u>I will</u> come to your room.

Not only–but also can be used both within and between sentences:

> <u>Not only</u> the coaches and players <u>but also</u> the fans had high hopes of defeating the Crimson Tide.
>
> <u>Not only</u> did the government's experts underestimate the economic downturn that 2001 would bring, <u>but</u> they <u>also</u> delayed in taking action to change its course.

This sentence would be equally grammatical with either *but* or *also,* rather than both.

Both–and does not connect complete sentences; it connects elements within the sentence only:

> Franco is a good sport, <u>both</u> on <u>and</u> off the playing field.
>
> <u>Both</u> Jeanne <u>and</u> Marie worked hard to get their manuscript finished on schedule.

Conjunctive Adverbs (Adverbial Conjunctions). As their name suggests, the **conjunctive adverbs** join sentences to form coordinate structures as other conjunctions do, but they do so with an adverbial emphasis. The following list also includes some of the most common simple adverbs and adverbial prepositional phrases that function as sentence connectors:

Result:	*therefore, so, consequently, as a result, of course*
Concession:	*nevertheless, yet, at any rate, still, after all, of course*
Apposition:	*for example, for instance, that is, namely, in other words*
Addition:	*moreover, furthermore, also, in addition, likewise, further*
Time:	*meanwhile, in the meantime*
Contrast:	*however, instead, on the contrary, on the other hand, in contrast, rather*
Summary:	*thus, in conclusion, then*
Reinforcement:	*further, in particular, indeed, above all, in fact*

Conjunctive adverbs differ from other conjunctions in that, like many other adverbials, they tend to be movable within their clause; they need not introduce the clause:

> My tax accountant is not cheap; <u>however</u>, the amount of tax she saves me is far greater than her fee.

> My tax accountant is not cheap; the amount of tax she saves me, <u>however</u>, is far greater than her fee.

The punctuation of coordinate sentences with conjunctive adverbs is explained on page 221. Their rhetorical effects are discussed in Chapter 14.

Subordinating Conjunctions. The subordinators are conjunctions too, although their function is not to connect independent ideas as equals but rather to show a relationship between two ideas in which one of them is a *dependent* or *subordinate clause*. Like the conjunctive adverbs, the **subordinating conjunctions** are both single words and phrases:

Time:	*when, whenever, after, as, before, once, since, till, until, now that, while, as long as, as soon as*
Concession:	*though, although, even though, if, while*
Contingency:	*if, once*
Condition:	*if, in case, as long as, unless, provided that*
Reason:	*because, since, as long as*
Result:	*so, so that*
Comparison:	*as, just as, as if*
Contrast:	*while, whereas*

Subordinate clauses come both before and after the main clause. This movability feature provides a test to differentiate between subordinators and coordinators. The coordinators—the conjunctive adverbs as well as the coordinating conjunctions—introduce only the second clause:

> We decided to walk because we missed the last bus.
>
> Because we had missed the last bus, we decided to walk.

> We decided to walk, for we had missed the last bus.
>
> *For we had missed the last bus, we decided to walk.

> We missed the bus, so we decided to walk.
>
> *So we decided to walk, we missed the bus.

When set off by commas, subordinate clauses can also come between the subject and the predicate, where they will get added emphasis:

> The City Council members, <u>before they adjourned their meeting</u>, voted to give a special award to the recycling center.
>
> None of the players, <u>as they sat in the dugout</u>, heard the fans fighting in the stands just above them.

In addition to these simple and phrasal subordinators, we have a small group of correlative subordinators—two-part structures, one of which is part of the main clause: *as–so, the–the, no sooner–than.*

> <u>As</u> General Motors goes, <u>so</u> goes the nation.
>
> <u>The</u> more I go on fad diets, <u>the</u> more weight I seem to add.
>
> He had <u>no sooner</u> arrived <u>than</u> he started to give orders.

Another two-part subordinator occurs in the clause of comparison:

> There were <u>more </u>people at the political rally <u>than</u> we expected.
>
> The governor gave a much <u>longer</u> speech <u>than</u> the program called for.

Adverbial subordinate clauses are discussed in Chapter 5. Subordinate clauses that are more clearly sentence modifiers and elliptical clauses are discussed in Chapter 8.

Relatives. **Relative pronouns**—*who (whose, whom), which,* and *that*—and **relative adverbs**—*where, when, why*—perform a dual function in the noun phrase: They introduce the relative, or adjectival, clause, connecting the clause to the noun it modifies; and they play a part in the clause, the pronouns as nominals and the adverbs as adverbials.

> The price *that* <u>we pay for sneakers</u> keeps going up.
>
> The man *who* <u>lives next door</u> rides a bicycle to work.

Nothing exciting ever happens in the small town <u>*where* I was born</u>.

Adjectival clauses are also introduced by the **indefinite relative pronouns**, such as *whoever* (*whomever, whosever*), *whichever, whatever,* and *what* (meaning "that which"). These pronouns are called "indefinite" because they have no specific referent; instead, they have a general, indefinite reference. (See page 303.)

Adjectival clauses are discussed in detail in Chapter 6.

INTERROGATIVES

As their name implies, the **interrogatives**—*who, whose, whom, which, what, how, why, when, where*—introduce questions:

<u>What</u> are you doing here?

<u>How</u> did you get here?

<u>When</u> are you leaving?

The function of such questions, of course, is to elicit particular information.

The interrogatives also introduce clauses that fill NP slots in the sentence patterns. Such clauses are sometimes referred to as *indirect questions:*

Tell me <u>why he came</u>.

I wonder <u>who came with him</u>.

<u>Whose car he drove</u> is a mystery to me.

These clauses, which function as nominals, are discussed in Chapter 7. (We should note that the interrogatives are the same words that in other contexts are classified as relative pronouns or relative adverbs. For that reason the term *interrogative* more accurately labels a function than a word class.)

EXPLETIVES

Rather than providing a grammatical or structural meaning as the other structure-word classes do, the **expletives**—sometimes defined as "empty words"—generally act simply as operators that allow us to manipulate sentences in a variety of ways. In the diagrams of these sentences, the expletives are independent of the basic sentence.

There. The *there* transformation, as we saw in Chapter 4, enables us to delay the subject in certain kinds of sentences, thus putting it in the position of main stress, which generally falls in the predicate half of the sentence:

An airplane is landing   →   There's an airplane landing
on the freeway.   on the freeway.

The expletive *there* plays no grammatical role in the sentence. To analyze the sentence, you have to discover its underlying form by eliminating the expletive and shifting the subject in front of the *be*.

The *there* transformation as a rhetorical tool is discussed in Chapter 14.

That. One of our most common expletives, *that,* introduces a nominal clause:

I hope that our exam is easy.

Unlike the relative pronoun *that,* which introduces adjectival clauses, the expletive *that* plays no part in the clause.

"Expletive" is not the only label given to this use of the word *that;* it is sometimes called a "nominalizer," because its function is to turn a clause into a nominal, that is, a noun phrase substitute. And sometimes it is called a "subordinator." The label "expletive" is used by traditional grammarians to emphasize the "empty word" quality of *that,* in that it serves strictly as an operator; it plays no role in the clause itself. The use of *that* in nominal clauses is taken up in detail in Chapter 7.

Or. The expletive *or* introduces an explanatory appositive:

The study of sentences, or syntax, helps us appreciate how much
we know when we know language.

The African wildebeest, or gnu, resembles an ox.

This *or* should not be confused with the conjunction *or,* which indicates an alternative (as in coffee or tea). The expletive introduces an equivalent in an appositive role.

The diagram shows its expletive role:

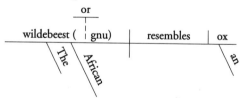

As. Another fairly common expletive introduces certain object complements in Patterns IX and X:

We elected him as president.

The diagram shows the role of *as* outside of the grammatical structure of the sentence:[2]

Leaving out the *as* does not change the meaning of this sentence; whether to choose it or not is usually a matter of emphasis or rhythm. With verbs like *refer to, think of,* and *know,* however, *as* is required with the object complement:

I refer to Professor Buck <u>as</u> a woman of character.

I think of her <u>as</u> a woman of many talents.

I think of her <u>as</u> exceptionally clever.

I know her <u>as</u> a friend.

If* and *Whether (or not). These two expletives serve as nominalizers, turning yes/no questions into nominal clauses:

I wonder <u>if the test will be easy</u>.

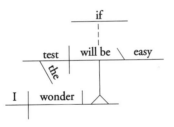

---

2. An alternative analysis for these phrases with *as* is to consider them prepositional phrases:

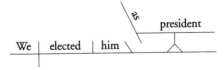

Admittedly, the word *as* presents something of a problem; however, to call it an expletive, or operator, does help alleviate the problem somewhat. First, it makes clear the membership of these sentences in Patterns IX and X, pointing out the optional nature of *as* with some of the verbs. It also avoids the introduction of what would be a deviant prepositional phrase: a preposition followed by an adjective (I consider him *as exceptionally clever*). Other prepositions do not take adjectives as objects. Finally, it acknowledges the resemblance between the role of *as* in these sentences and the expletive role of *or* and *that* in the previous sections, where the *or* and *that* have no grammatical role in the sentence itself.

It doesn't matter <u>whether I study or not</u>.

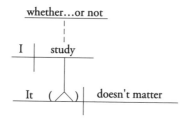

(You'll recall that for the other kind of questions—the information, or *wh-*questions—interrogative words act as nominalizers: I wonder <u>what I should study</u>.)

PARTICLES

The **particle**, which combines with a verb to produce a phrasal verb (look *up*, find *out*, turn *in*, look *into*), can be thought of as an alternative function that prepositions and adverbs perform rather than a word class of its own. Both transitive and intransitive verbs combine with particles:

> We <u>turned in</u> at midnight. (intransitive)

> The police <u>looked into</u> the allegations. (transitive)

Phrasal verbs are discussed on pages 37–38 and 40–41.

Exercise 55

Label the class of each underlined word.

1. I found some rare stamps <u>and</u> postmarks <u>on</u> <u>an</u> old envelope <u>in</u> the attic.

2. <u>Four</u> friends of mine <u>from</u> the dorm waited in line <u>for</u> sixteen hours, <u>for</u> they were determined to get tickets <u>for</u> the World Series.

3. <u>As</u> the experts predicted, the Republicans chose <u>an</u> ultraconservative <u>as</u> their party's candidate <u>at</u> the convention.

4. We should <u>be</u> arriving <u>by</u> six, <u>but</u> don't wait for us.

5. Our group <u>of</u> tourists will take <u>off</u> at dawn <u>if</u> the weather permits.

6. We <u>are</u> now studying the structure <u>of</u> sentences, <u>or</u> syntax, in <u>our</u> English class.

7. We <u>will</u> warm up <u>with</u> a game of one-on-one <u>while</u> we wait for the rest of the players.

8. We had <u>too</u> many problems with our <u>two</u> new puppies, so we gave them both <u>to</u> the neighbors.

CHAPTER 12
Key Terms

Adverbial conjunction

Article

Auxiliary

Conjunction

Conjunctive adverb

Coordinating conjunction

Correlative conjunction

Definite article

Demonstrative pronoun

Determiner

Expanded determiner

Explanatory appositive

Expletive

Indefinite article

Indefinite pronoun

Intensifier

Interrogative

Mass noun

Modal-like verb

Number

Particle

Phrasal preposition

Possessive noun

Possessive pronoun

Postdeterminer

Predeterminer

Preposition

Qualifier

Relative

Semi-auxiliary

Subject–verb agreement

Subordinating conjunction

QUESTIONS

?

for DISCUSSION

1. Prepositions and particles are among the most difficult words in the language for foreign speakers to master. Why do you suppose this is so? Look at the following sentences. How would you explain the selection of prepositions to a learner of English?

   Be sure to fill out the form carefully.

Be sure to fill in the form carefully.

I like to jog in the early morning.
I like to jog on a sunny morning.

Our house burned down last week.
All of my books burned up.

I'm working on my math.
I'm really working at it.

2. In what sense are *dare, get,* and *have to* modal-like? How do they differ from modals? In thinking about this question, consider their place in the verb-expansion rule.

   In what sense are these verbs *not* like the other modals? Consider the following examples:

   He has to work this afternoon.
   Does he have to work this afternoon?

   Do I dare walk alone?
   You dare not walk alone around here at night.

   He got fired.
   He was fired.
   He wasn't fired.
   He didn't get fired.

3. In answering an interviewer's question, an economist recently said, "I do not foresee any improvement in the economy, absent any change in the elements that are driving it." What part of speech is *absent?*

4. In an article entitled "The Big Nine" (*Atlantic,* March 1988), Cullen Murphy reports on a 1923 study in which the lexicographer G. H. McKnight identified nine words in our language that comprise one-quarter of all spoken words. (A list of forty-three accounts for one-half.) Here are the nine: *and, be, have, it, of, the, to, will,* and *you.* Identify their word classes.

   Murphy did his own research of written texts, ranging from an IRS document to the "Wizard of Id" comic strip and came up with similar results. You might find it interesting to evaluate your own writing. Then write a paragraph in which you use none of the nine—just to see if you can do it. Describe the difference—perhaps in tone or in rhythm—if any.

5. The *New Yorker* reported an apology printed by a Sydney, Australia, newspaper for inadvertently changing a word in a reader's letter to the editor. The correspondent had written, "The number of speakers became unmanageable." The paper changed *the* to *a*. How can one little structure word make such a difference?

CLASSROOM APPLICATIONS

1. Sometimes the source of ambiguity in headlines and telegrams is the lack of structure words. Demonstrate the double meaning of the following ambiguous passages by adding structure words:

PENTAGON REQUESTS CUT

SHIP SAILS TODAY

UNION DEMANDS CHANGE

POLICE PATROLS STRIP

Now come up with headlines of your own that have more than one meaning.

2. One of the assessment tools commonly used in the field of English as a Second Language (ESL) is the "Cloze" test, which consists of a prose passage with deletions at regular intervals. Language proficiency is then judged on the student's ability to fill in the blanks correctly. Here are two Cloze passages with every fifth word deleted. The first is from the opening paragraph of Shelby Foote's first volume of *The Civil War: A Narrative.* The second is the last paragraph in a *Time* article about weather on the occasion of the 1993 Mississippi flood. Fill in the blanks with what you think has been deleted; then compare your answers with those of your classmates. Is there more agreement among you on the form class words or on the structure words? Which blanks do you think would be the most difficult for a nonnative speaker?

1. It was a Monday _____ Washington, January 21; Jefferson Davis _____ from his seat in _____ Senate. South Carolina had _____ the Union a month _____ , followed by Mississippi, Florida, _____

Alabama, which seceded at _____ rate of one a
_____ during the second week _____ the new
year. Georgia _____ out eight days later;_____ and
Texas were poised _____ go; few doubted that
_____ would, along with others._____ more than
a decade _____ had been intensive discussion
_____ to the legality of _____, but now the argu-
ment _____ no longer academic.

2. What is new about _____ weather is that, for
_____ first time, some of _____ factors that help
shape _____ may be man-made. Experts _____ it
may be decades _____ we are certain what _____
the buildup of greenhouse _____ or the depletion of
_____ ozone layer has had _____ the global climate. Last _____ flooding and heat wave _____ as
a warning that _____ we wait for the _____ to tell
us what's _____ with the weather, it _____ be too
late to _____ anything about it.

CHAPTER 13

Pronouns

CHAPTER PREVIEW

Pronouns are among our most common words. You will rarely encounter a passage of two or more sentences that doesn't contain several pronouns. In fact, the sentence you just finished reading contains three.

We looked briefly at pronouns in earlier chapters when we substituted them for noun phrases in order to demonstrate where the subject ended and the predicate began:

The county commissioners (they) have passed a new ordinance.

The mayor's husband (he) spoke against it.

The mayor (she) was upset with him.

These substitutions—*they, he,* and *she*—are among the personal pronouns, the kind you probably recognize most readily. But there are many other classes of pronouns as well—reflexive, demonstrative, relative, indefinite, and others. In this chapter we will look at all of the pronouns, pointing out places where a conscious understanding of the system can be helpful to you as a writer.

As their name suggests, **pronouns** are words that stand for nouns. Perhaps a more accurate label would be *pronominal,* because they actually stand for any construction that functions as a nominal in the sentence. We refer to the noun or nominal that the pronoun stands for as its **antecedent.**

Most pronouns replace an entire noun phrase:

The pistachio nut ice cream at Meyer's Dairy is delicious.

   It   is delicious

My friend Jan, who lives in Houston, is coming to visit.

   She   is coming to visit.

Pronouns also substitute for other nominals, such as verb phrases and clauses:

The judge warned my brother to stay out of trouble.

He told me   that,   too.

Where you spend your time is none of my business.

$\left\{ \begin{matrix} \underline{That} \\ \underline{It} \end{matrix} \right\}$ is none of my business.

Not all pronouns are alike. The label *pronoun* actually covers a wide variety of words, many of which function in quite different ways. A brief description of the main classes of pronouns follows.

PERSONAL PRONOUNS

The **personal pronouns** are the ones we usually think of when the word *pronoun* comes to mind. We generally label them on the basis of person and number:

PERSON	NUMBER		
	Singular	*Plural*	
1st	I	we	[person(s) speaking]
2nd	you	you	[person(s) spoken to]
3rd	he she it	they	[person(s) spoken about]

For example, we refer to *I* as the "first-person singular" pronoun and *they* as the "third-person plural." In addition, the third-person singular pronouns include the feature of **gender:** masculine (*he*), feminine (*she*), and neuter (*it*).

The term **pronoun–antecedent agreement** describes our selection of the pronoun in reference to the noun or noun phrase (or nominal) it replaces: The personal pronoun "agrees with" its antecedent in both number and, for third-person singular, gender. Note that the second person (*you*) has neither gender nor number distinctions.

The forms given in the preceding set are in the **subjective** (traditionally called "nominative") case; this is the form used when the pronoun serves as the subject or subject complement. The personal pronouns also inflect for the **possessive** case, as nouns do, and the **objective** case, an inflection that nouns do not have.

Subjective:	I	we	you	he	she	it	they
Possessive:	my	our	your	his	her	its	their
	(mine)	(ours)	(yours)	(his)	(hers)		(theirs)
Objective:	me	us	you	him	her	it	them

The possessive forms of pronouns function as determiners. The objective case is used for pronouns in all the object slots: direct object, indirect object, and object complement. A pronoun as object of the preposition is also in the objective case, with one exception: The preposition *of* usually takes the possessive case, producing a structure called the "double possessive."

With common nouns we often use the *of* prepositional phrase in the place of the possessive noun:

the car's engine = the engine of the car

the day's end = the end of the day

But in the case of names and personal pronouns, we often use the possessive case in addition to *of:*

Tim's friend = a friend <u>of Tim's</u>

his friend = a friend <u>of his</u>

my class = a class <u>of mine</u>

Alternative forms of the possessive case, shown in parentheses in the previous chart, are used when the headword of the noun phrase is deleted:

This is <u>my book</u>.   This is <u>mine</u>.

This is <u>her book</u>.   This is <u>hers</u>.

Possessive nouns can also be used without headwords:

This is <u>John's book</u>.   This is <u>John's</u>.

<u>Mary's book</u> is missing.   <u>Mary's</u> is missing.

The third person singular *it*, the most neutral of the personal pronouns, is sometimes used as an "anticipatory" subject, as we saw in the discussion of cleft sentences and nominals. In some cases it has clear pronoun status, as in this passage from Robert Frost's poem "Stopping by Woods on a Snowy Evening":

> My little horse must think <u>it</u> queer
> <u>To stop without a farmhouse near.</u>

In other cases the *it*, while acting as a grammatical subject, remains essentially an empty word:

> It is raining
> It's a nice day.

The plural pronoun *they* can also have neutral status:

> They say best men are moulded out of faults. [Shakespeare]

We should also note that our system of personal pronouns—or, to be more accurate, a gap in the system—is the source of a great deal of the sexism in our language. Missing from the system is a singular third-person pronoun that refers to either gender. Our plural pronoun (*they*) includes both male and female; but when we need a pronoun to refer to an unidentified person, such as "the writer" or "a student" or "the doctor," the long-standing tradition has been to use the masculine (*he/his/him*):

> The writer of this news story should have kept <u>his</u> personal opinions out of it.

Attempts to promote *s/he* in recent years have been unsuccessful. Perhaps someday the plural pronoun will be accepted for both singular and plural, a usage that has become quite common in speech:

> Someone broke into our car last night; <u>they</u> stole our tape deck and all our tapes.

(This issue is discussed further on pages 338–343.)

Exercise 56

Substitute personal pronouns for the underlined nouns and noun phrases in the following sentences.

1. <u>Luis and Maria</u> have bought a new house.
2. <u>Bev and I</u> will be going to the game with <u>Otis</u>.
3. Betsy bought <u>that beautiful new car of hers</u> in Charlotte.
4. Both of <u>her cars</u> are gas guzzlers.
5. There have always been uneasy feelings between <u>the neighbors and my husband</u>.

6. I want <u>Tony</u> to approve of <u>the project</u>.

7. The kids gave <u>their father and me</u> a bad time.

8. <u>My brother, who works for the Navy in California</u>, spends <u>his weekends</u> in Las Vegas.

The difference between *who* and *whom* is identical to the difference between *I* and *me* or between *she* and *her* or between *he* and *him* or *they* and *them.* We say

    I know him.   and   He knows me.

    She helps them.   and   They help her.

We also say

    The man <u>who loves me</u> is coming to visit,

where *who* is the subject in its own clause, the subject of the verb *love,* and

    The man <u>whom I love</u> is coming to visit,

where *whom* is the direct object of *love.*

    The topic under discussion here, as you have probably guessed, is that of **case.** If you are a native speaker of English, nothing in the previous discussion comes as a surprise. Chances are you've never been tempted to say,

    *Him knows I.   or   *Them helps she.

However, you may have been tempted to say—you may even have heard yourself say—

    The stranger <u>who I helped this morning</u> was very grateful.

For some reason, that *who* doesn't sound as strange, or as ungrammatical, as

    *Amy knows I.   or   *They help she.

If you consider the position of *who* in its clause, you can probably figure out why that sentence about the stranger is so easy to say—and why it sounds o.k.

    The point is that we do *say* it. The fact that we do is one of the differences between speech and writing. But in writing, you'll want to figure out the appropriate case for the object position:

    The stranger <u>whom I helped this morning</u>…

You can use your understanding of case to edit yourself.

Objects of prepositions. The direct object slot, of course, is not the only object slot in our sentences. The slot following prepositions—the object of the preposition—is probably even more common than the direct object. And except for the preposition *of* (noted on page 295), this slot too requires the objective case when the object of the preposition is a pronoun:

> I bought this <u>for him</u>.   Pam bought this <u>for me</u>.
>
> I gave it <u>to them</u>.   They came <u>with her</u>.

Again, you're probably not tempted to say "for he" or "to they" or "for I" or "with she." You automatically use the objective case of personal pronouns after prepositions. And native speakers are probably never tempted to say,

> *This secret is just <u>between we</u>.

So why do you suppose it's so common to hear,

> *This secret is just <u>between Joe and I</u>
>
> *and*
>
> *This secret is just <u>between he and I</u>?

It's a question worth considering.

REFLEXIVE PRONOUNS

Reflexive pronouns are those formed by adding *-self* or *-selves* to a form of the personal pronoun:

PERSON	SINGULAR	PLURAL
1st	myself	ourselves
2nd	yourself	yourselves
3rd	himself herself itself	themselves

The reflexive pronoun is used as the direct object, indirect object, and object of the preposition when its antecedent is the subject of the sentence:

> John cut <u>himself</u>.

> I glanced at <u>myself</u> in the mirror.

I cooked dinner for Shelley and <u>myself</u>.

Joe cooked dinner for Gary and <u>himself</u>.

Investigating Language   *13.2*

For each of the italicized noun phrases in the following sentences, substitute either a personal pronoun or a reflexive pronoun. Assume that a name or noun phrase appearing more than once in a sentence refers to the same person or people in each instance:

1. Randall cut *Randall* while *Randall* was shaving.
2. The Kim sisters threw a party for *the Kim sisters.*
3. Although Selma ran a good race, two other runners finished ahead of *Selma.*
4. The wardrobe mistress gave *the wardrobe mistress* all the credit for the play's success.
5. The students said that *the students* understood the assignment.

Formulate a rule to explain the system you used to choose the class of pronoun. In what way do the following sentences depart from the system you described:

6. Joe cooked dinner for Gary and myself.
7. We decided that Gary and myself would do the dishes.

The rule you formulated for the first five sentences probably explains that the reflexive pronoun is used only when those identical noun phrases appear in the same clause, as in sentences 1, 2, and 4. In sentences 3 and 5, the repeated noun phrase appears in a second clause. However, in the last two examples, those requirements are absent: In 6 there is no antecedent for *myself* in the sentence; in 7, *Gary and myself* and its antecedent *we* are in separate clauses. While sentences like the last two are fairly common in speech, the written standard calls for personal pronouns:

Joe cooked dinner for Gary and me.

We decided that Gary and I would do the dishes.

Both versions are unambiguous; both forms of the first-person pronoun, *me* and *myself,* can refer only to the speaker. However, with third-person pronouns different forms produce different meanings:

Joe cooked dinner for Gary and <u>himself</u> (Joe).

Joe cooked dinner for Gary and <u>him</u> (someone else).

Exercise 57

Fill the blanks with the appropriate reflexive pronouns.

1. Gabrielle gave _____ a black eye when she fell.
2. Li and Mei-Ling cooked _____ salmon for dinner.
3. The ceramic figurine sat by _____ on the shelf.
4. We sat by _____ in the front row.
5. Paulo cooked a delicious Mexican feast for Rosa and _____ .
6. Wearing our new designer jeans, Sheila and I admired _____ in the mirror.

INTENSIVE PRONOUNS

Also known as the *emphatic reflexive pronouns,* the **intensive pronouns** have the same form as the reflexives. The intensive pronoun serves as an appositive to emphasize a noun, but it need not directly follow the noun:

I <u>myself</u> prefer chocolate.

I prefer chocolate <u>myself</u>.

<u>Myself</u>, I prefer chocolate.

Because *myself* is in apposition to *I* in all three versions, the diagram will not distinguish among them:

I (myself)	prefer	chocolate

RECIPROCAL PRONOUNS

Each other and *one another* are known as the **reciprocal pronouns.** They serve either as determiners (in the possessive case) or as objects, referring to previously named nouns. *Each other* generally refers to two nouns; *one another* to three or more.

Juan and Claudia help <u>each other</u>.

They even do <u>each other's</u> chores.

All the students in my study group help <u>one another</u> with their homework.

DEMONSTRATIVE PRONOUNS

In our discussion of determiners we noted that the selection of a determiner is based on certain inherent features, such as definite or indefinite, countable or noncountable. The **demonstrative pronouns**, one of the subclasses of determiners, include the features of "number" and "proximity":

PROXIMITY	NUMBER	
	Singular	*Plural*
Near	this	these
Distant	that	those

<u>That</u> documentary we saw last night really made me think, but <u>this</u> one is simply stupid.

<u>Those</u> trees on the ridge were almost destroyed by gypsy moths, but <u>these</u> seem perfectly healthy.

Like other determiner classes, the demonstrative pronoun can be a substitute for a nominal as well as a signal for one:

<u>These old shoes and hats</u>   will be perfect for the costumes.

<u>These</u>   will be perfect for the costumes.

To be effective as a nominal, the demonstrative pronoun must replace or stand for a clearly stated antecedent. In the following example, *that* does not refer to "solar energy"; it has no clear antecedent:

Our contractor is obviously skeptical about solar energy. <u>That</u> doesn't surprise me.

Such sentences are not uncommon in speech, nor are they ungrammatical. But when a *this* or *that* has no specific antecedent, the writer can usually improve the sentence by providing a noun headword for the demonstrative pronoun—by turning the pronoun into a determiner:

Our contractor is obviously skeptical about solar energy. <u>That attitude</u> (or <u>His attitude</u>) doesn't surprise me.

A combination of the two sentences would also be an improvement over the vague use of *that:*

Our contractor's skepticism about solar energy doesn't surprise me.

The vague reference of *this* and *that* has the same fuzzy quality as the broad-reference relative clause, which you read about in Chapter 8:

> Our contractor is skeptical about solar energy, <u>which doesn't surprise me</u>.

A singular demonstrative pronoun can also function as a qualifier:

> I can't imagine being <u>that</u> rich.

> I can't believe I weigh <u>this</u> much.

RELATIVE PRONOUNS

The **relative pronouns** are *who, which,* and *that*; they introduce clauses that modify the nouns that are the antecedents of these pronouns. *Who* inflects for both possessive and objective cases: *whose* (possessive) and *whom* (objective). The case of *who* is determined by the part it plays (its function) in its own clause:

> The man <u>who lives across the street</u> sold me his car.

In this sentence *who* renames *man*, its antecedent, and plays the part of subject in the relative (adjectival) clause. In the next sentence the relative pronoun is in the possessive case form, *whose*:

> The man <u>whose car I bought</u> was not very honest about the gas mileage.

Here *whose*, the possessive relative pronoun, again stands for *man;* in its own clause it acts as the determiner for *car*, the role that possessives normally play.

Whose also acts as the possessive form of *which:*

> The wooded ridge across the valley, <u>whose trees were infested by gypsy moths</u>, turned brown in mid-June.

The relative pronoun *that* is generally subjective or objective, never possessive:

> I lost the backpack <u>that I bought yesterday</u>.

That renames *backpack* and acts as the object within its own clause. In object position, *that* can be omitted:

> I lost the backpack <u>I bought yesterday</u>.

When *that* is the subject of the clause, however, it cannot be omitted:

> The route <u>that will get us there fastest</u> is straight across the mountain.

The *wh-* relative pronouns also have an expanded form with the addition of *-ever*, known as **indefinite relative pronouns**: *whoever, whosever, whomever,* and *whatever.* The expanded relatives have indefinite referents rather than specific ones as the simple relatives do:

I will give a bonus to <u>whoever works the hardest.</u>

I will pay you <u>whatever you deserve.</u>

I will call <u>whomever the doctor recommends.</u>

What is also considered an indefinite relative pronoun when it introduces adjectival clauses and means "that which":

I will pay you <u>what you deserve.</u>

The relative (adjectival) clauses are also discussed in Chapter 6.

INTERROGATIVE PRONOUNS

The list of **interrogative pronouns** is similar to that of the relatives: *who* (*whose, whom*), *which,* and *what.* The interrogatives, as their name suggests, are among the question words that produce information questions (in contrast to yes/no questions):

<u>What</u> do you want for lunch?

<u>Whose</u> car is that?

<u>Which</u> section of history did you get?

As we saw in Chapter 4, the interrogative word plays a part in the sentence. For example, in the first preceding sample sentence, *what* fills the direct object slot: "You do want *what* for lunch." In a sentence such as "What flavor do you prefer?" the interrogative *what* acts as a determiner for the noun *flavor.* In the other two examples listed, *whose* and *which* also act as determiners: *whose car, which section.* Because of this modifying function, *which, what,* and *whose* are sometimes classified as **interrogative adjectives**.

The interrogative pronouns also introduce nominal clauses and, like the relative pronouns, play a part in the clause. There is an indirect question involved in such clauses—either implied or stated, asked or answered:

Tell me <u>what you want for lunch.</u>

I know <u>who gave you that black eye.</u>

Nominal clauses are discussed in Chapter 7.

INDEFINITE PRONOUNS

The **indefinite pronouns** include a number of words listed earlier as determiners:

enough	many	all	either
few	much	both	neither
fewer	several	every	none
less	more	each	some
little	most	any	

One is also commonly used as a pronoun (as are the other cardinal numbers—*two, three,* etc.) along with its negative, *none.* As a pronoun, *one* often replaces only the headword, rather than the entire noun phrase:

> *The blue <u>shoes</u> that I bought yesterday* will be perfect for the trip.

> *The blue <u>ones</u> that I bought yesterday* will be perfect for the trip.

The personal pronoun, on the other hand, would replace the entire noun phrase:

> <u>They</u> will be perfect for the trip.

The pronouns *every, any, no,* and *some* can be expanded with *-body, -thing,* and *-one:*

some	body thing one	every	body thing one
any	body thing one	no	body thing one (two words)

(Note that *every* and *no,* which function as determiners, do not function as pronouns except in the expanded forms shown here.)

These pronouns can take modifiers in the form of clauses:

> <u>Anyone</u> *who wants extra credit in psych class* can volunteer for tonight's experiment.

They can also be modified by verb phrases:

> <u>Everyone</u> *reporting late for practice* will take fifteen laps.

And by prepositional phrases:

<u>Nothing</u> *on the front page* interests me anymore.

And, unlike most nouns, they can be modified by adjectives in posthead-word position:

I don't care for <u>anything</u> *sweet.*

I think that <u>something</u> *strange* is going on here.

Exercise **58**

Underline the pronouns in the following sentences. Identify the subclass to which each pronoun belongs.

1. When Roberto ordered a pizza with everything, I ordered one too.
2. Millie and Bev shopped at almost every store in the mall but couldn't find any shoes they liked.
3. Someone was standing in the shadows, but we couldn't see who it was.
4. All that I had for lunch was that overripe banana.
5. Booker and Marcus didn't eat much either, but they both ate more than I did.
6. I myself will go along with whatever you decide.
7. One hour of studying was enough for me.
8. Quarreling among themselves, the committee members completely disregarded one another's suggestions.
9. Tell me what color I should paint your sign.
10. The employment office will find a job for whoever wants one.

CHAPTER *13*
Key Terms

Antecedent	Indefinite pronoun
Case	Indefinite relative pronoun
Demonstrative pronoun	Intensive pronoun
Emphatic reflexive pronoun	Interrogative adjective
Gender	Interrogative pronoun

Number

Objective case

Person

Personal pronoun

Plural

Possessive case

Pronoun

Pronoun–antecedent agreement

Proximity

Reciprocal pronoun

Reflexive pronoun

Relative pronoun

Sexism

Singular

Subjective case

QUESTIONS
?
for DISCUSSION

1. The relative pronoun agrees with its antecedent in person and number but not necessarily in case. How do the following sentences illustrate that statement?

   I don't know the women who live next door.

   It was I whom you spoke with on the phone.

2. Comment on the choice of pronouns in the following sentence. Are they correct?

   I didn't know who felt worse: him or me.

3. In Chapter 2, Discussion Question 8, we looked at the following ambiguous sentence:

   Rosa called her mother.

   What is the source of the ambiguity? Would a sentence about Mario and father instead of Rosa and mother be equally ambiguous? What's the difference?

4. What is the difference in the meaning of *one* in the following sentences?

   One farmer told me there hadn't been rain in eight weeks.

   One can only hope that the weather changes soon.

5. The following sentences include clauses introduced by expanded, or indefinite, relative pronouns:

   I will give a bonus to whoever works hardest.

   I will pay you whatever you deserve.

   I will call whomever the doctor recommends.

Explain why a traditional diagram of such sentences would look like this:

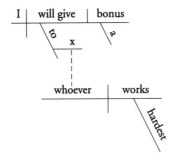

How should we diagram the sentences with *whatever* and *whomever?*

6. How do you explain the use of *we* and *us* in the following sentences?

> We graduates lined up to go into the gym.
>
> The speaker told us graduates that we were the hope of the future.

Is *we* used correctly in the following sentence?

> It wasn't a good idea for we dishwashers to go on strike.

7. Here's a statement with a single, straightforward meaning:

> I invited everyone in the class to my party.

The follow-up sentence is not quite as clear; in fact, it's ambiguous:

> Everyone didn't come.

Here's another ambiguous sentence:

> Everything doesn't cause cancer.

Paraphrase the two negative sentences in two ways to demonstrate their meanings. Then consider the meaning of *everyone* and *everything* and explain why their use with the negative should produce ambiguity.

8. Examine the following sentences; then explain the "rule" that a nonnative speaker learning English must understand in connection with *some* and *any*.

> Mario wants some dessert. Rosa doesn't want any.
>
> I lent someone my book. I didn't lend anyone my class notes.
>
> Are you going somewhere special for lunch? I'm not going anywhere.

Why would that student of English find the following sentences ungrammatical?

Anyone can have seconds on dessert.

I haven't given some of the volunteers their assignments yet.

What would happen to the meaning of those two sentences if that English student were to follow the "some/any rule"?

CLASSROOM APPLICATIONS

1. In this chapter you have seen eight subclasses of pronouns. Although they are all words you commonly use, you may not have realized they are all pronouns. Write a passage with as few sentences as possible using at least one pronoun from each of the eight subclasses: personal, reflexive, intensive, reciprocal, demonstrative, relative, interrogative, and indefinite.

2. The following passage, from "The Winter of Man," an essay by Loren Eiseley, was published in 1972, a time when the masculine pronoun was accepted as a generic singular. Note too the use of *man* in reference to humans in general.

> Students of the earth's climate have observed that man, in spite of the disappearance of the great continental ice fields, still lives on the steep edge of winter or early spring. The pulsations of these great ice deserts, thousands of feet thick and capable of overflowing mountains and valleys, have characterized the nature of the world since man, in his thinking and speaking phase, arose. The ice which has left the marks of its passing upon the landscape of the Northern Hemisphere has also accounted, in its long, slow advances and retreats, for movements, migrations and extinctions throughout the plant and animal kingdoms.
>
> Though man is originally tropical in his origins, the ice has played a great role in his unwritten history. At times it has constricted his movements, affecting the genetic selection that has created him. Again, ice has established conditions in which man has had to exert all his ingenuity in order to survive. By contrast,

there have been other times when the ice has withdrawn farther than today and then, like a kind of sleepy dragon, has crept forth to harry man once more. For something like a million years this strange and alternating context has continued between man and the ice.

Revise the passage in order to eliminate the sexist language.

PART V

Grammar for Writers

For some of you, this book has been your introduction to the study of grammar. Terms like *noun* and *adjective* and *predicate* and *participle* were completely new to you or, at best, distant echoes from a long-ago classroom. Others of you brought a fairly substantial understanding of parts of speech and sentences from grammar classes that may have begun in the fifth grade and continued through the twelfth, very likely starting every year with parts of speech and ending with complex sentences. The majority of you are probably somewhere in between, with memories of a grammar unit for a year or two, perhaps in the seventh and eighth grades.

Those differing backgrounds reflect actual differences in the way in which grammar is taught throughout this country. Grammar is not a subject area that curriculum experts agree on; it is, in fact, an area fraught with controversy and misunderstanding. Part of that misunderstanding lies in the problem of definition. What exactly do we mean by grammar?

In this book we have defined grammar as that unconscious system of rules that enables a speaker of the language to produce sentences. We have emphasized the automatic and unconscious nature of that system; we have encouraged you to make use of your subconscious expertise.

For many people, however, grammar is a set of do's and don't's, those traditional rules about correctness that they remember from their grammar classes. Grammar brings to mind red marks on essays pinpointing commas splices and spelling errors; it recalls warnings about ending sentences with prepositions or beginning them with conjunctions. It's understandable for people to assume that the purpose of studying grammar is to avoid error. This definition and this purpose—and the methods of teaching that reflect such a definition and purpose—contribute to the misunderstanding.

If the purpose of studying grammar is to avoid error, then it should follow that learning the "rules of grammar" will make you a better writer because you will avoid errors in your compositions. There are two problems with this assumption: First, the purpose for studying grammar goes far beyond that of avoiding error; and, second, composition teachers realized long ago that error-free writing is not necessarily effective writing. To write effectively, you must be sensitive to your readers, to take into account what they already know, what they expect, what they need to know. You must think about how the words and the structures you choose will accomplish your purpose.

Unfortunately, methods of teaching grammar have been slow to change. The traditional view of language as a set of rules to be memorized ignores all of the insights of twentieth-century linguistics. Instead, teachers should help their students recognize and explore their own innate competence and then help them use that knowledge when they write.

Composition teachers know that students who understand the structure of their language are in a position to recognize their own weaknesses and strengths as writers, to revise and edit their own writing; further, they can offer helpful evaluations in peer-review sessions. Students who have explored their own language expertise, who have acquired a vocabulary for discussing language, hold a decided advantage over those who have not.

We firmly believe that understanding English grammar—the title and theme of this book—does make a difference for writers and teachers of writing: It does so by enhancing a writer's confidence, by giving the writer control, by illuminating all the choices that are available. That control and those choices are the subject matter of Chapter 14, "Rhetorical Grammar."

Rhetorical Grammar

CHAPTER PREVIEW

Although the term *rhetorical* and its noun form, *rhetoric,* have not been used up to now, you'll find a description of rhetoric in Chapter 1 under the topic of Language Variety:

> In the written language, too, what is appropriate or effective in one situation may be inappropriate or ineffective in another. The language you use in letters to your family and friends is noticeably different from the language you use when applying for a job. Even the writing you do in school varies, depending on the situation. The language of the personal essay you write for your composition class has an informality that would be inappropriate for a business report or a history research paper. As with speech, the purpose and the audience make all the difference.

If this description of rhetoric sounds to you like plain old common sense, you're absolutely right. You've always understood that the person you're talking to or writing to—in other words, your audience—will have an effect on what you say and the way you say it.

In terms of writing, then, rhetoric means that the situation—the topic, the purpose, and the audience—will make a difference in the way you write. And to a great extent that rhetorical situation will determine the grammatical choices you make, choices about sentence structure and vocabulary, even about punctuation. Rhetorical grammar is about those choices.

In this final chapter we will discuss the ways you can use the grammar knowledge you have gained in the preceding chapters, the ways in which that knowledge can make a difference to you as a writer and, perhaps, as a teacher of writing. We will begin, as the book began, by considering sentence patterns; we will see how the features of those patterns, including their transformations and the choice of verbs, can heighten your awareness of the effect your writing has on your audience. We will then take up the grammatical choices and rhetorical effects of other sentence features.

SENTENCE PATTERNS

Cohesion. An important concept for helping you to understand sentence patterns back in Chapter 2 was the recognition that sentences consist of a series of slots, some required and some optional, filled by structures of various forms. Your understanding of the slots can be helpful in thinking about sentence **cohesion**, the ties that connect each sentence to what has gone before—the glue that gives a paragraph and an essay unity. Part of that glue is provided by information in the sentence that the reader knows or expects, information that has already been mentioned.

Let's look at the paragraph you just read as an example of that cohesive glue and reader expectation. The first sentence introduces the topic of sentence slots, with a brief description. You can be fairly certain that the next sentence will say something further about sentence slots. And, yes, it does: The subject of the next sentence is *Your understanding of the slots.* In other words, the sentence opens with old, or known, information. You don't expect to get to the new information, the purpose of the sentence, until you get to the predicate slot. And there it is in the predicate—new information, even a new term, *cohesion,* and the descriptive *glue.* And the third sentence? Again, you're not surprised to see known information—this time, *glue*—in the subject slot.

This known-to-new sequence is fairly typical for cohesive paragraphs, where the new information of one sentence becomes the known information of the next. In fact, the known–new sequence is so pervasive a feature of our prose that it is sometimes referred to as the **known–new contract.** The writer has an obligation, a contract of sorts, to fulfill expectations in the reader—to keep the reader on familiar ground. The reader has every right to expect each sentence to be connected in some way to what has gone before, to include a known element.

One of our most common known elements, certainly as strong as the repeated noun or noun phrase, is the pronoun. Consider how often the subject slot of the second sentence in a passage is filled by a pronoun, such as *she* or *he* or *it* or *they.* That pronoun is automatically tied to its antecedent, a previously mentioned nominal that it stands for. If there is no obvious antecedent, then the pronoun is not doing its cohesive job.

In the following passage, part of the opening paragraph of an essay by Annie Dillard, the first sentence introduces the topic, *a weasel,* in the subject slot. And, as you can see, the subject slots of the next three sentences are filled by the pronoun *he:*

> A weasel is wild. Who knows what **he** thinks? **He** sleeps in his underground den, his tail draped over his nose. Sometimes **he** lives in his den for two days without leaving. Outside, **he** stalks rabbits, mice, muskrats, and birds, killing more bodies than **he** can eat warm, and often dragging the carcasses home.

The pattern of known and new information in this passage, which is fairly common in descriptive writing, has a different schema from the earlier paragraph discussed. The earlier one, where the new information in one sentence becomes the known information of the next, might be diagrammed in this way:

$$A—B, B—C, C—D$$

In the weasel paragraph, where succeeding sentences repeated the subject, the schema would look like this:

$$A—B, A—C, A—D$$

Cohesion can also be enhanced by the information in an opening adverbial slot. For example, the opening of the fifth sentence in the weasel passage, *Outside,* provides a cohesive tie by contrasting with the "inside" designation *in his den* of sentence four. In narrative writing, adverbials of place or time often serve as the glue that connects sentences and paragraphs.

How can the known–new principle of cohesion help you as a writer? Are you supposed to stop after every sentence and estimate the cohesive power of your next subject? No, of course not. That's not the way writers work. But when you are revising—and by the way, revision goes on all the time, even during the first draft—you will want to keep in mind the issues of the known–new contract and reader expectation. You can learn to put yourself in your reader's shoes to see if you've kept your part of the bargain.

SENTENCE RHYTHM

One of the most distinctive features of any language—and one of the most automatic for the native speaker—is its sense of rhythm. Our language has a rhythm just as surely as music does—a regular beat. That sense of rhythm is tied up with the sentence patterns and with the known– new contract. If you read the opening sentence in this paragraph out loud, you'll hear yourself saying "one of the most" in almost a monotone; you probably don't hear a stressed syllable, a beat, until you get to *distinctive:*

one of the most disTINCtive

And you probably rush through those first four words so fast that you pronounce "of" without the *f*, making "one of" sound like the first two words in "won a prize."

The rhythm of sentences, what we call the **intonation** pattern, can be described as valleys and peaks, where the loudest syllables, those with stress, are represented by peaks:

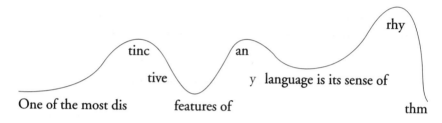

Not all the peaks are of the same height—we have different degrees of stress—but they do tend to come at fairly regular intervals. As listeners we pay attention to the peaks—that's where we'll hear the information that the speaker is focusing on. As speakers, we manipulate the peaks and valleys to coincide with our message, reserving the loudest stress, the highest peak, for the new information, which will be our main point of focus.

End Focus. The rhythm of a sentence is closely tied both to its two-part subject–predicate structure and to the known–new contract. The topic, or theme, stated in the subject will usually be a valley or low peak in the intonation contour, especially if it is known information; the prominent peak of stress, the focus on the new information, will come in the predicate; it will be close to the end of the sentence. Linguists describe this common rhythm pattern as **end focus**. It is a rhythm that experienced writers are sensitive to. Good writers, you can be sure, are tuned in to the rhythm of their own inner voice as they write; they understand how to manipulate sentences in order to control the way the reader reads them and to prevent misreading.

Read the following passage aloud and listen to the intonation pattern you give to the underlined sentence:

Did you hear what happened? Barbara wrecked her motorcycle yesterday. She was on her way to work when the car in front of her stopped suddenly—and she didn't.

You probably read that second sentence with the stress on *motor*. In a different context, however, the rhythm could change if the purpose of the sentence has changed. In the following passage, the known information has changed. Again, read it aloud and listen to the intonation:

> Sue told me that Barbara had an accident this morning on her way to work. But I think she got her facts wrong. <u>Barbara wrecked her motorcycle yesterday</u>.

This time you probably put the main stress on *yesterday*; in this context it would make no sense to stress *motorcycle*. Try reading the passage that way, and you'll easily recognize the problem: All the information in the last sentence up to the word *yesterday* is already known. In this context it is old information: "Barbara wrecked her motorcycle" is a repetition, albeit more specific, of "Barbara had an accident." As a reader, you know intuitively that it's not time to apply stress until you get beyond that old information, until you get to *yesterday*, the new focus.

You'll note, however, that the principle of end focus is still operating, with the main stress on the last sentence element. But imagine how awkward the sentence would be if the adverb *yesterday* were shifted to the beginning of the sentence. It would certainly be grammatical from a structural point of view; as you know, adverbials are movable, especially adverbials of time. Even in opening position the reader might recognize *yesterday* as the new information and give it main stress. But the sentence would certainly have lost its natural rhythm. Read the passage aloud, and you'll hear the problem:

> Sue told me that Barbara had an accident this morning on her way to work. But I think she got her facts wrong. Yesterday Barbara wrecked her motorcycle.

While sentence variety is certainly commendable, you won't want to shift an adverbial to the opening slot just for the sake of variety—certainly not if that adverbial is the new information.

Investigating Language *14.1*

Read the following passages, listening carefully to the intonation contour of each sentence. Indicate the words (or syllables) that get main stress. Compare your reading with that of your classmates. Identify the new information in each sentence. Does its position and emphasis fulfill the known–new contract?

1. <u>Never</u> invest in something you <u>don't</u> understand or in the <u>dream</u> of an artful salesperson. Be a <u>buyer, not a sellee</u>. <u>Figure</u> out what you want (be it life insurance, mutual funds or a vacuum cleaner)

and then shop for a good buy. Don't let someone else tell you what you need—at least not if he happens to be selling it. [Andrew Tobias, *Parade*]

2. Plaque has almost become a household word. It is certainly a household problem. But even though everyone is affected by it, few people really understand the seriousness of plaque or the importance of controlling it. Plaque is an almost invisible sticky film of bacteria that continuously forms on the teeth. Plaque germs are constantly multiplying and building up. Any dentist will tell you that controlling plaque is the single most important step to better oral health. [Advertisement of the American Dental Association]

3. To simulate chance occurrences, a computer can't literally toss a coin or roll a die. Instead, it relies on special numerical recipes for generating strings for shuffled digits that pass for random numbers. Such sequences of pseudorandom numbers play crucial roles not only in computer games but also in simulations of physical processes. [I. Peterson, *Science News*]

4. Frank evaluation of its [caffeine's] hazards is not easy. There is a vast literature on the effects of caffeine on the body, and for every study reaching one conclusion, seemingly there is another that contradicts it. Although most major health risks have been ruled out, research continues at a steady clip. [Corby Kummer, *Atlantic Monthly*]

SENTENCE TRANSFORMATIONS

Because end focus is such a common rhythm pattern, we can think of it as a part of the contract between writer and reader. The reader expects the main sentence focus to be in the predicate unless given a signal to the contrary. And we do have several such signals at our disposal.

Several of the sentence transformations we looked at in Chapter 4 allow the writer to shift the focus of the sentence, pointing the reader to a particular slot. The *it*-cleft transformation is one of the most versatile. Here are three variations of the sentence about Barbara, each of which guarantees that the reader will put the emphasis exactly where the writer intends for it to be:

1. It was Barbara who wrecked her motorcycle yesterday.

2. It was her motorcycle that Barbara wrecked yesterday.

3. It was yesterday that Barbara wrecked her motorcycle.

If sentence 3 had been included in that earlier passage about the accident, it would have been impossible for the reader to miss the new information; in the cleft transformation the emphasis is clearly on *yesterday*.

The *it*-cleft is not a structure you will want to overuse, but it certainly is useful—and almost foolproof—when it comes to controlling the rhythm of a sentence and directing the reader's focus.

Another cleft transformation, also described in Chapter 4, uses a *what* clause to direct the reader's attention. In the following sentence you will probably put the emphasis on *bothers:*

Mike's cynical attitude toward the customers really bothers me.

Here are two variations using the *what*-cleft:

What bothers me is Mike's cynical attitude toward the customers.

What bothers me about Mike is his cynical attitude toward the customers.

While all three versions mean essentially the same thing, the choice in a particular context will be determined in part by what the reader already knows—and consequently expects.

Another common sentence variation you saw in Chapter 4 is the *there* transformation, which allows the writer to focus on the subject by shifting it to the slot following *be*—either the predicating *be* or the auxiliary *be*:

Several hundred people were crowding the courtroom.

There were several hundred people crowding the courtroom.

Another big crowd was in the hallway.

There was another big crowd in the hallway.

The last paragraph in the previous Investigating Language exercise includes two *there* transformations in the second sentence:

There is a vast literature on the effects of caffeine on the body, and for every study reaching one conclusion, seemingly there is another that contradicts it.

Here the author undoubtedly wants the reader to put main stress on *vast literature* and on *another*.

Do writers consciously call up such rhythm-controlling devices from their grammar tool kits as they write? Do they tell themselves, "Time to use my trusty *it*-cleft, or should I delay this subject with the *there* transformation?" No, they probably don't. They may not even know labels like "transformation" and "cleft." But as experienced writers and readers, they're tuned in to sentence rhythm as they compose—especially as they revise. And you can be sure that in reading their own prose, whether silently or aloud, they are paying attention to sentence rhythm.

Unfortunately, the *there* and the cleft transformations are often misunderstood in handbooks and style manuals: They are seen as wordy, indirect ways of conveying ideas rather than as alternatives that give the writer a choice, that enable the writer to control the sentence focus. It's true, of course, that you won't want to overuse these transformations. You will want to consider the larger context, to pay attention to how many other *it* or *what* or *there* sentences occur in proximity. But certainly these kinds of sentence manipulations are valuable tools for the right occasion.

CHOOSING VERBS

Most writing teachers would probably agree that choosing verbs is one of the writer's most important jobs. The verb, after all, occupies the central, pivotal slot of the sentence pattern. A well-chosen verb not only heightens the drama of a sentence and makes its meaning clear; it can send a message to the reader that the writer has crafted the sentence carefully, that the idea matters.

Sometimes the culprit that keeps a sentence from sending that message is the phrasal verb, the verb + particle combination we saw in Chapter 2, known as an idiom: *turn down, bring about, put up with, take up, do away with, get on with, give up.* There's nothing wrong with these common idioms—and they certainly are common, part of our everyday speech. But the single-word synonym may be more precise—and it's always tighter:

> The legislature turned down the governor's compromise proposal.
> The legislature rejected. . .

> The lawyer turned down the prosecutor's offer of a plea bargain.
> The lawyer refused. . .

> The police are looking into the rumors about corruption.
> The police are investigating. . .

> The police are looking into the evidence.
> The police are analyzing. . .

Certainly another difference between the phrasal verb and its one-word counterpart is the level of formality: *To investigate* and *to analyze* sound more formal than *to look into.* In informal contexts, the idiom may be the best choice—for example, in a personal essay or narrative, or for a general audience, such as you might address in a letter to the editor of a newspaper. But for research papers or technical reports—and certainly for résumés and letters to prospective employers—the single-word version might be more effective. So one step in your revision process is to look carefully at (to *scrutinize*) the verbs that you have chosen—and recognize that you have a choice.

You may also have introduced some flabbiness simply by selecting a common garden-variety verb. In Chapter 3, you saw a list of the ten most frequently used verbs in English: *be, have, do, say, make, go, take, come, see,* and *get*. In many cases these are the verbs that take part in idioms. And because they have so many nuances of meaning, you can often find a more precise one.

Exercise 59

Revise the following passages by finding more precise alternatives to the italicized verbs. In some cases you will make changes other than just the verb substitution.

1. The small band of rebels *fought off* the army patrol for several hours, then *gave up* just before dawn. News reports about the event did not *give any specific details about* how many troops were involved.

2. The majority leader *has* a great deal of influence in the White House. He can easily *find a way around* the established procedures and go directly to the president, no matter what his party affiliation.

3. Several economists are saying that they *look forward to* an upturn in the stock market during the second half of the year. Others, however, maintain that interest rates must *stop their fluctuating* if the bull market is to prevail.

4. The night-shift workers took their complaints to the shop steward when the managers tried to *force* them into *giving up* their ten-cent wage differential.

5. The chairman of the Senate investigating committee *spoke against* the practice of accepting fees for outside speeches. He said that the new rules will *put a stop to* all such questionable fund raising. To some observers, such practices *are the same thing as* bribery. Several senators have promised to *come up with* a new compromise plan.

6. Dorm life changed drastically when colleges *did away with* their traditional "in loco parentis" role. In the old days, of course, there were always students who *paid no attention to* the rules. At some schools, where the administration would not *put up with* violations, students were routinely *kicked out*.

The Overuse of *Be*.   Another major culprit contributing to flabbiness is the overuse of *be* as the main verb. *Be* sentences commonly serve not only as topic sentences (as in the paragraph you're now reading), but as supporting sentences throughout the paragraph. You might be surprised, in checking a paragraph or two of your own prose, at how often you've used a form of *be* as the link between the known and the new information. An abundance of such examples—say, more than two or three in a paragraph—may constitute a clear "revise" message.

Sometimes you can eliminate *be* simply by substituting a different verb. We used this technique in rewriting the second sentence of the previous section:

> Most writing teachers would probably agree that choosing verbs
>
> is one of the writer's most important jobs. The verb, after all, i̶s̶ *occupies*
>
> the central, pivotal slot of the sentence pattern.

You may have noticed *be* in the first sentence too, which we didn't change. We could have written, "choosing verbs *constitutes* one of the writer's most important jobs," but that sounds a bit forced; it interferes with the natural rhythm.

Another technique for eliminating the flabbiness that *be* often brings with it is [Oops! There it is again!] to make use of appositives and absolute phrases and other kinds of modifiers to combine sentences, to combine ideas. For example, in the following passage the second and third sentences can become appositives, nominals that rename another nominal, which you studied in Chapter 7.

> Last year scientists announced the discovery of the smallest known primate. It is one of several species of Eosimias (dawn monkey). This extinct animal was no longer than a human thumb.

> *Revision:* Last year scientists announced the discovery of the smallest known primate, one of several species of Eosimias (dawn monkey), an extinct animal no longer than a human thumb.

In combining the following sentences, we have turned the subject complement of the second one, where *be* is the main verb, into a sentence appositive, punctuated with a dash:

> The play opened to rave reviews and standing-room-only crowds; it was a smashing success.

Revision: The play opened to rave reviews and standing-room-only crowds—a smashing success.

The sentence appositive acts as a summary statement that gives special focus to the idea of the main clause.

The Passive Voice. In Chapter 3 you learned how to transform a sentence in the active voice into the passive voice by adding *be + -en* to the verb and shifting the object to subject position. Here's one of the examples you studied:

> Active: *The committee discussed the report.*
>
> Passive: *The report was discussed by the committee.*

It's certainly possible that everything you've read in other books or heard from teachers about the passive voice has been negative—admonitions to avoid it because of wordiness or vagueness. In fact, however, the passive voice has a legitimate role to play in every kind of writing.

As with cleft sentences and the *there* transformation, the passive voice enables the writer to shift emphasis in the sentence, so that the reader will put the focus where it should be—on the new information. That passive shift can also provide transition between sentences. When the object of the action is the known information, the passive transformation can shift that information to the subject slot, where we generally find it.

In the earlier discussion of cohesion, on page 314, we looked at the pattern of known and new information in the paragraph about sentence slots. The subject of the third (and last) sentence includes the word *glue*, the known information from the previous sentence:

> Part of that glue is provided by information in the sentence that the reader knows or expects, information that has already been mentioned.

Part of that glue functions as the subject—but it's not the agent. We put the agent, the "doer" of the verb provided, in end-focus position because it is the new information. We used the passive transformation to do so.

Here's another example, the opening of a paragraph from *Time* about the destruction of the Brazilian rain forests. Note that in the second sentence, which is passive, the known information of the subject provides transition:

> If Americans are truly interested in saving the rain forests, they should move beyond rhetoric and suggest *policies* that are practical—and acceptable—to the understandably wary Brazilians. *Such policies* cannot be presented as take-them-or-leave-them propositions. If

the U.S. expects better performance from Brazil, Brazil has a right to make demands in return. [emphasis added]

Michael D. Lemonick

In the first sentence, *policies* is new information; in the second it is known.

The passive voice may also be appropriate if the identity of the agent is obscured in history or simply has no bearing on the discussion:

> In 1905 the streets of Patterson, California, were laid out in the shape of a wheel.

> Oregon's economy is closely tied to the lumber industry.

The passive voice is especially common—and deliberate—in technical and scientific writing, in legal documents, and in lab reports, where the researcher is the agent but to say so would be inappropriate:

> I increased the temperature to 450° for one hour. (*Active*)

> The temperature was increased to 450° for one hour. (*Passive*)

In some instances the passive voice is simply more straightforward:

> Joe was wounded in Vietnam.

In many situations, of course, the purpose of the passive is simply to avoid mentioning the agent:

> It was reported today that the federal funds to be allocated for the power plant would not be forthcoming as early as had been anticipated. Some contracts on the preliminary work have been canceled and others renegotiated.

Such "officialese" or "bureaucratese" takes on a nonhuman quality because the agent role has completely disappeared from the sentences. In the foregoing example the reader does not know who is reporting, allocating, anticipating, canceling, or renegotiating.

This kind of agentless passive is especially common in official news conferences, where press secretaries and other government officials explain what is happening without revealing who is responsible for making it happen. The faceless passive does an efficient job of obscuring responsibility, but it is neither efficient nor graceful for the writing that most of us do in school and on the job.

Sometimes student writers resort to the passive voice in order to avoid using *I*, perhaps because the paper has too many of them already or because the teacher has ruled out the first-person point of view:

> The incessant sound of foghorns could be heard along the waterfront.

But English is a versatile language: First person is not the only alternative. Here's a version of the sentence using *sound* as the verb:

> The foghorn sounded along the waterfront.

Here's one that describes the movement of the sound:

> The incessant sound of foghorns floated across the water.

Many times, of course, the writer simply doesn't realize that the passive voice may be the culprit producing the vagueness or wordiness of that first draft. For example, the writer of the following sentence ended a family Christmas story with no awareness of voice at all:

> That visit from Santa was an occurrence that would never be forgotten by the family.

The active version produces a tight, straightforward sentence:

> The family would never forget that visit from Santa.

The writer could also have found an active sentence that retains *visit* as the subject:

> That visit from Santa became part of our family legend.

The passive voice certainly has a place in every kind of prose. To avoid it simply for the sake of avoiding it often results in a stilted, unnatural voice. The choices we make when we write should always be made on the basis of rhetorical effectiveness, not on the misguided notion that certain structures are inherently weak or wordy or vague. When we read in our handbooks,

> The passive voice should be avoided,

we should celebrate the fact that the authors have found a way to put their most important word, *avoided*, in the position of end-focus and have used an efficient tool for doing so: the passive voice.

THE ABSTRACT SUBJECT

As you know from your study of the passive voice, the agent—the perpetrator—is not always the subject of the sentence; in some passive sentences it doesn't appear at all. However, the more concrete and active the sentence, the more likely the agent will function as the subject—or at least make an appearance. The more abstract and passive the sentence, the more likely the agent will be missing.

One common cause of abstraction is **nominalization, verbs that have been turned into nouns.** The word *occurrence* in the previous discussion about Santa's visit is one such example; we saw other nominalizations in Chapters 10 and 11 in connection with derivational affixes, the word endings that change the class of the word. Remember that a verb is an action word. A verb *shows* the action; but a noun simply *names* the action:

> The governor's <u>opposition</u> to abortion has caused many pro-choice organizations to work against his reelection.

> There is a growing <u>recognition</u> that forests are more valuable when left standing.

Our language, of course, is filled with nominalized verbs—most of which are useful, legitimate ways of expressing ideas. In the second sentence of this paragraph, for example, you'll see *discussion* and *connection*, both of which began as verbs (*discuss, connect*) and are now ordinary, everyday nouns.

But because nominalized verbs are so common and so easy to produce, they can become a trap for the unwary writer, introducing abstraction where concrete ideas belong. It's during the revision stage of writing that you'll want to be on the lookout. Ask yourself, Is the agent there and, if so, is it functioning as the subject? In other words, does the sentence explain *who is doing what*? If the answer is no, your sentence may be a prime candidate for revision.

Another source of abstraction and flabbiness is the sentence with a verb phrase or a clause as subject, rather than the usual noun phrase. You learned in Chapter 7 that these structures are grammatical, common substitutes for noun phrases. But because they are abstractions, they too may be pitfalls for the unwary writer. Again, the source of the problem may be that of the missing or misplaced agent:

> The <u>buying</u> of so many American companies and so much real estate by the Japanese is causing concern on Wall Street.

> With the opening of China to certain aspects of capitalism, <u>what is happening</u> is that American companies are looking for ways of expanding their markets and their product lines to take advantage of the situation.

> <u>Analyzing</u> the situation in the Far East has shown that opportunities for investment are growing.

Although we need context to tell us the best way to revise these sentences, we can see and hear a problem. The sentences seem to be about actions—but they can't show the action in a strong and concrete way because the agents of those actions are not there in subject position. This kind of agentless sentence should send up a red flag—a signal that here's a possible candidate for revision.

Exercise 60

Here are some sentences that might sound familiar—that is, you may write like this yourself. Try to achieve a more direct style and tone as you revise the sentences. Be especially alert to nominalizations and passives. The first three items are the examples from the preceding discussion. Remember to ask yourself, "Who is doing what?"

1. The buying of so many American companies and so much real estate by the Japanese is causing concern on Wall Street.

2. With the opening of China to certain aspects of capitalism, what is happening is that American companies are looking for ways of expanding their markets and their product lines to take advantage of the situation.

3. Analyzing the situation in the Far East has shown that opportunities for investment are growing.

4. In the biography of Lyndon Johnson by Robert Caro, an account of the Senate election of 1948 is described in great detail.

5. When Julie filled out an application for a work-study job, she was surprised to learn that a detailed financial statement would have to be submitted by her parents.

6. Getting his new pizza parlor to finally turn a profit has meant a lot of hard work and long hours for Tim.

7. The broadening of one's view of life and the establishment of worthy goals are both important aims of education.

8. The encouragement of the thinking process is also an important educational aim. Strategies should be developed by students for the understanding of problems and for their solutions.

THE SHIFTING ADVERBIALS

One of the writer's most versatile sentence elements is the adverbial, in terms of both form and position. As you recall from Chapter 5, the adverbs and prepositional phrases and noun phrases and verb phrases and clauses that add adverbial information can open the sentence or close it, or they can interrupt it somewhere in the middle. Sentence variety by itself is, of course, not a reason for opening or closing a sentence with an adverbial structure. Rather, you should understand the effects on cohesion and reader expectation that adverbials will have in different positions.

In Chapter 2 we labeled the adverbial function as "optional," but that label is somewhat misleading. Even though an adverbial is rarely needed from a grammatical point of view, the adverbial information is often the main idea—the new information of the sentence. For example, in the sentence,

I got up <u>early to study for my Spanish test,</u>

the two adverbials are optional in terms of the sentence pattern: *I got up* is a grammatical Pattern VI sentence. But the person saying or writing that sentence probably does so to convey time or purpose. It's the information in one or both adverbials that actually provides the main focus of the sentence.

<u>The decision about placement of adverbials, then, is connected to sentence focus and to the concept of known and new information.</u> If the adverbial is the main focus, it probably belongs at or near the end of the sentence. We saw an example of this situation earlier in this chapter with the sentence "Barbara wrecked her motorcycle yesterday," where the adverb *yesterday* supplied the new information. In opening position, the adverbial will usually tie the sentence to what has gone before, either because it is the known information or because it is providing a cohesive element, such as time sequence, with an adverbial like *then* or *later that day* or *on the following afternoon.*

The opening adverbial in the sentence you just read provides that cohesive tie: *In opening position* contrasts with the discussion in the previous sentence about closing position. In a sense it is known information, even though opening position had not been discussed in the paragraph up to that point: Common sense tells us that a sentence has an opening as well as a closing position.

The versatility of adverbials lies not only in the variety of positions they can occupy; it lies also in the variety of their forms. They can be short and brisk, or they can be long and relaxed, changing the tone and pace of the sentence.

I haven't been feeling well <u>lately.</u>

I haven't been feeling well <u>since September.</u>

I haven't been feeling well <u>since the beginning of the semester.</u>

I haven't been feeling well <u>since September, when the semester started.</u>

The Adverbial Clause. In Chapters 5 and 8 we emphasized the movable nature of adverbial and subordinate clauses. They are both movable and versatile: Our long list of subordinators enables us to connect ideas for a wide variety of reasons. Certainly subordinate clauses are common structures in our language: In speech we use them often and automatically. In writing, of course, they are not automatic, nor are they always used as effectively as they could be. Two problems that show up fairly often are related to the meaning of the sentence: (1) The wrong idea gets subordinated; and (2) the meaning of the subordinator is imprecise.

Here, for example, are two related ideas that a writer might want to combine into a single sentence:

> We worked hard for the candidates.
>
> We suspected they didn't stand a chance.

Here are some possibilities for connecting them:

> <u>While</u> we worked hard for the candidates, we suspected they didn't stand a chance.
>
> <u>Although</u> we worked hard for the candidates, we suspected they didn't stand a chance.
>
> We worked hard for the candidates, <u>even though</u> we suspected they didn't stand a chance.

We need context, of course, to know precisely what the connection between the two ideas should be, but given no other information, the last version expresses what would appear to be the logical relationship.

Perhaps an even more common problem than the imprecise subordinator is the compound sentence with no subordination—the sentence with two independent clauses, two equal focuses, that would be more accurate and effective with a single focus. The most common culprit is the compound sentence connected by *but:*

> The prime rate went down two percentage points during the last quarter, but government economists are still worried about high inflation and low productivity.

Because *but* is a coordinating conjunction, just as *and* is, the sentence has two ideas that, by reason of the structure, can be considered only as equals. But are they? Probably not.

Here's another compound sentence with *but*, a paragraph opener in an article about sleep. The paragraph preceding this one gives examples of accidents on the job connected with work schedules:

> The biological clock is flexible enough to adjust to slight changes in a person's work schedule, *but* in many industries rotations in shift work are so drastic that they play havoc with body rhythms, leaving employees unable to sleep at home and impairing their productivity at work. [emphasis added]

ERIK ECKHOLM, *New York Times Magazine*

Here the two clauses are clearly not equal: The main idea is the second clause. The idea in the first clause, although it has not previously appeared in the article, is presented as understood, as information the reader is assumed to know—the known information. The new information is in the second clause. Making the first clause subordinate will help the reader focus on the new idea:

> *Although* the biological clock is flexible enough to adjust to slight changes in a person's work schedule, in many industries rotations in shift work are so drastic that they play havoc with body rhythms, leaving employees unable to sleep at home and impairing their productivity at work.

Remember that a compound sentence has two points of focus that, in terms of structure, are equal. The compound sentence is effective only when that structure accurately reflects the relationship of the two ideas. If a single point of focus would be more accurate, then a subordinating conjunction should introduce one of the two ideas.

Exercise *61*

Combine each of the following groups of sentences into a single sentence by using subordination. In some cases you will want to reword the sentence. Remember that the subordinator you select will signal the relationship between the two ideas. You can probably come up with more than one possibility for each.

Although 1. The famous Gateway Arch is in St. Louis,
Kansas City claims the title "Gateway to the West."

Because 2. Our spring semester doesn't end until the second week of June,
Many students have a hard time finding summer jobs.

When 3. Thomas Jefferson acquired the Ozark Mountains for the United States in 1803,
That was the year of the Louisiana Purchase. *when*
We bought the Louisiana Territory from Napoleon.

Because 4. Many attorneys are unacquainted with oil and gas laws,
They are unable to offer advice concerning oil and gas leases to their clients.

Because 5. The neighbors added a pit bull to their pet population, which now numbers three unfriendly four-legged creatures,
We have decided to fence in our backyard.

Although 6. The human circulatory system is a marvel of efficiency,
It is still subject to a wide variety of degenerative diseases.

7. Carbohydrates ~~and~~ starches ~~and~~ are the body's prime source of energy. *and*
   Fad diets that severely restrict the intake of starches are nearly always ineffective. *and*
   ~~Such diets~~ can also be dangerous. *because*

8. Our congressman knows that the majority of voters in this district are upset with their tax rates. *because*
   They also don't like the way their tax dollars are being spent.
   He has made "No New Taxes" the main theme of his reelection campaign. *and*

9. Auto companies offered enticing cash rebates to buyers of new cars last January.
   Car sales increased dramatically. *when*

10. By 1890 the buffalo population of the West had been nearly wiped out.
    It now numbers about 60,000.
    About 400 ranchers in Colorado are raising buffalo for meat.

The Adverbs of Emphasis. As you know, the adverbials are versatile structures. They provide their information of time, place, manner, and the like in a variety of shapes; and they give the writer special flexibility because they can fill so many different slots—at the beginning, the middle, and the end of sentences. But there's another group of adverbials, mainly single-word adverbs, whose purpose is to emphasize a particular structure and thus control the pace and rhythm of the sentence.

Read the following sentences and note where you apply the main stress:

I hardly slept last night.

I slept hardly at all last night.

My roommate never has trouble sleeping.

Some people are always looking for trouble.

Joe tells me that he rarely stays awake past midnight.

You probably put the emphasis on *hardly, all, never, always,* and *rarely*

Given these examples, you can think of other words that you use for emphasis: other negatives, such as *seldom, barely, scarcely;* other time and frequency words, such as *afterwards, finally, sometimes;* and others expressing duration, such as *already, no longer, still.*

It's possible, of course, to write sentences in which these words would not have main stress, where the principle of end focus, for example, would still be in effect. But certainly these are words that you, as a writer, need

to recognize; they often wield the power in a sentence, controlling its intonation contour and making a difference in the message.

The Common *Only*. One of our most versatile—but also most frequently
misused—adverbials of emphasis is the common *only*. Like other empha-
sizers, *only* can change the focus of the sentence by directing the reader's
attention to a particular word:

> I'm taking <u>only twelve</u> credits this semester.
>
> The car <u>only looks</u> old; it's really quite new.
>
> Joe isn't <u>only handsome</u>; he's rich too.
>
> Paul cleans house <u>only on Saturdays</u>.

When you read these sentences, you'll find yourself putting nearly equal
emphasis on both *only* and the word that follows it.

But there's also a common problem with *only*: It's frequently misplaced—and most of the time we don't even notice!

> I'm only taking twelve credits this semester.
>
> Paul only cleans house on Saturdays.
>
> We're only going to be gone for two or three days.
>
> Jane refuses to watch the Super Bowl; she only likes baseball.

Even songwriters get it wrong:

> I only have eyes for you.

A well-placed *only* can strengthen the sentence focus. It sends a message to the reader that the writer has crafted the sentence carefully.

STYLE

Everything we write, we write "with style," in one sense of the word—
when the word refers simply to an individual's way of writing. You have
your own style of writing, just as you have your own style of walking and
whistling and wearing your hair. We also use the word *style* to characterize the overall impression of a piece of writing, such as the plain style, the
pompous style, the official style. When you follow advice about being brief
and using simple words, the outcome will be a plain style; words that are
too fancy will probably result in a pompous style.

The word *style* is also used in connection with variations in sentence
structure, with the structural and punctuation choices that you as a writer
can use to your advantage. For example, in the second sentence of the

previous paragraph, three verb phrases in a series are connected with two *and*s and no commas:

> walking and whistling and wearing your hair

It could have been written with two commas and only one *and:*

> walking, whistling, and wearing your hair

Or only commas

> walking, whistling, wearing your hair

Such stylistic variations have traditionally occupied an important place in the study of rhetoric. In fact, the Greeks had names for every deviation from ordinary word order and usage, and Greek orators practiced using them. Some of the more common ones you're familiar with, such "figures of speech" as simile, metaphor, and personification. But many of them, you probably don't even notice—such as the shift, in both this sentence and the previous one, of the direct object to opening position. In this section we will examine the rhetorical effects that these and other variations in sentence structure and punctuation can have.

Word Order Variation. Variation from the standard subject–verb–object word order is fairly common in poetry; it can be effective in prose as well, partly because it is uncommon. In the following sentence, Charles Dickens made sure that the reader would hear the contrast between *has* and *has not:*

> Talent, Mr. Micawber has; money, Mr. Micawber has not.

Another fairly common rearrangement occurs when a clause as direct object opens the sentence, as you saw in the previous paragraph.

> Which of these calls seemed more mysterious, it is not possible to say.
>
> JAMES AGEE

Robert Frost used this variation, too, in the first line of his famous poem "Stopping by Woods on a Snowy Evening":

> Whose woods these are, I think I know.

Notice that all these variations put special emphasis on the verb, the slot that would normally be in a valley when the sentence has a direct object.

With certain adverbs in opening position, the subject and the auxiliary can be reversed:

> Never before had I seen such an eerie glow in the night sky.
> Rarely do I hear such words of praise.

You'll notice that the opening adverbial is a peak of stress.

The following sentence, written by Winston Churchill, illustrates another kind of shift in word order. Here the very last noun phrase in the sentence is the grammatical subject:

> Against Lee and his great Lieutenant [Stonewall Jackson], united for a year of intense action in a comradeship which recalls that of Marlborough and Eugene, were now to be marshaled *the overwhelming forces of the Union.* [emphasis added]

When you read this sentence aloud, you can hear your voice building to a peak of stress on *overwhelming forces,* just as Churchill planned. In fact, it's hard to read the sentence without sounding Churchillian.

Ellipsis. Another fairly common stylistic variation is the use of ellipsis, where part of the sentence is simply left out, or "understood," usually for the purpose of avoiding repetition. In the following description of Stonewall Jackson, Churchill used ellipsis in both sentences. In the first, he left out the linking verb in all but the first clause. The tightness of the sentence actually reflects the description of Jackson's character:

> His character was stern, his manner [was] reserved and usually forbidding, his temper [was] Calvinistic, his mode of life [was] strict, frugal, austere.

> Black-bearded, pale-faced, with thin, compressed lips, aquiline nose, and dark, piercing eyes, he slouched in his weather-stained uniform a professor-warrior; yet [he was] greatly beloved by the few who knew him best, and [he was] gifted with that strange power of commanding measureless devotion from the thousands whom he ruled with an iron hand.

Notice also in the last sentence that in the clause after the semicolon both the subjects and the verbs are understood.

The Coordinate Series. Many of the structural variations that writers use for special effects occur in connection with coordinate structures—pairs and series of sentences and sentence parts. One effective way of changing the emphasis in coordinate structures entails a small deviation from the usual way of using conjunctions, as you saw in the example about "walking, whistling, and wearing your hair." In a series of three or more structures, we generally use commas between the parts of the series, and we use a conjunction before the final member. Here's another example:

> At the class reunion, we laughed, reminisced, and sang the old songs.

Here are two variations. Read them aloud and listen to the differences.

> At the class reunion we laughed and reminisced and sang the old songs.

> At the class reunion we laughed, reminisced, sang the old songs.

The differences are subtle, but meaningful. The first variation puts emphasis on each verb with a fairly equal beat: / and / and /. It also puts a lilt in your voice. The second variation, the one without conjunctions, has an open-ended quality, as though the list were incomplete. The writer seems to be saying, "I could go on and on; I could tell you much more."

The following sentence, from Churchill's description of Stonewall Jackson, includes that second technique. The phrases themselves have no conjunctions, as a regular series would, nor does the final series of adjectives:

> His character was stern, his manner reserved and usually forbidding, his temper Calvinistic, his mode of life strict, frugal, austere.

The omission of the conjunction contributes to the strictness and frugality of style that echo the words themselves. With conjunctions, the sentence would lose that echo:

> His mode of life was strict and frugal and austere.

The Introductory Appositive Series. In the following passages, the sentence opens with a series of noun phrases that act as appositives to the subject. In the first example, Churchill describes Queen Victoria:

> High devotion to her royal task, domestic virtues, evident sincerity of nature, a piercing and sometime disconcerting truthfulness—all these qualities of the Queen's had long impressed themselves upon the mind of her subjects.

The following description is from a *Time* article on the Vikings, written by Michael D. Lemonick and Andrea Dorfman:

> Ravagers, despoilers, pagans, heathens—such epithets pretty well summed up the Vikings for those who lived in the British Isles during medieval times.

Often the noun phrase series is in apposition to a pronoun as subject, as in this example from William Golding:

> Political and religious systems, social customs, loyalties and traditions, they all came tumbling down like so many rotten apples off a tree.

Notice, too, in these examples that the series does not include a conjunction before the last member.

The Deliberate Sentence Fragment. The sentence fragments that composition teachers flag with a marginal "frag" are the unintentional kind, usually the result of punctuation errors, the most common being the subordinate clause punctuated as a full sentence. But not all fragments are errors. Experienced writers know how to use them effectively—noun phrases or verb phrases that invariably call attention to themselves. The first two examples are from novels of John le Carré:

> They remembered the tinkling of falling glass all right, and the timid brushing noise of the young foliage hitting the road. <u>And the mewing of people too frightened to scream.</u>
>
> *The Little Drummer Girl*

> Our Candidate begins speaking. <u>A deliberate, unimpressive opening.</u>
>
> *A Perfect Spy*

In the following paragraph from *Love Medicine* by Louise Erdrich, we are hearing fragmented thoughts—ideal candidates for sentence fragments. You'll notice that some are simple noun phrases, some are absolutes—a noun with a modifier following—and some are subordinate clauses. But, obviously, all are deliberate:

> <u>Northern lights</u>. Something in the cold, wet atmosphere brought them out. I grabbed Lipsha's arm. We floated into the field and sank down, crushing green wheat. We chewed the sweet kernels and stared up and were lost. Everything seemed to be one piece. <u>The air, our faces, all cool, moist, and dark, and the ghostly sky</u>. Pale green licks of light pulsed and faded across it. <u>Living lights</u>. Their fires lobbed over, higher, higher, then died out in blackness. At times the whole sky was ringed in shooting points and puckers of light gathering and falling, pulsing, fading, rhythmical as breathing. <u>All of a piece</u>. <u>As if the sky were a pattern of nerves and our thought and memories traveled across it</u>. <u>As if the sky were one gigantic memory for us all</u>. <u>Or a dance hall</u>. And all the world's wandering souls were dancing there. I thought of June. She would be dancing if there were a dance hall in space. She would be dancing a two-step for wandering souls. <u>Her long legs lifting and falling</u>. <u>Her laugh an ace</u>. <u>Her sweet perfume the way all grown-up women were supposed to smell</u>. <u>Her amusement at both the bad and the good</u>. <u>Her defeat</u>. <u>Her reckless victory</u>. <u>Her sons</u>.

Repetition. Repetition has come up before in these pages—in both a positive and a negative sense. On the positive side, repetition gives our sentences cohesion: The known–new contract calls for the repetition, if not of words, then of ideas. It is part of the glue that holds sentences together. But we also have a negative label for repetition when it has no purpose, when it gets in the reader's way: Then we call it redundancy. If you've heard warnings about redundancy, if you've seen "red" in the margins of your essays, you might hesitate to use repetition deliberately. But don't hesitate. It's easy to distinguish redundancy from good repetition, from repetition as a stylistic tool.

The Greek rhetoricians had labels for every conceivable kind of good repetition—from the repetition of sounds and syllables to that of words and phrases in various locations in the sentence. We'll confine our discussion to repetition in coordinate structures that will make the reader sit up and take notice.

Consider the Gettysburg Address. Which of Lincoln's words, other than "Fourscore and seven years ago," do you remember? Probably "government of the people, by the people, and for the people." It's hard to imagine those words without the repetition: "Of, by, and for the people" just wouldn't have the same effect. And think about President Kennedy's stirring words, with his repetition of *any:*

> [W]e shall pay any price, bear any burden, meet any hardship, support any friend, oppose any foe to assure the survival and the success of liberty.

Notice, too, that the conjunction has been omitted before the last member of the series. He seems to be saying, "I could go on and on with my list."

You don't have to be a president to use that kind of repetition, nor do you have to reserve it for formal occasions. Whenever you use a coordinate structure, there's an opportunity for you to add to its impact with repetition, simply by including words that wouldn't have to be included. The following sentence, from an essay in *Time* by Charles Krauthammer, could have been more concise, but it would have lost its drama:

> There is not a single Western standard, there are two: what we demand of Western countries at peace and what we demand of Western countries at war.

And here is the second paragraph of the *Time* article about the Vikings by Michael D. Lemonick and Andrea Dorfman, with four repetitions of *they were.* The first paragraph began with that opening appositive series we saw earlier:

> But that view is wildly skewed. The Vikings were indeed raiders, but they were also traders whose economic network stretched from today's Iraq all the way to the Canadian Arctic. They were democrats who

founded the world's oldest surviving parliament while Britain was still mired in feudalism. They were master metalworkers, fashioning exquisite jewelry from silver, gold and bronze. Above all, they were intrepid explorers whose restless hearts brought them to North American some 500 years before Columbus.

In the following one-sentence paragraph from *Undaunted Courage,* Stephen E. Ambrose describes the birthplace of Meriwether Lewis with repeated *where* clauses:

Lewis was born in a place where the West invited exploration but the East could provide education and knowledge, where the hunting was magnificent but plantation society provided refinement and enlightenment, where he could learn wilderness skills while sharpening his wits about such matters as surveying, politics, natural history, and geography.

Notice, too, the parallelism of the *where* clauses, each including a contrasting pair of descriptors.

These uses of repetition, as well as the other stylistic devices we have taken up in this chapter, will invariably call attention to themselves. For that reason, you will reserve these structures for important ideas, for those times when you want your reader to sit up and take notice. But, like the gourmet cook who knows that too many spices can overwhelm a dish, you won't want to overwhelm your reader. But you will want to recognize that, like the spice that turns a bland sauce into fine cuisine, these stylistic tools can make the difference between ordinary and powerful prose.

AVOIDING SEXISM IN LANGUAGE

As you learned in Chapter 13, the system of personal pronouns has a gap. And it is that gap—the lack of a gender-neutral pronoun in the third-person singular slot—that is responsible for a great deal of the sexism in our language. You'd think that *he* and *she* and *it* would be up to the task of covering all the contingencies, but they're not. When we need a pronoun to refer to an unidentified person, such as "the writer" or "a student" or just "someone," our long-standing tradition has been to use the masculine:

The writer of this news story should have kept <u>his</u> personal opinion out of it.

Someone left <u>his</u> book on the table.

But that usage is no longer automatically accepted. Times and attitudes change, and we have come to recognize the power of language in shaping those attitudes. So an important step in reshaping society's view of women has been to eliminate the automatic use of *he* and *his* and *him* when the gender of someone referred to could just as easily be female.

In a paragraph we looked at earlier in this chapter in connection with sentence rhythm, the writer has made an effort to avoid sexism with the generic *salesperson,* a title that has all but replaced the masculine *salesman.* But notice the pronoun in the last sentence:

> Never invest in something you don't understand or in the dream of an artful salesperson. Be a buyer, not a sellee. Figure out what you want (be it life insurance, mutual funds or a vacuum cleaner) and then shop for a good buy. Don't let someone else tell you what you need—at least not if <u>he</u> happens to be selling it.
>
> ANDREW TOBIAS

In speech we commonly use *they* for both singular and plural:

> Don't let someone else tell you what you need—at least not if <u>they</u> happen to be selling it.

Eventually, perhaps, the plural pronoun will take over for the singular; in the second person (*you/your/you*), we make no distinction between singular and plural, so it's not unreasonable to do the same in the third person. But such changes come slowly. What should we do in the meantime?

One common, but not necessarily effective, way to solve the problem of the pronoun gap is with *he or she:*

> . . . at least not if <u>he or she</u> happens to be selling it.

An occasional *he or she* will work in most situations like this one, but more than one in a paragraph will change the rhythm of the prose, slow the reader down, and call attention to itself when such attention is simply uncalled for.

The awkwardness of *he or she* in a passage becomes even more obvious when the possessive and objective case pronouns are also required. Avoiding sexist language by using *his or her* and *him or her* as well as *he or she* will quickly render the solution worse than the problem. Here, for example, is a passage from a 1981 issue of *Newsweek:*

> To the average American, the energy problem is mainly his monthly fuel bill and the cost of filling up his gas tank. He may also remember that in 1979, and way back in 1974, he had to wait in long lines at gasoline stations. For all of this, he blames the "Arabs" or the oil companies or the government, or perhaps all three. Much of the information that he gets from the media, as well as his own past

experience, tells him that energy prices will continue to go up sharply and that gas lines are going to come back whenever a conflict flares up in the Middle East.

FRED SINGER, *"Hope for the Energy Shortage"*

Now imagine a version in which the problem of sexism has been solved with *he or she*:

~~To the~~ average American, the energy problem is mainly ~~his or her~~ monthly fuel bill and the cost of filling up ~~his or her~~ gas tank. He or she may also remember that in 1979, and way back in 1974, ~~he or she~~ had to wait in long lines at gasoline stations. For all of this, ~~he or she~~ blames the "Arabs" or the oil companies or the government, or perhaps all three. Much of the information that ~~he or she~~ gets from the media, as well as from ~~his or her~~ own past experience, tells ~~him or her~~ that energy prices will continue . . . *Enough!*

[handwritten annotations: "as an" above "To the"; "your" above "his or her" multiple times; "you" in left margin multiple times]

That's only one short paragraph. Imagine reading a whole essay! Clearly, there are better solutions to the problem.

Because we do have a gender-neutral pronoun in the plural, often that singular noun can be changed to plural. In the *Newsweek* article, for example, the writer could have started out by discussing "average Americans":

To average Americans, the energy problem is mainly their monthly fuel bills and the cost of filling up their gas tanks.

That revision, of course, has changed the relationship of the writer to the reader: The writer is no longer addressing the reader as an individual—a change the writer may not want. Often, however, the plural is an easy and obvious solution. For example, in the following passages from books about language, the change to plural does not affect the overall meaning or intent:

Of all the developments in the history of ~~man~~ *the human race*, surely the most remarkable was language, for with it ~~he was~~ *our ancestors were* able to pass on ~~his~~ *their* cultural heritage to succeeding generations who then did not have to rediscover how to make a fire, where to hunt, or how to build another wheel.

CHARLES B. MARTIN and CURT M. RULON

It has been said that whenever ~~a person~~ speaks, ~~he is~~ either mimick-

ing or analogizing.

CHARLES HOCKETT

We should emphasize that these three examples of sexist language were written at least two decades ago, when the masculine pronoun was the norm. Chances are, none of them would have been written in this way today. All of us who are involved with words, who are sensitive to the power of language, have gone through a consciousness-raising in the matter of sexist language.

Let's assume that Fred Singer, the *Newsweek* writer, insists on maintaining the singular "average American." What other means would he have for eliminating the sexism of the masculine pronouns? In some cases, he could use different determiners. For example, he needn't write "*his* monthly fuel bill" and "*his* gas tank"; *the* will do the job. And in the last sentence, "his own past experience" could become "past experience" or, simply, "experience" without losing any information; "tells him" could become "says" or "suggests." He could probably get by with a single *he or she*, to replace the *he* of the second sentence; the other sentences with *he* can be revised with different subjects. Here's one possibility:

> To the average American, the energy problem is mainly the monthly fuel bill and the cost of filling up the gas tank. He or she may also remember in 1979, and way back in 1974, waiting in long lines at the gasoline stations. Who gets the blame for all of this? The "Arabs" or the oil companies or the government, or perhaps all three. The media, as well as the consumer's past experience, suggest that energy prices will continue to go up sharply and that gas lines are going to come back whenever a conflict flares up in the Middle East.

In the last sentence we've substituted "the consumer" for "the average American."

Here, then, are some of the ways in which you can make up for the pronoun gap when you write and/or revise your own sentences:

1. USE THE PLURAL:
   Every writer should be aware of the power of language when <u>he</u> chooses <u>his</u> pronouns.
   Revision: Writers should be aware of the power of language when <u>they</u> choose <u>their</u> pronouns.

2. USE *HE OR SHE* IF YOU CAN USE IT ONLY ONCE.
   Revision: Every writer should be aware of the power of language when <u>he or she</u> chooses pronouns.

3. AVOID *HIS* AS A DETERMINER, EITHER BY SUBSTITUTING ANOTHER ONE OR, IN SOME CASES, DELETING THE DETERMINER:
   The writer of the news story should have kept <u>his</u> opinion out of it.
   Revision: The writer of the news story should have kept (<u>all</u>) opinion out of it.

4. TURN THE CLAUSE INTO A VERB PHRASE, THUS ELIMINATING THE PROBLEM SUBJECT:
   Every writer should be aware of the power of language when <u>choosing pronouns</u>.

This fourth method of revision is often a good possibility because the offending pronoun nearly always shows up in the second clause of a passage, often as part of the same sentence. In our example, we have turned the complete subordinate clause into an elliptical clause—that is, a clause with something missing. In this case what's missing is the subject. (The elliptical clause, which has some hidden pitfalls, is discussed in Chapter 8.)

5. REWRITE THE ADVERBIAL CLAUSE AS A RELATIVE (WHO) CLAUSE:
   When <u>a person</u> buys a house, <u>he</u> should shop carefully for the lowest interest rate.
   Revision: <u>A person who</u> buys a house should shop carefully for the lowest interest rate.

The relative clause with its neutral *who* eliminates the necessity of a personal pronoun to rename *a person.*

6. CHANGE THE POINT OF VIEW:
   2nd person: As a writer <u>you</u> should be aware of the power of language when you choose (your) pronouns.
   1st person: As writers, <u>we</u> should be aware of the power of language when we choose (our) pronouns.

Exercise   62

1. Rewrite the *Newsweek* passage using the second person. (Note: You might begin with "If you are an average American. . .")

2. The following passage was written in 1944, a time when the masculine pronoun was accepted as the generic singular. Revise it to reflect today's concerns about sexism in language.

   Of all born creatures, man is the only one that cannot live by bread alone. He lives as much by symbols as by sense report, in a realm compounded of tangible things and virtual images, of actual events and ominous portents, always between fact and fiction. For he sees not only actualities but meanings. He has, indeed, all the impulses and interests of animal nature; he eats, sleeps, mates, seeks comfort and safety, flees pain, falls sick and dies, just as cats and bears and fishes and butterflies do. But he has something more in his repertoire, too—he has laws and religions, theories and dogmas, because he lives not only through sense but through symbols. That is the special asset of his mind, which makes him the master of earth and all its progeny.

SUSANNE K. LANGER, "The Prince of Creation"

THE RHETORIC OF PUNCTUATION

In the preceding chapters you have studied the structure of sentences: both their basic slots and the ways we expand and combine them. In this chapter you have learned about the effect of those options on the reader— hence the word *rhetorical* in its title. Rhetorical choices and their effects apply also to punctuation within the boundaries of conventional rules. To organize the details of punctuation, we will begin with whole sentences, then move to the sentence slots and the structures that fill them.

Punctuation of Sentences. The main question concerning sentences arises when we coordinate them: S + S. What are the punctuation options? There are three possibilities: (1) a comma with a coordinating conjunction; (2) a semicolon; and (3) a colon. Here's a simple example to illustrate the first two:

1. The family held a reunion on the Fourth of July, and everyone had a great time.

2. The family held a reunion on the Fourth of July; everyone had a great time.

The semicolon works well here—perhaps better than the first option— because it means *and* without saying so. It produces a tighter connection. It also gives extra emphasis to the second clause.

We should emphasize the importance in option 1 of the comma. You might think that the conjunction would be connection enough. But it isn't. With the *and* alone, the reader, who has no way of knowing that a full sentence follows, is likely to assume that the *and* signals an internal coordinate pair. Here, for example, is a sentence that requires the reader to reread:

> Robin was having a serious conversation with Julie and Todd, who was sitting across the room, kept interrupting with snide remarks.

We should also mention that to use the comma without the conjunction produces a nonconventional connection called the "comma splice." Writers do use comma splices on certain occasions, especially when combining two or three short sentences for special attention:

> They graduated on Saturday, they got married on Sunday, they moved to Alaska on Monday.

But there are conditions: The sentences must be fairly short, and they must be closely and logically connected.

With a series of three or more short sentences, the punctuation is like that of any series—with a comma and conjunction before the final sentence:

> We swam, we played softball, and we feasted on every picnic casserole ever created.

Again, these could be connected with semicolons to produce a tighter, more controlled effect. In this case, however, the first version may fit the topic better: The commas and the *and* produce a more leisurely pace.

Our third connection, the colon (an example of which you'll find in the preceding sentence) will not work for the reunion sentences, 1 and 2. Colons and semicolons are not interchangeable. The colon does not mean "and"; rather, it means "namely" or "that is" or "in fact." Here are some examples:

> Rats and Rabbits, to those who injected, weighed and dissected them, were little different from cultures in a petri dish: they were just things to manipulate and observe.
>
> STEVEN ZAK

> My mother was not prodigal: she was unnaturally frugal.
>
> BARBARA GRIZZUTI HARRISON

> The 1988 election confirmed the split-level rule in American politics: The higher the office, the more ideology matters.
>
> WILLIAM SCHNEIDER

Notice how the first clause sets up an expectation in the reader. The colon says, "Here comes the information that you're expecting" or "Here's what I promised." In the second passage, the *not* in the first clause sets the reader up for a contrast in the second.

Two other common situations that the colon signals are questions and direct quotations:

Everyone had the same question in mind: Will he run?

Libby finally let us in on her secret: "We're getting married next week."

There is one detail of punctuation in these compound sentences that varies. Except for direct quotations, you have the choice of using either a capital or a lowercase letter when a full sentence follows the colon. The first word of a direct quotation is always capitalized, even when the quotation is not a full sentence. Some publications capitalize the first letter of all full sentences following colons (the style of this book); others capitalize only questions; some use lowercase for all sentences except direct quotations. Whichever style you choose, be consistent.

The Sentence Slots. You'll recall from Chapter 2 that we do not separate the sentence slots with punctuation. With one exception, there are no commas between the subject and verb, the verb and direct object, the verb and subject complement, the direct and indirect object, or the direct object and the object complement. The one exception occurs when the direct object is a direct quotation following a verb like *say* or *reply.* In this circumstance, we follow the verb with a comma or a colon:

He said, "I love you."

The candidate replied adamantly: "I am not a crook."

You may remember also that the direct quotation can be turned into an indirect quotation with a *that* clause:

He said that he loved her.

The candidate replied adamantly that he was not a crook.

The convention also calls for the indirect quotation to be in the past tense, even though as a direct quotation it is in the present.

The optional adverbial slot in opening position, which you saw first in Chapter 2 and later in Chapter 5, will always be set off by a comma *if it contains a verb.* This means that not only subordinate clauses, but also participial phrases, infinitive phrases, and prepositional phrases with gerunds as objects will always be followed by commas:

When you leave, please close the door. (subordinate clause)

To end the tension between us, I decided to apologize. (infinitive phrase)

Finding the door unlocked, I got worried. (participial phrase)

After finding the house empty, I checked with the neighbors. (prepositional phrase with gerund)

Generally the only adverbials set off at the end of the sentence are certain subordinate clauses. (See pages 200–201.)

Other sentence openers—those without verbs—will be set off only if they are long or clearly parenthetical or if they rate special emphasis. However, even a short prepositional phrase may need a comma to make the meaning clear:

> During the summer, vacation plans become a scheduling problem for our family.

The writer should make these punctuation decisions with the reader in mind.

Within the Sentence Slots. When you studied the systematic nature of the noun phrase in Chapter 6, you learned that on some occasions the modifiers call for commas. In preheadword position a string of two or more adjectives of the same class (e.g., subjective qualities) requires separation:

> an industrious, energetic salesman

You'll recall that you can test the need for the comma by inserting *and*. If the result is grammatical,

> an industrious and energetic salesman,

then the comma can replace *and*. The *and* test is extremely reliable.

The modifiers in postheadword position—appositives, prepositional phrases, participial phrases, and relative clauses—will need commas if the information is not necessary to clarify the identity of the headword. It helps to think of the commas as parentheses setting off optional information. This important punctuation issue is discussed on pages 155–159.

The Colon with Appositives. In the discussion of sentence punctuation, we saw the colon as a connector in a compound sentence, where the colon introduces a following clause with the meaning of "namely." That same meaning applies in the colon's more common role of connecting smaller units to a complete sentence, often in the form of a list:

> Three committees were set up to plan the convention: program, finance, and local arrangements.

Here the list is actually a list of appositives renaming the noun *committees*. The colon is a way of saying, "Here it comes, the list I promised." Sometimes the list following the colon includes internal punctuation other than commas:

> The study of our grammar system includes three areas: phonology, the study of sounds; morphology, the study of meaningful combinations of sounds; and syntax, the study of sentences.

Here the list includes three nouns, each of which has a nonrestrictive post-noun modifier of its own. This is one of the two occasions in our writing system that call for the semicolon. (The other, the joining of clauses in compound sentences, is discussed on pages 220–221.)

Avoiding Colon Errors. The use of the colon with appositives is the source of a common punctuation error, but one simple rule can resolve it:

A COMPLETE SENTENCE PRECEDES THE COLON.

Notice in the examples that the structure preceding the colon is a complete sentence pattern, with every slot filled:

Three committees were set up to plan the convention.

The study of our grammar system includes three areas.

Because the colon so often does precede a list, the writer may assume that every list should be preceded by one, but that is not the case. In the following sentences, the colons are misused:

*The committees that were set up to plan the convention are: program, finance, and local arrangements.

*The three areas of the grammar system are: phonology, morphology, and syntax.

Your understanding of the sentence patterns will tell you that a subject complement is needed to complete these sentences in which a form of *be* is the predicating verb.

One common variation for the sentence with a list includes the phrase *the following*:

The committees that were set up to plan the convention are the following: program, finance, and local arrangements.

That noun phrase, *the following,* fills the subject complement slot, so the sentence is indeed grammatical. But it is not necessarily the most effective version of the sentence. If you want to use a colon in such a sentence for purposes of emphasis, the earlier version is smoother and more concise:

Three committees were set up to plan the convention: program, finance, and local arrangements.

The Versatile Dash. The rules of both syntax and punctuation enable writers to convey meanings that go beyond the message in the words themselves. We've seen variations in word order that change the rhythm and emphasis of the sentence; we've seen alternatives to the standard use of commas for punctuating the series. Among our most versatile tools is the dash, which can substitute for both the comma and the colon under certain circumstances, a choice that nearly always sends a message that says

"Pay attention! This is important." The dash also adds an air of informality to a text—in both tone and looks.

The following sentences are from a *New Yorker* article by Sol Wachtler ("Crime and Punishment," July 15, 1996). In each case the dash represents what might be called alternative punctuation, substituting for the mainstream comma or colon in several different situations:

To highlight an appositive:

The experience has only confirmed my view of the criminal-justice system—that the system must work to punish the guilty without lessening the constitutional protections accorded all citizens.

But his sentence—forty years without possibility of parole—bordered on the uncivilized.

To highlight an adjectival modifier:

If our judicial system has a single outstanding feature, it is its attempt to apply the law fairly and with an even hand—free from the passions of the moment and free from the passions of the crowd.

The question is one that is repeated today—not quite so artfully phrased—by public-office holders and seekers from both political parties.

To set off an adverbial:

They've all heard it before—on TV or when they were last arrested.

He was ecstatic—for a while.

To highlight the second clause of a compound sentence:

The kingpins rarely deal directly with the drugs—those are handled by lower-ranking participants.

They tend to allow their agendas to be shaped by the publicity that an arrest will bring—and the publicity is enhanced by the number of arrests the charges will bring.

To highlight a compound predicate:

A woman who steals powdered milk to feed her baby has committed the same crime—and may receive the same punishment—as a man who steals powdered milk to cut heroin.

Like any attention-getter, the dash should be used sparingly, as it is in this article: Seventeen of its thirty paragraphs, most of which are quite long, contain only one dash; two paragraphs contain two; the remaining eleven have none.

Exercise 63

The following passages are punctuated according to our conventional rules. However, the proliferation of commas tends to detract from their readability. Revise the punctuation with the reader in mind:

1. During the second two-year stretch of a president's term in office, he may find himself on the defensive, even with his own party, and, when, as frequently happens, his party loses a number of Senate and House seats in the midterm election, that second stretch can become even more defensive.

2. In recent years, the public attitude toward smoking, except perhaps in the tobacco-growing states, has changed so fast, with smoke-free zones everywhere, including restaurants, office buildings, and shopping malls, it could almost be called a revolution, and even outdoor stadiums, such as Oriole Park at Camden Yards and Jacobs Field in Cleveland, have established a no-smoking policy.

Exercise 64

Experiment with commas, colons, and dashes as you revise and/or combine the following sentences.

1. The cost of repairs to the nation's public transportation facilities is an expenditure that cannot be delayed much longer if the system is to survive: Roads, bridges, and railroads are all in need of repair.

2. To many people, the mushroom is a lowly fungus. It has little food value. To other people, it is a gourmet's delight.

3. In the early 1980s the Chinese banned the import of certain American goods, such as cotton, synthetic fibers, and soybeans. The restriction had an adverse effect on the U.S. economy, especially on the farmers.

4. According to fashion experts, the crew cut will be back in style before long. That particular haircut was more or less the hallmark of the 1950s.

5. My favorite activities are skiing, playing golf, and bowling; unfortunately, they cost more than my budget can stand.

6. Alexander Graham Bell is remembered as the inventor of the telephone. Most people probably don't know that Bell succeeded his father-in-law as president of the National Geographic Society.

7. Cypress Gardens, Florida, comprises thirty acres of flowers, exotic plants, and wildlife. It is a year-round extravaganza of nature's bounty and beauty.

8. Many scientists believe that sightings of "cryptids" are mistakes. Cryptids include Big Foot, the Loch Ness monster, and Yeti, known as the Abominable Snowman. Mistaken sightings can be attributed to unfamiliarity with known animals, rather than to delusions.

CHAPTER *14*

Key Terms

Absolute phrase

Abstract subject

Adverbial clause

Adverbial of emphasis

Appositive

Cohesion

Colon

Compound sentence

Coordinate series

Dash

Ellipsis

End focus

Intonation

Introductory appositive series

Known–new contract

Nominalization

Passive voice

Punctuation

Repetition

Rhetorical grammar

Rhythm

Sentence rhythm

Sexist language

Shifting adverbial

Style

Word-order variation

PART VI

Glossary of Grammatical Terms

(For further explanation of the terms listed here, check the Index for page references.)

Absolute adjective. An adjective with a meaning that is generally not capable of being intensified or compared, such as *unique* or *perfect* or *square.* Careful writers avoid such usages as "very perfect" or "more unique."

Absolute phrase. A noun phrase related to the sentence as a whole that includes a postnoun modifier (often a participial phrase). One kind of absolute explains a cause or condition ("*The weather being warm,* we decided to have a picnic"); the other adds a detail or a point of focus to the idea in the main clause ("He spoke quietly to the class, *his voice trembling*").

Accusative case. The Latin term denoting the case of nouns and pronouns functioning as direct objects and as objects of certain prepositions.

Active voice. A feature of transitive verb sentences in which the subject is generally the agent and the direct object is the goal or objective of the action. Voice refers to the relationship of the subject to the verb. See also *Passive voice.*

Adjectival. Any structure, no matter what its form, that functions as a modifier of a noun—that is, that functions as an adjective normally functions. See Chapter 6.

Adjectival clause. See *Relative clause.*

Adjective. One of the four form classes, whose members act as modifiers of nouns; most adjectives can be inflected for comparative and superlative degree (*big, bigger, biggest*); they can be qualified or intensified (*rather big, very big*); they have characteristic derivational endings such as *-ous* (*famous*), *-ish* (*childish*), *-ful* (*graceful*), and *-ary* (*complementary*).

Adverb. One of the four form classes, whose members act as modifiers of verbs, contributing information of time, place, reason, manner, and the like. Like adjectives, certain adverbs can be qualified (*very quickly, rather fast*); some can be inflected for comparative and superlative degree (*more quickly, fastest*); they have characteristic derivational endings such as *-ly* (*quickly*), *-wise* (*lengthwise*), and *-ward* (*backward*).

Adverbial. Any structure, no matter what its form, that functions as a modifier of a verb—that is, that functions as an adverb normally functions. See Chapter 5.

Adverbial objective. The traditional label given to the noun phrase that functions adverbially: "Joe went *home*"; "It was cold *last night.*"

Affix. A morpheme, or meaningful unit, that is added to the beginning (prefix) or end (suffix) of a word to change its meaning or its grammatical role or its form class: (prefix) *un*likely; (suffix) unlike*ly*.

Agent. The initiator of the action in the sentence, the "doer" of the action. Usually the agent is the subject in an active sentence: "*John* groomed the dog"; "*The committee* elected Pam." In a passive sentence the agent may be the object of the preposition *by*: "Pam was elected by *the committee.*"

Agreement. (1) Subject–verb. A third-person singular subject in the present tense takes the -s form of the verb: "*The dog barks* all night"; "*He bothers* the neighbors." A plural subject takes the base form: "*The dogs bark*"; "*They bother* the neighbors." (2) Pronoun–antecedent. The number of the pronoun (whether singular or plural) agrees with the number of its antecedent: "*The boys* did *their* chores"; "*Each girl* did *her* best."

Allomorph. A variation of a morpheme, usually determined by its environment. For example, the three allomorphs of the regular plural morpheme are determined by the final sound of the nouns to which they are added: /s/ *cats;* /z/ *dogs;* and /əz/ *churches.*

Ambiguous. The condition in which a structure has more than one possible meaning. The source may be lexical ("She is *blue*") or structural ("*Visiting relatives* can be boring") or both ("The detective looked *hard*").

Antecedent. The noun or nominal that a pronoun stands for.

Anticipatory *it*. The use of the pronoun *it* in subject position in order to delay the actual subject: "It was Mary who had the accident in Phoenix." See also *Cleft sentence.*

Appositive. A structure, often a noun phrase, that renames another structure: "My neighbor, *a butcher at Weis Market*, recently lost his job." Clauses ("It is nice *that you could come*") and verb phrases ("My favorite hobby, *collecting stamps*, is getting expensive") can also function as appositives.

Article. One of the determiner classes, including the indefinite *a*, or *an*, which signals only countable nouns, and the definite *the*, which can signal all classes of nouns.

Aspect. The perfect (*have* + *en*) and progressive (*be* + *ing*) auxiliaries, which denote such features of verbs as completion, duration, and repetition—time elements not related to past, present, or future.

Attributive adjective. The adjective in prenoun position: "my *new* coat"; "the *big* attraction."

Auxiliary. One of the structure-class words, a marker of verbs. Auxiliaries include forms of *have* and *be*, as well as the modals, such as *will*, *shall*, and *must*.

Base form of the verb. The uninflected form of the verb. In all verbs except *be*, the base form is the present tense: *go*, *help*. The base form also serves as the infinitive, usually preceded by *to*.

Base morpheme. The morpheme that gives a word its primary lexical meaning: *help*ing, re*flect*.

Be patterns. The sentence patterns in which a form of *be* is the main verb: Patterns I, II, and III.

Bound morpheme. A morpheme that cannot stand alone as a word. Most affixes are bound (help*ing*; *re*act); some base morphemes are also bound (con*cise*; *leg*al).

Case. A feature of nouns and certain pronouns that denotes their relationship to other words in a sentence. Pronouns have three case distinctions: subjective (e.g., *I*, *they*, *who*); possessive (e.g., *my*, *their*, *whose*); and objective (e.g., *me*, *them*, *whom*). Nouns have only one case inflection, the possessive (*John's*, the *cat's*). The case of nouns other than the possessive is sometimes referred to as common case.

Catenative verb. A transitive verb that can take another verb as its object: "I *like* to jog"; "We *enjoy* jogging."

Clause. A structure with a subject and a predicate. The sentence patterns are clause patterns. Clauses are either independent or dependent.

Cleft sentence. A sentence variation that provides a way of shifting the stress or focus of the sentence: "A careless bicyclist caused the accident" → "It was a careless bicyclist who caused the accident"; "What caused the accident was a careless bicyclist."

Cohesion. The grammatical, lexical, and semantic connections between sentences. Cohesive ties are furnished by pronouns that have antecedents in previous sentences, by adverbial connections, by known information, and by knowledge shared by the reader.

Collective noun. A noun that refers to a collection of individuals: *group, team, family.* Collective nouns can be replaced by both singular and plural pronouns, depending on the meaning.

Command. See *Imperative sentence.*

Common case. See *Case.*

Common noun. A noun with general, rather than unique, reference (in contrast to proper nouns). Common nouns may be countable (*house, book*) or noncountable (*water, oil*); they may be concrete (*house, water*) or abstract (*justice, indifference*).

Comparative degree. See *Degree.*

Complement. A structure that "completes" the sentence. The term includes those slots in the predicate that complete the verb: direct object, indirect object, subject complement, and object complement. Certain adjectives also have complements—clauses and phrases that pattern with them: "I was certain *that he would come;* I was *afraid to go.*"

Complementary infinitive. An infinitive that functions as the main verb. "I'm going *to move* next week"; "I have *to find* a new apartment." There is a modal-like quality in "going to" and "have to."

Complex sentence. A sentence that includes at least one dependent clause.

Compound sentence. A sentence with two or more independent clauses.

Compound–complex sentence. A sentence that includes at least two independent clauses and one dependent clause.

Conditional mood. The attitude of probability designated by the modal auxiliaries *could, may, might, would,* and *should.*

Conjunction. One of the structure classes, which includes connectors that coordinate structures of many forms (e.g., *and, or*), subordinate sentences (e.g., *if, because, when*), and coordinate sentences with an adverbial emphasis (e.g., *however, therefore*).

Conjunctive adverb. A conjunction that connects two sentences with an adverbial emphasis, such as *however, therefore, moreover,* and *nevertheless.*

Coordinating conjunction. A conjunction that connects two or more sentences or structures within a sentence as equals: *and, but, or, nor, for,* and *yet.*

Coordination. A way of expanding sentences in which two or more structures of the same form function as a unit. All the sentence slots and modifiers in the slots, as well as the sentence itself, can be coordinated. See Chapter 9.

Correlative conjunction. A two-part conjunction that expresses a relationship between the coordinated structures: *either–or, neither–nor, both–and.*

Countable noun. A noun whose referent can be identified as a separate entity; the countable noun can be signaled by the indefinite article, *a,* and numbers: *a house; an experience; two eggs; three problems.*

Declarative sentence. A sentence in the form of a statement (in contrast to a command, a question, or an exclamation).

Deep structure. A term from transformational generative grammar that refers to the underlying semantic and syntactic relationships of the sentence, in contrast to surface structure, the sentence as it is actually written or spoken.

Definite article. The determiner *the,* which generally marks a specific or previously mentioned noun: " the man on *the* corner"; "*the* blue coat I want for Christmas."

Degree. The variations in adjectives that indicate the simple quality of a noun, or positive degree ("Bill is a *big* boy"); its comparison to another, the comparative degree ("Bill is *bigger* than Tim"); or to two or more, the superlative degree ("Bill is the *biggest* person in the whole class"). Certain adverbs also have degree variations, usually designated by *more* and *most.*

Demonstrative pronoun. The pronouns *this* (plural *these*) and *that* (plural *those*), which function as nominal substitutes and as determiners. They include the feature of proximity: near (*this, these*); distant (*that, those*).

Dependent clause. A clause that functions as an adverbial, adjectival, nominal, or sentence modifier (in contrast to an independent, or main, clause).

Derivational affix. A morpheme that is added to a form-class word, either to change its class (*friend* → *friendly; act* → *action*) or to change its meaning (*legal* → *illegal; boy* → *boyhood*).

Determiner. One of the structure-class words, a marker of nouns. Determiners include articles (*a, the*); possessive nouns and pronouns (e.g., *Chuck's, his, my*); demonstrative pronouns (*this, that*); quantifiers (e.g., *many, several*); indefinite pronouns (e.g., *each, every*); and numbers.

Dialect. The shared linguistic features of a group, often one from a particular region or of a particular ethnic or social background.

Direct address. see *Vocative.*

Direct object. A nominal slot in the predicate of the transitive sentence patterns. The direct object names the objective or goal or the receiver of the verb's action: "We ate *the peanuts*"; "The boy hit *the ball*"; "I enjoy *playing chess.*"

Do **support.** The addition of the stand-in auxiliary *do* to a verb string that has no other auxiliary. The question, the negative, and the emphatic transformations all require an auxiliary. *Do* also substitutes for a repeated verb phrase in compound sentences: "Bryan liked the movie, and I *did* too."

Dynamic. Words that exhibit features related to qualities capable of change. Dynamic verbs can combine with the progressive aspect, *be* + *-ing:* "I *am leaving* now"; dynamic adjectives can follow the progressive form of *be:* "He is being *silly.*" See also *Stative.*

Edited American English. The variety of English usage that is widely accepted as the norm for the public writing of school essays, newspapers, magazines, and books. It is sometimes referred to as EAE.

Elliptical clause. A clause in which a part has been left out but is "understood"; "Chester is older *than I (am old)*"; "Bev can jog farther *than Otis (can jog)*"; " *When (you are) planning your essay,* be sure to consider the audience."

Emphatic sentence. A statement in which the main stress has been shifted to the auxiliary: "I AM trying." When there is no auxiliary, the "stand-in auxiliary" *do* is added to carry the stress: "I DO want to go."

End focus. The common rhythm pattern in which the prominent peak of stress falls on or near the final sentence slot.

Exclamatory sentence. A sentence that expresses excitement or emotion. It may include a shift in the word order of a basic sentence that focuses on a complement: "What a beautiful day we're having!" It is characterized by heightened pitch and stress and is usually punctuated with an exclamation point.

Expanded determiner. The determiner, together with pre- and postdeterminers that qualify and quantify and in other ways alter its meaning.

Expletive. A word that enables the writer or speaker to shift the stress in a sentence or to embed one sentence in another: "A fly is in my soup → *There is* a fly in my soup"; "I know *that* he loves me." The expletive is sometimes called an "empty word" because it plays a structural rather than a lexical role.

Finite verb. The main verb of the clause, one that fills the last slot in the verb-expansion formula. See also *Nonfinite verb.*

Flat adverb. A class of adverb that is the same in form as its corresponding adjective: *fast, high, early, late, hard, long,* etc.

Form. The inherent features, the shapes, of words and phrases and clauses, as distinguished from their function in the sentence, characterized in words by prefixes and suffixes, in phrases by headwords and their objects or complements or modifiers, and in clauses by subjects and predicates.

Form classes. The large, open classes of words that provide the lexical content of the language: nouns, verbs, adjectives, and adverbs. Each has characteristic derivational and inflectional morphemes that distinguish its forms. See Chapter 11.

Free morpheme. A single morpheme that is also a complete word (in contrast to a bound morpheme, which is not).

Function. The role that a particular structure plays, or the slot that it fills, in a sentence (or in any larger structure). In "The book on the table is mine," "table" functions as the *object of a preposition* in the prepositional phrase "on the table"; the prepositional phrase functions as an *adjectival*, modifying book. The entire noun phrase "the book on the table" functions as the *subject* in its sentence.

Functional shift. The conversion of one word class to another, simply by changing its function. He *bottled* the wine (noun to verb); She *lowered* the curtain (adjective to verb); We took a *swim* (verb to noun).

Gender. A feature of personal pronouns and certain nouns that distinguishes masculine (*he*), feminine (*she*), and neuter (*it*). Nouns with gender distinctions include *waiter, waitress, actor, actress, girl, boy, man, woman, ewe, ram.*

Genitive case. The Latin term for possessive case.

Gerund. An *-ing* verb functioning as a nominal: "I enjoy *jogging*"; "*Running* is good exercise."

Gerund phrase. A gerund together with all of its complements and modifiers.

Grammatical. Usage that conforms to the rules that native speakers follow or that native speakers would find acceptable in a given situation. See also *Ungrammatical.*

Headword. The word that fills the noun slot in the noun phrase: "the little *boy* across [the *street*]." The verb is the headword of the verb phrase; the preposition is the headword of the prepositional phrase.

Helping verb. See *Auxiliary.*

Homonyms. Words and morphemes that have the same sound and the same spelling but have different meanings: *saw / saw;* farm*er* / bright*er.*

Homophones. Words that have the same sound, but with both different meanings and different spellings: *sale / sail; to / too / two.*

Idiom. A combination of words, a set phrase, whose meaning cannot be predicted from the meaning of the individual words.

Imperative sentence. The sentence in the form of a command. The imperative sentence includes the base form of the verb and usually an understood subject (*you*): "*Eat* your spinach"; "*Finish* your report as soon as possible"; "You *go* on without me."

Indefinite article. The determiner *a*, or *an*, which marks an unspecified count noun. See also *Definite article*.

Indefinite pronoun. A large category that includes quantifiers (e.g., *enough, several, many, much*), universals (*all, both, every, each*), and partitives (*any, either, neither, no, some*). Many of the indefinite pronouns can function as determiners.

Indefinite relative pronoun. The relative pronouns with -*ever* added, which have indefinite referents; they introduce adjectival clauses: "I will give a bonus to *whoever* works the hardest" (i.e., to the person who works the hardest).

Independent clause. The main clause of the sentence; a compound sentence has more than one independent clause.

Indicative mood. The expression of an idea as fact (as opposed to probability). Verb phrases without modal auxiliaries and those with *will* and *shall* are considered the indicative mood: "We *will* go soon"; "We *are going* tomorrow." "When *are* you *going*?" See also *Subjunctive mood* and *Conditional mood*.

Indirect object. The nominal slot following the verb in a Pattern VIII sentence. In a sentence with a verb like *give*, the indirect object is the recipient; the direct object is the thing given: "We gave *our friends* a ride home." The indirect object can be shifted to the slot following the direct object with the preposition *to* or *for*: "Joe gave a message to Kim"; "Sam bought a ticket for his dad."

Infinitive. The base form of the verb (present tense), usually expressed with *to*, which is called the "sign of the infinitive." The infinitive can function adverbially ("I stayed up all night *to study* for the exam"); adjectivally ("That is no way *to study*"); or nominally ("*To stay up* all night is foolish"). The only verb with an infinitive form separate from the present tense is *be*.

Infinitive phrase. The infinitive together with all of its complements and modifiers.

Inflection. See *Inflectional suffix*.

Inflectional suffix. Morphemes that are added to the form classes (nouns, verbs, adjectives, and adverbs) to change their grammatical role in some way. Nouns have two inflectional suffixes (-*s* plural and -*'s* possessive); verbs have four (-*s*, -*ing*, -*ed*, and -*en*); adjectives and some adverbs have two (-*er* and -*est*).

Intensifier. See *Qualifier.*

Intensive pronoun. A pronoun that serves as an appositive to emphasize a noun or pronoun. It is formed by adding *-self* or *-selves* to a personal pronoun: "I *myself* prefer chocolate."

Interjection. A word considered independent of the main sentence, often punctuated with an exclamation point: "*Ouch!* My shoe pinches"; "*Oh!* Is that what you meant?"

Interrogative. One of the structure classes. Sometimes referred to as "*wh*-words," the interrogatives—*where, when, who, what,* and *how*—introduce questions and nominal clauses, filling the roles of pronouns, adjectives, and adverbs in their clauses: "*Where* is she going?" "I wonder *who* is going with her."

Interrogative sentence. A sentence that is a question in form: "Are you leaving now?" "When are you leaving?"

Intonation. The rhythmic pattern of a spoken sentence, affected by its stress and pitch and pauses.

Intransitive verb. The verbs of Pattern VI sentences, most of which require no complement to be complete.

Irregular verb. Any verb in which the *-ed* and *-en* forms are not that of the regular verb; in other words, a verb in which the *-ed* and *-en* forms are not simply the addition of *-d, -ed,* or *-t* to the base form.

It-cleft. See *Cleft sentence.*

Known–new contract. A common feature of prose in which the known information opens the sentence and the new information occupies the point of main focus at or near the end of the sentence.

Linking verb. The verbs of Patterns IV and V, which require a subject complement to be complete.

Main verb. The finite verb that fills the last slot in the verb-expansion formula.

Manner adverb. An adverb that answers the question of "how" or "in what manner" about the verb. Most manner adverbs are derived from adjectives with the addition of *-ly: quickly, merrily, candidly.*

Mass noun. See *Noncountable noun.*

Modal auxiliary. The auxiliary that occupies the opening slot in the verb-expansion rule and may affect what is known as the mood of the verb, conveying probability, possibility, obligation, and the like.

Mood. A quality of the verb denoting fact (indicative), a condition contrary to fact (subjunctive), and probability or possibility (conditional).

Morpheme. A sound or combination of sounds with meaning.

Morphology. The study of morphemes. See Chapter 10.

Nominal. Any structure that functions as a noun phrase normally functions. See Chapter 7.

Nominal clause. A clause that fills a noun phrase (NP) slot.

Nominalization. The process of producing a noun by adding derivational affixes to another word class, commonly a verb: *legalize–legalization; regulate–regulation; friendly–friendliness.*

Nominative case. The Latin term for subjective case.

Noncountable noun. Nouns referring to what might be called an undifferentiated mass—such as *wood, water, sugar, glass*—or an abstraction—*justice, love, indifference.* Whether or not you can use the indefinite article, *a,* is probably the best test of countability: If you can, the noun is countable.

Nonfinite verb. A verb that functions other than as the main (finite) verb. Verbs and verb phrases acting as adjectivals, adverbials, and nominals within the sentence are called nonfinite verbs.

Nonrestrictive modifier. A modifier in the noun phrase that comments about the noun rather than defines it. Nonrestrictive modifiers following the noun are set off by commas.

Noun. One of the four form classes, whose members fill the headword slot in the noun phrase. Most nouns can be inflected for plural and possessive (*boy, boys, boy's, boys'*). Nouns have characteristic derivational endings, such as *-tion* (*action, compensation*), *-ment* (*contentment*), and *-ness* (*happiness*). Nouns can also function as adjectivals and adverbials (The *neighbor* children went *home*).

Noun clause. See *Nominal clause.*

Noun phrase (NP). The noun headword with all of its attendant pre- and postnoun modifiers.

Number. A feature of nouns and pronouns, referring to singular and plural.

Object complement. The slot following the direct object, filled by an adjectival (Pattern IX) or a nominal (Pattern X). The object complement has two functions: (1) It completes the idea of the verb; and (2) it modifies (if an adjective) or renames (if a nominal) the direct object: "I found the play *exciting*"; "We consider Pete *a good friend.*"

Object of preposition. The nominal slot—usually filled by a noun phrase—that follows the preposition to form a prepositional phrase.

Objective case. The role in a sentence of a noun phrase or pronoun when it functions as an object—direct object, indirect object, object complement, or object of the preposition. Although nouns do not have a special form for objective case, many of the pronouns do; personal pronouns and the relative pronoun *who* have separate forms when they function as objects. See Chapter 13.

Optional slot. The adverbial information that can be added to all the sentence patterns; such information is not required for grammaticality.

Parallel structure. A coordinate structure in which all the coordinate parts are of the same grammatical form.

Participial phrase. A participle together with all of its complements and modifiers.

Participle. The *-ing* and *-en* verb (or verb phrase) functioning as an adjectival or adverbial. See also *Present participle* and *Past participle.*

Particle. A word that combines with a verb to form a phrasal verb: look *up*, look *into*, put *up with*.

Passive voice. A feature of transitive sentences in which the direct object (the objective or goal) is shifted to the subject position and *be* + *-en* is added to the verb. The term *passive* refers to the relationship between the subject and verb: "Ed ate the pizza" → "The pizza *was eaten* by Ed."

Past participle. The *-en* form of the verb.

Past tense. The *-ed* form of the verb, usually denoting a specific past action.

Person. A feature of personal pronouns that distinguishes the speaker or writer (first person), the person or thing spoken to (second person), and the person or thing spoken of (third person).

Personal pronoun. The pronoun that refers to a specific person or thing: In the subjective case the personal pronouns are *I, you, he, she, we, you, they,* and *it.* The personal pronouns have variant forms for objective and possessive case.

Phoneme. The smallest unit of sound that makes a difference in meaning.

Phonology. The study of phonemes.

Phrasal preposition. A preposition consisting of two or more words, a simple preposition preceded by a word from another category, such as an adverb or adjective: *according to, aside from, because of, prior to.*

Phrasal verb. A verb–particle combination that produces a meaning that cannot be predicted from the meaning of the parts: *look up, put up with, make up.*

Phrase. A word or group of words that functions as a unit within the sentence.

Plural. A feature of nouns and pronouns denoting more than one, usually signaled in nouns by the inflectional ending *-s* (or *-es*).

Positive degree. See *Degree.*

Possessive case. The inflected form of nouns (*John's, the dog's*) and pronouns (*my, his, your, her, their*, etc.) usually indicating ownership.

Predicate. One of the two principal parts of the sentence, the comment made about the subject. The predicate includes the verb, together with its complements and modifiers.

Predicate adjective. The adjective that functions as a subject complement.

Predicate nominative. The noun or nominal that functions as a subject complement.

Predicating verb. The function of the verb slot in the sentence patterns, consisting of the main verb together with its auxiliaries. The verb-expansion rule in Chapter 3 accounts for the auxiliary–verb combinations of the predicating verb.

Predicative adjective. The adjective that occupies a complement slot in the sentence as subject or object complement.

Prefix. An affix added to the beginning of the word to change its meaning (*un*likely, *il*legal, *pre*scribe, *re*new) or its class (*en*able, *be*little).

Preposition. A structure-class word found in pre-position to—that is, preceding—a nominal. Prepositions can be classed according to their form as simple (*above, at, in, of,* etc.) or phrasal (*according to, instead of,* etc.).

Prepositional phrase. The combination of a preposition and a nominal, which is known as the object of the preposition.

Prescriptivism. An approach to teaching grammar, the purpose of which is to prescribe "proper" usage, rather than to describe how the language is actually used. It is sometimes referred to as "linguistic etiquette."

Present participle. The *-ing* form of the verb.

Present tense. The base form and the *-s* form of the verb: *help, helps.* The present tense denotes a present point in time ("I *understand* your position"), a habitual action ("I *jog* five miles a day"), or the "timeless" present ("Shakespeare *helps* us understand ourselves").

Pronoun. A word that substitutes for a noun—or, more accurately, for a nominal—in the sentence.

Pronoun–antecedent agreement. See *Agreement.*

Proper noun. A noun with individual reference to a person, a historical event, or other name. Proper nouns are capitalized.

Qualifier. A structure-class word that qualifies or intensifies an adjective or adverb: "We worked *rather* slowly"; "We worked *very* hard."

Reciprocal pronoun. The pronouns *each other* and *one another*, which refer to previously named nouns.

Referent. The thing (or person, event, concept, action, etc.)—in other words, the reality—that a word stands for.

Reflexive pronoun. A pronoun formed by adding *-self* or *-selves* to a form of the personal pronoun, used as an object in the sentence to refer to a previously named noun or pronoun: "I gave *myself* a haircut."

Regular verb. A verb in which the *-ed* form (the past tense) and the *-en* form (the past participle) are formed by adding *-ed* (or, in some cases, *-d* or *-t*) to the base. These two forms of a regular verb are always identical. "I *walked* home"; "I have *walked* home every day this week."

Relative adverb. The adverbs *where, when,* and *why,* which introduce adjectival clauses.

Relative clause. A clause introduced by a relative pronoun (*who, which, that*) or a relative adverb (*when, where, why*) that generally modifies a noun. The broad-reference *which* clause functions as a sentence modifier.

Relative pronoun. The pronouns *who* (*whom, whose*), *which,* and *that* in their role as introducers of a relative clause.

Restrictive modifier. A modifier in the noun phrase whose function is to restrict the meaning of the noun. A modifier is restrictive when it is needed to identify the referent of the headword. The restrictive modifier is not set off by commas.

Retained object. The direct object of a Pattern VIII sentence that is retained in its original position when the sentence is transformed into the passive voice: "The judges awarded Mary the prize" → "Mary was awarded *the prize.*"

Sentence. A word or group of words based on one or more subject–predicate, or clause, patterns. The written sentence begins with a capital letter and ends with terminal punctuation—a period, question mark, or an exclamation point.

Sentence modifier. A word or phrase or clause that modifies the sentence as a whole. See Chapter 8.

Sentence patterns. The simple skeletal sentences, made up of two or three or four required elements, that underlie our sentences, even the most complex among them. Ten such patterns will account for almost all the possible sentences of English. See Chapter 2.

Serial comma. The comma that is used before the conjunction in a series: *On our fishing trip to Alaska, we caught salmon, halibut,* **and** *the elusive Arctic grayling.* Some publications, as a matter of policy, omit the serial comma.

Simple preposition. A one-word preposition. See also *Phrasal preposition.*

Singular. A feature of nouns and pronouns denoting one referent.

Standard English. See *Edited American English.*

Stand-in auxiliary. The auxiliary *do* (*does, did*), which we add to sentences when we transform them into questions, negatives, and emphatic statements when there is no auxiliary in the original.

Stative. Words that exhibit features relating to an unchanging state, in contrast to those that change. Stative verbs do not pattern with the progressive aspect: *I am *resembling* my mother. Stative adjectives generally do not follow the progressive form of be: *He is *being tall.* See also *Dynamic.*

Structuralism. An approach to analyzing grammar, associated with mid-twentieth-century linguists, in which the purpose is to describe how the language is actually used in its various dialects, not to prescribe a "correct" version.

Structure classes. The small, closed classes of words that explain the grammatical or structural relationships of the form classes. See Chapter 12.

Subject. The opening slot in the sentence patterns, filled by a noun phrase or other nominal, that functions as the topic of the sentence.

Subject complement. The nominal or adjectival in Pattern II, III, IV, and V sentences following the verb, which renames or modifies the subject. The passive version of a Pattern IX or X sentence will also have a subject complement, the nominal or adjectival that in the active voice functions as the object complement.

Subjective case. The role in the sentence of a noun phrase or a pronoun when it functions as the subject of the sentence. Personal pronouns have distinctive forms for subjective case: *I, he, she, they*, etc.

Subject–verb agreement. See *Agreement.*

Subjunctive mood. An expression of the verb in which the base form, rather than the inflected form, is used (1) in certain *that* clauses conveying strong suggestions or resolutions or commands ("We suggest that Mary *go* with us"; "I move that the meeting *be* adjourned"; "I demand that you *let* us in"), and (2) in the expression of wishes or conditions contrary to fact ("If I *were* you, I'd be careful"; "I wish it *were* summer"). The subjunctive of the verb *be* is expressed by *were* or *be*, even for subjects that normally take *is* or *was*.

Subordinate clause. A dependent clause introduced by a subordinating conjunction, such as *if, since, because,* and *although.*

Subordinating conjunction. See *Subordinator.*

Subordinator. A subordinating conjunction that turns a complete sentence into a subordinate clause and expresses the connection between the subordinate clause and the main clause.

Substantive. A structure that functions as a noun; a nominal.

Suffix. An affix added to the end of a form-class word to change its class (act → act*ion;* laugh → laugh*able*) with derivational suffixes or to change its grammatical function (boy → boy*s;* walk → walk*ing*) with inflectional suffixes. See also *Derivational affix* and *Inflectional suffix.*

Superlative degree. See *Degree.*

Surface structure. A term used by transformational grammarians to designate the sentences of the language as they are spoken and written. See also *Deep structure.*

Syntax. The structure of sentences; the relationship of the parts of the sentence.

Tense. A grammatical feature of verbs and auxiliaries relating to time. Three verb forms indicate tense: the base form and the *-s* form (present) and the *-ed* form (past). Note that "tense" in relation to the modal auxiliaries refers only to form, not to time.

Tensed verb. A verb string that includes T, also known as a finite verb. In contrast, gerunds, infinitives, and participles have no tense marker.

***There* transformation.** A variation of a basic sentence in which the expletive *there* is added at the beginning and the subject is shifted to a position following *be:* "A fly is in my soup" → "*There is a fly in my soup.*"

Third-person singular. The personal pronouns *he, she,* and *it.* The term is also used in reference to the *-s* form of the verb.

Transformational grammar (also called Transformational Generative, or T-G). A theory of grammar that attempts to account for the ability of native speakers to generate and process the sentences of their language. See Appendix.

Transitive verb. The verbs of Patterns VII through X, which require at least one complement, the direct object, to be complete. With only a few exceptions, transitive verbs are those that can be transformed into the passive voice.

Ungrammatical. Usage that does not conform to the rules that native speakers follow. Usage that varies from one dialect or speech community to another is not necessarily ungrammatical. "I ain't coming" is an unacceptable usage to many, although it follows the "rules." However, it is not part of the prestige, or standard, dialect and would be inappropriate in most formal and business situations. See also *Grammatical* and *Edited American English.*

Verb. One of the four form classes, traditionally thought of as the action word in the sentence. A better way to recognize the verb, however, is by its form, its *-s* and *-ing* ending; verbs also have an *-ed* and an *-en* form, although in the case of some irregular verbs these forms are not readily apparent. And every verb, without exception, can be marked by auxiliaries. Many verbs also have characteristic derivational forms, such as *-ify* (*typify*), *-ize* (*criticize*), and *-ate* (*activate*).

Verb phrase (VP). A verb together with its complements and modifiers; the predicate of the sentence is a verb phrase. See also *Gerund phrase, Infinitive phrase,* and *Participial phrase.*

Verb-expansion rule. The formula that describes our system for expanding the verb with auxiliaries to express variations in meaning. See Chapter 3.

Vocative. The noun or noun phrase of direct address, considered a sentence modifier: "*Mike,* is that you?"

***What*-cleft.** See *Cleft sentence.*

***Wh*-question.** A question that is introduced by an interrogative, such as *who, which, when, where, why,* or *how,* that asks for information of content, in contrast to a *yes/no* question.

***Yes/no* interrogative.** The words *if* and *whether* (*or not*) that introduce nominal clauses that ask or suggest a *yes/no* question: "I wonder *if Kim is coming*"; "I wonder *whether or not she's coming.*"

***Yes/no* question.** A question that calls for a *yes* or *no* response. It is characterized by the opening auxiliary, in contrast to the interrogative that opens the *wh*-question: "*Are* you being served?" "*Did* the Orioles win?"

An Introduction to Transformational Grammar

The theory of **transformational generative grammar** (often abbreviated T-G or called simply transformational grammar) has itself gone through several stages of transformation since 1957, when it was first presented by Noam Chomsky in his book *Syntactic Structures* (The Hague: Mouton). But despite the changes that the field of linguistics has undergone, the goal of linguists remains the same: to account for the ability that native speakers of a language share in generating and processing sentences, to account for our knowledge of language.

Although its purpose was not pedagogical or practical like that of traditional and structural theory, transformational theory has practical value for the student of grammar. Many of the ideas in this book are taken directly from transformational grammar: the verb-expansion rule in Chapter 3, for example, and the idea of sentence transformations discussed in Chapter 4 and elsewhere.

One of the most useful concepts from early transformational theory is the idea that a sentence has both a "deep structure" and a "surface structure." The **deep structure** consists of the semantic and grammatical relationships that underlie the surface structure; the **surface structure** is the form the sentence takes when we speak it. This concept of a deep structure underlying all our sentences accounts for our ability to perceive more than one meaning when a sentence is ambiguous. Consider the following sentence:

Visiting relatives can be boring.

Who is doing the visiting, you or your relatives? The sentence is structurally ambiguous because there is more than one possible deep structure underlying the opening noun phrase, *visiting relatives*. In one, *relatives* is the subject of *visiting*; in the other, it is the object. The transformations that the two different deep structures go through result in the same surface structure:

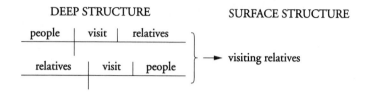

DEEP STRUCTURE   SURFACE STRUCTURE

| people | visit | relatives |
| relatives | visit | people |

→ visiting relatives

Investigating Language   *A.1*

If you have studied the nominals in Chapter 7 and the adjectivals in Chapter 6, you understand the difference between gerunds and participles. One way to illustrate the two possible deep structures underlying these sentences is to diagram each of them in two ways.

> Flying planes can be dangerous.
>
> I don't like burping babies.

However, the traditional diagram will not illustrate the ambiguity of this third sentence. What is different about it?

> The shooting of the hunters was astonishing.

The passive transformation illustrates the opposite situation—two different surface structures that mean the same thing:

> Howard Hughes built *The Spruce Goose.*
>
> *The Spruce Goose* was built by Howard Hughes.

We are able to recognize these two sentences, these two different surface structures, as synonymous because they share the same deep structure. The relationship between Howard Hughes and *The Spruce Goose* remains the same no matter what the surface structure: Howard Hughes is the agent or actor (in this case, the builder); *The Spruce Goose* is the object of the action.

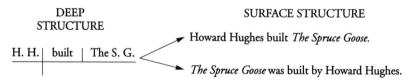

DEEP STRUCTURE   SURFACE STRUCTURE

| H. H. | built | The S. G. |

→ Howard Hughes built *The Spruce Goose.*

→ *The Spruce Goose* was built by Howard Hughes.

It was Chomsky's belief that the descriptive methods of the traditional and structural grammarians were simply inadequate to account for or explain this important aspect of language: this intuitive recognition of ambiguity and synonymy in sentences. One of his classic examples illustrates still another aspect of this inadequacy. The following sentences, neither ambiguous nor synonymous, are outwardly identical in structure:

John is easy to please.

John is eager to please.

A traditional analysis confirms their similarity:

But think about the underlying meaning. Think about the relationship of *John* and *please* in the two sentences. They are not the same. In one sentence John is doing the pleasing; in the other, someone is pleasing him. The first sentence can be paraphrased:

It is easy to please John.

The second cannot:

*It is eager to please John.

The theory attempts to describe how it is that a native speaker knows that those two sentences have different meanings. It is concerned with the underlying logical relations and the way in which the deep structure, the meaning, gets transformed into the outward surface structure.

The sentences about John are similar to the ambiguous sentence about the shooting that you considered in the Investigating Language exercise:

The shooting of the hunters was astonishing.

Both interpretations of this sentence—whether the hunters did the shooting or were themselves shot—will produce the same traditional diagram: In both, *shooting* is a gerund. Transformational grammar, however, will account for the ambiguity by generating two different deep structures underlying this one surface structure.

Deep structure is described in terms of *phrase-structure* rules such as the following:

RULE 1: S → NP + VP

This rule says that a sentence can be rewritten as, or consists of, a noun phrase and a verb phrase. We used the branching diagram of this rule in Chapter 2 to describe the sentence patterns:

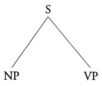

Our second rewrite rule describes the noun phrase, which begins with the determiner. We know that not every noun takes a determiner: Proper nouns do not, nor do all plural nouns. So we'll show the determiner as optional. Of course many of our noun phrases include modifiers; we commonly add adjectives and prepositional phrases. All of the following formulas represent possible noun phrases:

1. N (students)
2. Det + N (the students)
3. Det + Adj + N (the weary students)
4. Adj + N (weary students)
5. Det + N + Prep Phr (the students in the dorm)
6. Det + Adj + N + Prep Phr (the weary students in the dorm)

The one thing that all of these noun phrase variations have in common is, obviously, the noun headword. So taking advantage of parentheses, which mean "optional," we can come up with a rule that will account for all of them:

RULE 2: NP → (Det) + (Adj) + N + (Prep Phr)

You'll recall that we used this same technique in the verb-expansion rule in Chapter 3. Now the NP rule says that the one requirement is the noun, the headword—the only element without parentheses; we can add a determiner and/or an adjective in prenoun position and a prepositional phrase in postnoun position if we wish.

We haven't quite finished the rewrite rule for NPs. We'll come back to it after we examine the expanded VP.

The VP rule describes how to generate a grammatical verb phrase.

RULE 3: VP → AUX + V + (COMP) + (ADV)

The required components are the auxiliary and the verb; the complement and the adverbial are optional, as indicated by the parentheses. The rule simply states in terms of a single formula what you have learned in your study of the sentence patterns: Some sentence patterns have a complement (a noun phrase or an adjective), and some don't, depending on the class of the verb.

You will understand why the AUX is shown as required instead of optional when you consider the next phrase-structure rule:

RULE 4: AUX → T + (M) + (have + -en) + (be + -ing)

This rule should look familiar. It is, of course, the verb-expansion rule without the main-verb slot at the end. In other words, it is the rule that describes how the auxiliary is generated. AUX is shown in the VP rule as required because, as you will recall from Chapter 3, every verb phrase includes tense, T. And in this rule, T is a component of the auxiliary.

Two more rules, which rewrite the complement and the adverbial, will enable us to generate skeletal versions of most of our sentence patterns:

RULE 5: COMP → $\begin{Bmatrix} NP \\ Adj \end{Bmatrix}$

RULE 6: ADV → $\begin{Bmatrix} Adv \\ Prep\ Phr \end{Bmatrix}$

The complement will be either an adjective or a noun phrase; the adverbial will be either an adverb or a prepositional phrase. Our final two rules describe the form of the prepositional phrase and the choice of tense:

RULE 7: Prep Phr → Prep + NP

RULE 8: T → $\begin{Bmatrix} Pres \\ Past \end{Bmatrix}$

The clearest way to picture how the phrase-structure rules work is to draw a branching tree. Here, for example, is a tree that represents the deep structure of our sample Pattern VII sentence from Chapter 2: *The students studied their assignment.*

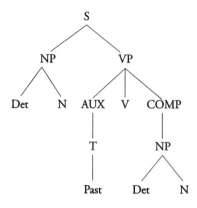

None of the symbols now at the bottom of the tree can be rewritten; that is, none of them appear on the left side of the arrows in the phrase-structure rules. We have thus generated what is known as a *terminal string*:

Det + N + Past + V + Det + N

We now insert words from our lexicon—the inventory, or dictionary, we have in our heads—and produce "The students studied their assignment." If we had wanted to generate the deep structure of "The students studied their assignment in the library," we would have selected ADV as well as COMP in rewriting the VP, then Prep Phrase in rewriting the ADV:

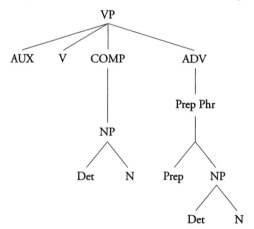

Exercise *A-1*

Follow the phrase-structure rules to generate terminal strings that represent the deep structures of the following sentences. You will find it helpful to identify the sentence pattern and the forms of the structures that fill each slot. Do a branching tree. (Answers to the odd-numbered items are on pages 377–378.)

1. The soup tastes salty.
2. My new car should be in the shop.
3. The car has developed a strange noise in the engine.
4. My roommate became a good friend immediately.

The eight phrase-structure rules enable us to generate most of our sentence patterns—certainly the first seven. When we select *be* as the predicating verb, we can generate I, II, and III by selecting the ADV for I, an adjective as COMP for II, and an NP as COMP for III. To generate Patterns IV and V, again we choose an adjective or an NP as the complement. For VI we can choose an adverbial if we wish. But a bare Pattern VI such as "The children giggled" would require only the following:

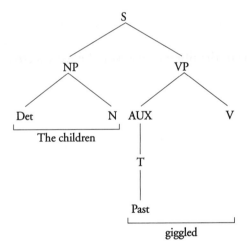

To generate Pattern VII, we can simply select COMP in the VP and rewrite the complement as a noun phrase.

Pattern VIII is a little trickier. You'll recall that it has two NPs in the predicate—an indirect object, followed by a direct object. You'll recall, too, that the indirect object sometimes appears as the object of a preposition:

Pam gave *Joe* a present → Pam gave a present *to Joe*.

We could make the case that the version with *to* is the deep structure and that the one with the indirect object is the transformation. Clearly, the two sentences mean the same thing; they have the same deep structure. So to generate Pattern VIII, we will select both the COMP and the ADV:

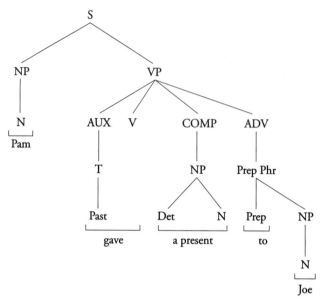

We would have to go beyond this limited introduction to transformational theory to include the rules that generate Patterns IX and X and to generate such structures as gerunds, nominal clauses, appositives, coordinate structures, sentence modifiers, as well as adverbials other than adverbs and prepositional phrases. However, we will add one more detail to the phrase-structure rules to illustrate the embedding feature that underlies a great many of our sentence expansions.

Consider the postnoun modifier in the subject noun phrase of the following sentence:

The people <u>who live across the street</u> are noisy.

Who live across the street is clearly a sentence in form; we can pick out its subject and predicate; we can identify its sentence pattern; and in the traditional diagram we analyze it as a sentence:

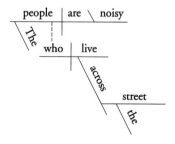

The simple addition of an optional S to our NP rewrite rule will produce the modifying clause. So here is the final form for Rule 2:

RULE 2: NP → (Det) + (Adj) + N + (Prep Phr) + (S)

We can now recognize the noun phrase with the *who* clause in the previous example as Det + N + S:

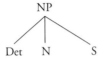

the people [the people live across the street]

The relative pronoun *who* is a feature of the surface structure only; its antecedent, *the people*, is what underlies it in the deep structure of the clause. The embedded S, the modifier, will always include an occurrence of the N headword, the noun being modified, although not necessarily as the subject. In the following sentence the N appears as the direct object in the embedded S:

The neighbors <u>whom we met yesterday</u> are nice.

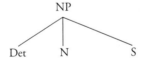

the   neighbors   [we met the neighbors yesterday]

Even when we leave out *whom* from the surface structure, as we probably would in this sentence, we recognize it as a part of the deep structure. The traditional diagram, too, you will recall, includes a slot for the relative pronoun even though it does not appear in the surface structure:

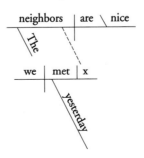

Not all modifiers in the noun phrase, of course, are clauses. The same information, or nearly so, can be conveyed if we reduce the clause to a participial phrase:

The people <u>living across the street</u> are noisy.

We can still identify the sentence pattern of the modifier, however, because sentence patterns are, in effect, verb phrase patterns; this one is Pattern VI, the intransitive verb pattern. Its subject is the noun being modified, *the people*. These two forms of modifiers, the clause and the participial phrase, have the same deep structure; only their surface structures are different. The participial phrase has undergone a transformational operation that deletes the subject.

The notion of the participle or participial phrase as a sentence should be obvious; in Chapter 6 we identified the sentence patterns underlying both pre- and postnoun participles. And we saw that the diagram of the participial phrase looks just like the verb half of a sentence:

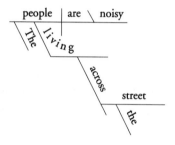

Exercise **A-2**

Draw a tree to illustrate the deep structure of the following sentences. Make sure that you have reached a terminal string—i.e., that none of the elements at the bottom of the tree can be rewritten. (Answers to the odd-numbered items are on pages 378–379.)

1. The car that my sister bought in June needs four new tires already.
2. Peter recognized that man standing at the edge of the crowd.
3. Our house was designed by my father.
4. The neighbors are building their new puppy an elegant doghouse.
5. That young woman rowing the boat toward the pier is holding a rabbit on her lap.
6. The woman with the rabbit looks familiar.

The following sentences are ambiguous. Illustrate their two possible deep structures by doing a phrase-structure tree to illustrate one meaning and a traditional diagram to illustrate the other. (Answers to the odd-numbered items are on pages 380–381.)

1. Mary washed the stones she found in the river.
2. We discussed our problem with the teacher.
3. My roommate is always entertaining.
4. My parents live near the school on Main Street.

In Chapter 1 we labeled transformational grammar as a revolutionary method of examining language. For the first time linguists were interested, not simply in examining the sentences we speak, their surface structures, but rather in examining grammar knowledge, our innate ability to generate and process language. And even though the early version of transformational grammar described here has long since been replaced by much more intricate, and constantly evolving, linguistic theories, this brief overview does explain the branching diagram, now commonly used in linguistic descriptions, as well as the important concepts of deep and surface structure. It also explains the origin of the verb-expansion rule, which you studied in Chapter 3, and gives you another view of the transformations and reduced clauses that are introduced in Chapter 4 and elsewhere.

ANSWERS TO THE APPENDIX EXERCISES

Exercise A-1

1.

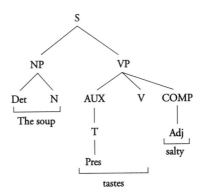

3.

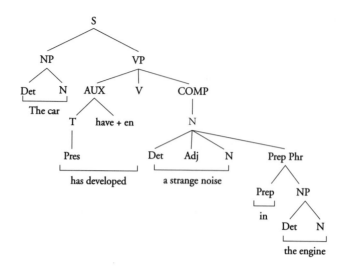

Exercise A-2

1.

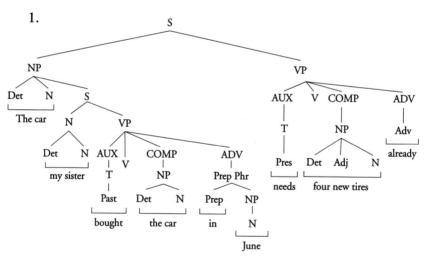

3.

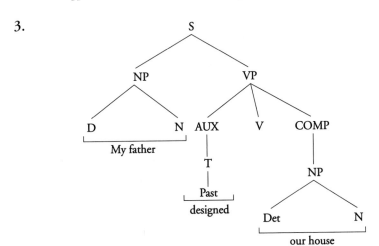

5.

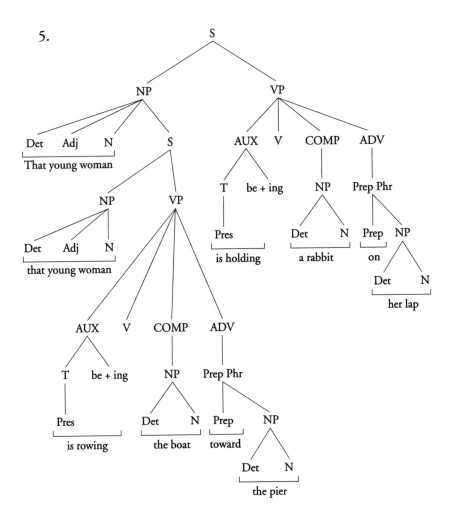

Exercise A-3

1.

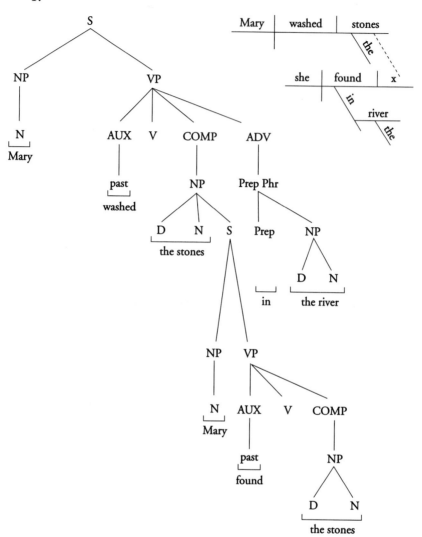

3.

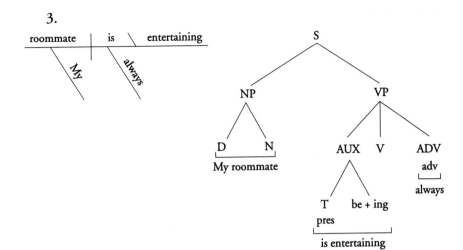

Answers to the Exercises

CHAPTER 2

Exercise 1, page 25
1. commissioners, husband, mayor, residents, merchants, law
2. of the community, in town (prepositional phrases)

Exercise 2, page 31
1. Brian's problem | is | serious. (Pattern II)
   NP   be   adj
   subj   pred   subj comp
           vb

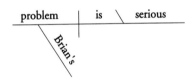

2. The workers | are | on the roof. (Pattern I)
   NP   be   prep phr
   subj   pred   ADV/TP
           vb

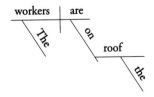

3. The excitement of the fans | is | really contagious. (Pattern II)

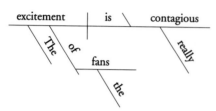

4. Brevity | is | the soul of wit. (Pattern III)

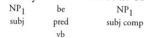

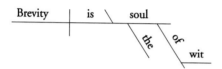

5. The final exam | was | at four o'clock. (Pattern I)

6. The kids | are | very silly. (Pattern II)

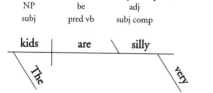

7. The Wongs | were | quiet neighbors. (Pattern III)

NP₁   be   NP₁
subj   pred vb   subj comp

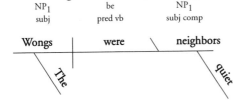

8. Those joggers | are | out of shape. (Pattern II)

NP   be   prep phr
subj   pred   subj comp
     vb

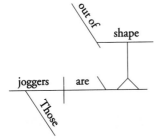

9. The basketball team | is | on a roll. (Pattern II)

NP   be   prep phr
subj   pred   subj comp
     vb

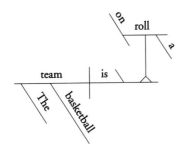

10. A foolish consistency | is | the hobgoblin of little minds. (Pattern III)

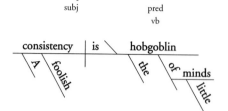

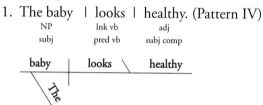

Exercise 3, page 33

1. The baby | looks | healthy. (Pattern IV)

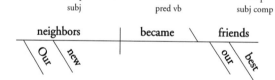

2. Our new neighbors | became | our best friends. (Pattern V)

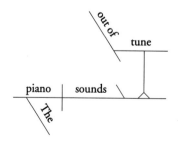

3. The piano | sounds | out of tune. (Pattern IV)

4. Ryan | looks | like his older brother. (Pattern IV)
     NP   lnk vb   prep phr
     subj   pred vb   subj comp

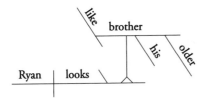

5. You | look | a mess! (Pattern V)
     pro   lnk vb NP_1
     subj   pred vb subj comp
   (NP_1)

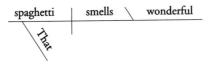

6. That spaghetti | smells | wonderful. (Pattern IV)
       NP   lnk vb   adj
       subj   pred vb subj comp

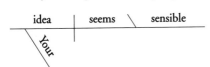

7. Your idea | seems | sensible. (Pattern IV)
       NP   lnk vb   adj
      subj   pred vb subj comp

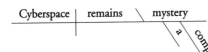

8. Cyberspace | remains | a complete mystery. (Pattern V)
     NP_1 lnk vb NP_1
     subj   pred vb   subj comp

Exercise 4, page 36

1. The rug in the dining room is dirty.   (II)
    adj

2. On sunny days we lounge on the lawn between classes.   (VI)
    adv   adv   adv

3. The break between classes seems very short on sunny days.   (IV)
    adj   adv

4. At the diner on Water Street, we chatted aimlessly until midnight.   (VI)
    adj   adv
    adv

5. Daylilies grow wild in our backyard.   (VI—or, perhaps, IV)
    adv

6. In 1638 a young philanthropist of Puritan background became the
    adv   adj
    founder of the oldest university in the U.S.   (V)
    adj
    adj

7. The name of that young man was John Harvard.   (III)
    adj

8. My cousin from Iowa City works for a family with seven children.   (VI)
    adj   adj
    adv

Exercise 5, page 38

1.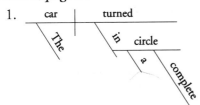

car | turned
The | in circle / a \ complete

2.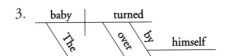

boys | turned in
The | at midnight

3.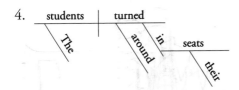

baby | turned
The | over / by himself

4.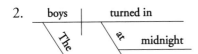

students | turned
The | around / in seats \ their

5.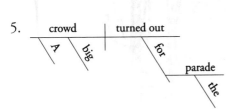

crowd | turned out
A \ big | for parade \ the

6.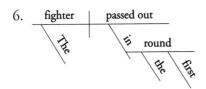

fighter | passed out
The | in round \ the \ first

7.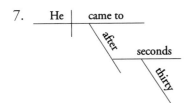

He | came to
after seconds \ thirty

8.

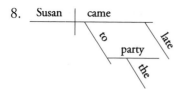

9.

10.

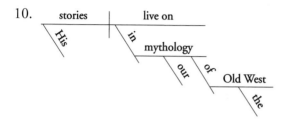

Exercise 6, page 41

1. The boys | prepared | a terrific spaghetti dinner. (VII)
    NP₁   tr vb   NP₂
    subj   pred vb   dir obj

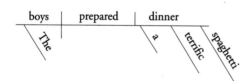

2. An old jalopy | turned | into our driveway. (VI)
    NP   int vb   prep phr
    subj   pred vb   opt ADV

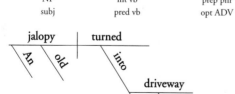

3. The ugly duckling | turned into | a beautiful swan. (V)
   NP₁ — subj   lnk vb — pred vb   NP₁ — subj comp

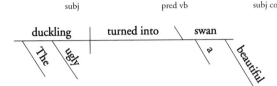

4. The fog | comes | on little cat feet. (VI)
   NP — subj   int vb — pred vb   prep phr — opt ADV

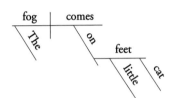

5. On Sundays | the neighbor across the hall | walks | his dog |
   prep phr — opt ADV   NP₁ — subj   tr vb — pred vb   NP₂ — dir obj

   at 6:00 A.M. (VII)
   prep phr
   opt ADV

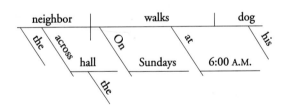

6. Betsy | often | jogs | with her dog. (VI)
   NP — subj   adv — opt ADV   int vb — pred vb   prep phr — opt ADV

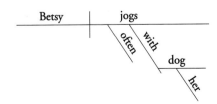

7. After two months | the teachers | called off | their strike. (VII)
    prep phr   NP₁   tr vb   NP₂
    opt ADV   subj   pred vb   dir obj

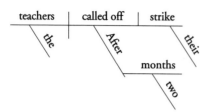

8. The whole gang | reminisced | at our class reunion |
       NP   int vb   prep phr
      subj   pred vb   opt ADV

about the good old days. (VI)
    prep phr
    opt ADV

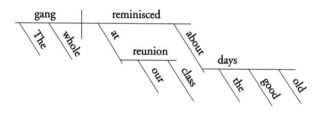

9. My best friend from high school | arrived | on Friday |
            NP   int vb   prep phr
           subj   pred vb   opt ADV

for the weekend. (VI)
    prep phr
    opt ADV

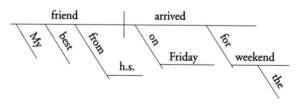

10. The mass of men │ lead │ lives of quiet desperation. (VII)
      NP₁   tr vb   NP₂
      subj   pred vb   dir obj

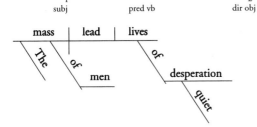

Exercise 7, page 44

1. Jessica │ made │ her new boyfriend │ some cookies. (VIII)
    NP₁   tr vb   NP₂   NP₃
    subj   pred vb   ind obj   dir obj

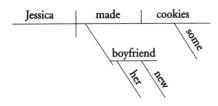

2. I │ made │ an A │ on my research paper. (VII)
   pro   tr vb   NP₂   prep phr
   subj   pred vb   dir obj   opt ADV
   (NP₁)

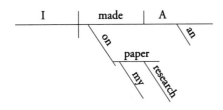

3. For lunch | Manny | made | himself | a humongous sandwich. (VIII)

prep phr	NP₁	tr vb	pro	NP₃
opt ADV	subj	pred vb	ind obj	dir obj
			(NP₂)	

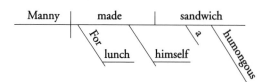

4. The kids | made up | a story about Pokemon monsters. (VII)

NP₁	tr vb	NP₂
subj	pred vb	dir obj

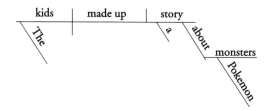

5. The teacher | wrote | a lot of comments | in the margins. (VII)

NP₁	tr vb	NP₂	prep phr
subj	pred vb	dir obj	opt ADV

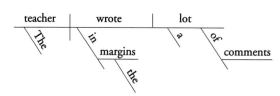

6. My advisor | wrote | a letter of recommendation | for me. (VIII)

NP₁	tr vb	NP₂	prep phr
subj	pred vb	dir obj	ind obj

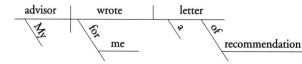

7. I | wrote down | the assignment | very carefully. (VII)

   pro   tr vb   NP₂   adv phr

   subj   pred vb   dir obj   opt ADV

   (NP₁)

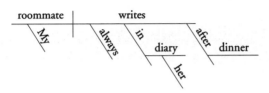

8. My roommate | always | writes | in her diary | after dinner. (VI)

    NP   adv   intr vb   prep phr   prep phr

    subj   opt ADV   pred vb   opt ADV   opt ADV

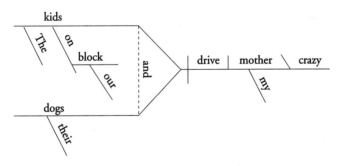

Exercise 8, page 47

1. The kids on our block and their dogs | drive | my mother | crazy. (IX)

            NP₁   tr vb   NP₂   adj

     compound subj   pred vb dir obj obj comp

2. She | calls | them | a menace to the neighborhood. (X)

   pro   tr vb   pro   NP$_2$

   subj   pred vb   dir obj   obj comp

   (NP$_1$)   (NP$_2$)

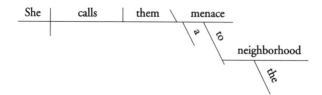

3. On Friday | the weather | suddenly | turned | cold and blustery. (IV)

   prep phr   NP   adv   lnk vb   compound adj

   opt ADV   subj   opt ADV   pred vb   subj comp

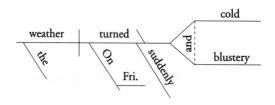

4. Yesterday | Luis | bought | himself | an expensive leather coat |

   adv   NP$_1$ tr vb   pro   NP$_3$

   opt ADV   subj   pred vb   ind obj   dir obj

                       (NP$_2$)

at Nordstrom. (VIII)

   prep phr

   opt ADV

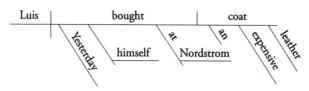

5. England's soccer fans | have | a reputation for wild behavior. (VII)

         NP$_1$ tr vb   NP$_2$

         subj   pred vb   dir obj

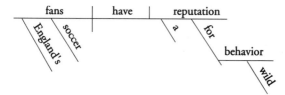

6. My boss at the pizza parlor | promised | me | a raise. (VIII)

       NP₁   tr vb   pro   NP₃

       subj   pred vb   ind obj   dir obj

                                               (NP₂)

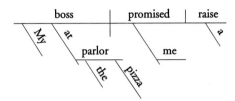

7. Hector's party | broke up | at midnight. (VI)

       NP   int vb   prep phr

       subj   pred vb   opt ADV

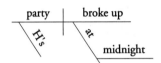

8. The Green Party | chose | Ralph Nader | as its candidate |

       NP₁   tr vb   NP₂   NP₂

       subj   pred vb   dir obj   obj comp

in 2000. (X)

  prep phr

  opt ADV

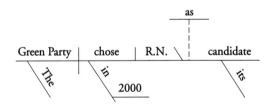

9. Joe | cut | himself | a huge piece of cake. (VIII)

NP₁   tr vb   pro   NP₃

subj   pred vb   ind obj   dir obj

               (NP₂)

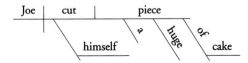

10. Alaska | became | the forty-ninth state | in 1959. (V)
   NP₁   lnk vb   NP₁   prep phr
   subj   pred vb   subj comp   opt ADV

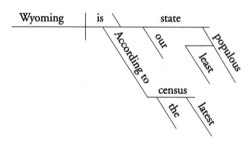

11. According to the latest census, | Wyoming | is |
    prep phr   NP₁   be
    opt ADV   subj   pred vb

our least populous state. (III)
   NP₁
   subj comp

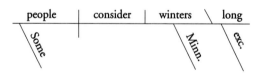

12. Some people | consider | Minnesota's winters | excessively long. (IX)
    NP₁   tr vb   NP₂   adj phr
    subj   pred vb   dir obj   obj comp

13. Our team | plays | Indiana | in the HIT | on Saturday night. (VII)
    NP₁   tr vb   NP₂   prep phr   prep phr
    subj   pred vb   dir obj   opt ADV   opt ADV

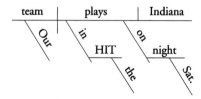

14. I | ordered | you | a large Coke and a cheeseburger with onions. (VIII)

pro   tr vb   pro   NP₃
subj   pred vb   ind obj   compound dir obj
(NP₁)   (NP₂)

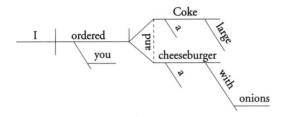

15. Professor Moore | assigned | the class | six chapters |

NP₁   tr vb   NP₂   NP₃
subj   pred vb   ind obj   dir obj

for Monday. (VIII)

prep phr
opt ADV

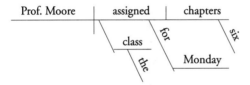

CHAPTER 3

Exercise 9, page 62

1. have	has	had	having	had
2. do	does	did	doing	done
3. say	says	said	saying	said
4. make	makes	made	making	made
5. go	goes	went	going	gone
6. take	takes	took	taking	taken
7. come	comes	came	coming	come
8. see	sees	saw	seeing	seen
9. get	gets	got	getting	got, gotten
10. move	moves	moved	moving	moved
11. prove	proves	proved	proving	proved, proven
12. put	puts	put	putting	put

13.	think	thinks	thought	thinking	thought
14.	beat	beats	beat	beating	beat, beaten
15.	meet	meets	met	meeting	met

Exercise 10, page 68
A.

1. has worked
2. was working
3. will be playing
4. was being
5. is having
6. should have had
7. had had
8. could have been
9. may have been trying
10. might have been being

B.

1. past + be + -ing + study
2. pres + have + -en + find
3. past + lose
4. pres + have + -en + be + -ing + skip
5. past + can + be
6. past + crash
7. pres + seem
8. pres + will + be + -ing + have
9. pres + may + be + -ing + graduate
10. past + shall + have + -en + study

Exercise 11, page 78

1. The lead article in today's *Collegian* was written by my roommate.
2. Some of our most intricate fugues were composed by Bach.
3. The most expensive houses in town are built by my brother-in-law.
4. That expensive apartment complex on Allen Street is being built by him.
5. A new tax collection system will be discussed by the county commissioners at their next meeting.

6. Power lines in three counties have been knocked down by heavy thunderstorms.
7. The fire could be seen by people on neighboring farms.
8. Our conversation was being recorded by a hidden microphone.
9. Your plan of study should have been approved by an advisor.
10. The classroom is decorated by (with) brightly colored posters.

Exercise 12, page 79

1. The cheerleading squad led the football team onto the field. (VII)
2. A committee chooses the cheerleaders in the spring. (VII)
3. The managing editor had warned the new reporters about late submissions. (VII)
4. Someone has burglarized several apartments in our building recently. (VII)
5. UPS should deliver a shipment of fresh lobsters soon. (VII)
6. Someone manufactured dental floss for the first time in 1882. (VII)
7. People are discussing the abortion question around the country. (VII)
8. The bank must have granted Gabrielle an extension on her loan payment. (VIII)
9. The critics called the play a smashing success. (X)
10. Someone has rendered the poison harmless. (IX)

CHAPTER 4

Exercise 13, page 98

1.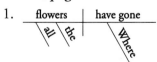

2.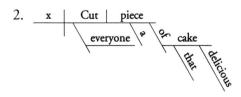

3.

4.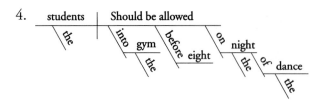

5.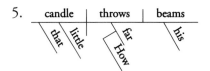

6.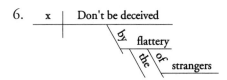

7.

8.

Exercise 14, page 101

1. expletive (Pattern VII)
2. adverb (Pattern I)
3. expletive (Pattern I)
4. expletive (Pattern I)
5. adverb (Pattern I)
6. adverb (Pattern VI)
7. expletive (Pattern I)
8. adverb (Pattern VI)

CHAPTER 5

Exercise 15, page 116

1. 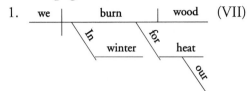 (VII)

2. 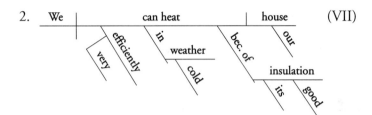 (VII)

3. 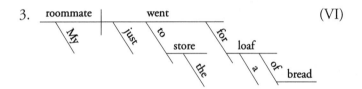 (VI)

4. 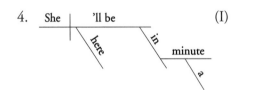 (I)

5. (VII)

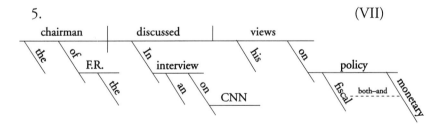

6.   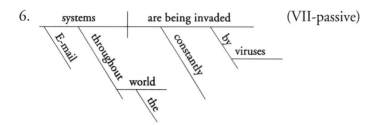   (VII-passive)

7.   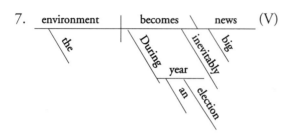   (V)

8.   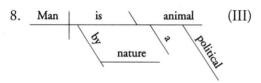   (III)

Exercise 16, page 117

1. I'm going to wax the car parked in the garage.
   I'm going into the garage to wax the car.
2. We watched the game from the porch.
   We watched the game being played on the porch.
3. I hid from the neighbors who live upstairs.
   I went upstairs to hide from the neighbors.
4. Fred tripped his teammate who was holding the bat.
   Fred stuck the bat out and tripped his teammate.
5. Susan washed the stones she found in the riverbed.
   Susan went to the river to wash the stones she found.

Exercise 17, page 119

1. Pete is working <u>nights</u> <u>this week</u>. (Pattern VI)
                 N   NP

2. I was awake <u>the whole night</u>. (Pattern II)
                NP

3. I'll see you <u>soon</u>. (Pattern VII)
            adv

4. <u>This morning</u> Pam threw away the leftover spaghetti. (Pattern VII)
   NP

5. George will do dishes <u>next time</u>. (Pattern VII)
                        NP

6. I love weekends (Pattern VII)

7. Bill works <u>weekends</u>. (Pattern VI)
             N

8. <u>At the first sign of winter</u> the birds flew <u>south</u>. (Pattern VI)
        prep phr   adv

Exercise 18, page 123

1. Our cat <u>often</u> jumps <u>up</u> <u>on the roof</u> <u>to reach the attic window</u>. (main clause: Pattern VI; infinitive: Pattern VII)

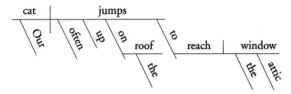

2. <u>Sometimes</u> she <u>even</u> climbs the ladder <u>to get there</u>. (main clause: Pattern VII; infinitive: Pattern VI)

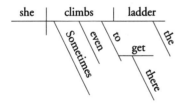

3. <u>Last night</u> my computer blinked <u>ominously</u> <u>during an electrical storm</u>. (Pattern VI)

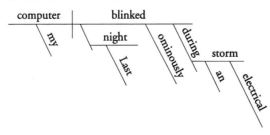

4. I <u>immediately</u> turned it off. (Pattern VII)

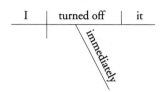

5. We went <u>to the mall</u> <u>last Saturday</u> <u>to check out the big sales</u>.
   (main clause: Pattern VI; infinitive: Pattern VII)

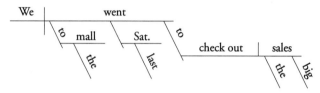

6. <u>Afterwards</u> we stayed <u>home</u> <u>to watch the playoff game with Uncle</u>
   <u>Dick</u>. (main clause: Pattern VI; infinitive: Pattern VII)

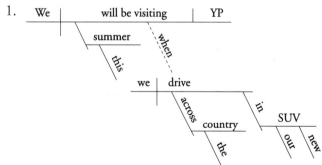

Exercise 19, page 125

1.

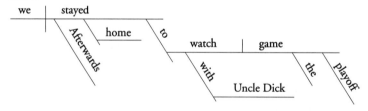

2.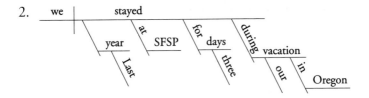

3.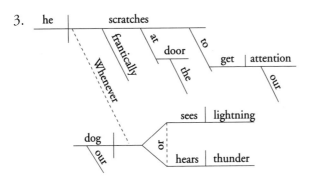

4.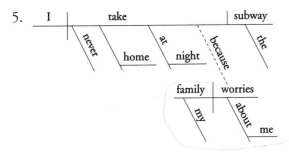

(Note: The adverbial clause could also be interpreted as a modifier of the main verb.)

5.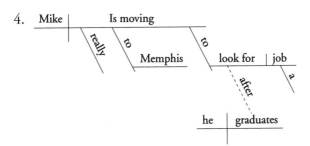

6.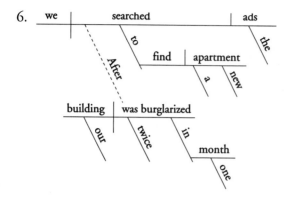

CHAPTER 6

Exercise 20, page 138

A. 1. <u>a</u> highly successful land <u>speculator</u>
(D)   (qualified adj)   (n)   (H)

2. <u>today's</u> <u>standards</u>
(D)   (H)

3. <u>his</u> entire <u>fortune</u>
(D)   (adj)   (H)

4. <u>This</u> financial <u>disaster</u>
(D)   (adj)   (H)

5. <u>a</u> local <u>newspaper</u>
(D) (adj)   (H)

6. <u>their</u> newly discovered <u>eccentric</u>
(D)   (modified part.)   (H)

7. <u>an</u> old blue military <u>uniform</u>
(D) (adj) (adj)   (adj)   (H)

8. <u>every</u> public <u>function</u> and <u>meeting</u>
(D)   (adj)   (H)   (H)

9. <u>a</u> large upholstered <u>chair</u>
(D) (adj)   (part)   (H)

10. <u>the</u> state <u>legislature</u>
(D)   (n)   (H)

11. <u>his</u> own imperial <u>bonds</u>
(D)   (adj)   (adj)   (H)

12. <u>each</u> <u>note</u>
(D)   (H)

13. the face value
    (D)   (n)   (H)

14. a scientific conference
    (D)   (adj)   (H)

15. His lavish funeral
    (D)   (adj)   (H)

B. 1. The department's personnel committee
       (D)   (n)   (H)

    the main office   this morning
    (D)   (adj)   (H)   (D)   (H)

2. Our whole family   the new Sunday brunch menu   the cafeteria
   (D)   (adj) (H)   (D)   (adj)   (n)   (n)   (H)   (D)   (H)

3. Serena's daughter   an expensive-looking copper-colored bracelet
   (D)   (H)   (D)   (adj)   (part)   (n)   (part)   (H)

   the subway station
   (D)   (n)   (H)

4. The bicycle safety commission   the new regulations
   (D)   (n)   (n)   (H)   (D)   (adj)   (H)

   their regular meeting   this noon
   (D)   (adj)   (H)   (D)   (H)

5. Her lovely, gracious manner   the start
   (D)   (adj)   (adj)   (H)   (D)   (H)

6. Any mother   the job   several air-traffic controllers
   (D)   (H)   (D) (H)   (D)   (n)   (n)   (H)

7. The rising interest rates   a serious concern
   (D)   (part)   (n)   (H)   (D)   (adj)   (H)

   every cost-conscious citizen
   (D)   (n)   (adj)   (H)

Exercise 21, page 141

1. with a cast on his left foot
2. of the museum (*near the visitors' information booth* could modify either *museum* or *meet*)
3. after the game (*at Bob's house* could modify either *party* or *game*)
4. of computer viruses
5. from within
6. for my science course, from Stanford
7. in the United States, of money
8. with the weakest qualifications, about the selection process

Exercise 22, page 144

1. that doesn't bite; modifies *rattlesnake; that* = subj; VI
2. who died in 1994; modifies *Jacqueline Kennedy Onassis; who* = subj; VI
3. that the jazz club is sponsoring; modifies *concert; that* = dir obj; VII
4. [that] she gave the bride and groom; modifies *gift; [that]* = dir obj; VIII
5. whose virtues . . . discovered; modifies *plant; whose* = det; VII (passive)
6. who have everything but good sense; modifies *kids; who* = subj; VII
7. whom she had not seen in years; modifies *people; whom* = dir obj; VII
8. in which the connection . . . explained; modifies *article; which* = obj of prep; VII (passive)
9. which was damp and drafty; modifies *shed; which* = subj; III
10. that killed the rat; modifies *cat; that* = subj; VII
    that ate the malt; modifies *rat; that* = subj; VII
    that lay in the house; modifies *malt; that* = subj; VI
    that Jack built; modifies *house; that* = dir obj; VII

Exercise 23, page 149
Here are some possibilities; you will think of others.

1. Bill owns that expensive sports car standing in the driveway. (Note that the indefinite *an* becomes definite with *that*.)
2. I am babysitting for the baby sleeping upstairs in the crib.
3. Some of the fans lining up at the ticket office will probably be disappointed.
4. The students searching the Internet want to find material for their research projects.
5. The defense could not stop the fullback charging through the line.
6. The teachers walking the picket line have been on strike for eight days.

Exercise 24, page 151

1. The award <u>given every year to the outstanding volunteer</u> has
                        VIII (passive)

   been announced.

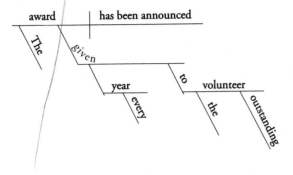

2. <u>Being a philosopher</u>, she can propose a problem for every solution.
      III

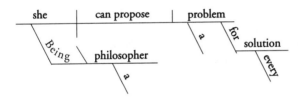

3. He has all the gall of a shoplifter <u>returning an item for a refund</u>.
                                    VII

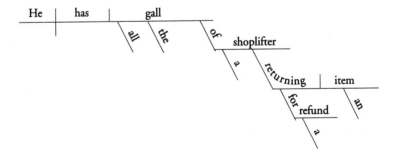

4. The hostess gave the <u>departing</u> guests some leftover food for
                   VI

their pets.

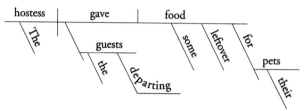

(The prepostional phrase could also be interpreted as adverbial)

5. <u>Finding the price reasonable</u>, they rented the apartment on the spot.
        IX

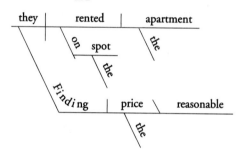

6. Congress shall make no law <u>abridging the freedom of speech or</u>
                                   VII

<u>of the press.</u>

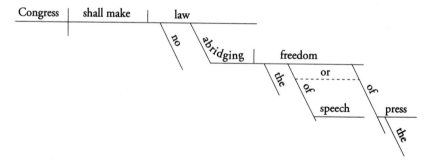

7. They planned the class picnic for Saturday, <u>hoping for good weather</u>.
$$\text{VI}$$

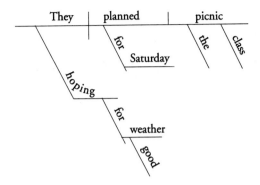

8. The university will not fund research <u>involving genetic manipulation</u>.
$$\text{VII}$$

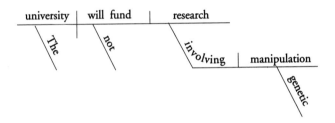

9. The special computer workshops <u>held on campus last weekend</u>
$$\text{VII (passive)}$$
were designed for students <u>majoring in business</u>.
$$\text{VI}$$

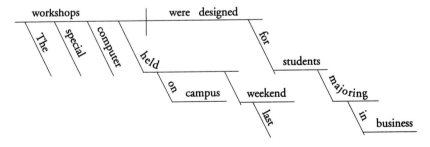

10. The teachers' union has finally approved the last two <u>disputed</u>
VII (passive)
sections of the contract <u>offered by the school district</u>.
VII (passive)

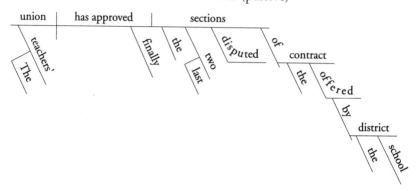

Exercise 25, page 155
Here are some possibilities; you will probably think of others.

1. Because the house needed considerable repair, my parents were able to buy it for little money.
2. When installing a new program, you should turn off all other applications.
3. Having misunderstood the assignment, I got a low grade on my paper.
4. The archeologists could not decipher the inscription, which was covered with the grime of centuries.
5. The bus left without the woman who was still searching for change in her purse.
6. The patient spent four hours on the operating table while doctors performed a double bypass on her (or his) severely blocked arteries.
7. Once considered only an average player, Chris has greatly improved his game in the last three months.
8. The dean of men surprised several members of the football team as they were breaking in through the window of the girls' dormitory.
9. I'll eat anything that's pickled.
10. Seen from miles away, the mountain might be mistaken for a cloud.

Exercise 26, page 159

1. Samuel Johnson, who published his famous dictionary in 1755, defined . . .
2. The town where I was born, which has a population of 3,000, offers . . .
3. standing . . . window—*restrictive*, no comma
4. Naphtha, which is highly flammable, is . . .
5. that are . . . employees—*restrictive*, no comma
6. . . . is called an incunabulum, which literally means "swaddling clothes."
7. bearing down on Florida—*restrictive*, no commas; who live . . . coast—*restrictive*, no comma
8. My Aunt Hazel, who is an expert shopper, spends . . .
9. who are . . . foolish—*restrictive*, no comma
10. Ozzie Smith, leaping high in the air, speared . . .; that would . . . game—*restrictive*, no comma

Exercise 27, page 162

1. in which players . . . target (relative clause)
2. which originated . . . Netherlands (relative clause); of bowling and shuffleboard (prep phrase); of billiards and chess (prep phrase)
3. that is 42 . . . wide (relative clause); of four players to a side (prep phrase); to a side (prep phrase)
4. that is . . . away (relative clause)
5. called Blue Hone (participial phrase); which is . . . resiliency (relative clause)
6. of the wrist (prep phrase); imparting . . . named (participial phrase); for which . . . named (relative clause)
7. on a team (prep phrase); to knock . . . bounds (infinitive phrase)
8. of curling equipment (prep phrase); used by players . . . stone (participial phrase); of a teammate's stone (prep phrase)
9. whose stones . . . target (relative clause); of the target (prep phrase); that is closer (relative clause)
10. where there are . . . circuit (relative clause); who play . . . circuit (relative clause)

CHAPTER 7

Exercise 28, page 172

1. simple ballads sung to guitar music
2. son of the legendary songwriter Woody Guthrie
3. An offbeat film about illegal trash dumping
4. the search for personal freedom
5. a contemporary folk singer and songwriter; *Revival* and *Hell Among the Yearlings*
6. Casey

Exercise 29, page 177

A. 1. Flying a supersonic jet—Pattern VII, subject; main clause: Pattern III

2. playing practical jokes on his players—Pattern VII, direct object; main clause: Pattern VII

3. telling a few jokes—Pattern VII, object of preposition; main clause: Pattern VI

4. staying awake in my eight o'clock class—Pattern IV, subject complement; main clause: Pattern III

5. Leaving the scene of the accident—Pattern VII, subject; main clause: Pattern III

6. seeing the suspect near the entrance of the bank—Pattern VII, direct object; main clause: Pattern VII

7. winning a fourth World Championship—Pattern VII, appositive; main clause: Pattern VI

8. going to college—Pattern VI, object of preposition; main clause: Pattern VI

9. Thinking a problem through—Pattern VII, subject; main clause: Pattern VII

10. being a good wife and homemaker—Pattern III, subject complement; main clause: Pattern III

1.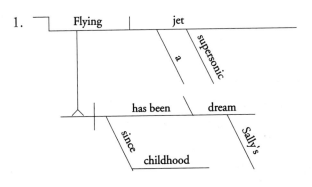

2.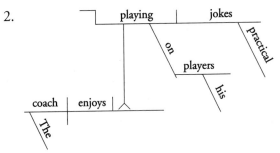

3.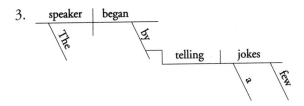

4.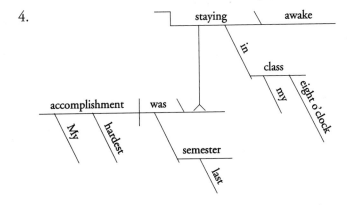

5.

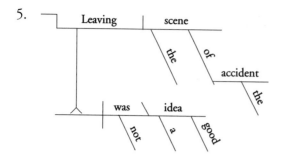

6.

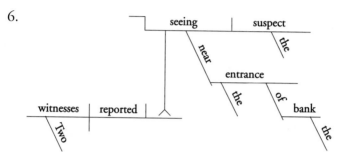

7.

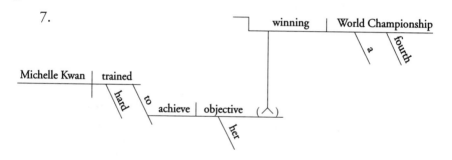

8.

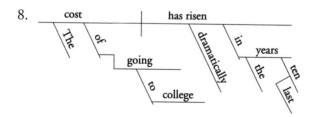

9.

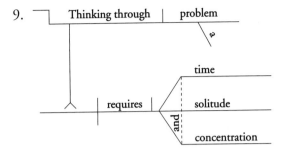

10.

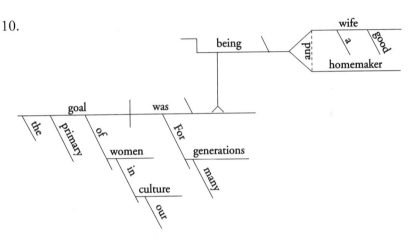

B. Here are some possibilities; you will probably think of others.

Taking grammar tests makes some people nervous. (subj)

Other people like taking grammar tests. (direct obj)

Being punctual is a rare virtue. (subj)

My father has pointed out to me the advantages of being punctual. (obj of prep)

Giving people a helping hand makes me feel useful. (subj)

There are many good reasons for giving people a helping hand. (obj of prep)

Lying on the beach is not everyone's idea of the best way to spend a vacation. (subj)

I enjoyed lying on the beach last summer. (direct obj)

Exercise 30, page 179
Here are some possibilities; you may come up with others.

1. After we had finished the decorations, the ballroom looked beautiful.
2. You will reduce your revising time by following a few helpful pointers.
3. In making a career decision, you will find your counselor a big help.
4. By signing this waiver, you give up any right to make claims against the owner.
5. Our backpacks got really heavy after we hiked up that steep mountain trail.

Exercise 31, page 181

1. to give . . . Christmas—Pattern VIII, direct obj
2. To side with the truth—Pattern VI, subj
3. to beg for mercy—Pattern VI, subj comp
4. To walk . . . night—Pattern VI, subj
5. to become president—Pattern V, direct obj
6. never to take . . . lunch—Pattern VII, appositive
7. to shock . . . views—Pattern VII, direct obj
8. to be . . . times—Pattern II, subj comp
9. to be . . . friendship—Pattern II, subj comp
10. To know him—Pattern VII, subj; to love him—Pattern VII, subj comp

1.

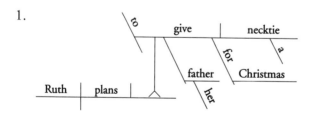

2.

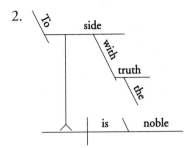

3.

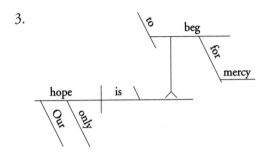

4.

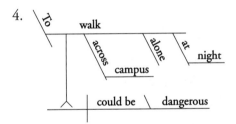

5.

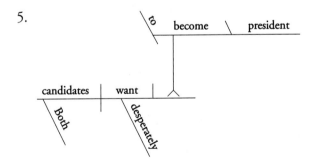

6.

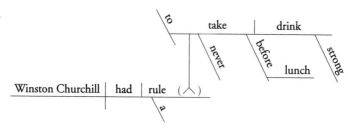

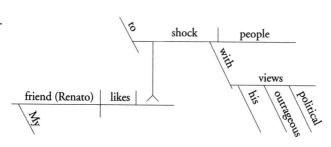

7.

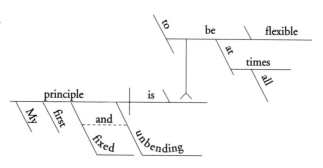

8.

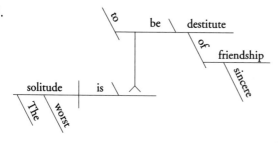

9.

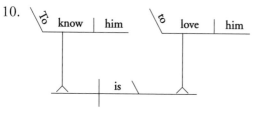

10.

Exercise 32, page 183

1. <u>for you to tell the truth</u>, infinitive (subj comp)
2. <u>remaining silent</u>, gerund (obj of prep)
3. <u>To ignore . . .order</u>, infinitive (subj)
4. <u>to welcome . . . company</u>, infinitive (direct obj)
5. <u>to buy up . . . stocks</u>, infinitive (appositive)
6. <u>Raising . . . profile</u>, gerund (subj)
7. <u>to write . . . assignment</u>, infinitive (direct obj)
8. <u>your proofreading . . . me</u>, gerund (direct obj)
9. <u>to extend the deadline</u>, infinitive (direct obj)
10. <u>The baby's crying</u>, gerund (subj)

1.

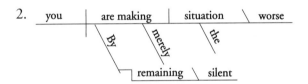

2.

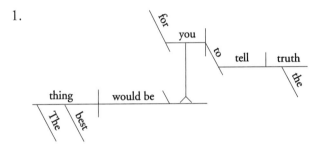

3.

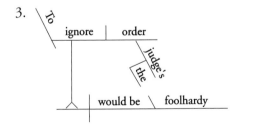

4.

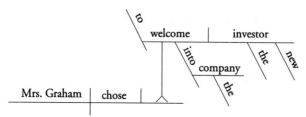

5.

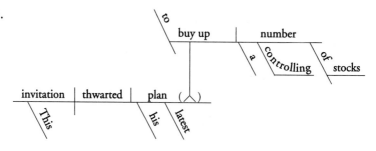

6.

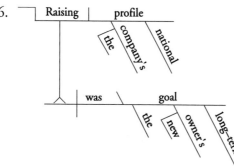

7.

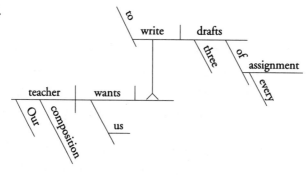

8.

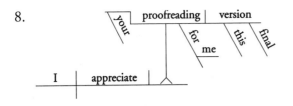

9.

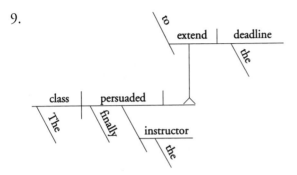

10.

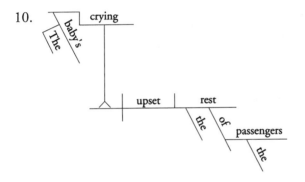

Exercise 33, page 185

Here are some possibilities; you will undoubtedly think of others.

1. You should know <u>that this flight has been cancelled</u>. (direct obj)

2. <u>That the airlines overbook their flights</u> makes everyone angry. (subj)

3. My parents are expecting <u>that I will call them from the airport</u>. (direct obj)

4. <u>That my flight will be late</u> has not occurred to them. (subj)

5. The truth is <u>that they never asked me about my travel plans</u>. (subj comp)

6. The fact <u>that I might keep them waiting</u> disturbs me. (appositive)

Exercise 34, page 188

1. Main clause: Pattern VII; nominal *where* clause (direct obj): Pattern VII

2. Main clause: Pattern VII; adverbial *when* clause: Pattern VII

3. Main clause: Pattern IV; adverbial *when* clause: Pattern VI

4. Main clause: Pattern III; nominal *when* clause (subj): Pattern VI

5. Main clause: Pattern VI; adverbial *where* clause: Pattern VI

6. Main clause: Pattern VIII; adverbial *when* clause: Pattern VII; nominal *where* clause (direct obj): Pattern VII

7. Main clause: Pattern VI; adverbial *where* clause: Pattern VI

8. Main clause: Pattern VII; nominal *where* clause (direct obj): Pattern VII (passive)

9. Main clause: Pattern VII; adverbial *when* clause: Pattern III

10. Main clause: Pattern VII; nominal *where* clause (direct obj): Pattern I; adverbial *when* clause: Pattern VI

Exercise 35, page 188

1. how awesome a redwood tree could be (direct obj)

2. that it was too short (subj comp)

3. What Carlos said about his cousin (subj)

4. why people fear intimacy (obj of prep)

5. that they could have a dog (direct obj)

6. Who invented calculus (subj)

7. which twin was Elaine (direct obj)

8. when the play would end (direct obj)

9. he would explain his explanation (direct obj)

10. that they should replay the point (appositive)

1.

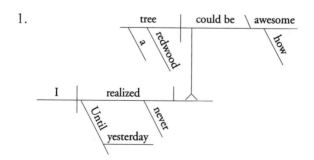

2.

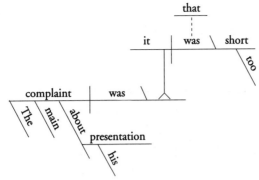

3.

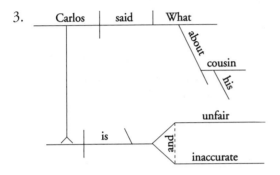

4.

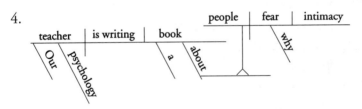

5.

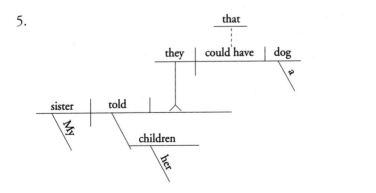

6.

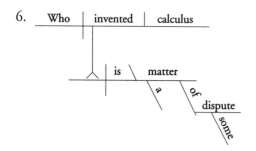

7.

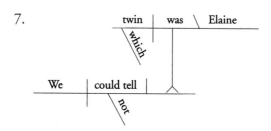

8.

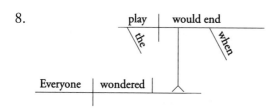

9.

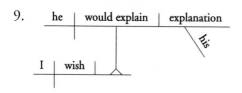

10.

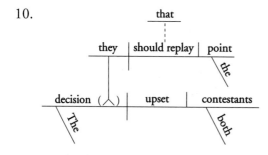

Exercise 36, page 189

1. <u>clipping . . . magazine</u>, gerund (obj of prep)
2. <u>To search . . . scores</u>, infinitive (subj)
3. <u>that we . . . house</u>, nom clause (direct obj)
4. <u>when he would arrive</u>, nom clause (direct obj)
5. <u>to raise their fares</u>, infinitive (direct obj)
6. <u>that they . . . fares</u>, nom clause (direct obj); <u>to raise their fares</u>, infinitive (direct obj)
7. <u>falling asleep at the wheel</u>, gerund (subj comp)
8. <u>Why the Backstreet Boys. . . popular</u>, nom clause (subj)
9. <u>that the semester is almost over</u>, nom clause (appositive)
10. <u>to make . . . class</u>, infinitive (direct obj)
11. <u>how higher tuition . . . enrollments</u>, nom clause (obj of prep)
12. <u>I had studied the wrong chapters</u>, nom clause (direct obj)

CHAPTER 8

Exercise 37, page 199

1. <u>Amazingly</u>
2. (none)
3. <u>Well</u>
4. (none)
5. <u>Strangely</u>
6. (none)
7. <u>Without a doubt</u>
8. <u>no doubt</u>
9. (none)
10. <u>my friend</u>

Exercise 38, page 201

1. (no commas)
2. us, although
3. over, we
4. coffee, since (optional)
5. rent, even
6. (no commas)
7. apartment, even (optional)
8. heat, get

Exercise 39, page 203

A 1. When you are late for work, the subway is better than the bus.
   2. If bread is kept too long in hot weather, mold will grow on it.

3. While we were driving to the game on Saturday, an accident tied up traffic for over an hour.

B. 1. I picked up a Midwestern accent while *I was* living in Omaha.

2. My accent is not as noticeable as Carlo's *accent is* [noticeable].

3. Holmes hit Ali harder than Norton (*hit Ali* or *Holmes hit Norton*).

4. If *it is* necessary, strain the juice before adding the sugar.

5. While *I was* waiting . . .

6. If *your paper is* handed in late . . .

7. Love goes toward love, as schoolboys *go* from their books. But love *goes* from love, *as schoolboys go* toward school with heavy looks.

8. The weather in Little Rock is not as humid *as it is in* New Orleans.

Exercise 40, page 206

1. her tail . . . metronome (participle)

2. their arms . . . shoulders (participle)

3. The rain having . . . hour (participle)

4. her book . . . floor (adjective phrase); her eyes . . . flames (adjective phrase)

5. the streets . . . light (noun phrase); the planet . . . edges (participle); the sky . . . infinity (noun phrase)

6. bunched shirt . . . blades (prepositional phrase); his toes . . . floor (participle); the aunt's arms . . . shoulders (prepositional phrase)

Exercise 41, page 208

1. Cleaning the basement this morning wasn't very much fun.

2. It surprised me that Otis didn't want to stay for the second half of the game.

3. The president criticized the Congress rather severely in his press conference; some observers considered his criticism quite inappropriate.

4. Contrary to the prediction of the weather service, the first snowstorm of the season in Denver was both early and severe.

5. Our having company for dinner three times this week probably means hot dogs for the rest of the month.

CHAPTER 9

Exercise 42, page 215

1. (no commas)
2. now, I
3. tires, shock absorbers, and brake linings
4. 1970s, a 1959 Chevy, required
5. (no commas)
6. Corvette, the car

Exercise 43, page 219

There's more than one possibility in each case.

1. I can't decide which activity I prefer: swimming . . . or jogging . . .
2. I almost never watch television. Either there is nothing on that appeals to me or the picture . . .
3. I don't enjoy flying, and I don't feel like taking the train.
4. Either the superintendent or the members of the school board make the final decision.
5. Either the recipe was printed wrong, or I misread it.
6. I was unhappy with what he said and how he said it.
7. The coach announced an extra hour of drill on Saturday and no practice on Sunday.
8. My history class, as well as both English classes, requires. . .
9. For my birthday dinner, Aunt Rosa has promised to fix her famous lasagna and to bake my favorite cake.
10. For the picnic we brought lemonade and baskets of chicken.

CHAPTER 10

Exercise 44, page 234

nov | a	aud | it | or
re | nov | at | ion	aud | ience
in | nov | ate	in | aud | ible
nov | ice	aud | it | or | ium
nov | el | ist	aud | io
nov = new	aud = hear

dur | able   con | ceive

en | dure   cap | able

dur | ation   sus | cept | ible

dur | ing   cap | ture

en | dur | ance   inter | cept

   dur = hard   cap (cept) = take

Exercise 45, page 235
Check your answers with the dictionary and/or your instructor.

Exercise 46, page 240

1. pre cis ion (bound + bound + bound; affix, base, affix)
    d   d

   (note: d = derivational; i = inflectional)

2. candid ate (free + bound; base, affix)
        d

3. de tour ed (bound + free + bound; affix, base, affix)
   d   i

4. ex cess ive ly (bound + bound + bound + bound; affix, base, affix, affix)
   d   d d

5. un a ware (bound + bound + free; affix, affix, base)
    d d

6. money (free; base)

7. side walk s (free + free + bound; base, base, affix)
        i

8. pro mot ion (bound + bound + bound; affix, base, affix)
    d   d

9. il leg al (bound + bound + bound; affix, base, affix)
   d   d

10. weal th y (free + bound + bound; base, affix, affix)
      d d

11. tele vis ion (bound + bound + bound; affix, base, affix)
    d   d

12. re vis es (bound + bound + bound; affix, base, affix)
    d   i

CHAPTER 11

Exercise 47, page 245

1. pleasure
2. regulation, regulator
3. stealth
4. health, healer
5. derivation
6. inflection
7. formula, formation
8. revival
9. seizure
10. retirement, retiree

Exercise 48, page 246

1. teacher's, teachers'
2. horse's, horses'
3. sister's husband's, sisters' husbands'
4. son's, sons'

Exercise 49, page 248

1. Price's
2. Hedges'
3. James's (or James')
4. Massachusetts'
5. Linus's
6. neighbor's
7. neighbors'
8. Miss Piggy's
9. women's
10. Confucius'

Exercise 50, page 258

friendly	friendlier	friendliest
helpful	more helpful	most helpful
wise	wiser	wisest
awful	more awful	most awful
rich	richer	richest
mellow	mellower	mellowest
expensive	more expensive	most expensive
valid	more valid	most valid
pure	purer	purest
able	abler (more able)	ablest (most able)

Exercise 51, page 262

grief	grieve	grievous	grievously
variation	vary	variable	variably
variance		various	variously
variety			
ability	enable	able	ably
defense	defend	defensive	defensively
economy	economize	economical	economically
		economic	
pleasure	please	pleasant	pleasantly
type	typify	typical	typically
prohibition	prohibit	prohibitive	prohibitively
critic	criticize	critical	critically
criticism			
validation	validate	valid	validly
validity			
appreciation	appreciate	appreciative	appreciatively
beauty	beautify	beautiful	beautifully
acceptance	accept	acceptable	acceptably
purity	purify	pure	purely
continuation	continue	continuous	continuously
continuity		continual	continually

(**Note:** You may think of other possibilities.)

CHAPTER 12

Exercise 52, page 271

1. my, enough, her
2. John's, the
3. Every, this, a
4. more, the week's
5. less, last
6. either, no

Exercise 53, page 275

1. <u>have been</u> (having)
2. <u>used to</u> (use)
3. <u>should have</u> (eaten)
4. <u>can't</u> (look)
5. <u>will be</u> (helping)
6. <u>has to</u> (leave)
7. <u>are</u> (frustrating)
8. <u>can</u> (be)
9. <u>should</u> (continue)
10. <u>am</u> (keeping)

Exercise 54, page 281

1. in, since
2. because of
3. in spite of
4. Prior to, in
5. According to, of, in
6. with (on = particle)
7. Except for, in, of , out of
8. Thanks to, on
9. Between, until
10. within

Exercise 55, page 288

1. <u>and</u>—coordinating conjunction; <u>on</u>—preposition;
   <u>an</u>—determiner; <u>in</u>—preposition
2. <u>Four</u>—determiner; <u>from</u>—preposition; <u>for</u>—preposition;
   <u>for</u>—coordinating conjunction; <u>for</u>—preposition
3. <u>As</u>—subordinating conjunction; <u>an</u>—determiner; <u>as</u>—expletive;
   <u>at</u>—preposition
4. <u>be</u>—auxiliary; <u>by</u>—preposition; <u>but</u>—coordinating conjunction
5. <u>of</u>—preposition; <u>off</u>—particle (part of verb);
   <u>if</u>—subordinating conjunction
6. <u>are</u>—auxiliary; <u>of</u>—preposition; <u>or</u>—expletive; <u>our</u>—determiner
7. <u>will</u>—auxiliary; <u>with</u>—preposition;
   <u>while</u>—subordinating conjunction
8. <u>too</u>—qualifier; <u>two</u>—determiner; <u>to</u>—preposition

CHAPTER 13

Exercise 56, page 296

1. They	4. them	6. him, it
2. We, him	5. them *or*	7. us
3. it	them and him	8. He, them

Exercise 57, page 300

1. herself	3. itself	5. himself
2. themselves	4. ourselves	6. ourselves

Exercise 58, page 305

1. everything—indefinite; I—personal; one—indefinite
2. every—indefinite; any—indefinite; they—personal
3. Someone—indefinite; we—personal; who—interrogative; it—personal
4. All—indefinite; that—relative; I—personal; that—demonstrative
5. much—indefinite; they—personal; both—indefinite; more—indefinite; I—personal
6. I—personal; myself—intensive; whatever—indefinite relative; you—personal
7. enough—indefinite; me—personal
8. themselves—reflexive; one another's—reciprocal
9. me—personal; what—interrogative; I—personal; your—personal
10. whoever—indefinite relative; one—indefinite

CHAPTER 14
There is no one correct answer for any of the exercise items in this chapter. The answers given here are simply suggestions.

Exercise 59, page 321

1. The small band of rebels *resisted* the army patrol for several hours, then *surrendered* just before dawn. News reports . . . did not *specify* . . . .
2. The majority leader *wields* a great deal of influence in the White House. He can easily *circumvent* . . . .

3. Several economists are saying that they *anticipate* an upturn. . . . Others, however, maintain that interest rates must *stabilize* if. . . .

4. The night-shift workers . . . tried to *compel* them to *relinquish*. . . .

5. The chairman. . . *denounced* the practice. . . . He said that the new rules will *eliminate* . . . . To some observers, such practices *signify* [or *constitute*] bribery. Several senators have promised to *formulate*. . . .

6. Dorm life changed drastically when colleges *abrogated* [or *abolished*]. . . . In the old days. . . students who *defied* [or *disregarded, disobeyed*] the rules. At some schools . . .would not *tolerate*. . . routinely *expelled*.

Exercise 60, page 327

1. Investors on Wall Street are concerned because the Japanese are buying so many American companies and so much real estate.

2. Now that China has opened its doors to certain aspects of capitalism, American companies are looking for ways to expand their markets and their product lines.

3. Analysts of the situation in the Far East agree that opportunities for investment there are growing.

4. In his biography of Lyndon Johnson, Robert Caro describes the 1948 Senate election in great detail.

5. When Julie applied for a work-study job, she was surprised to learn that her parents would have to submit a detailed financial statement.

6. Tim worked long and hard before his new pizza parlor finally turned a profit.

7. Two important aims of education are to broaden one's view of life and to establish worthy goals.

8. Another important aim of education is to help students learn to think: to develop strategies for understanding and solving problems.

Exercise 61, page 330

1. Even though the famous Gateway Arch is in St. Louis, it is Kansas City that claims the title "Gateway to the West."

2. Many students have a hard time finding summer jobs because our spring semester doesn't end until the second week of June.

3. Thomas Jefferson acquired the Ozark Mountains for the United States when he negotiated the Louisiana Purchase with Napoleon in 1803.

4. Many attorneys are unable to offer advice to their clients concerning oil and gas leases because they are unacquainted with the relevant laws.

5. When the neighbors added a pit bull to their pet population, which now numbers three unfriendly four-legged creatures, we decided to fence in our backyard.

6. Even though the human circulatory system is a marvel of efficiency, it is still subject to a wide variety of degenerative diseases.

7. Because carbohydrates are the body's prime source of energy, fad diets that severely restrict them are not only ineffective, they are often dangerous.

8. Because our congressman knows that the majority of voters are upset with both their tax rate and the way their taxes are spent, he has made "No New Taxes" the main theme of his reelection campaign.

9. When the auto companies offered cash rebates last January, sales of new cars increased dramatically.

10. Although the buffalo population of the West had nearly been wiped out by 1890, it now numbers about 60,000, with some 400 Colorado ranchers raising buffalo for meat.

Exercise 62, page 342

1. If you are an average American, the energy problem is mainly your monthly fuel bill and the cost of filling up the gas tank. You may also remember that in 1979, and way back in 1974, you had to wait in long lines at gasoline stations. For all of this, you may have blamed the "Arabs" or the oil companies or the government, or perhaps all three. Much of the information in the media, as well as your past experience, probably tells you that energy prices will continue to go up. . . .

2. Of all born creatures, we humans are the only ones that cannot live by bread alone. We live as much by symbols as by sense report. . . . For we see not only actualities but meanings. We have, indeed, all the impulses and interests of animal nature; we eat, sleep. . . . That is the special asset of the human mind, which makes Homo sapiens the master of earth and all its progeny.

Exercise 63, page 349

1. During the second two-year stretch of a president's term in office, he may find himself on the defensive, even with his own party; when—as frequently happens—his party loses a number of Senate and House seats in the midterm election, that second stretch can become even more defensive.

2. In recent years, the public attitude toward smoking (except perhaps in the tobacco-growing states) has changed so fast, with smoke-free zones everywhere, including restaurants, office buildings, and shopping malls, it could almost be called a revolution; even outdoor stadiums, such as Oriole Park at Camden Yards and Jacobs Field in Cleveland, have established a no-smoking policy.

Exercise 64, page 349

1. The cost of repairs to the nation's public transportation facilities—roads, bridges, and railroads—is an expenditure that cannot be delayed much longer if the system is to survive.

2. To many people, the mushroom is a lowly fungus with little food value; to others, it is a gourmet's delight.

3. In the early 1980s, a Chinese restriction on importing certain American goods, such as cotton, synthetic fibers, and soybeans, had an adverse effect on the U.S. economy—especially on the farmers.

4. According to fashion experts, the crew cut—the haircut that was more or less the hallmark of the 1950s—will be back in style before long.

5. Unfortunately, my favorite activities—skiing, playing golf, and bowling—cost more than my budget can stand.

6. Most people probably don't know that Alexander Graham Bell, the inventor of the telephone, succeeded his father-in-law as president of the National Geographic Society.

7. With its thirty acres of flowers, exotic plants, and wildlife, Cypress Gardens, Florida, is a year-round extravaganza of nature's bounty and beauty.

8. Many scientists believe that sightings of "cryptids"—including Big Foot, the Loch Ness monster, and Yeti, the Abominable Snowman—are simply mistakes, attributable to unfamiliarity with known animals, rather than to delusions.

Index